GENIUS 132: SUPER COMBO

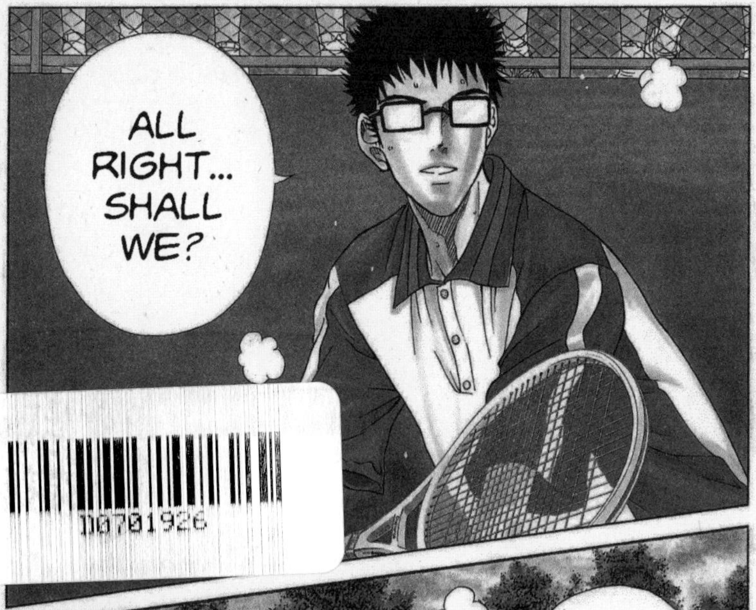
ALL RIGHT... SHALL WE?

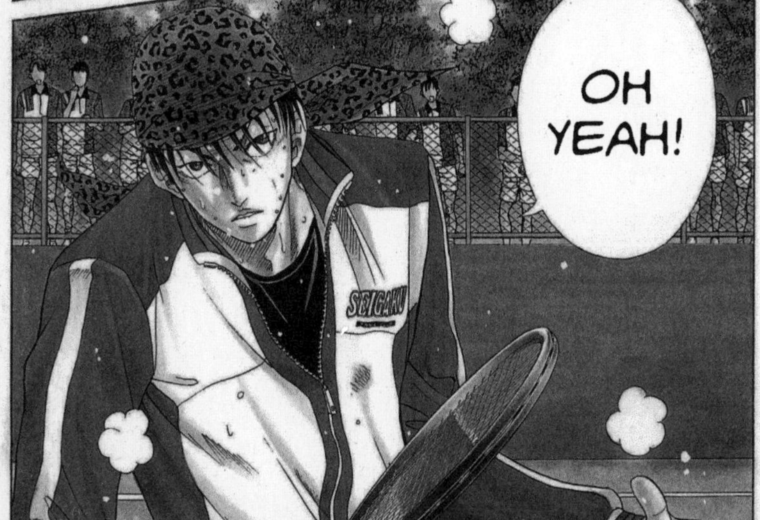
OH YEAH!
SEIGAKU

THE PRINCE OF TENNIS

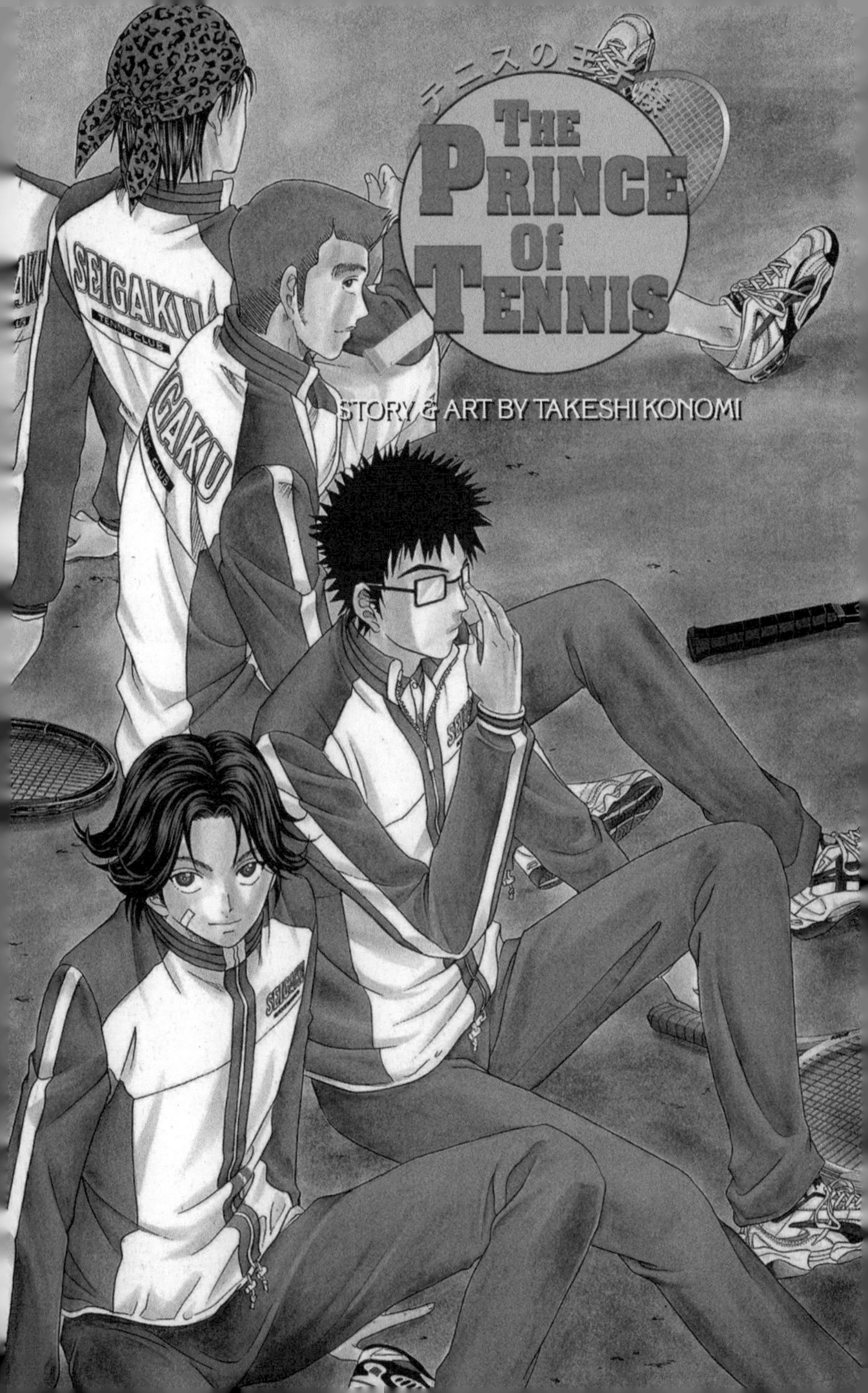
テニスの王子様
THE PRINCE OF TENNIS
STORY & ART BY TAKESHI KONOMI

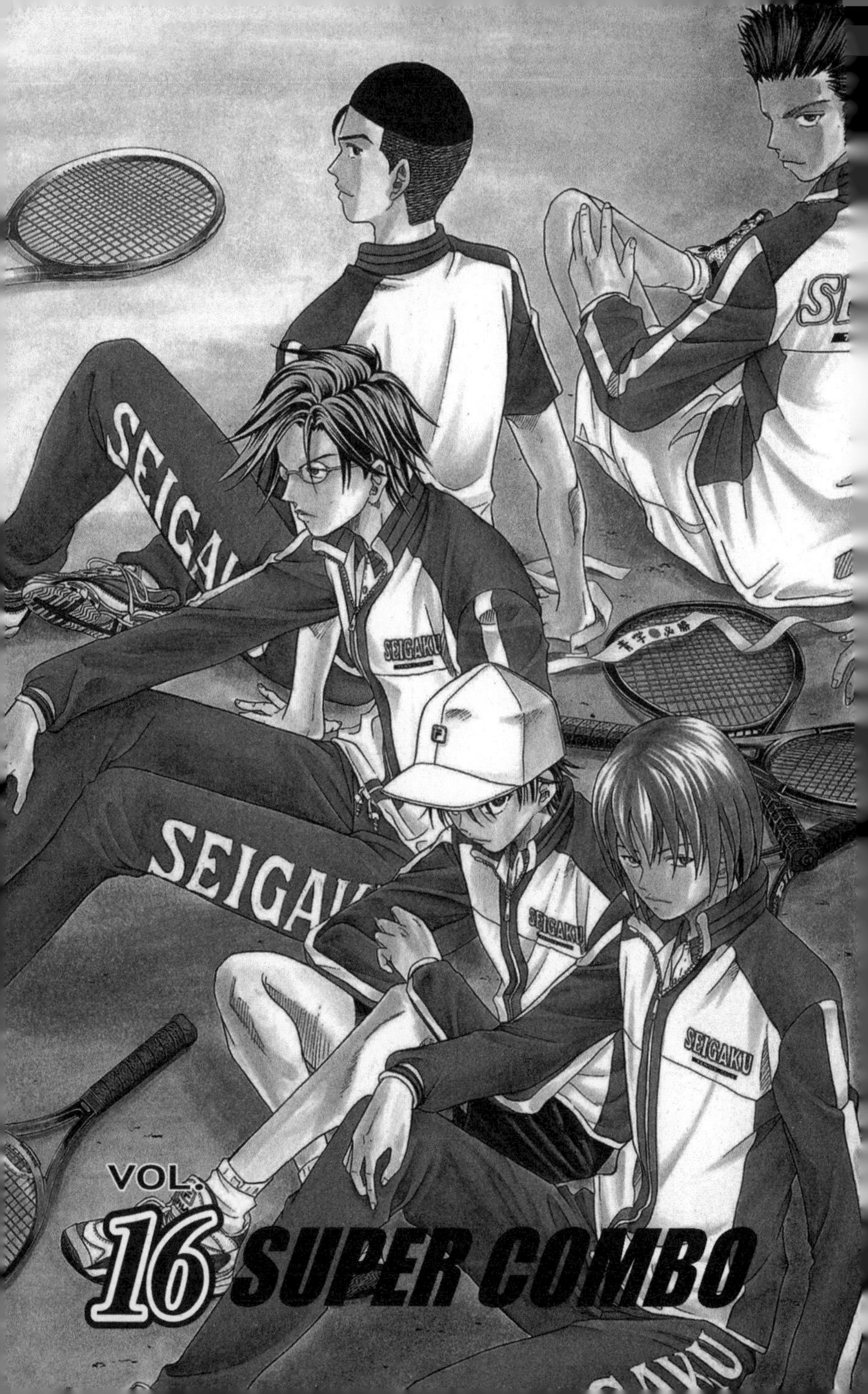
VOL. 16
SUPER COMBO

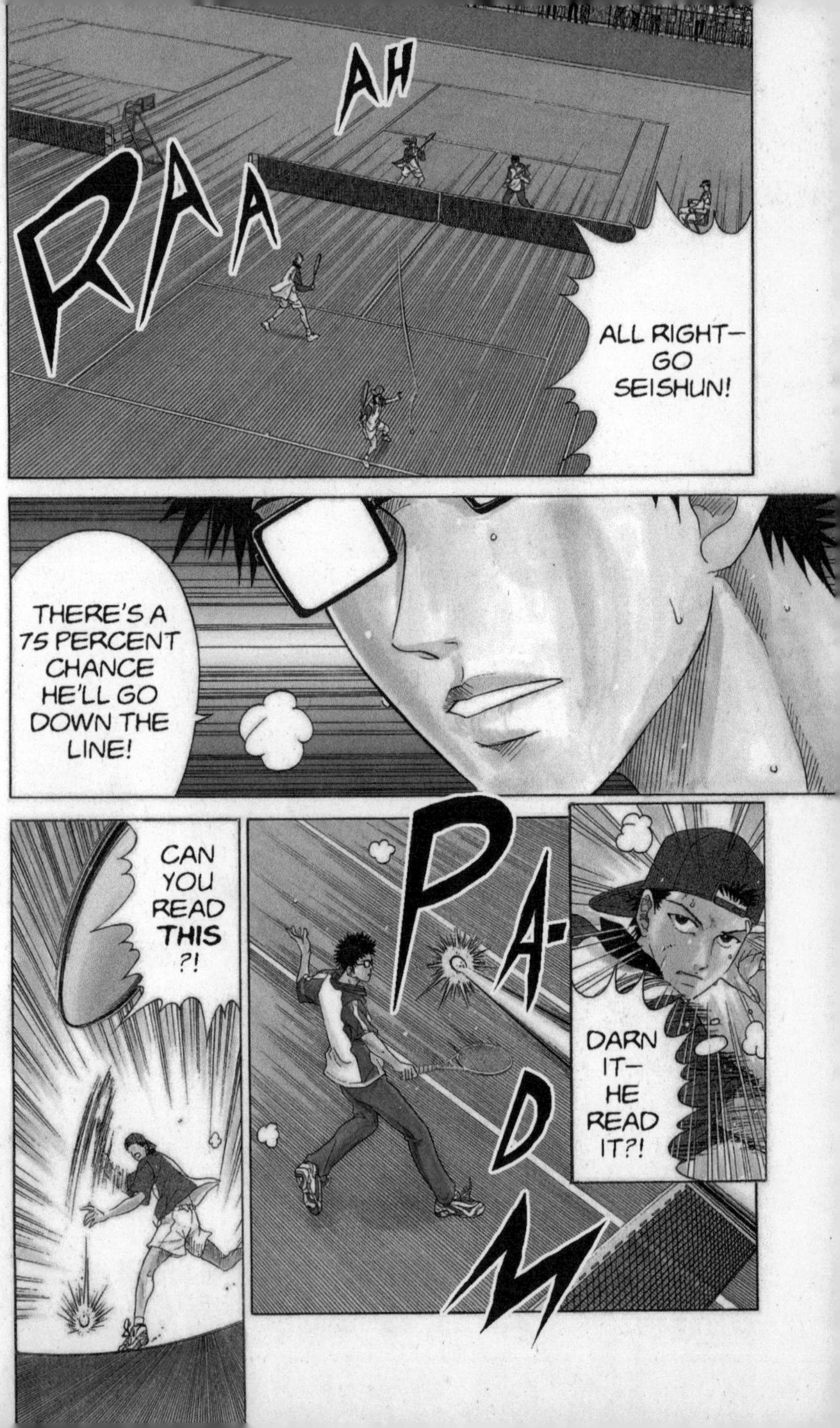
RAAAH
ALL RIGHT— GO SEISHUN!
THERE'S A 75 PERCENT CHANCE HE'LL GO DOWN THE LINE!
DARN IT— HE READ IT?!
PA-DM
CAN YOU READ **THIS** ?!

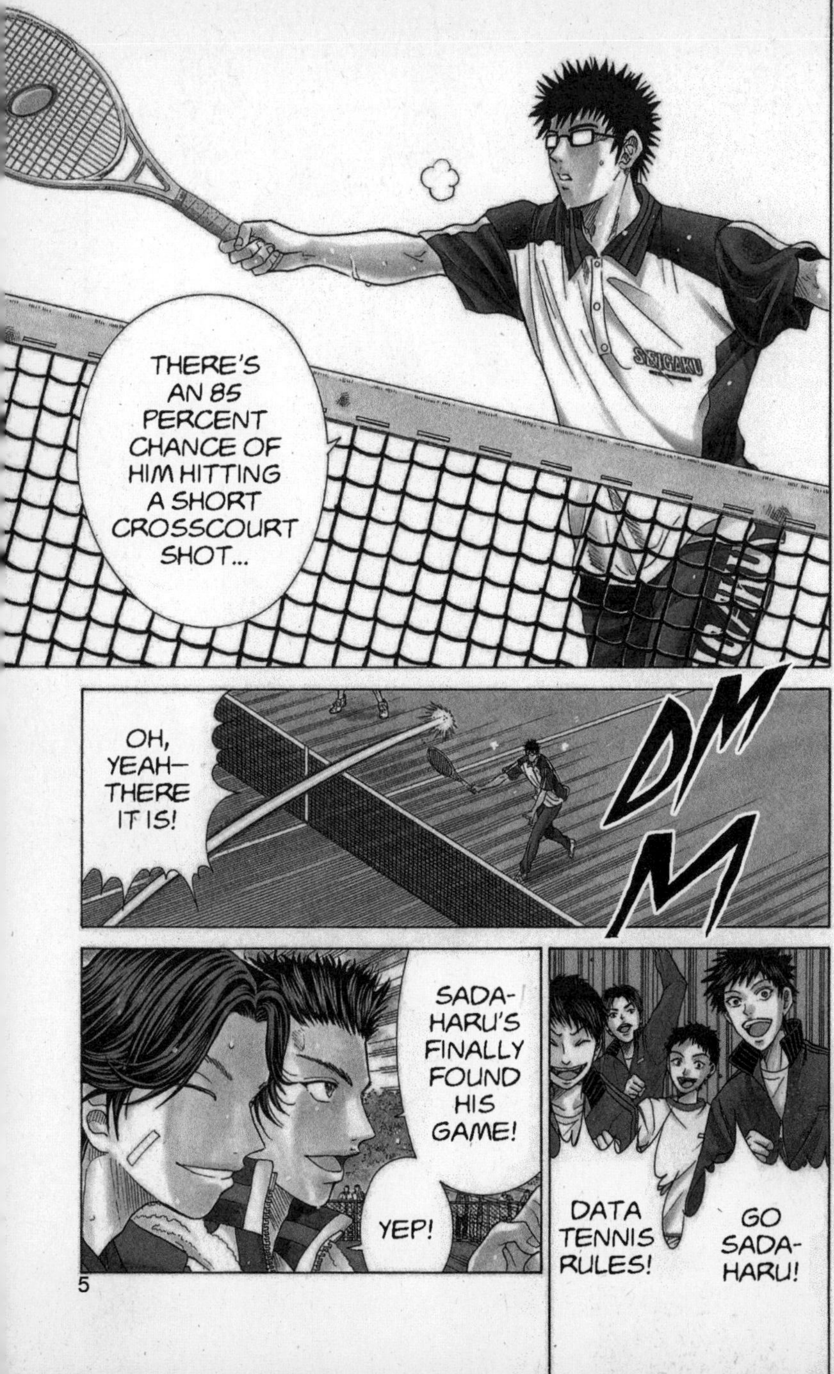
THERE'S AN 85 PERCENT CHANCE OF HIM HITTING A SHORT CROSSCOURT SHOT...
DMM
OH, YEAH— THERE IT IS!
GO SADA-HARU!
DATA TENNIS RULES!
SADA-HARU'S FINALLY FOUND HIS GAME!
YEP!

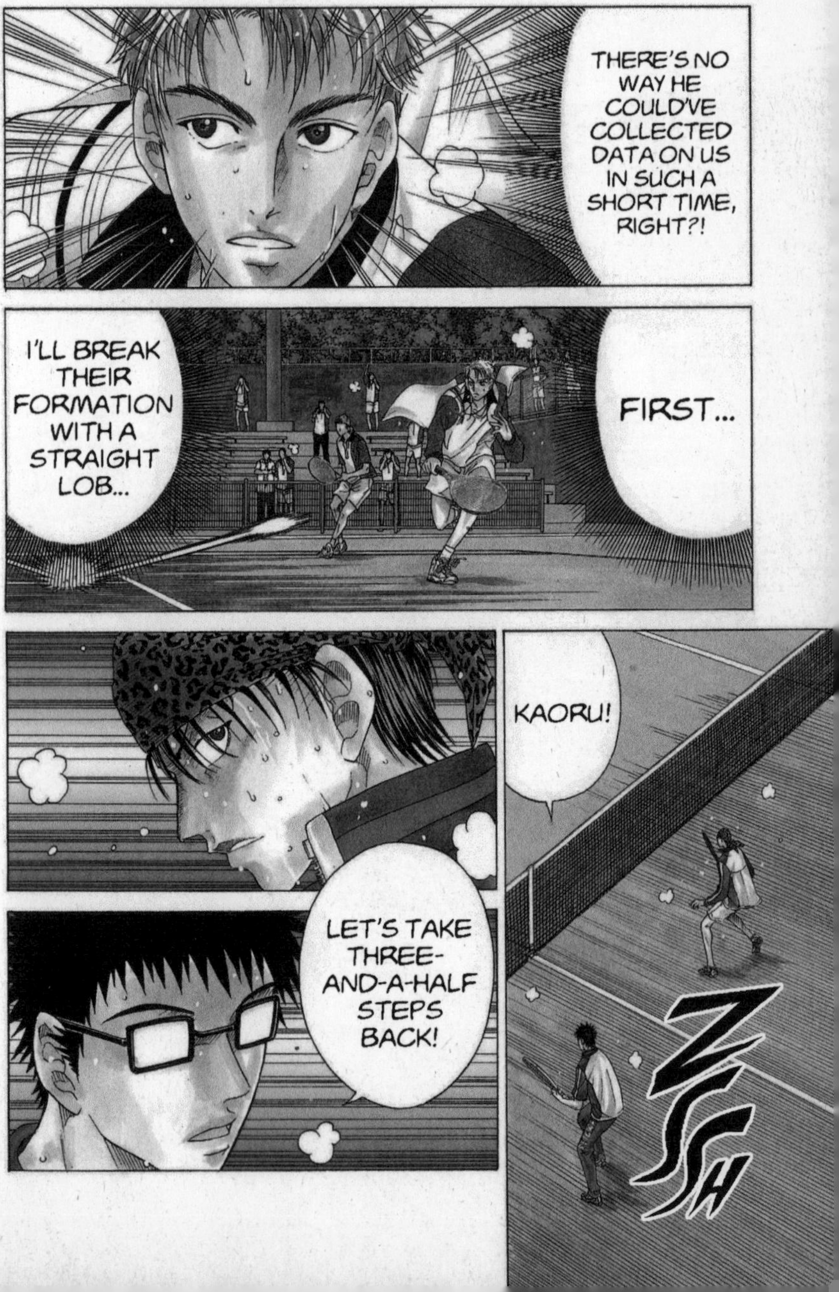
THERE'S NO WAY HE COULD'VE COLLECTED DATA ON US IN SUCH A SHORT TIME, RIGHT?!
FIRST...
I'LL BREAK THEIR FORMATION WITH A STRAIGHT LOB...
KAORU!
LET'S TAKE THREE-AND-A-HALF STEPS BACK!
ZSSH

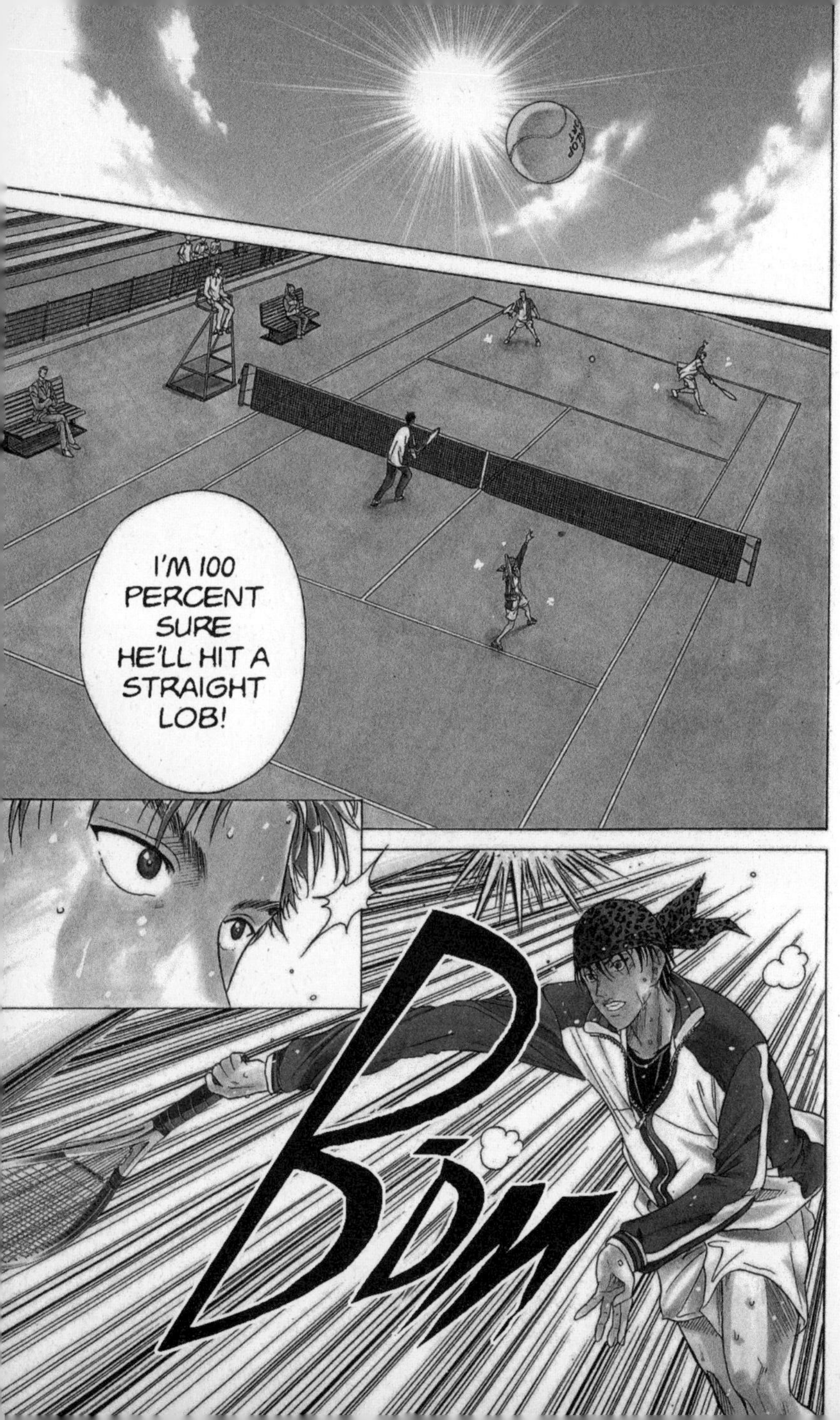
I'M 100 PERCENT SURE HE'LL HIT A STRAIGHT LOB!
BAM

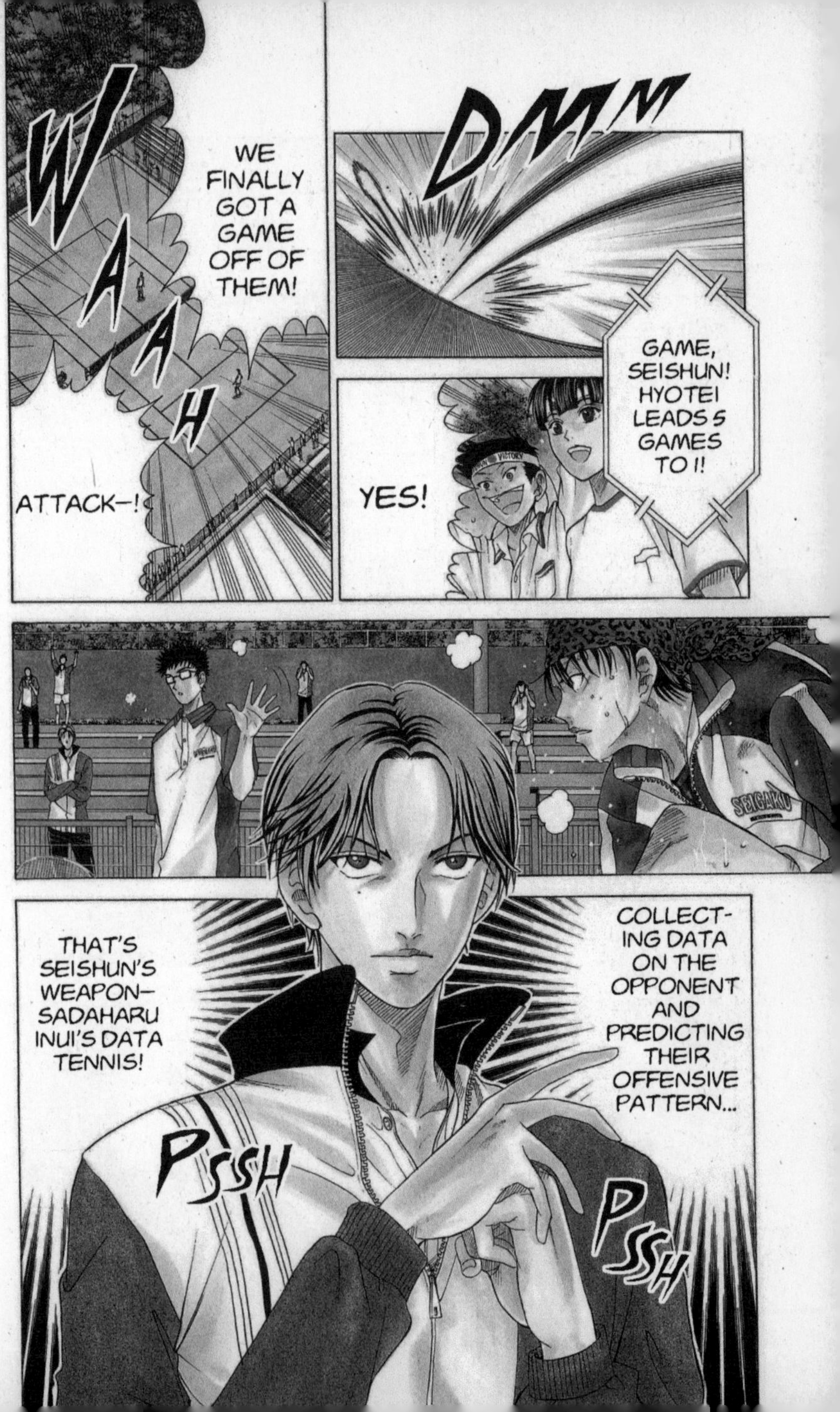
DMM
GAME, SEISHUN! HYOTEI LEADS 5 GAMES TO 1!
YES!
WAAH
WE FINALLY GOT A GAME OFF OF THEM!
ATTACK—!
SEIGAKU
COLLECTING DATA ON THE OPPONENT AND PREDICTING THEIR OFFENSIVE PATTERN...
THAT'S SEISHUN'S WEAPON— SADAHARU INUI'S DATA TENNIS!
PSSH
PSSH

READ THIS WAY

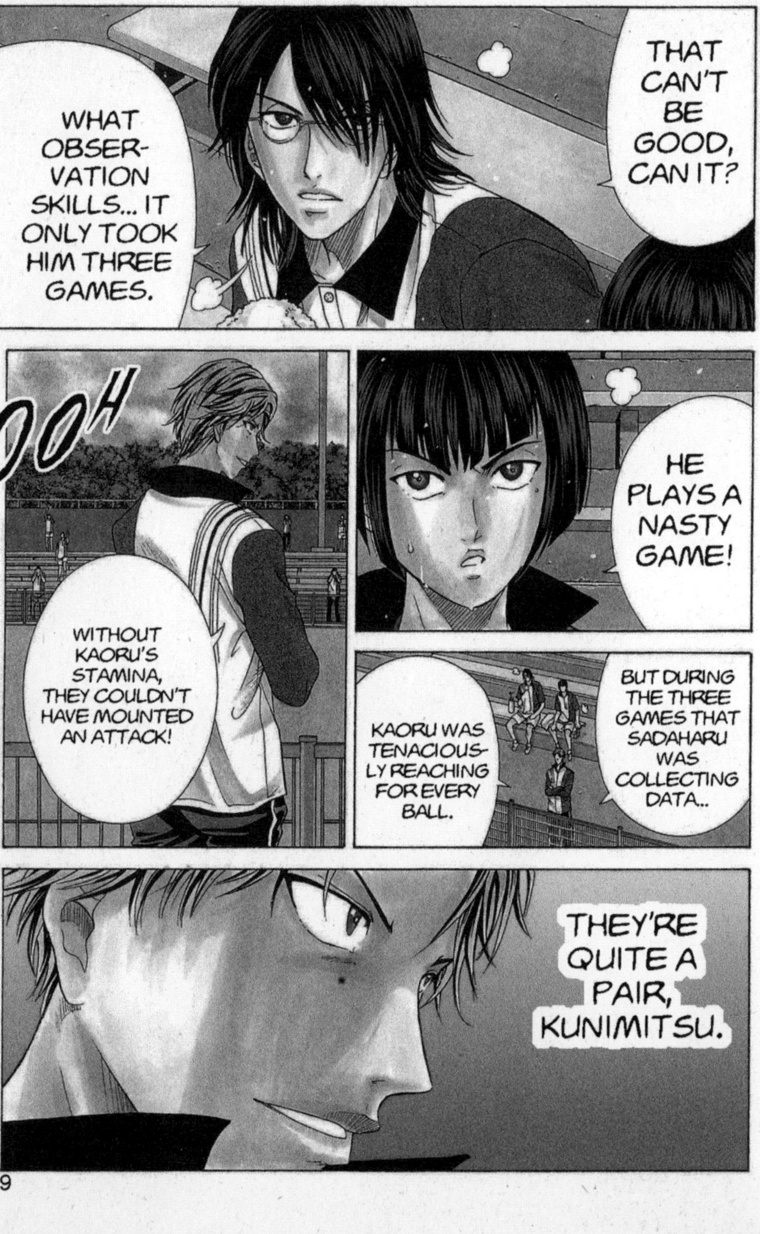
THAT CAN'T BE GOOD, CAN IT?
WHAT OBSERVATION SKILLS... IT ONLY TOOK HIM THREE GAMES.
HE PLAYS A NASTY GAME!
BUT DURING THE THREE GAMES THAT SADAHARU WAS COLLECTING DATA...
KAORU WAS TENACIOUSLY REACHING FOR EVERY BALL.
OOH
WITHOUT KAORU'S STAMINA, THEY COULDN'T HAVE MOUNTED AN ATTACK!
THEY'RE QUITE A PAIR, KUNIMITSU.

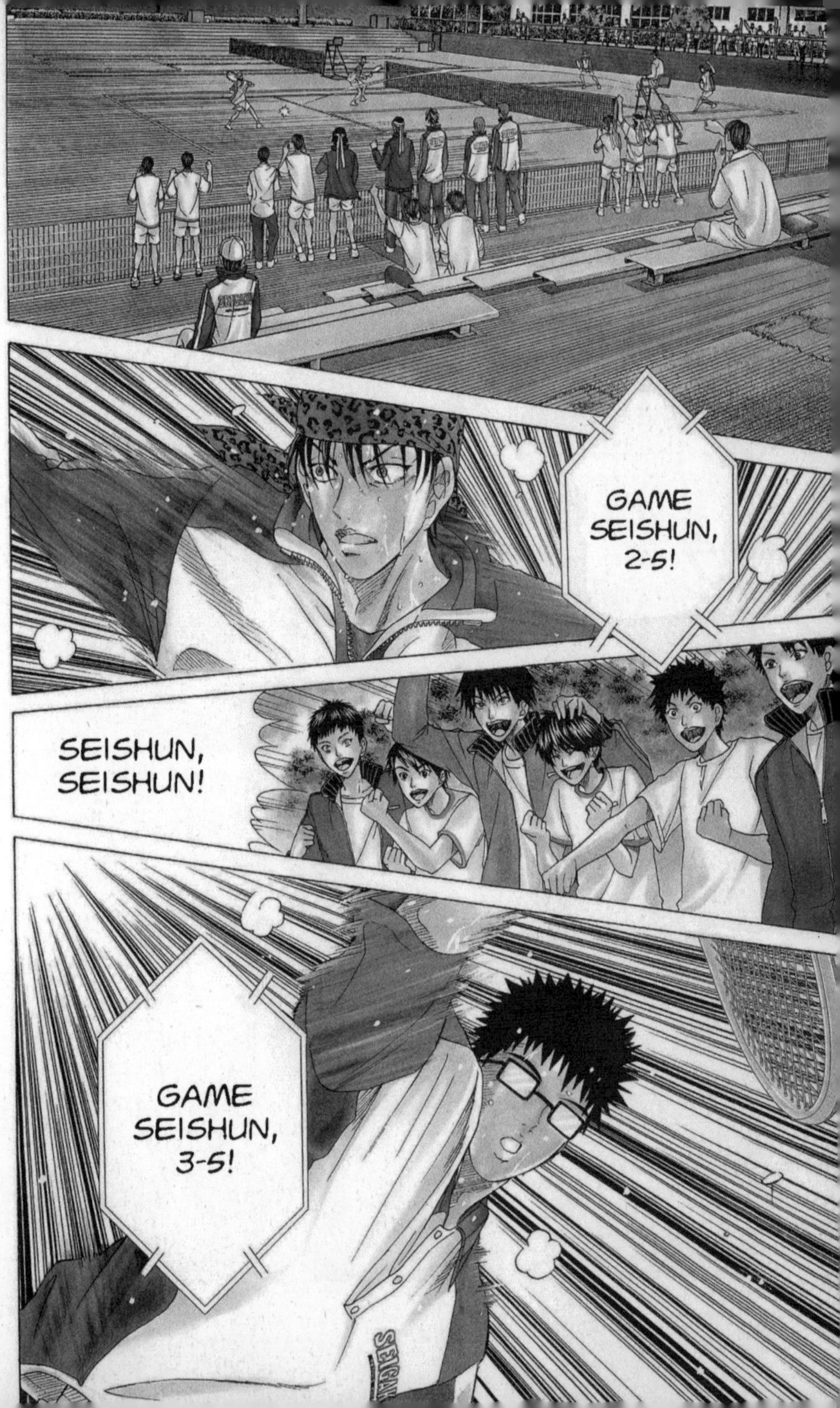
GAME SEISHUN, 2-5!
SEISHUN, SEISHUN!
GAME SEISHUN, 3-5!

READ THIS WAY

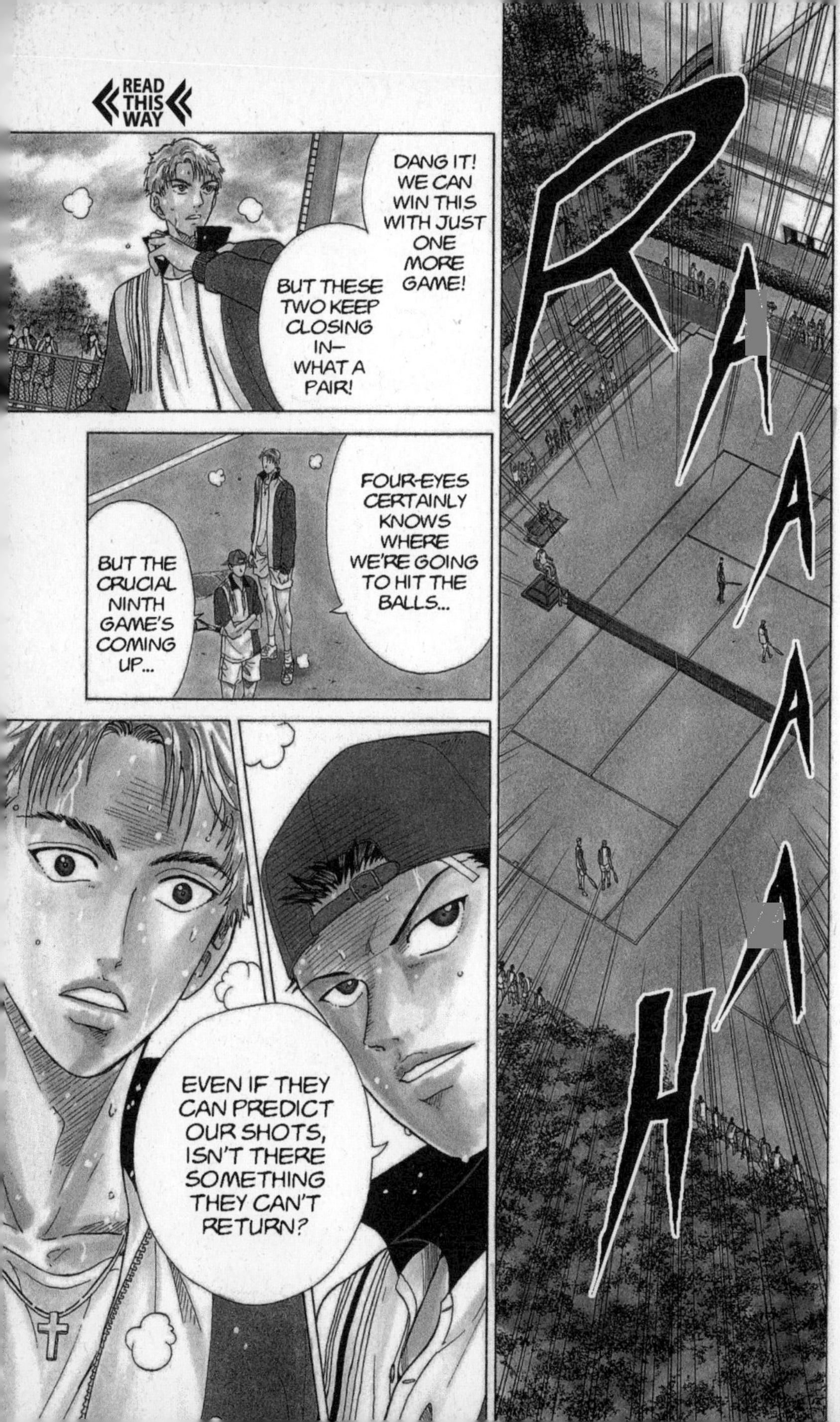
RAAAAH
DANG IT! WE CAN WIN THIS WITH JUST ONE MORE GAME!
BUT THESE TWO KEEP CLOSING IN— WHAT A PAIR!
FOUR-EYES CERTAINLY KNOWS WHERE WE'RE GOING TO HIT THE BALLS...
BUT THE CRUCIAL NINTH GAME'S COMING UP...
EVEN IF THEY CAN PREDICT OUR SHOTS, ISN'T THERE SOMETHING THEY CAN'T RETURN?

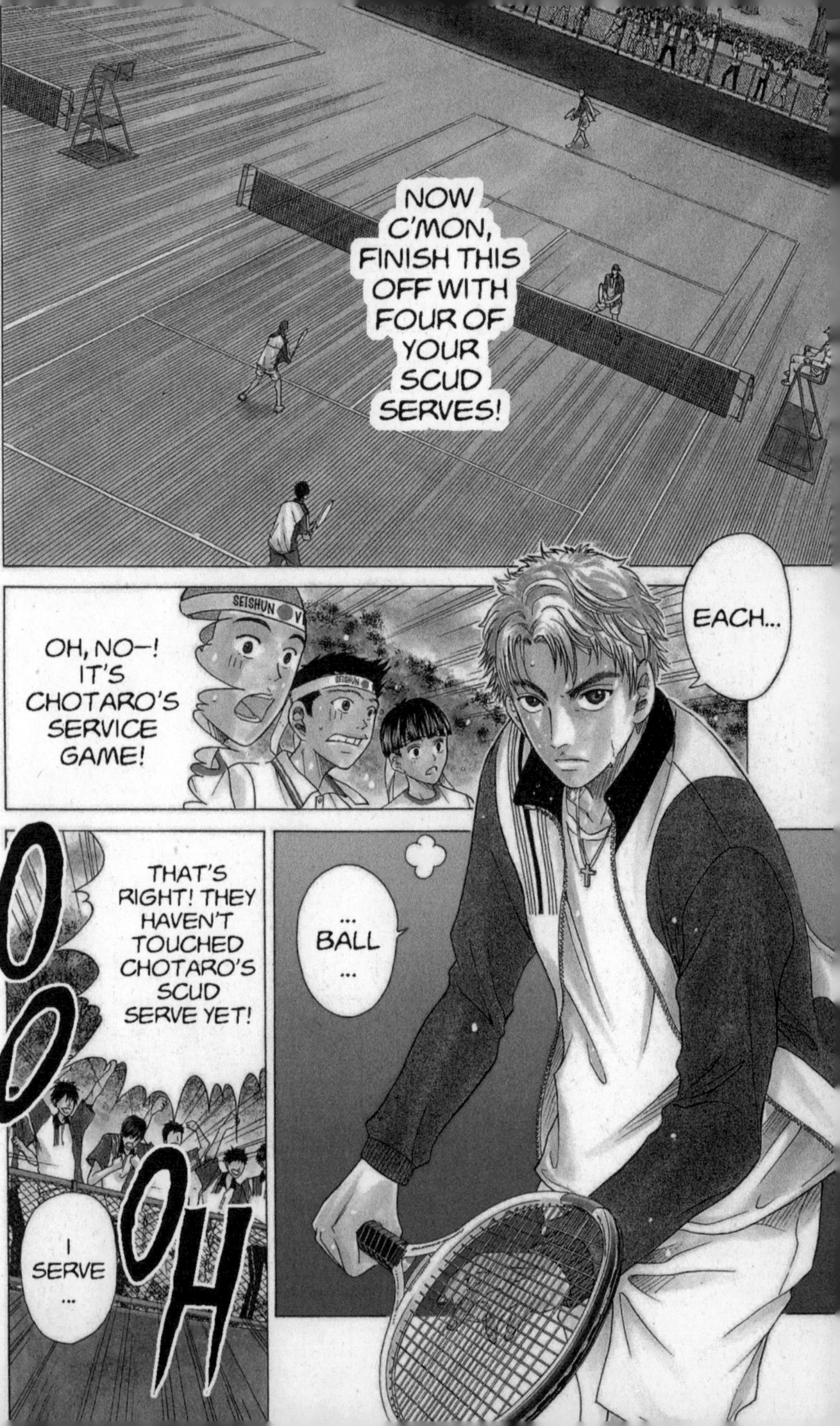
NOW C'MON, FINISH THIS OFF WITH FOUR OF YOUR SCUD SERVES!
SEISHUN
OH, NO–! IT'S CHOTARO'S SERVICE GAME!
THAT'S RIGHT! THEY HAVEN'T TOUCHED CHOTARO'S SCUD SERVE YET!
OOOOH
I SERVE ...
EACH...
... BALL ...

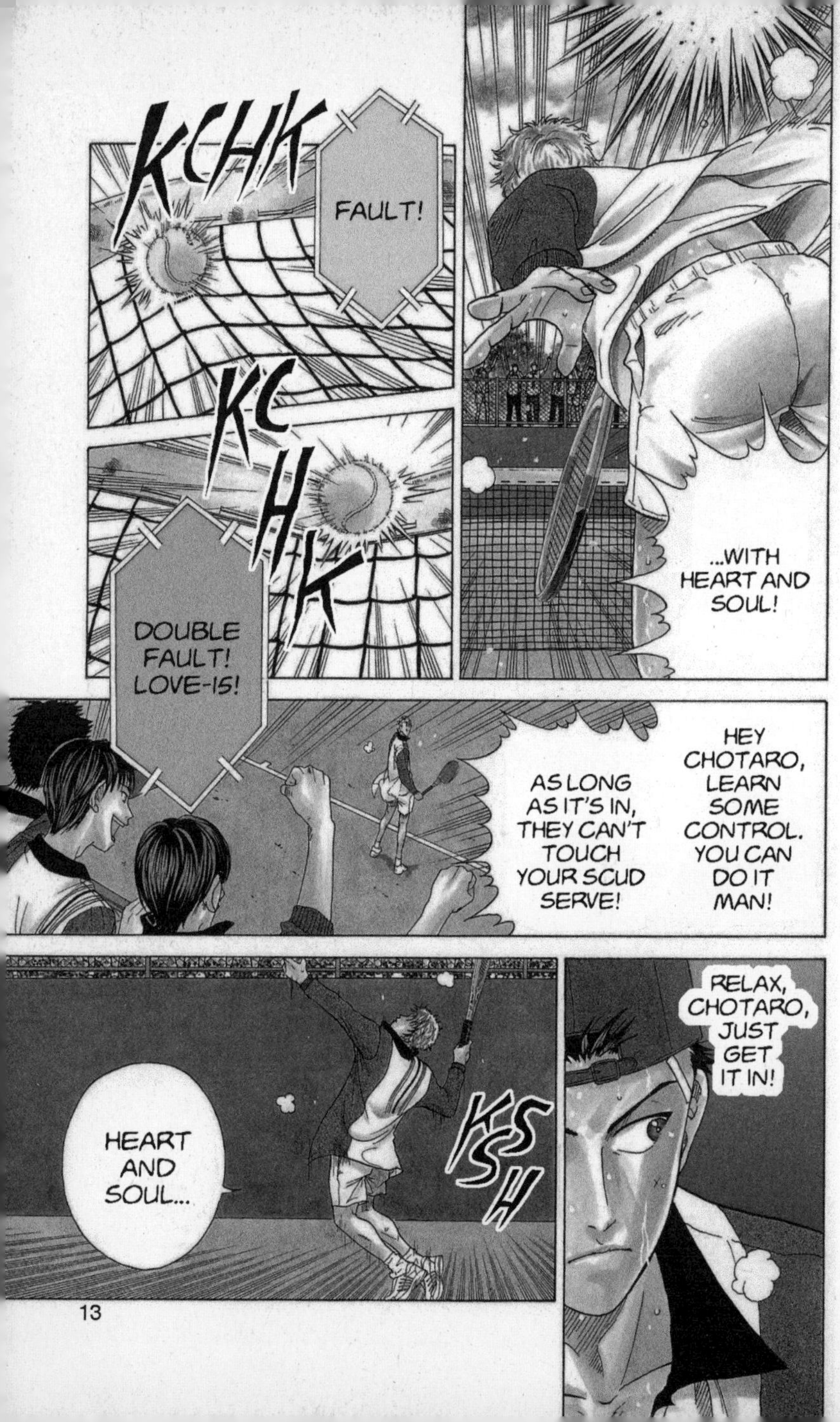
...WITH HEART AND SOUL!
KCHK
FAULT!
KCHK
DOUBLE FAULT! LOVE-15!
HEY CHOTARO, LEARN SOME CONTROL. YOU CAN DO IT MAN!
AS LONG AS IT'S IN, THEY CAN'T TOUCH YOUR SCUD SERVE!
RELAX, CHOTARO, JUST GET IT IN!
HEART AND SOUL...
KSSH

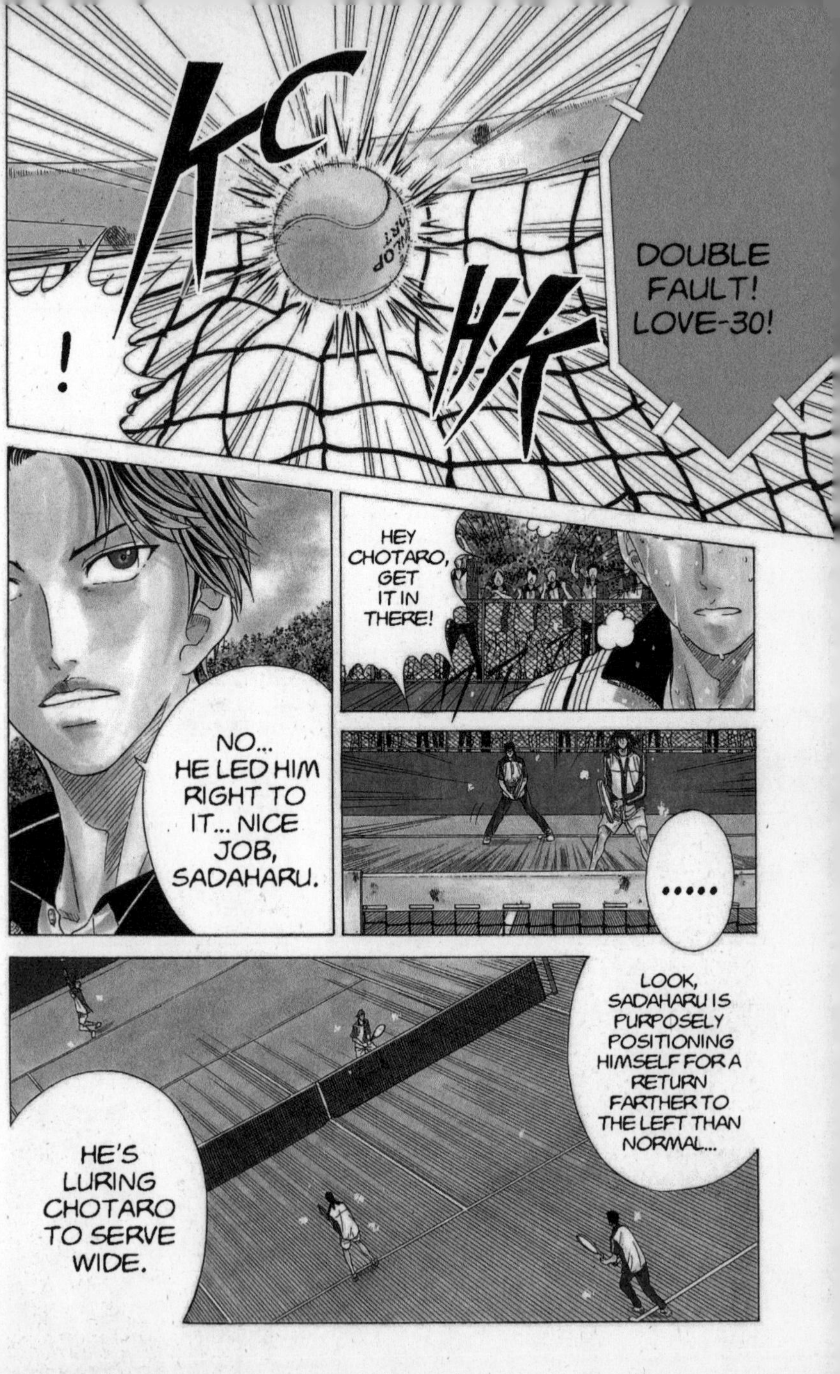
DOUBLE FAULT! LOVE-30!
KCHK
!
HEY CHOTARO, GET IT IN THERE!
NO... HE LED HIM RIGHT TO IT... NICE JOB, SADAHARU.
.....
LOOK, SADAHARU IS PURPOSELY POSITIONING HIMSELF FOR A RETURN FARTHER TO THE LEFT THAN NORMAL...
HE'S LURING CHOTARO TO SERVE WIDE.

READ THIS WAY

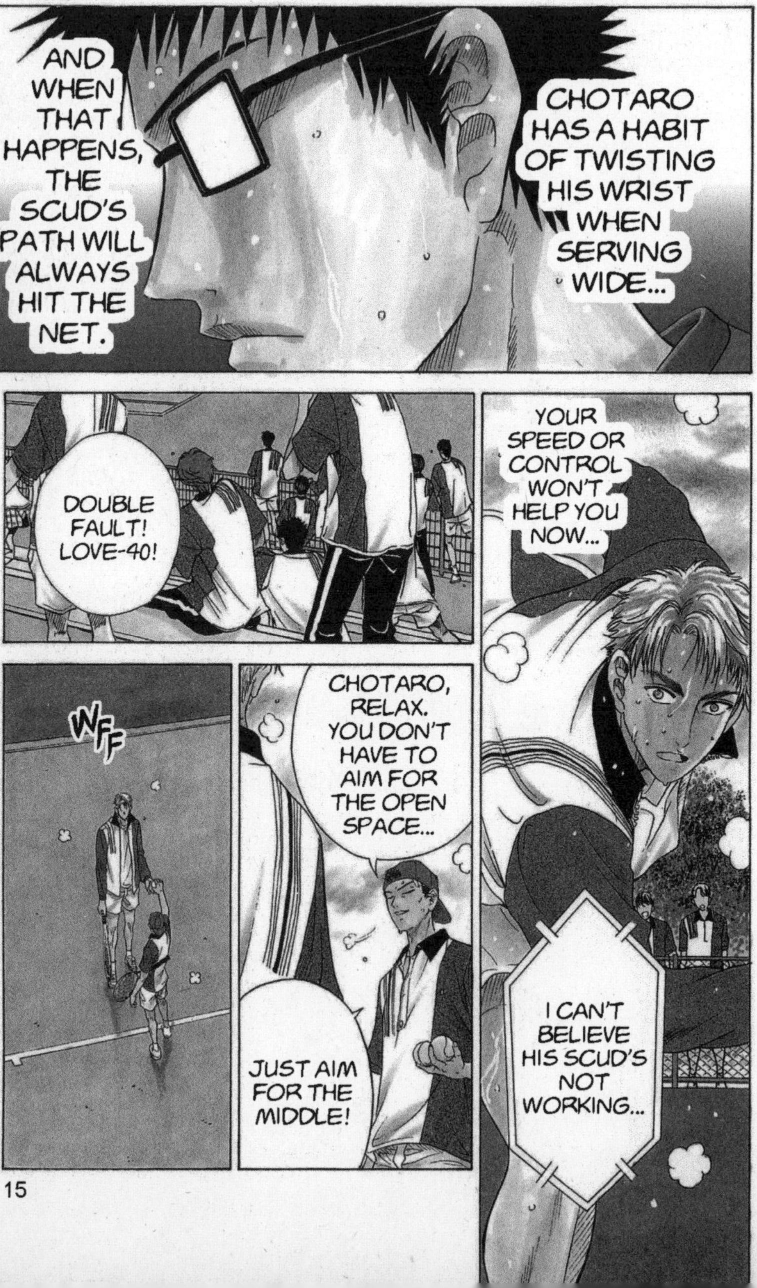
CHOTARO HAS A HABIT OF TWISTING HIS WRIST WHEN SERVING WIDE...
AND WHEN THAT HAPPENS, THE SCUD'S PATH WILL ALWAYS HIT THE NET.
YOUR SPEED OR CONTROL WON'T HELP YOU NOW...
I CAN'T BELIEVE HIS SCUD'S NOT WORKING...
DOUBLE FAULT! LOVE-40!
CHOTARO, RELAX. YOU DON'T HAVE TO AIM FOR THE OPEN SPACE...
JUST AIM FOR THE MIDDLE!
WFF

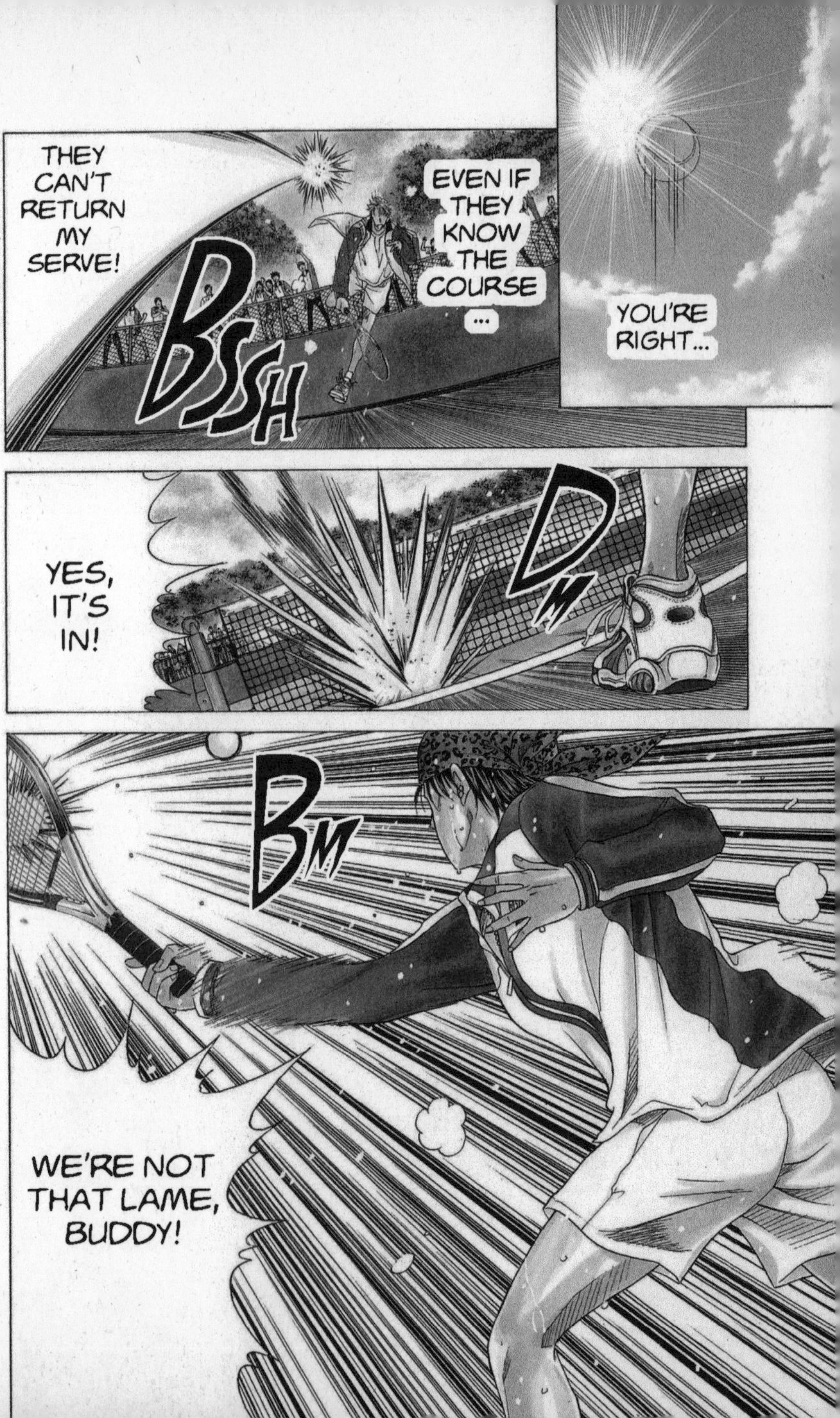
YOU'RE RIGHT...
EVEN IF THEY KNOW THE COURSE ...
THEY CAN'T RETURN MY SERVE!
BSSH
DM
YES, IT'S IN!
BM
WE'RE NOT THAT LAME, BUDDY!

READ THIS WAY

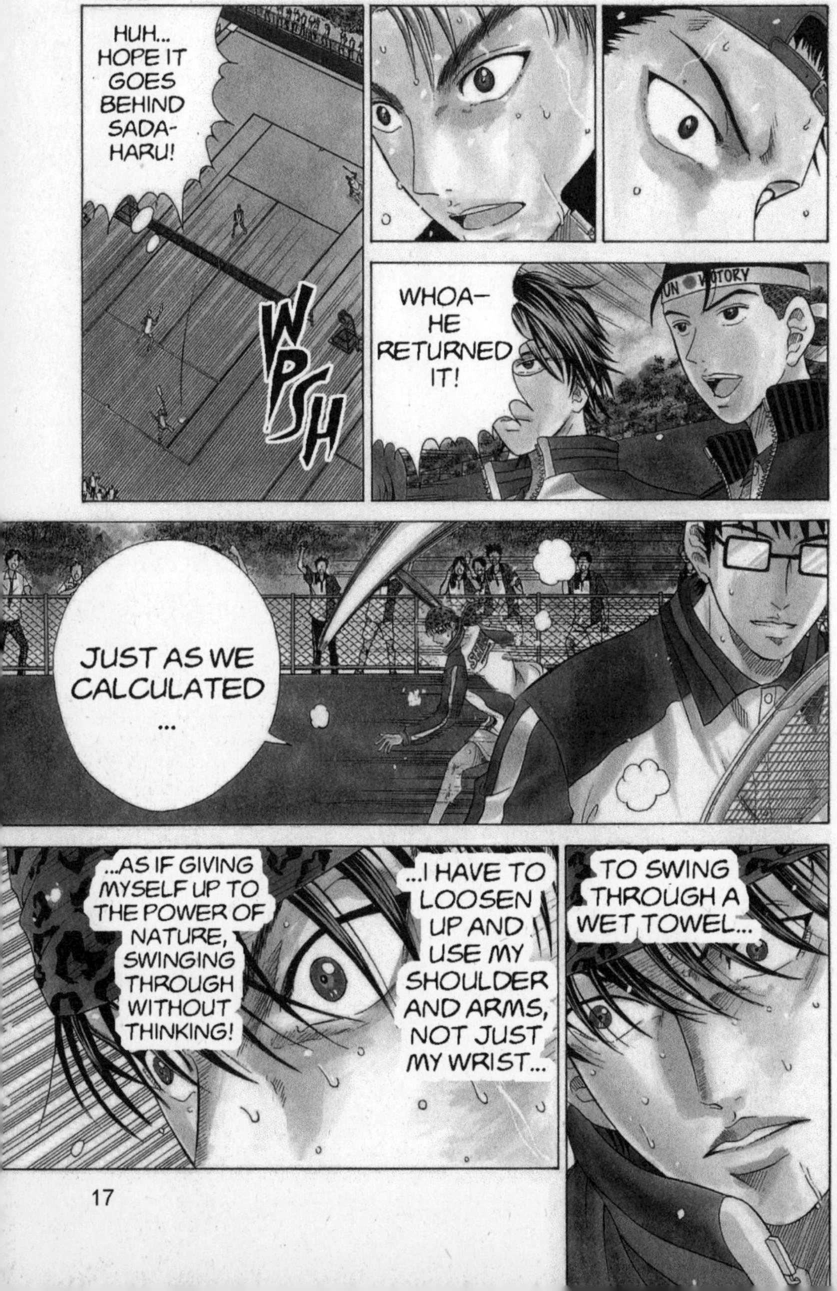

WHOA—HE RETURNED IT!
HUH... HOPE IT GOES BEHIND SADA-HARU!
WPSH
JUST AS WE CALCULATED...
TO SWING THROUGH A WET TOWEL...
...I HAVE TO LOOSEN UP AND USE MY SHOULDER AND ARMS, NOT JUST MY WRIST...
...AS IF GIVING MYSELF UP TO THE POWER OF NATURE, SWINGING THROUGH WITHOUT THINKING!

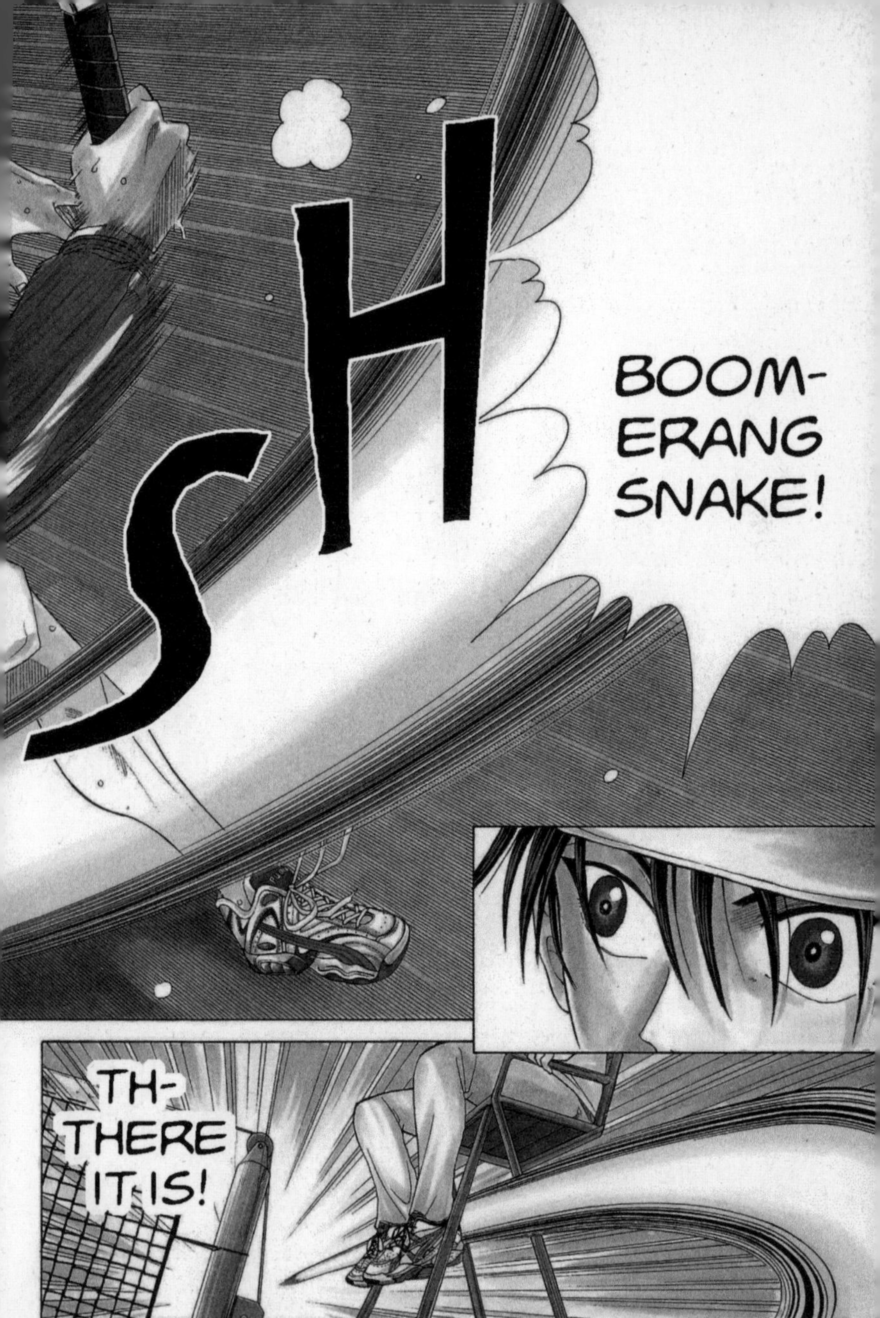
SH
BOOM-
ERANG
SNAKE!
TH-
THERE
IT IS!

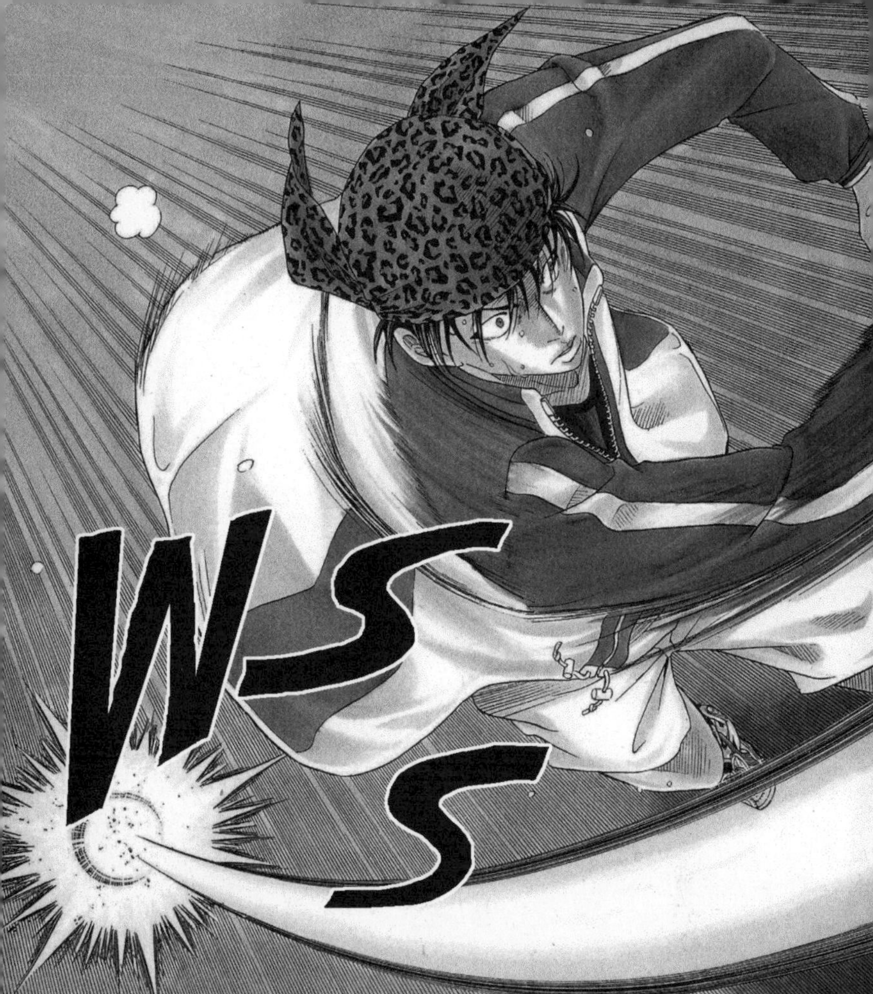
WSS
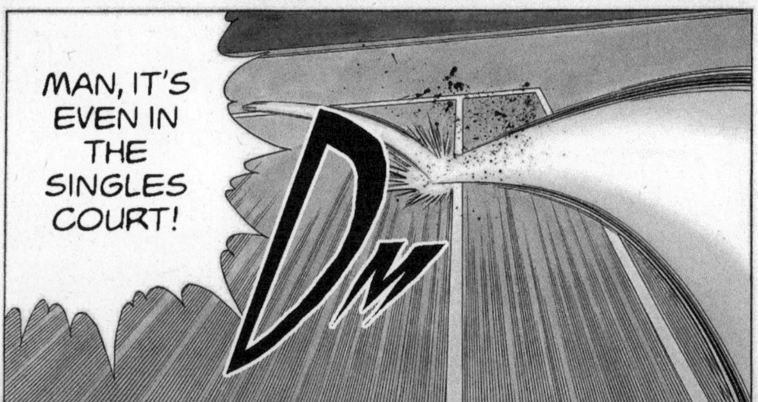
MAN, IT'S EVEN IN THE SINGLES COURT!
DM

CONTENTS

**Vol.16
Super Combo**

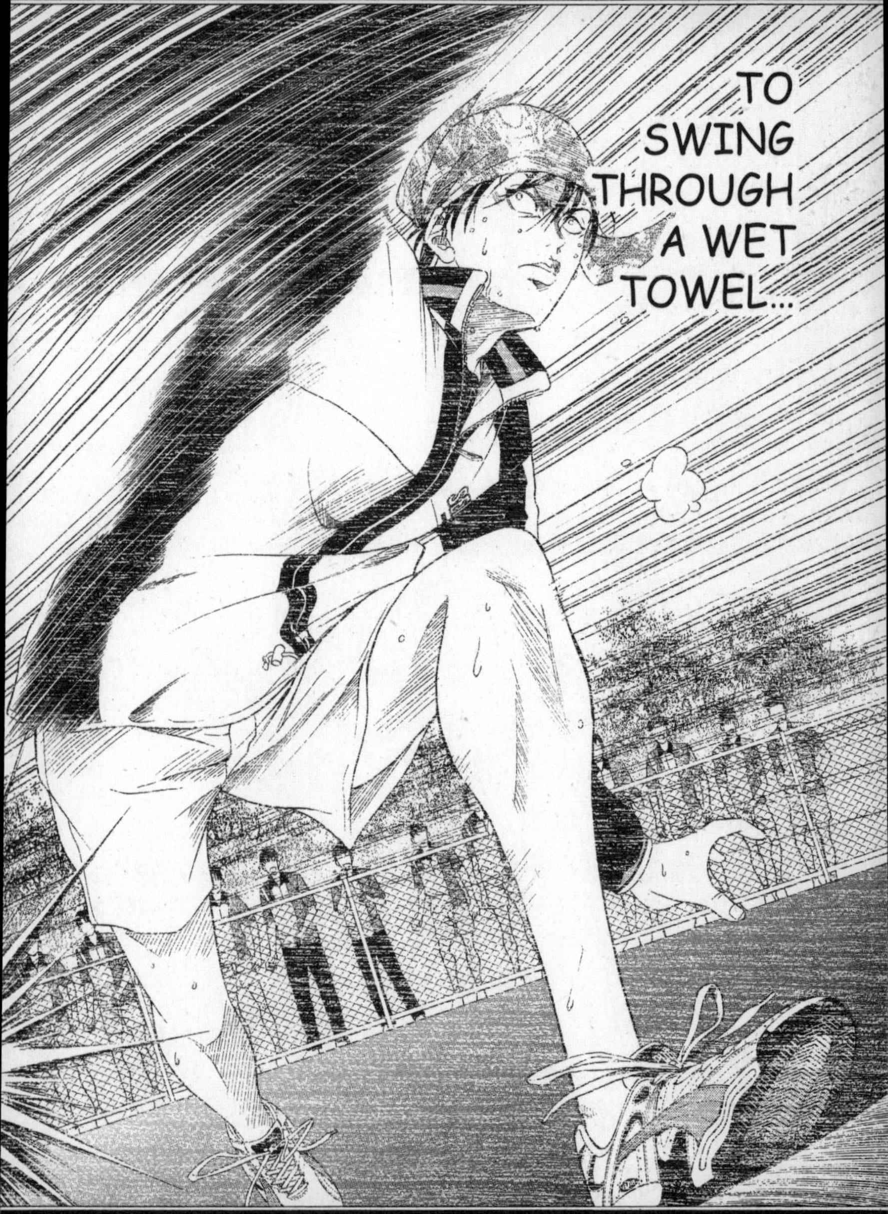
TO SWING THROUGH A WET TOWEL...

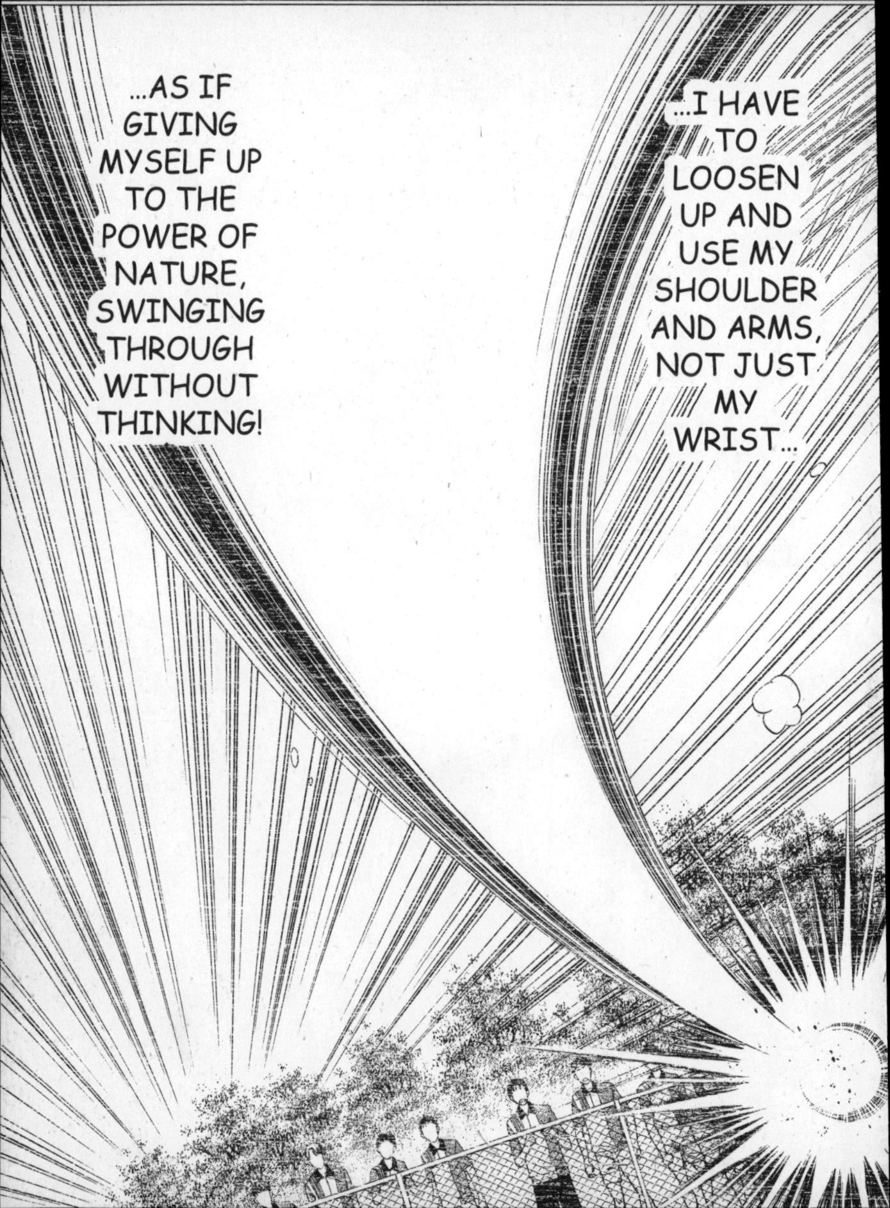
...I HAVE TO LOOSEN UP AND USE MY SHOULDER AND ARMS, NOT JUST MY WRIST...
...AS IF GIVING MYSELF UP TO THE POWER OF NATURE, SWINGING THROUGH WITHOUT THINKING!

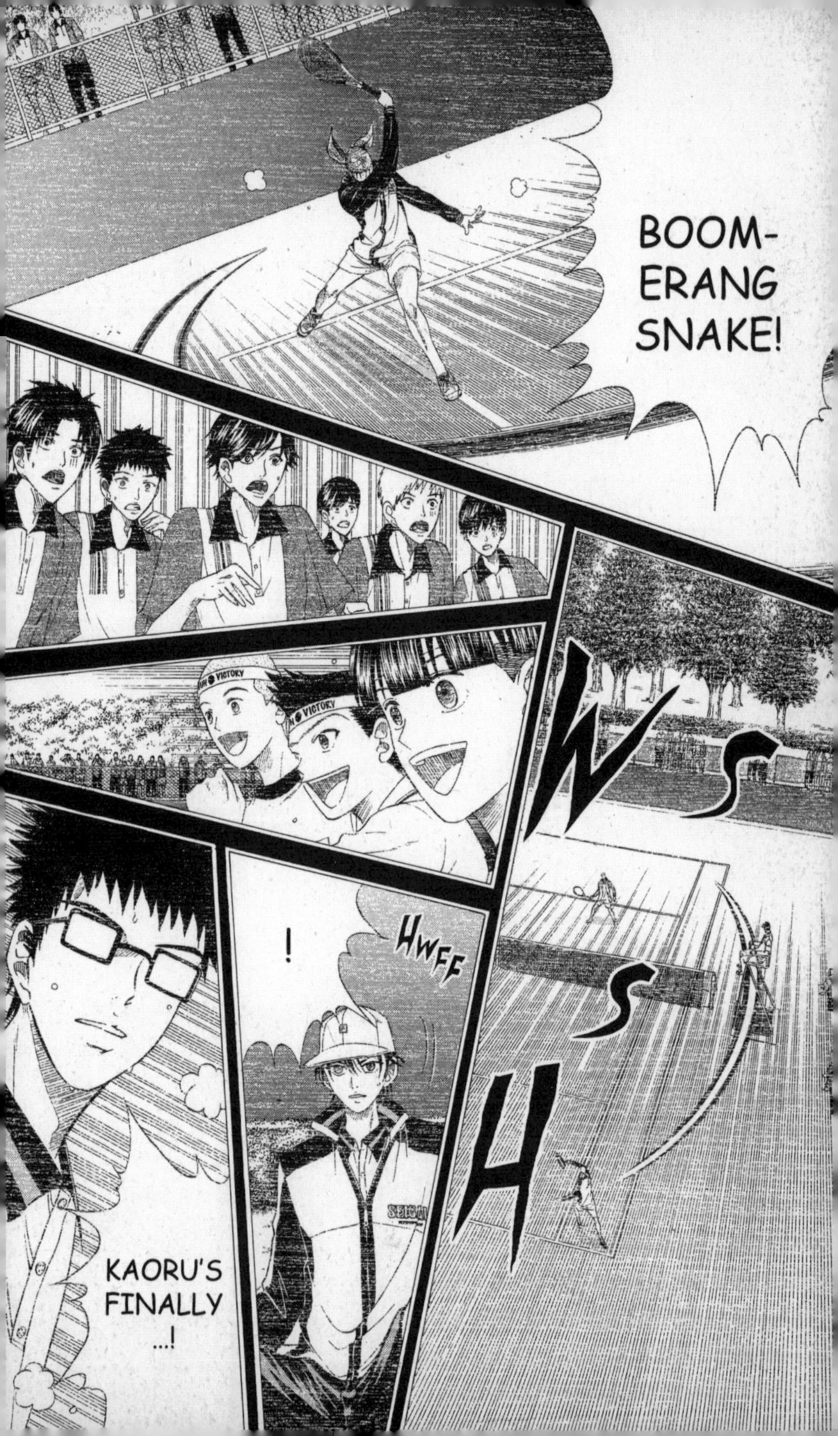
BOOM-
ERANG
SNAKE!
WSSH
!
HWFF
KAORU'S
FINALLY
...!

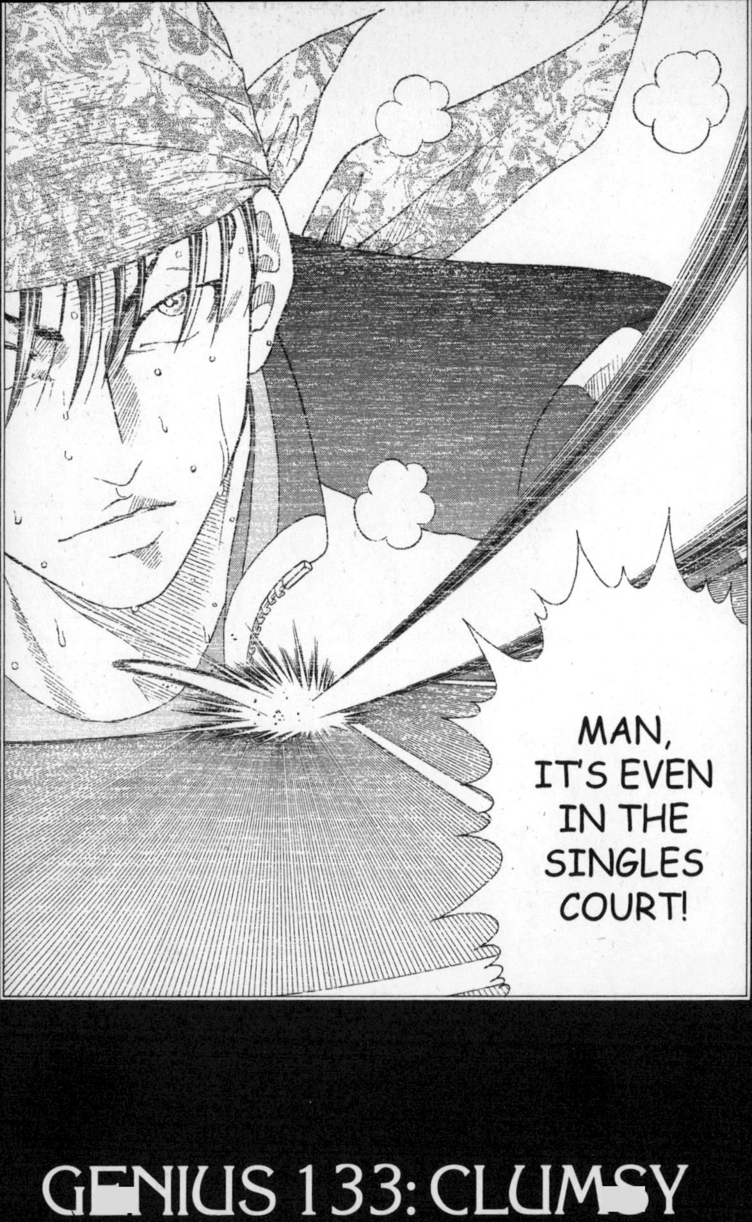
MAN, IT'S EVEN IN THE SINGLES COURT!

GENIUS 133: CLUMSY

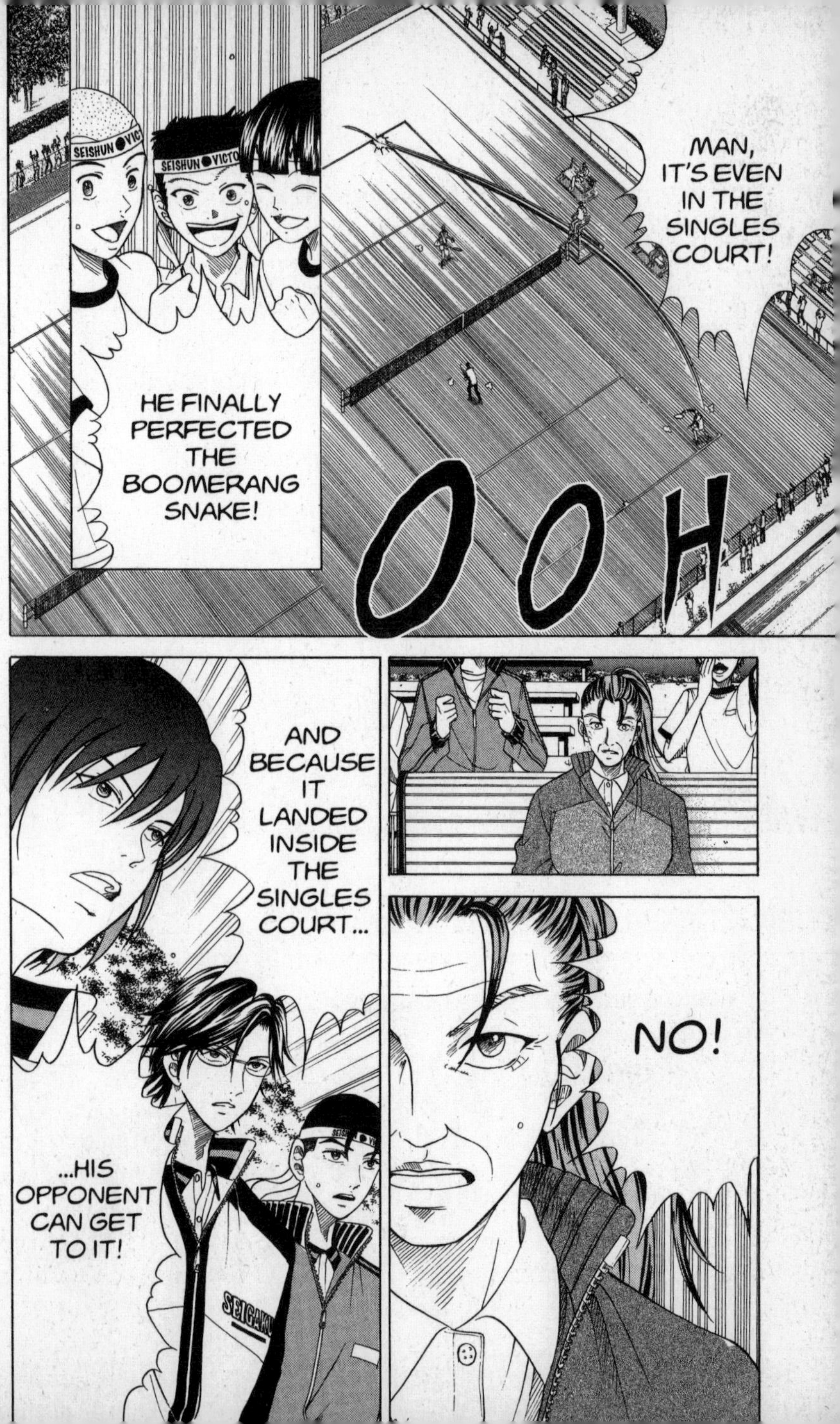
MAN, IT'S EVEN IN THE SINGLES COURT!
OOH
HE FINALLY PERFECTED THE BOOMERANG SNAKE!
AND BECAUSE IT LANDED INSIDE THE SINGLES COURT...
...HIS OPPONENT CAN GET TO IT!
NO!

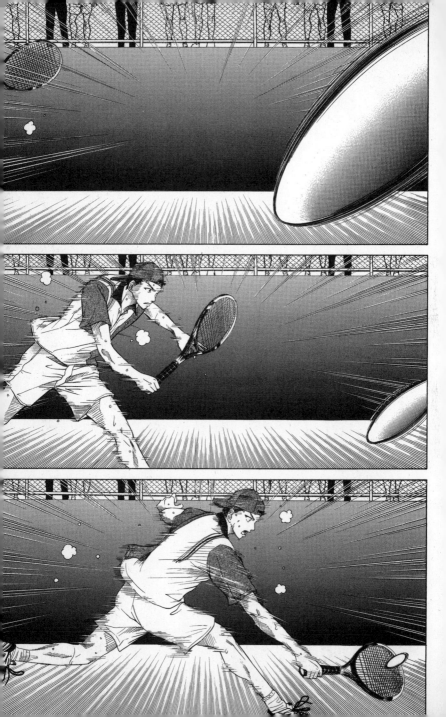

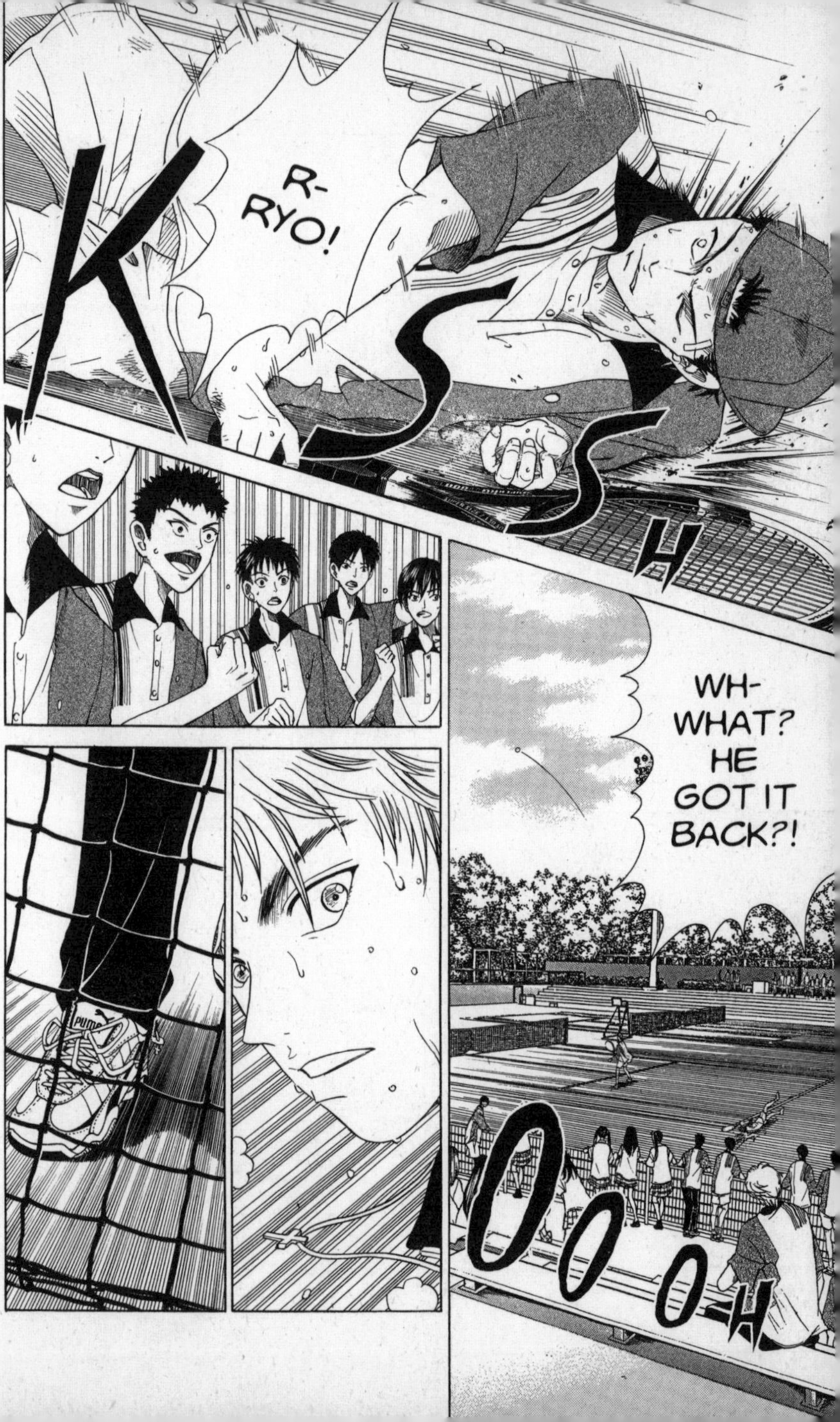
R-RYO!
KSSH
WH-WHAT? HE GOT IT BACK?!
OOOOH

READ THIS WAY

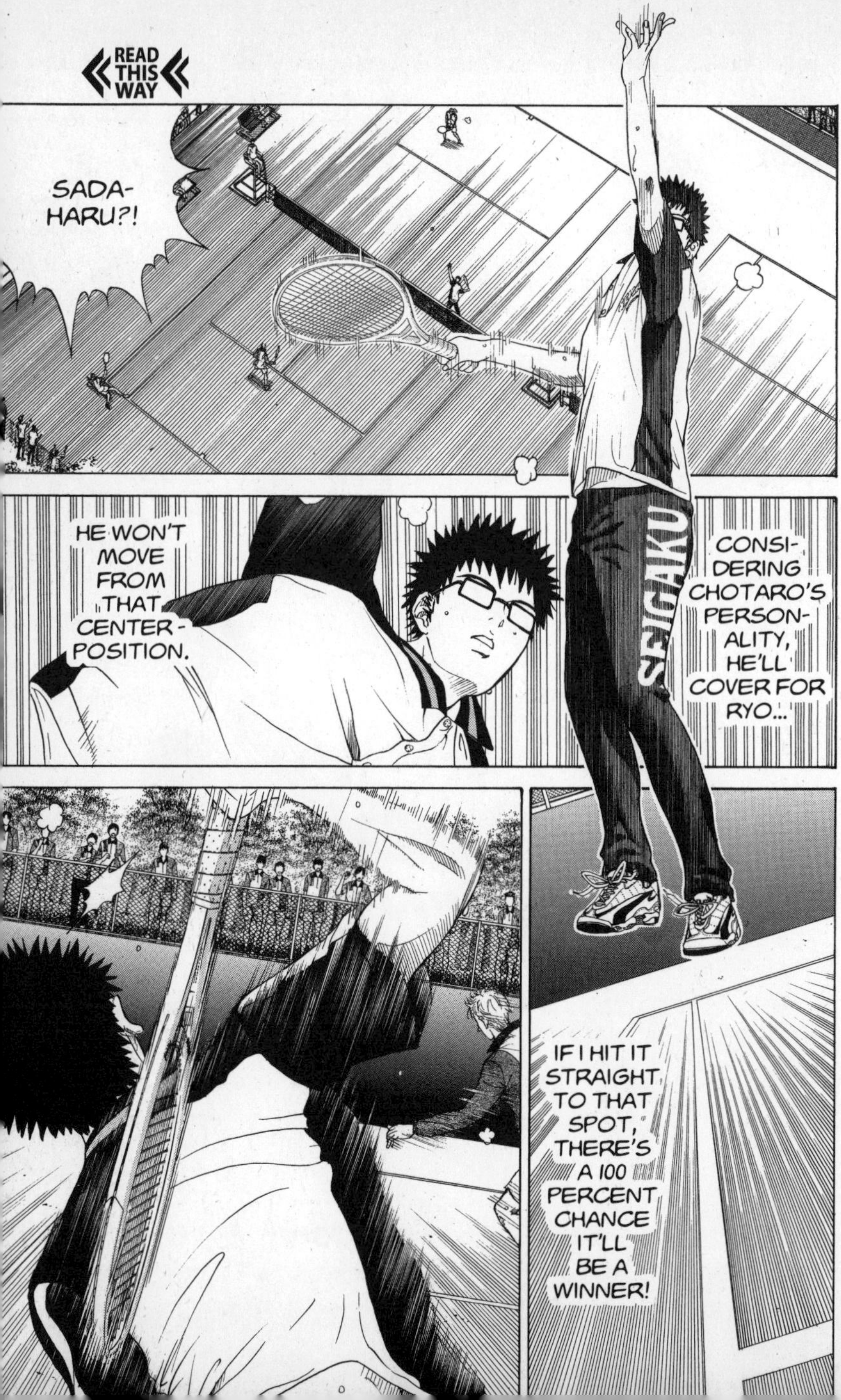
SADA-HARU?!
SEIGAKU
CONSI-DERING CHOTARO'S PERSON-ALITY, HE'LL COVER FOR RYO...
HE WON'T MOVE FROM THAT CENTER-POSITION.
IF I HIT IT STRAIGHT TO THAT SPOT, THERE'S A 100 PERCENT CHANCE IT'LL BE A WINNER!

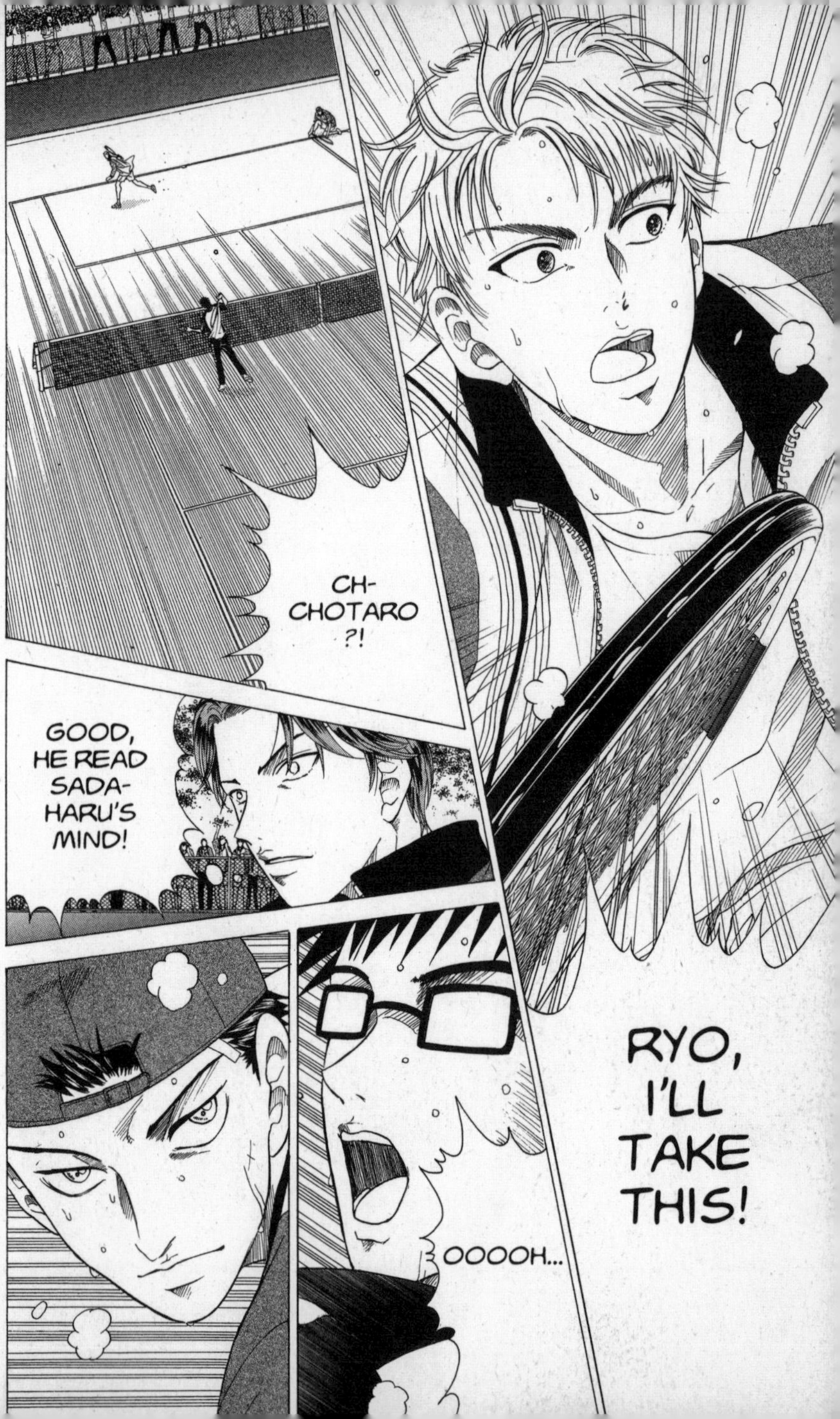
RYO, I'LL TAKE THIS!
CH-CHOTARO?!
GOOD, HE READ SADAHARU'S MIND!
OOOOH...

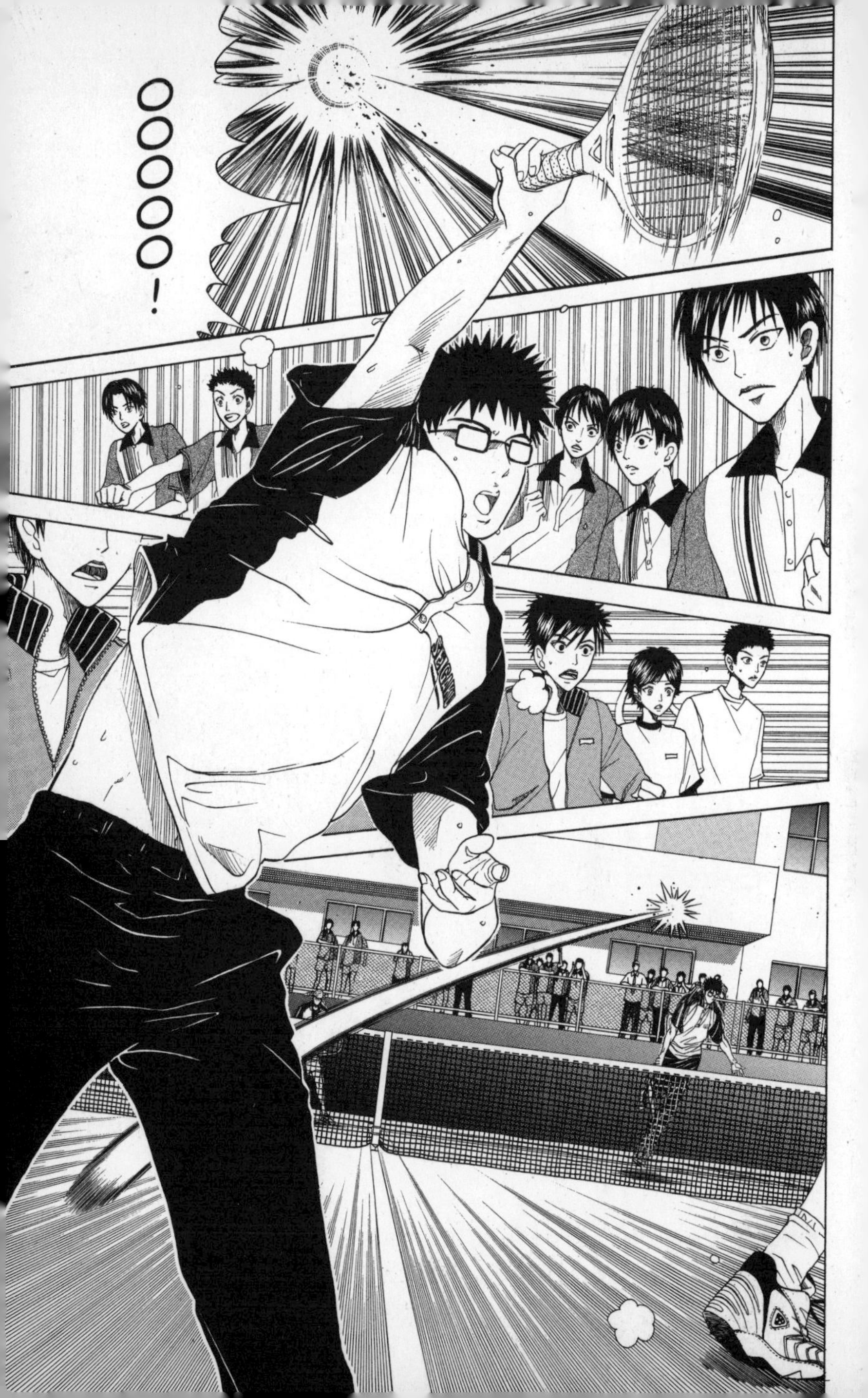
OOOOOO!

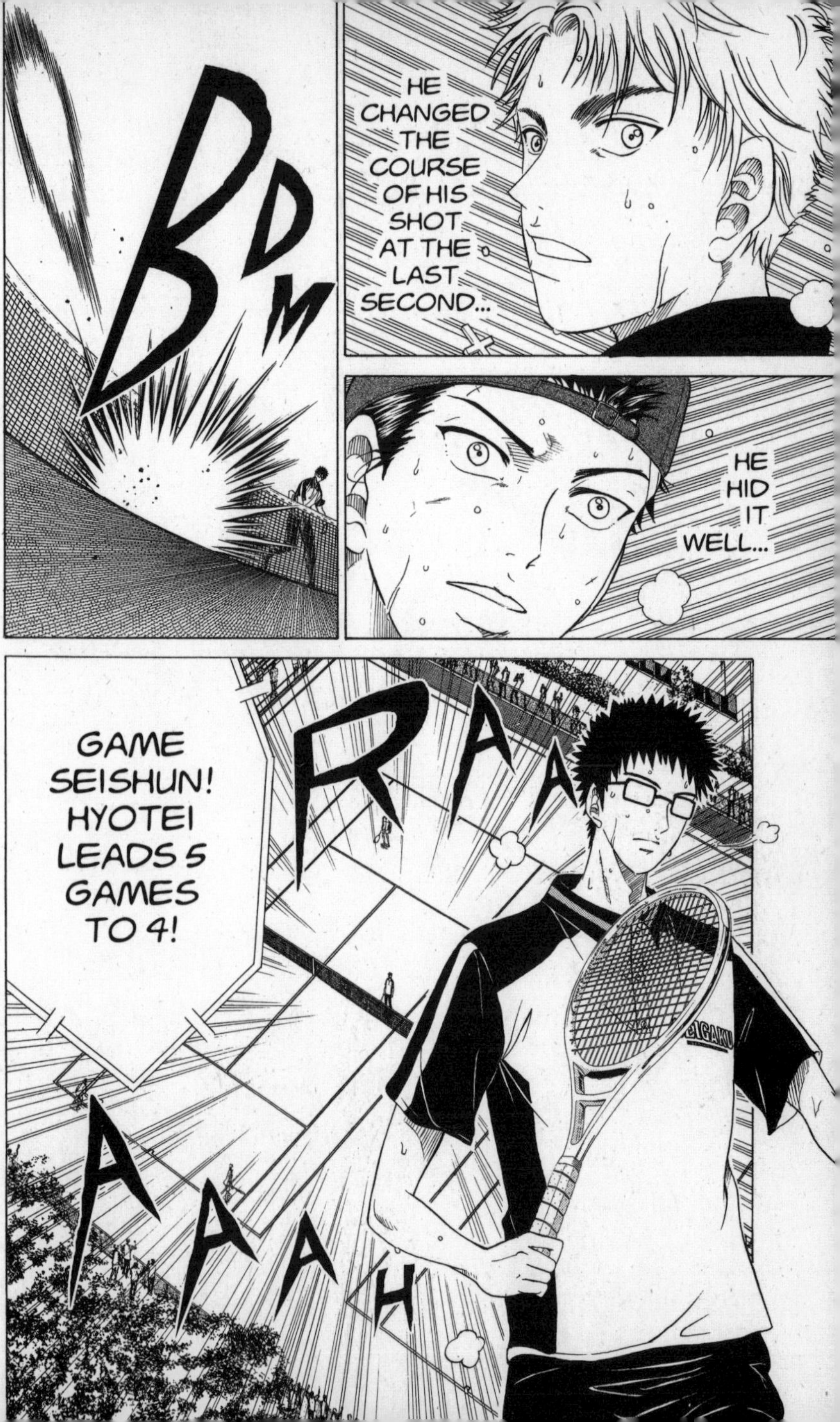
HE CHANGED THE COURSE OF HIS SHOT AT THE LAST SECOND...
HE HID IT WELL...
BDM
GAME SEISHUN! HYOTEI LEADS 5 GAMES TO 4!
RAAAAAH

READ THIS WAY

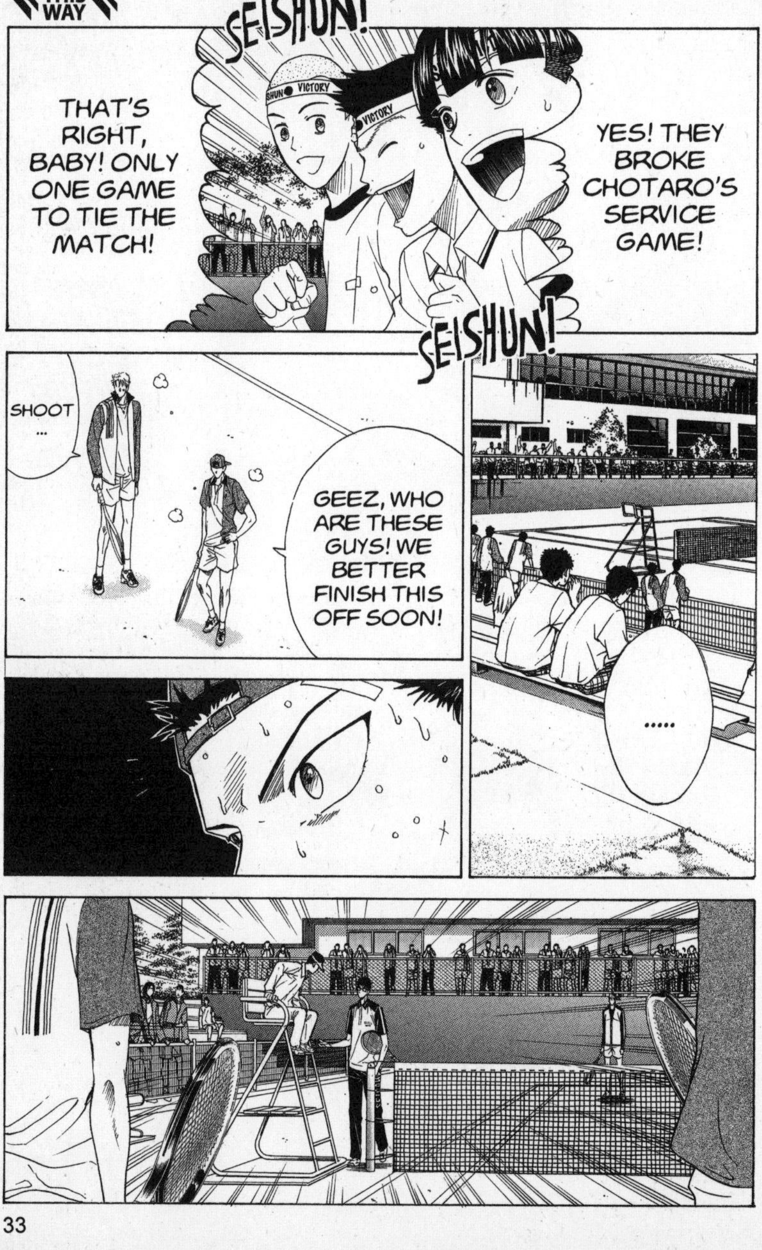
SEISHUN!
YES! THEY BROKE CHOTARO'S SERVICE GAME!
THAT'S RIGHT, BABY! ONLY ONE GAME TO TIE THE MATCH!
SEISHUN!
.....
GEEZ, WHO ARE THESE GUYS! WE BETTER FINISH THIS OFF SOON!
SHOOT ...

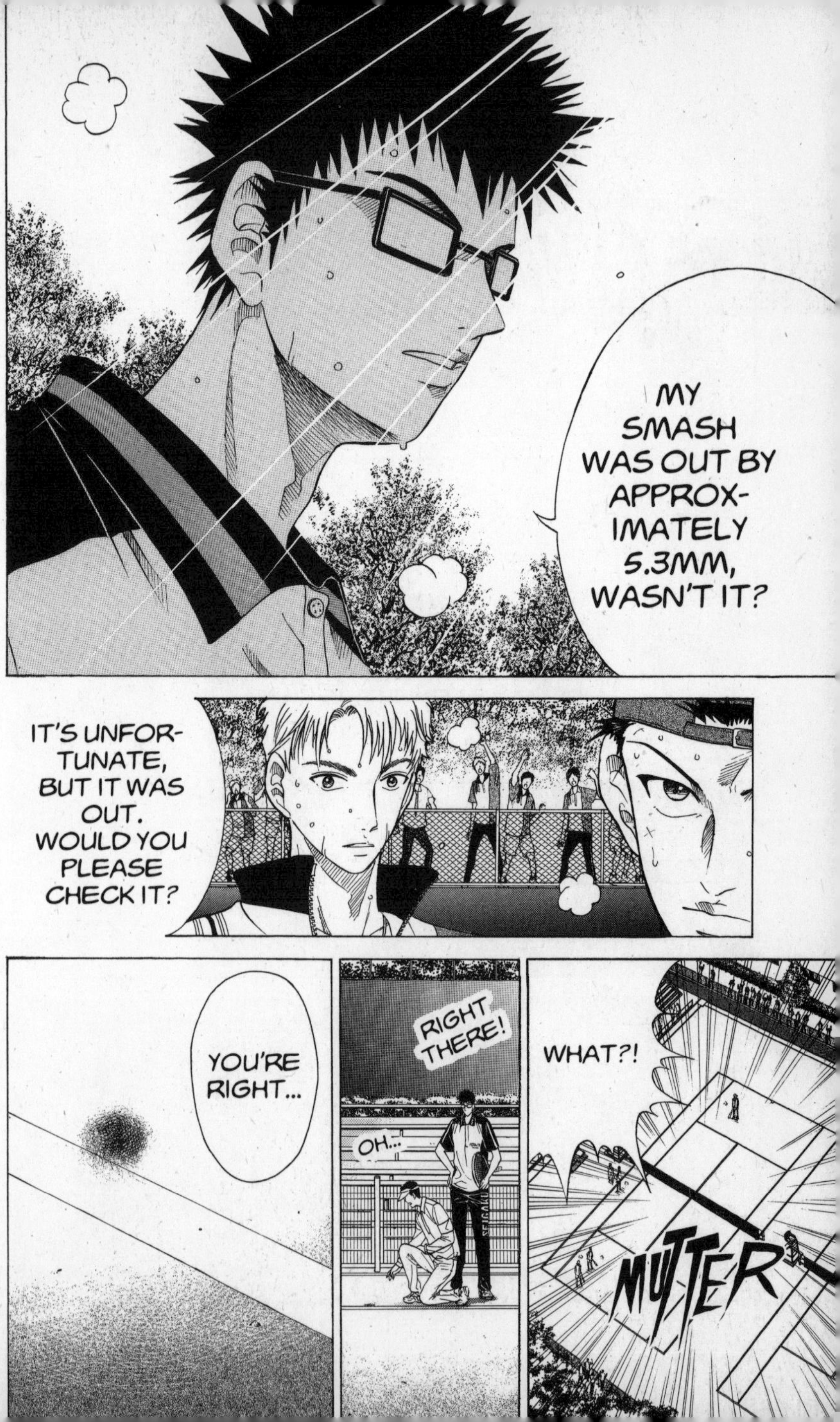
MY SMASH WAS OUT BY APPROX-IMATELY 5.3MM, WASN'T IT?
IT'S UNFOR-TUNATE, BUT IT WAS OUT. WOULD YOU PLEASE CHECK IT?
WHAT?!
MUTTER
RIGHT THERE!
OH...
YOU'RE RIGHT...

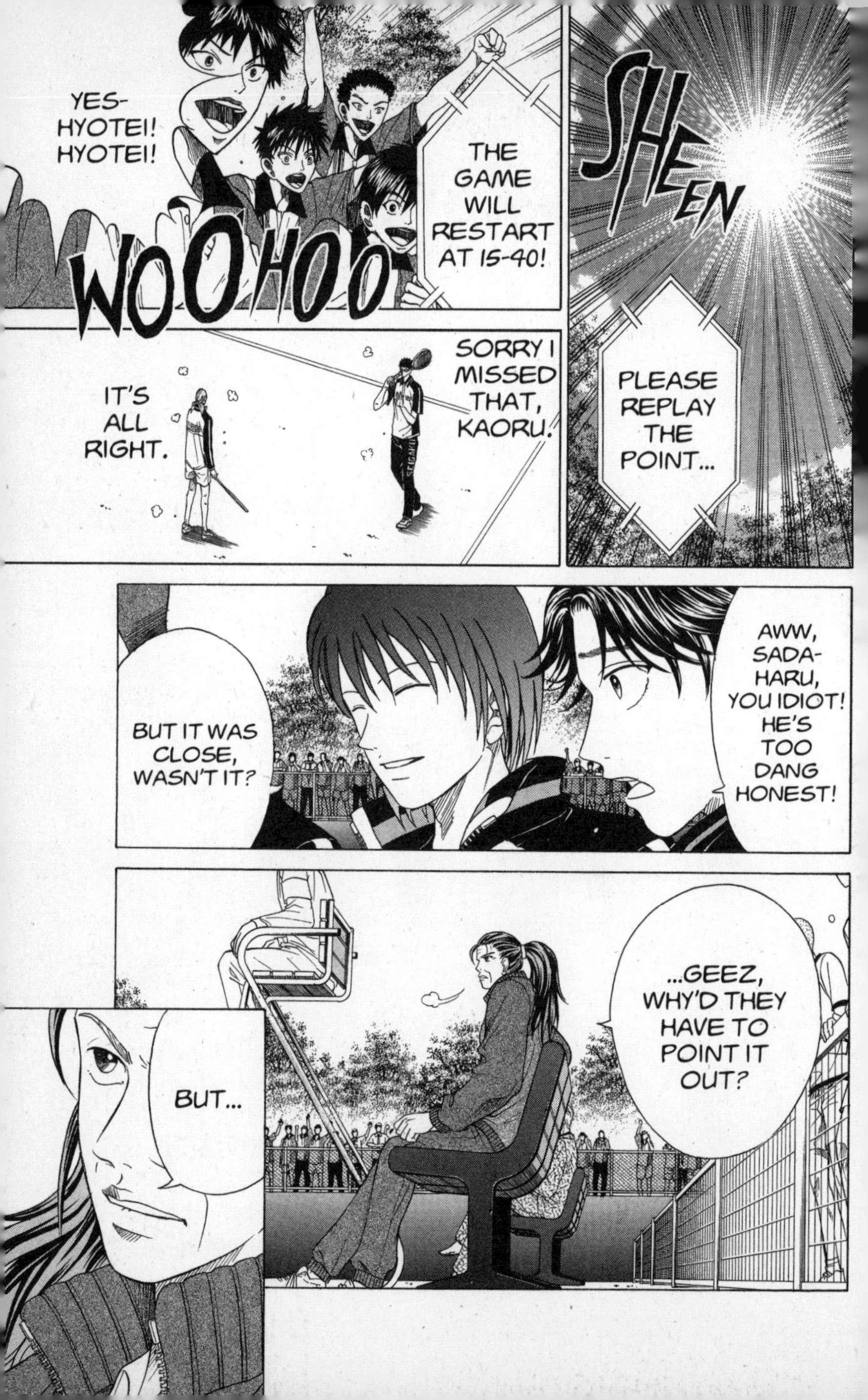
SHEEN
PLEASE REPLAY THE POINT...
THE GAME WILL RESTART AT 15-40!
WOOHOO
YES-HYOTEI! HYOTEI!
SORRY I MISSED THAT, KAORU.
IT'S ALL RIGHT.
AWW, SADAHARU, YOU IDIOT! HE'S TOO DANG HONEST!
BUT IT WAS CLOSE, WASN'T IT?
...GEEZ, WHY'D THEY HAVE TO POINT IT OUT?
BUT...

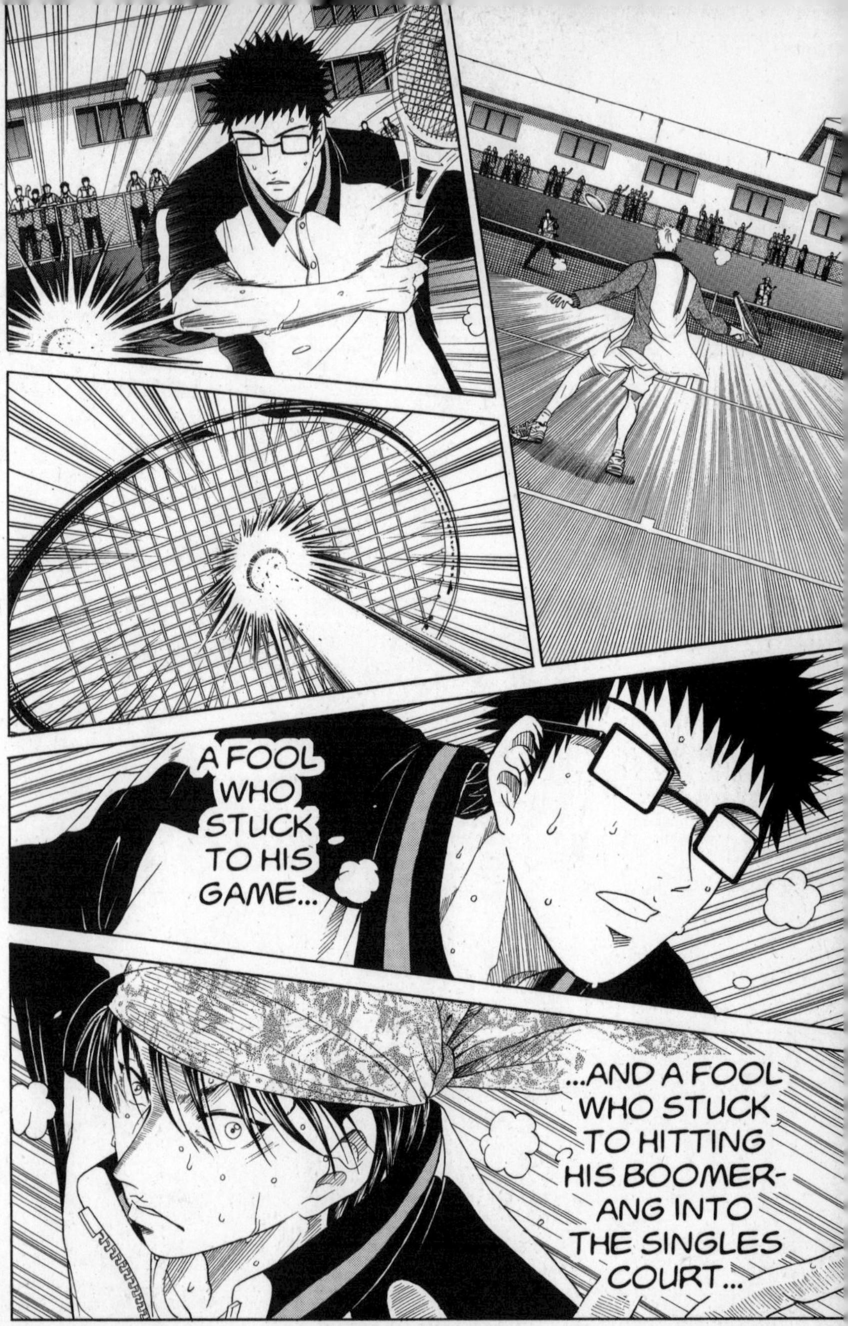
A FOOL WHO STUCK TO HIS GAME...
...AND A FOOL WHO STUCK TO HITTING HIS BOOMER-ANG INTO THE SINGLES COURT...

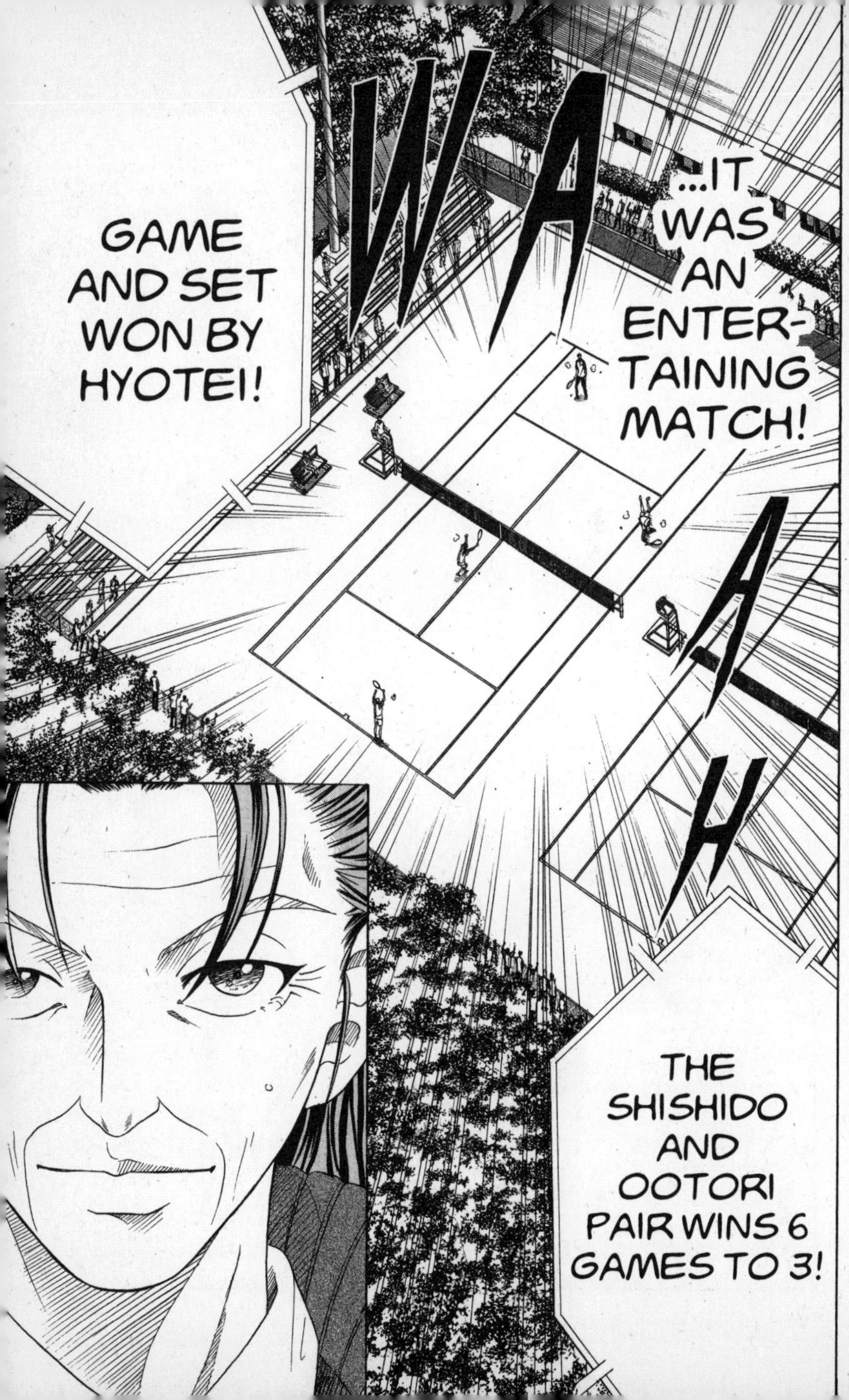
WA
...IT WAS AN ENTER-TAINING MATCH!
GAME AND SET WON BY HYOTEI!
AAH
THE SHISHIDO AND OOTORI PAIR WINS 6 GAMES TO 3!

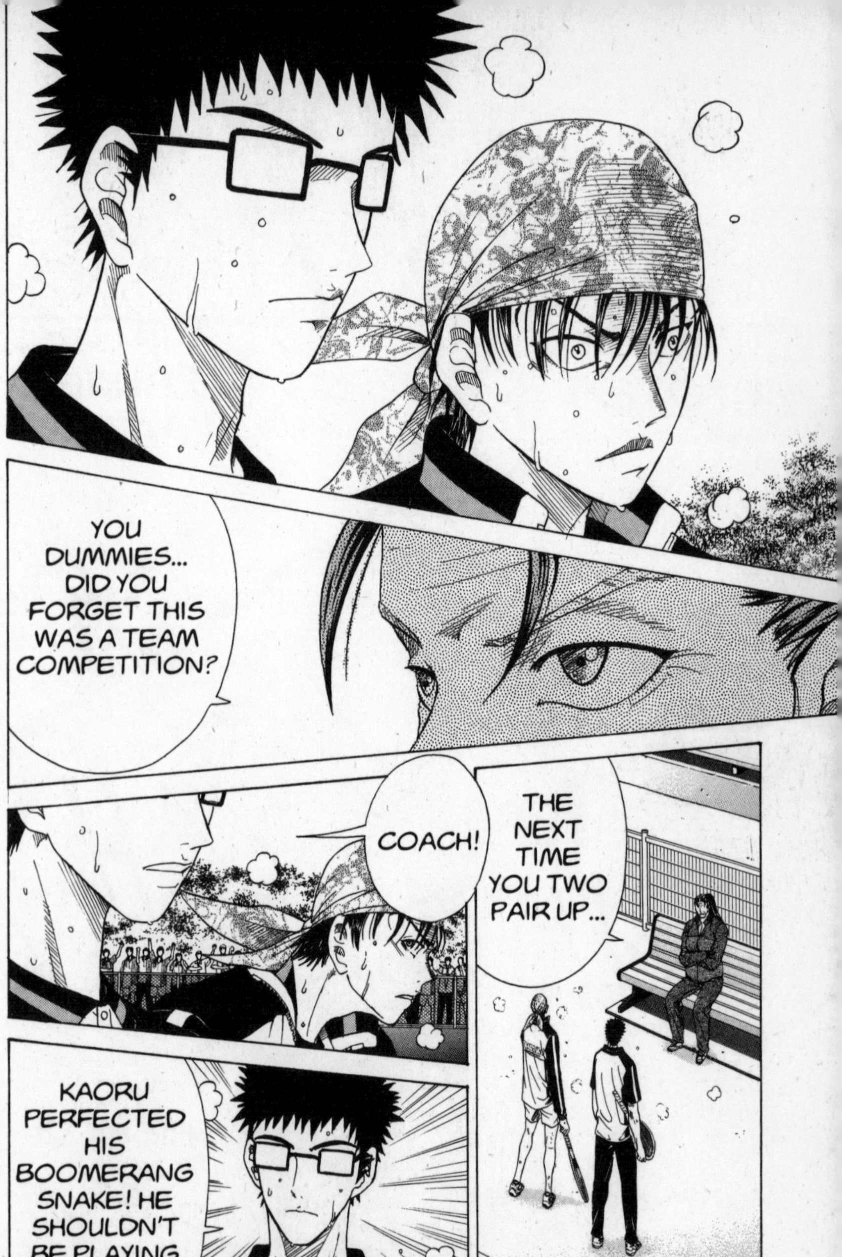
YOU DUMMIES... DID YOU FORGET THIS WAS A TEAM COMPETITION?
COACH!
THE NEXT TIME YOU TWO PAIR UP...
KAORU PERFECTED HIS BOOMERANG SNAKE! HE SHOULDN'T BE PLAYING DOUBLES...

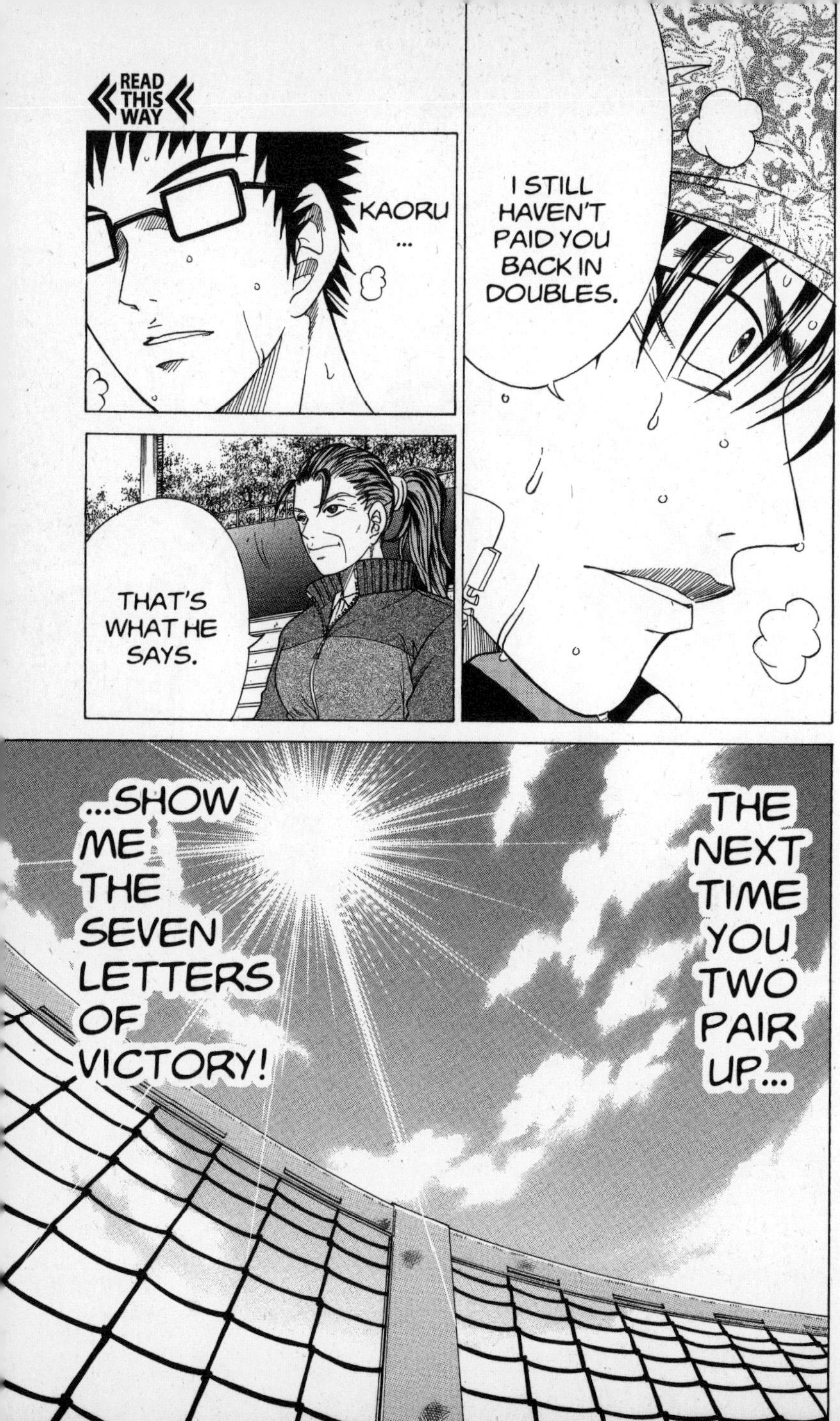
READ THIS WAY
I STILL HAVEN'T PAID YOU BACK IN DOUBLES.
KAORU ...
THAT'S WHAT HE SAYS.
THE NEXT TIME YOU TWO PAIR UP...
...SHOW ME THE SEVEN LETTERS OF VICTORY!

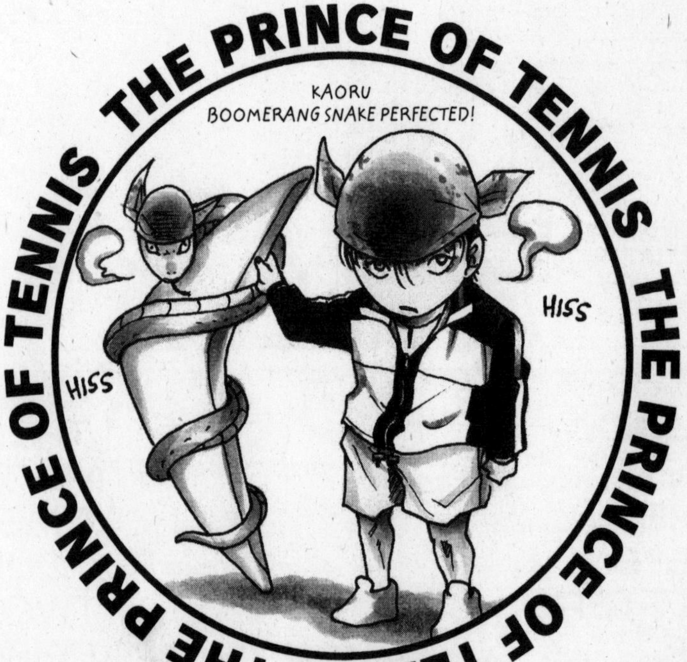
THE PRINCE OF TENNIS THE PRINCE OF TENNIS THE PRINCE OF TENNIS
KAORU
BOOMERANG SNAKE PERFECTED!
HISS
HISS

GENIUS 134: LAST TENNIS

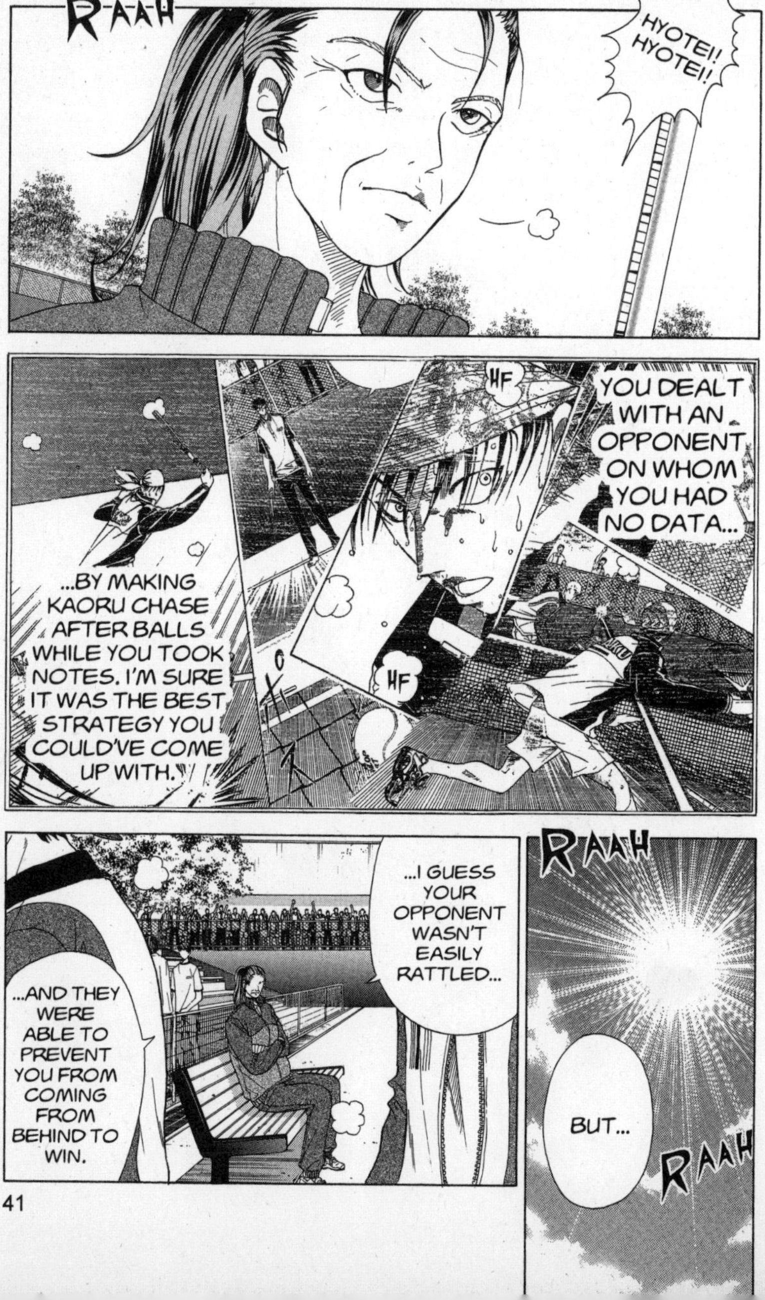
HYOTEI!! HYOTEI!!
RAAH
YOU DEALT WITH AN OPPONENT ON WHOM YOU HAD NO DATA...
HF
HF
...BY MAKING KAORU CHASE AFTER BALLS WHILE YOU TOOK NOTES. I'M SURE IT WAS THE BEST STRATEGY YOU COULD'VE COME UP WITH.
RAAH
BUT...
RAAH
...I GUESS YOUR OPPONENT WASN'T EASILY RATTLED...
...AND THEY WERE ABLE TO PREVENT YOU FROM COMING FROM BEHIND TO WIN.

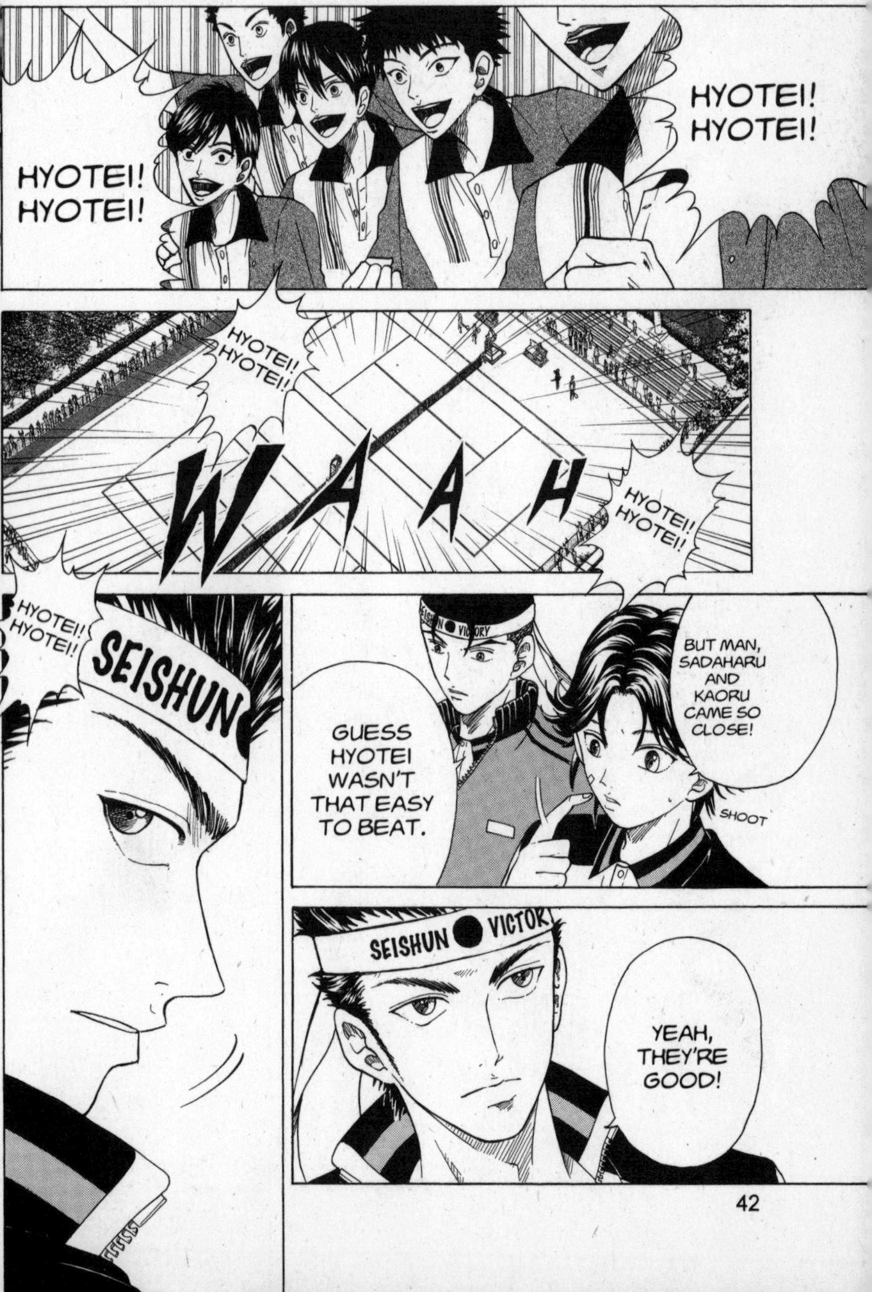
HYOTEI! HYOTEI!
HYOTEI! HYOTEI!
HYOTEI!! HYOTEI!!
WAAH
HYOTEI!! HYOTEI!!
BUT MAN, SADAHARU AND KAORU CAME SO CLOSE!
SHOOT
GUESS HYOTEI WASN'T THAT EASY TO BEAT.
SEISHUN VICTOR
YEAH, THEY'RE GOOD!
HYOTEI!! HYOTEI!!
SEISHUN

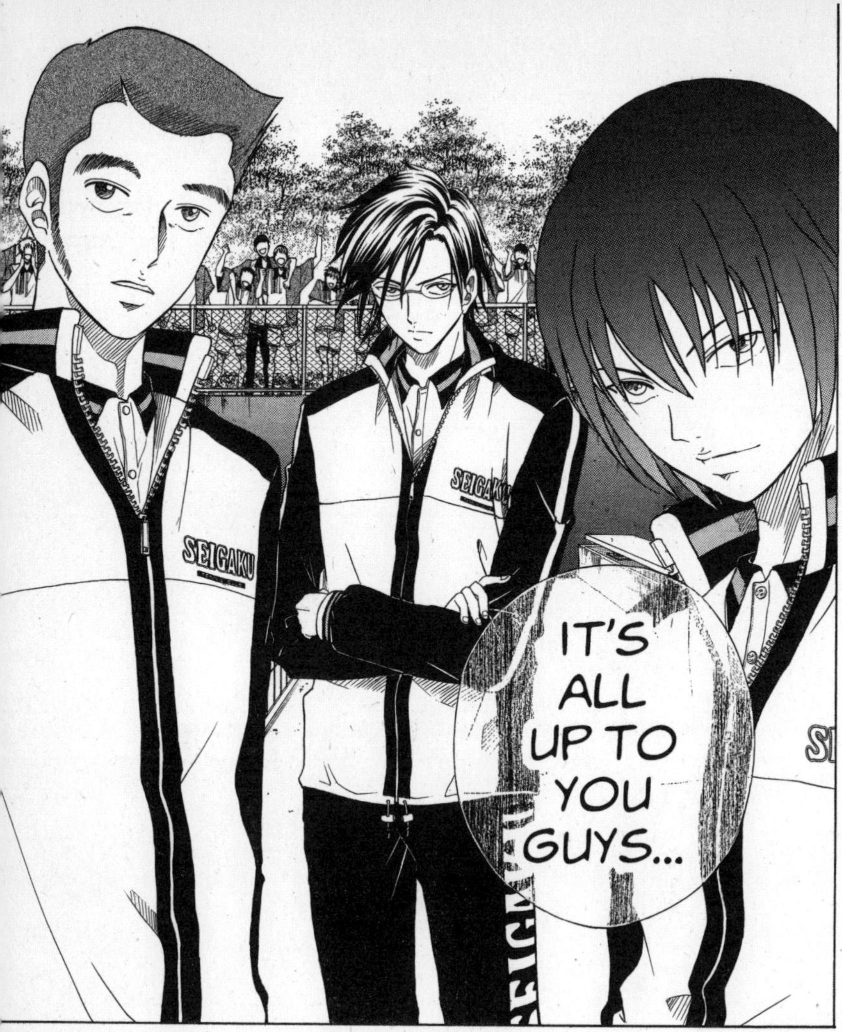
IT'S ALL UP TO YOU GUYS...

GENIUS 134:

LAST TENNIS?

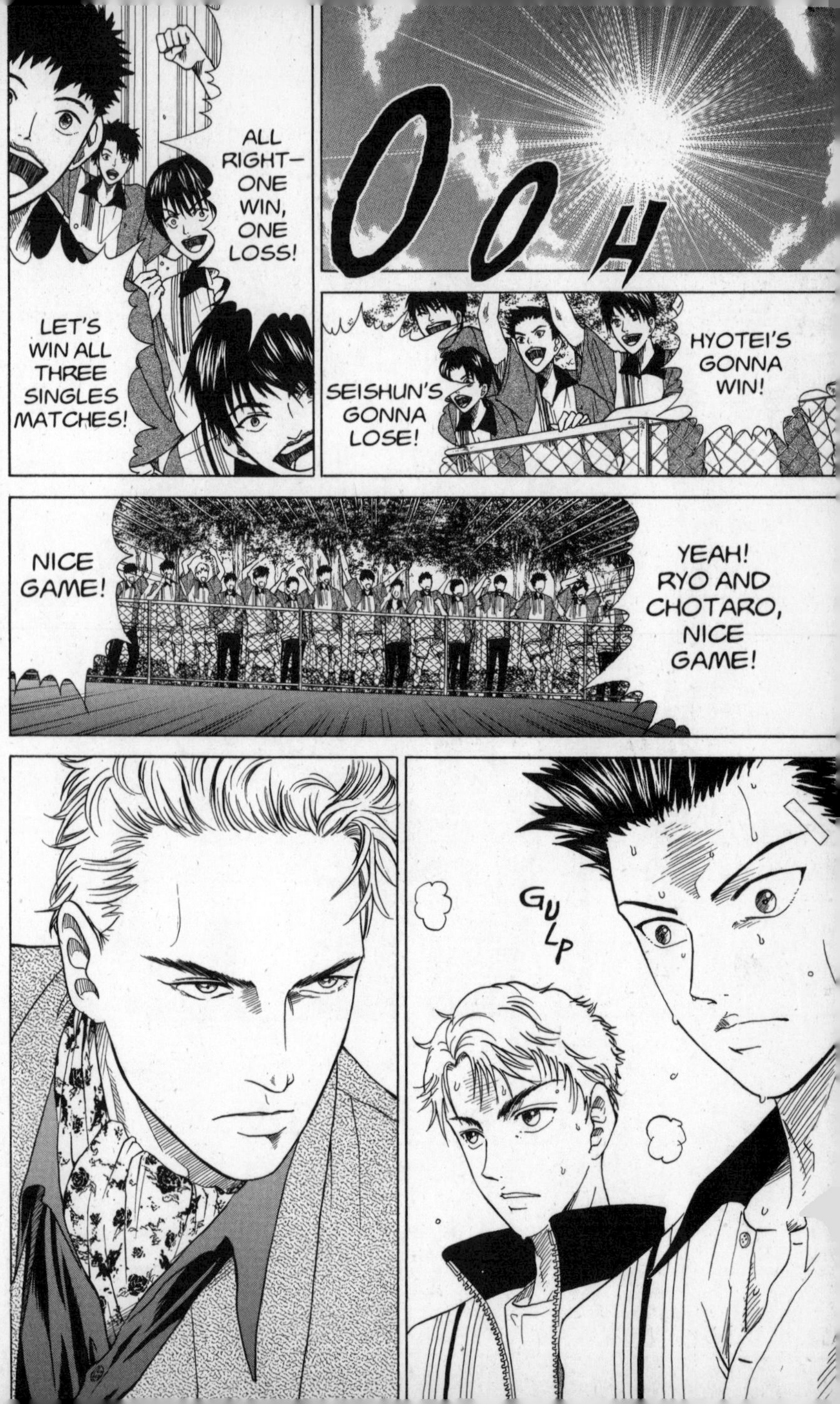
OOOH
HYOTEI'S GONNA WIN!
SEISHUN'S GONNA LOSE!
ALL RIGHT— ONE WIN, ONE LOSS!
LET'S WIN ALL THREE SINGLES MATCHES!
YEAH! RYO AND CHOTARO, NICE GAME!
NICE GAME!
GULP

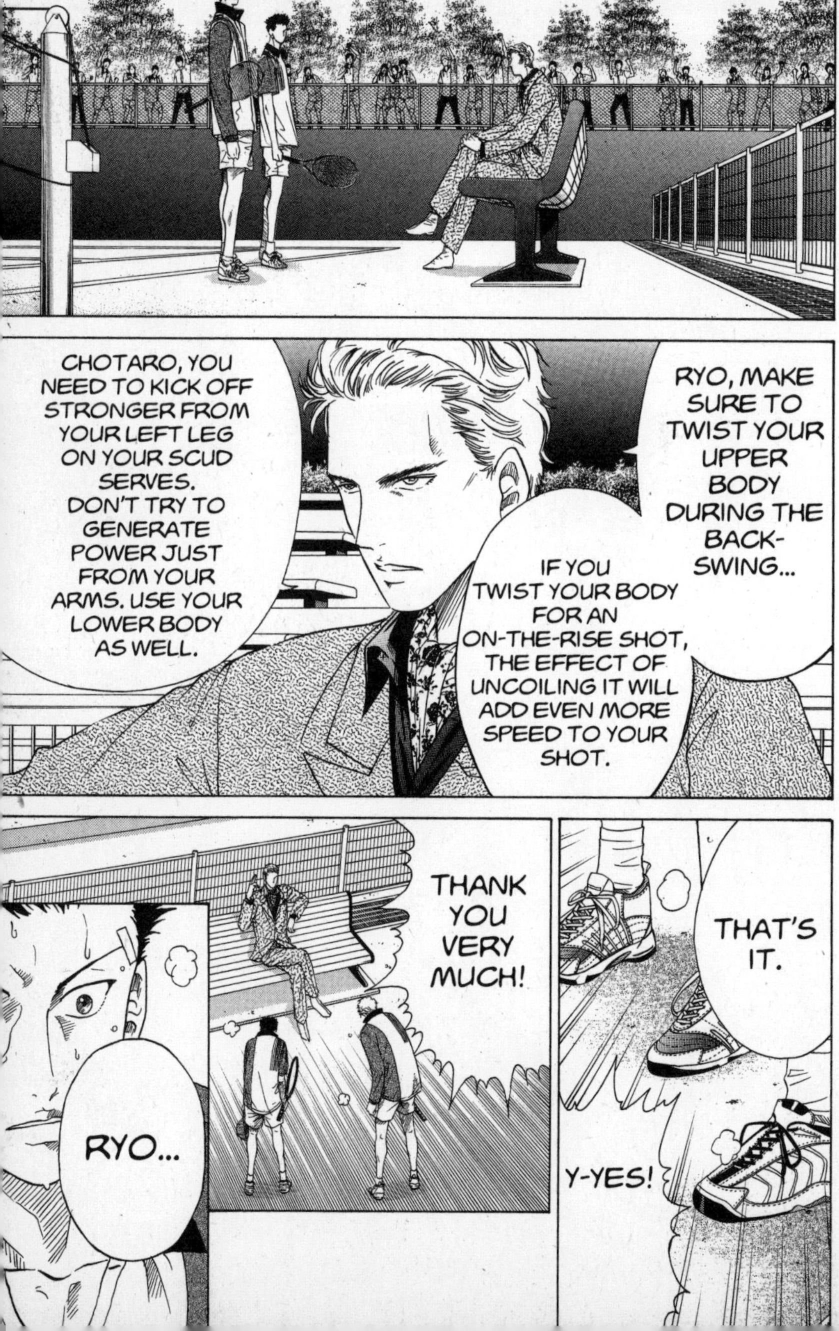
RYO, MAKE SURE TO TWIST YOUR UPPER BODY DURING THE BACK-SWING...
IF YOU TWIST YOUR BODY FOR AN ON-THE-RISE SHOT, THE EFFECT OF UNCOILING IT WILL ADD EVEN MORE SPEED TO YOUR SHOT.
CHOTARO, YOU NEED TO KICK OFF STRONGER FROM YOUR LEFT LEG ON YOUR SCUD SERVES. DON'T TRY TO GENERATE POWER JUST FROM YOUR ARMS. USE YOUR LOWER BODY AS WELL.
THAT'S IT.
Y-YES!
THANK YOU VERY MUCH!
RYO...

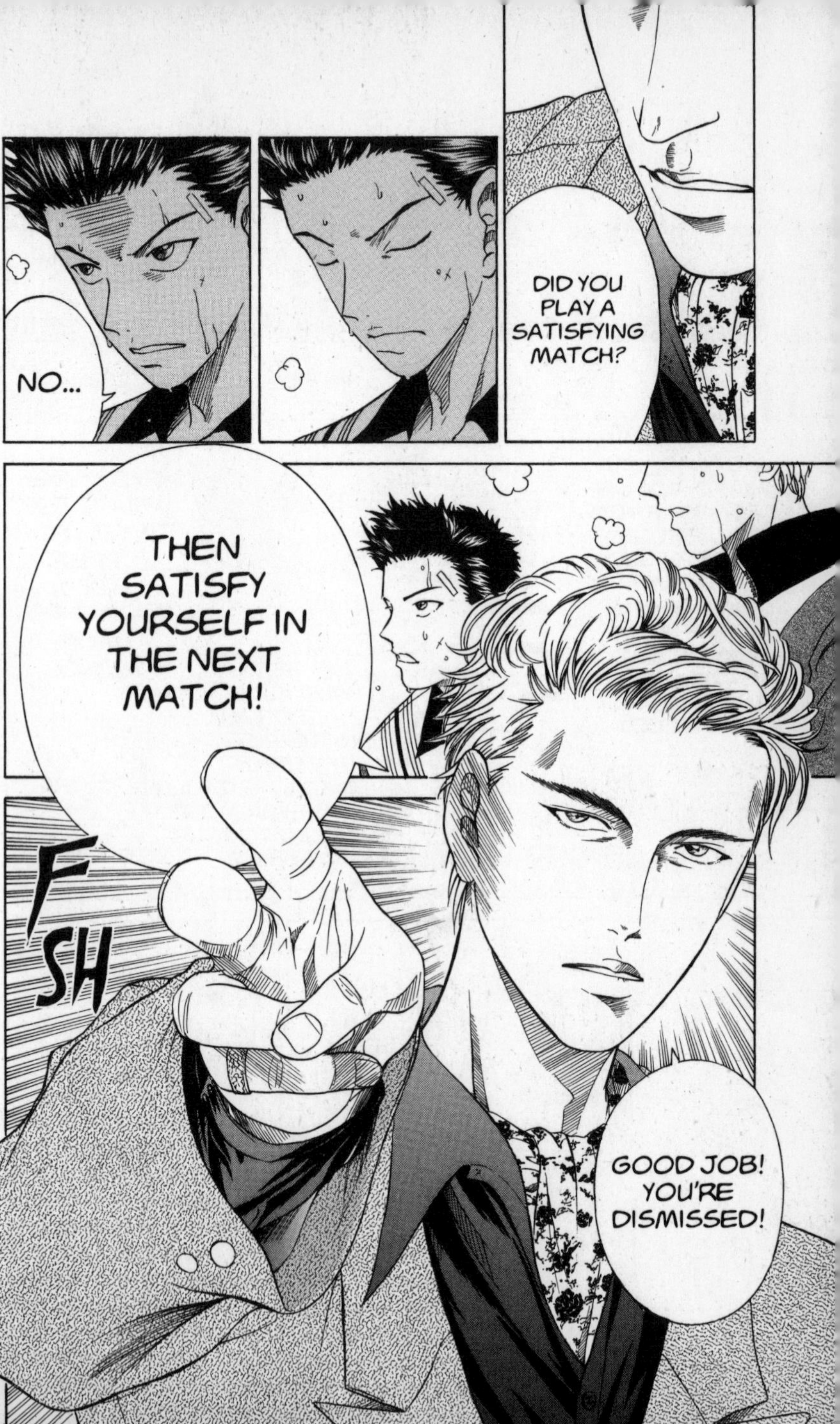
DID YOU PLAY A SATISFYING MATCH?
NO...
THEN SATISFY YOURSELF IN THE NEXT MATCH!
FSH
GOOD JOB! YOU'RE DISMISSED!

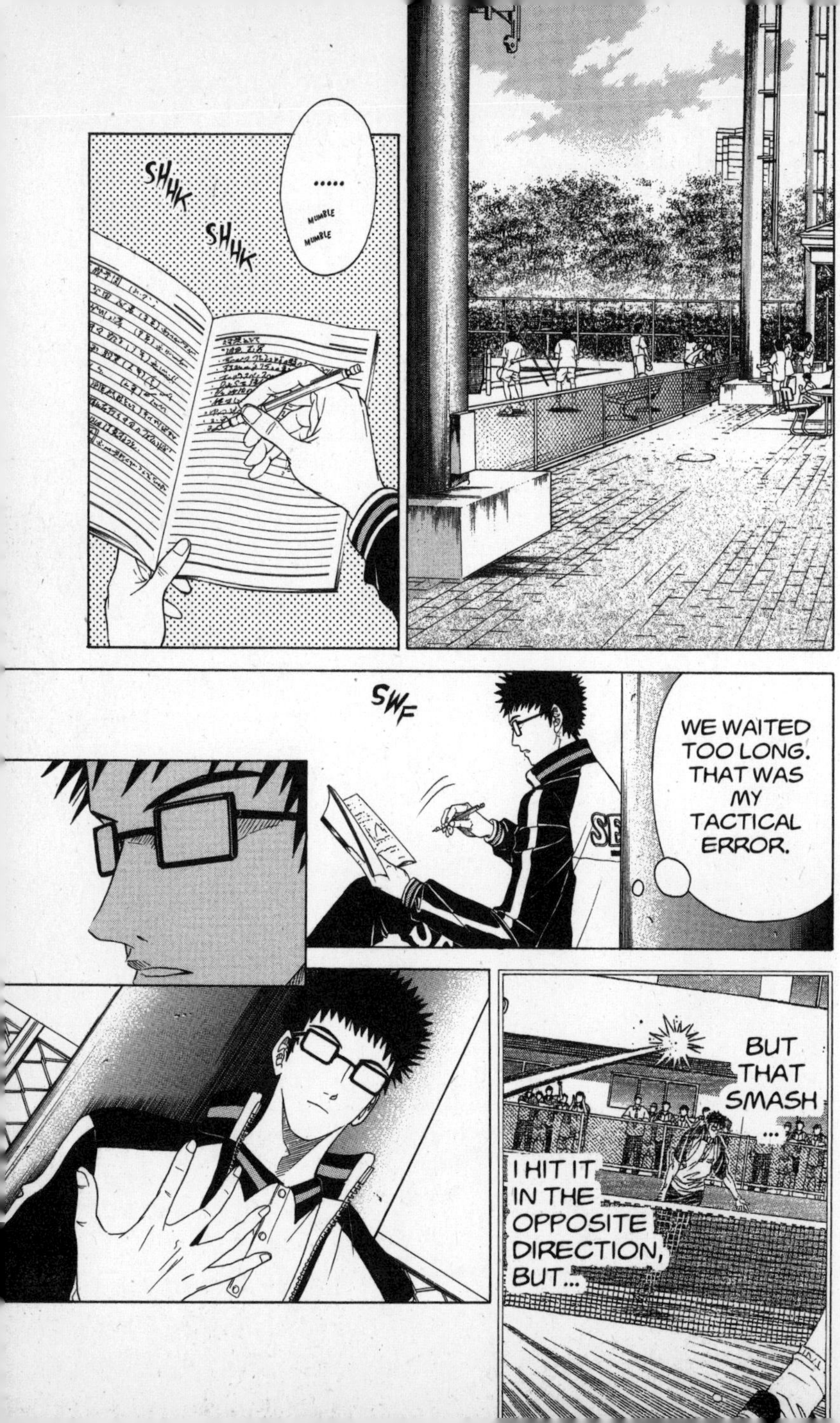
SHHK
SHHK
......
MUMBLE
MUMBLE
WE WAITED TOO LONG. THAT WAS MY TACTICAL ERROR.
SWF
BUT THAT SMASH ...
I HIT IT IN THE OPPOSITE DIRECTION, BUT...

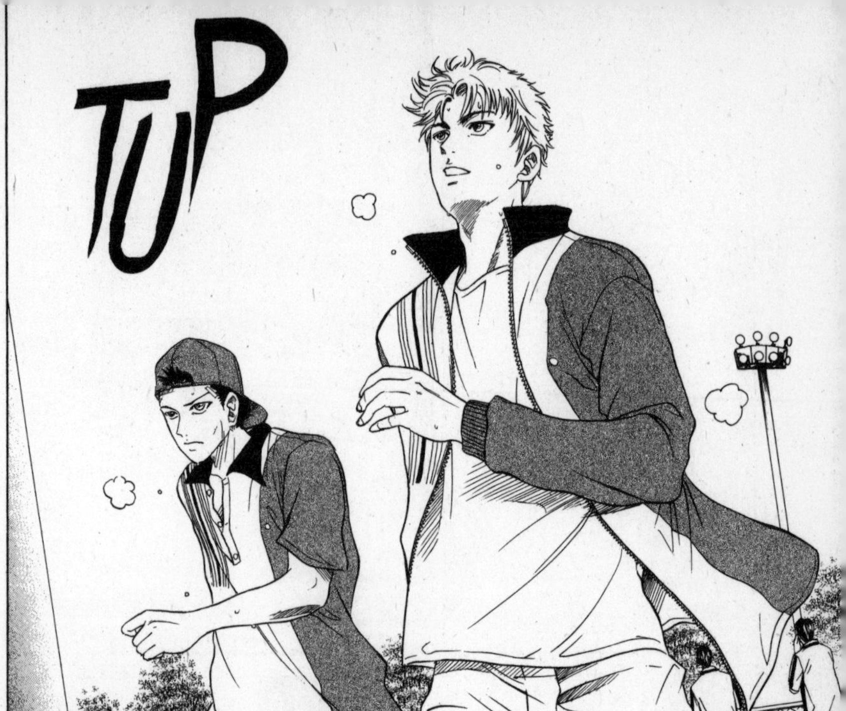
TUP
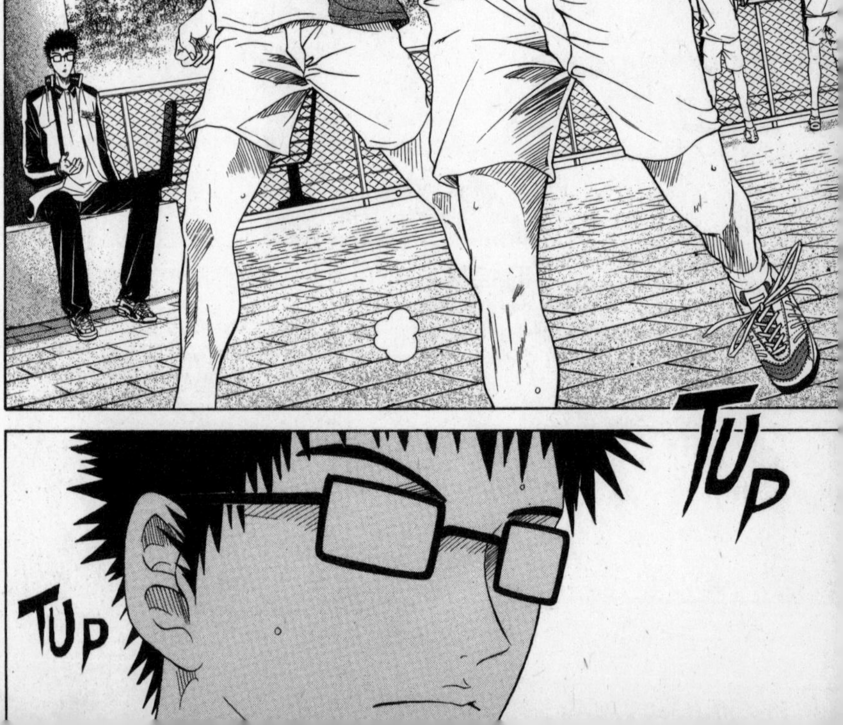
TUP
TUP

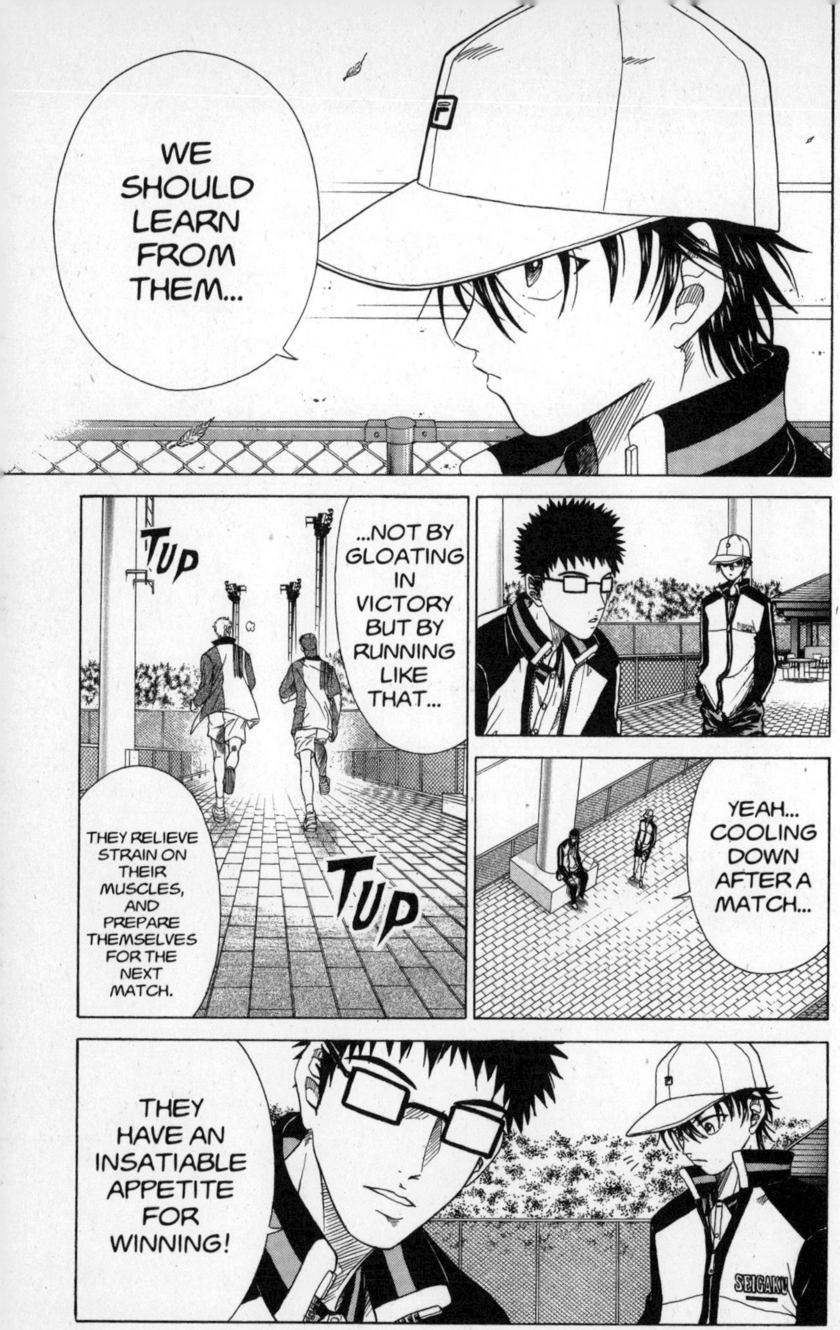
WE SHOULD LEARN FROM THEM...
YEAH... COOLING DOWN AFTER A MATCH...
...NOT BY GLOATING IN VICTORY BUT BY RUNNING LIKE THAT...
TUP
TUP
THEY RELIEVE STRAIN ON THEIR MUSCLES, AND PREPARE THEMSELVES FOR THE NEXT MATCH.
THEY HAVE AN INSATIABLE APPETITE FOR WINNING!
SEIGAKU

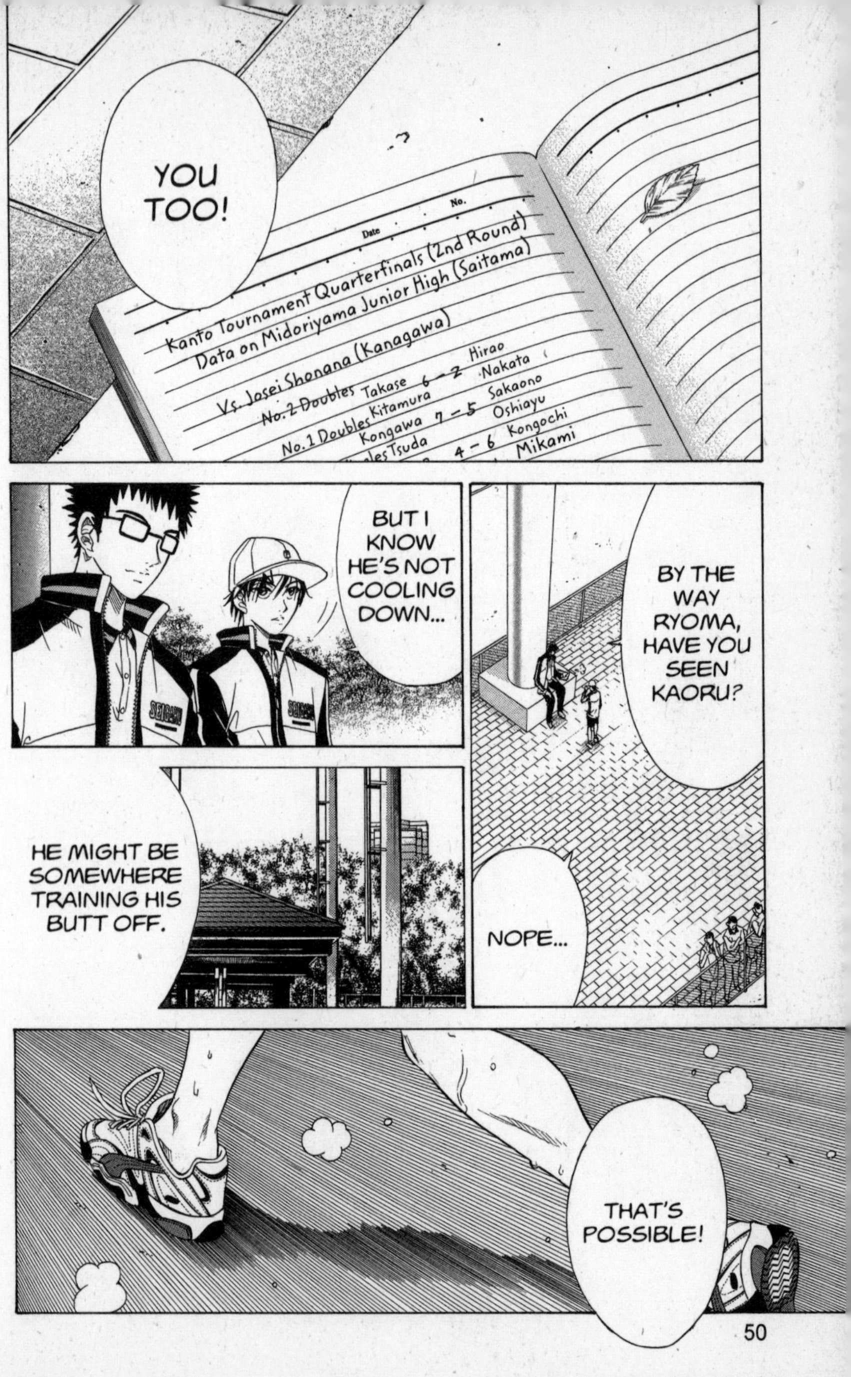
YOU TOO!
Date
No.
Kanto Tournament Quarterfinals (2nd Round)
Data on Midoriyama Junior High (Saitama)
Vs. Josei Shonana (Kanagawa)
No. 2 Doubles Takase 6-2 Hirao
Kitamura Nakata
No. 1 Doubles Kongawa 7-5 Sakaono
Tsuda Oshiayu
4-6 Kongochi
Mikami
BY THE WAY RYOMA, HAVE YOU SEEN KAORU?
NOPE...
BUT I KNOW HE'S NOT COOLING DOWN...
HE MIGHT BE SOMEWHERE TRAINING HIS BUTT OFF.
THAT'S POSSIBLE!

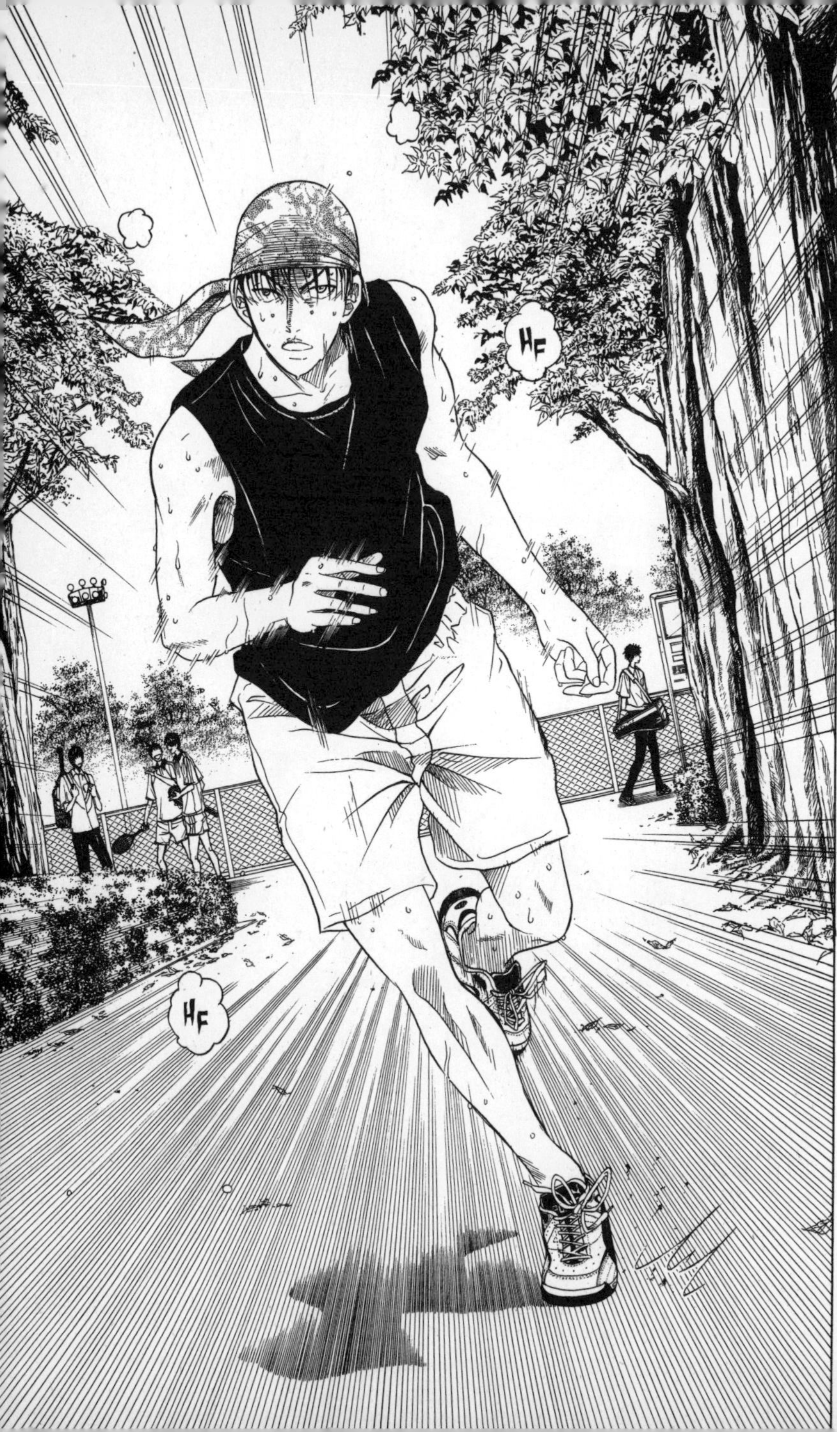
HF
HF

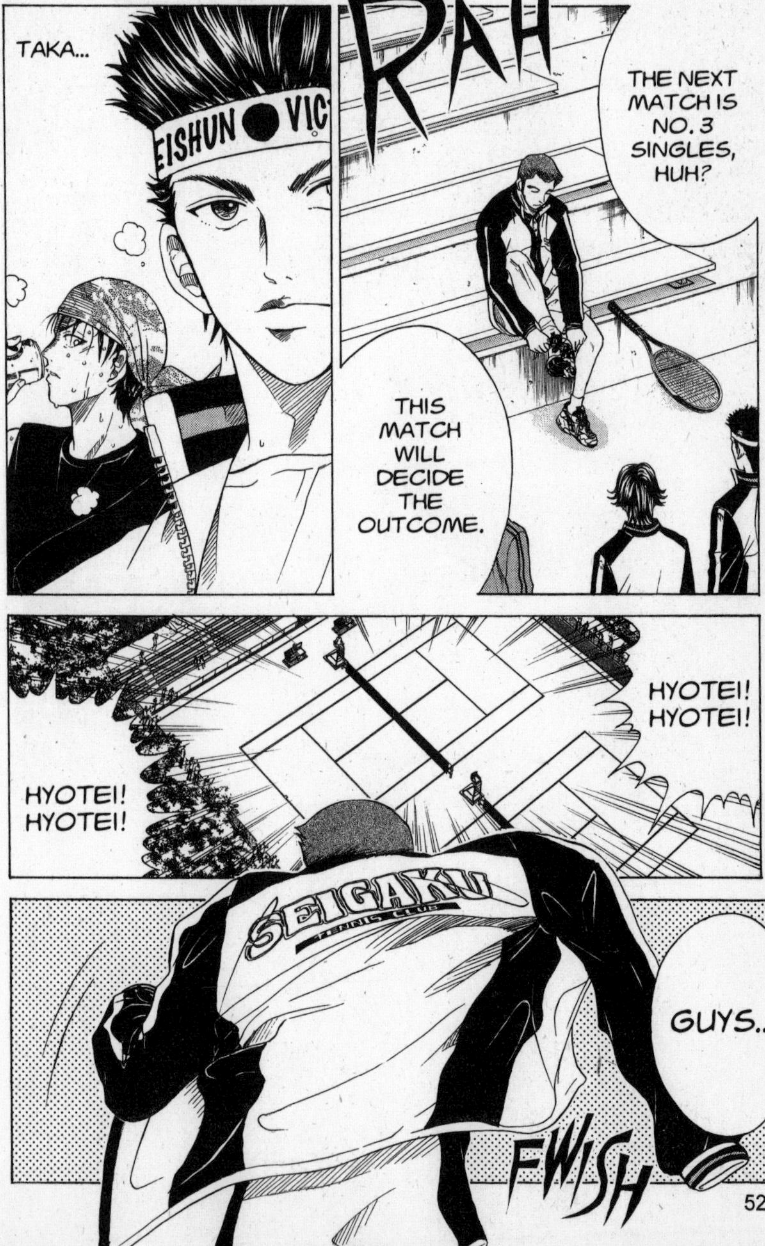
RAH
THE NEXT MATCH IS NO. 3 SINGLES, HUH?
THIS MATCH WILL DECIDE THE OUTCOME.
TAKA...
HYOTEI! HYOTEI!
HYOTEI! HYOTEI!
SEIGAKU TENNIS CLUB
GUYS...
FWISH

READ THIS WAY

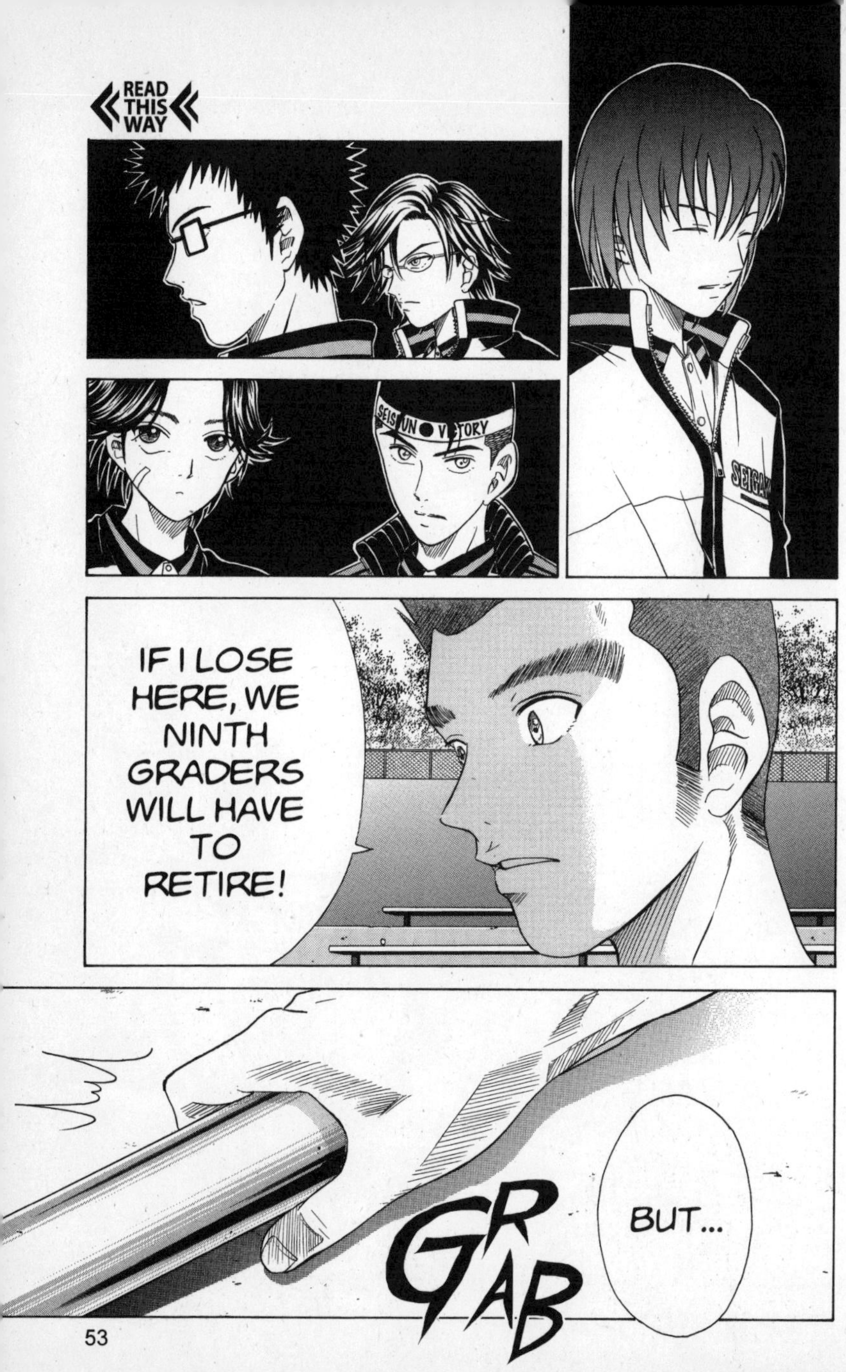
IF I LOSE HERE, WE NINTH GRADERS WILL HAVE TO RETIRE!
BUT...
GRAB

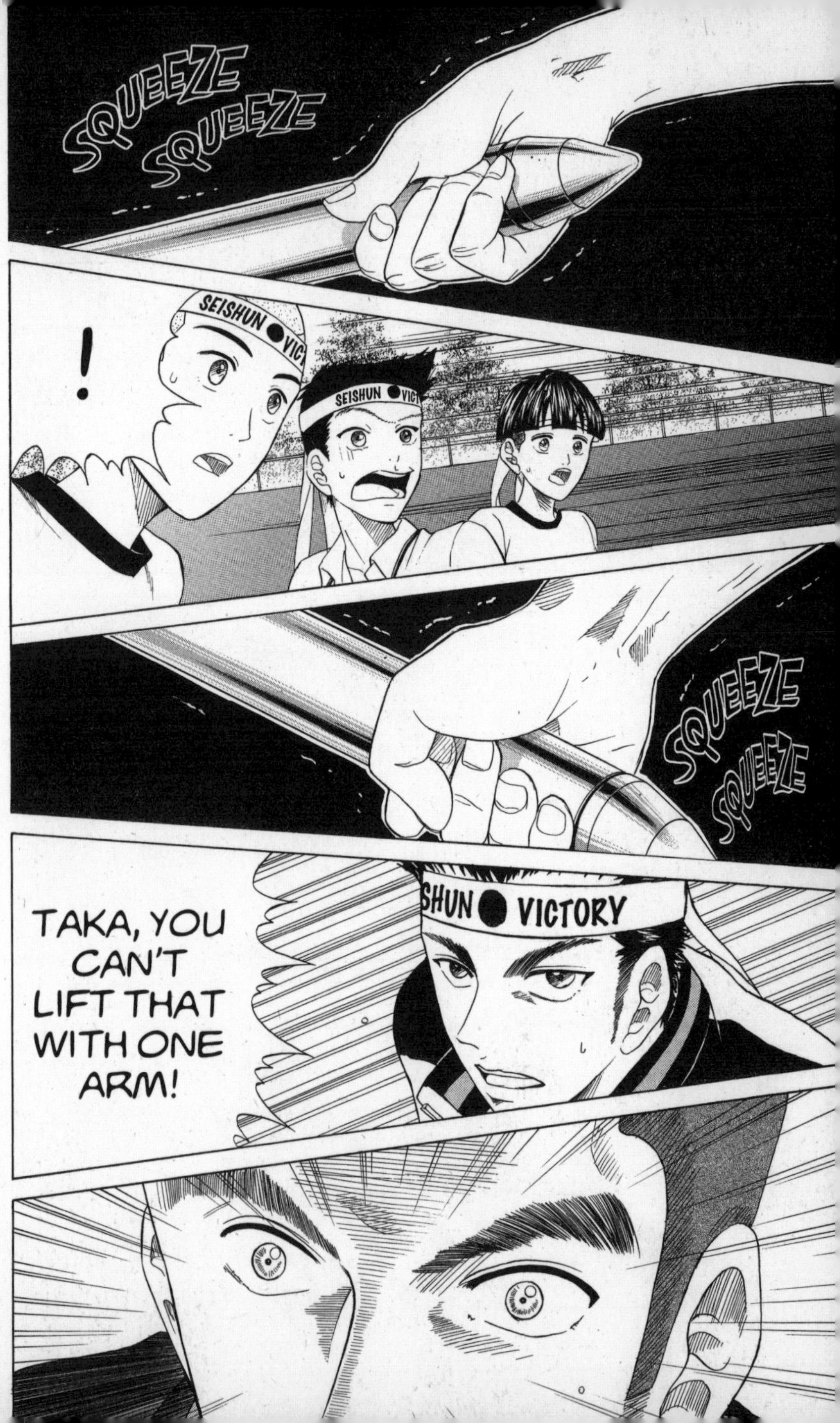

SQUEEZE SQUEEZE
SEISHUN
!
SEISHUN
SQUEEZE SQUEEZE
SHUN VICTORY
TAKA, YOU CAN'T LIFT THAT WITH ONE ARM!

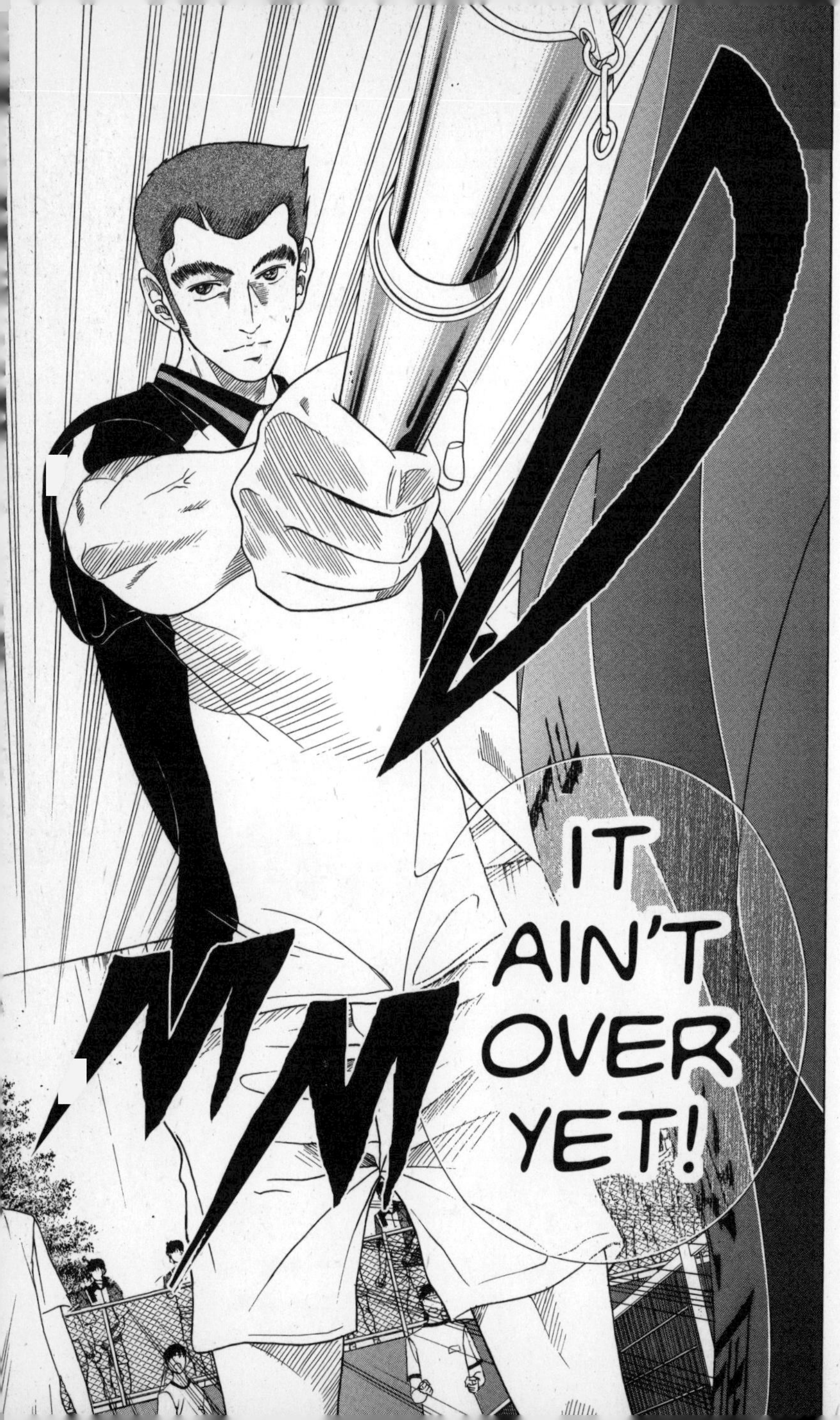
IT AIN'T OVER YET!

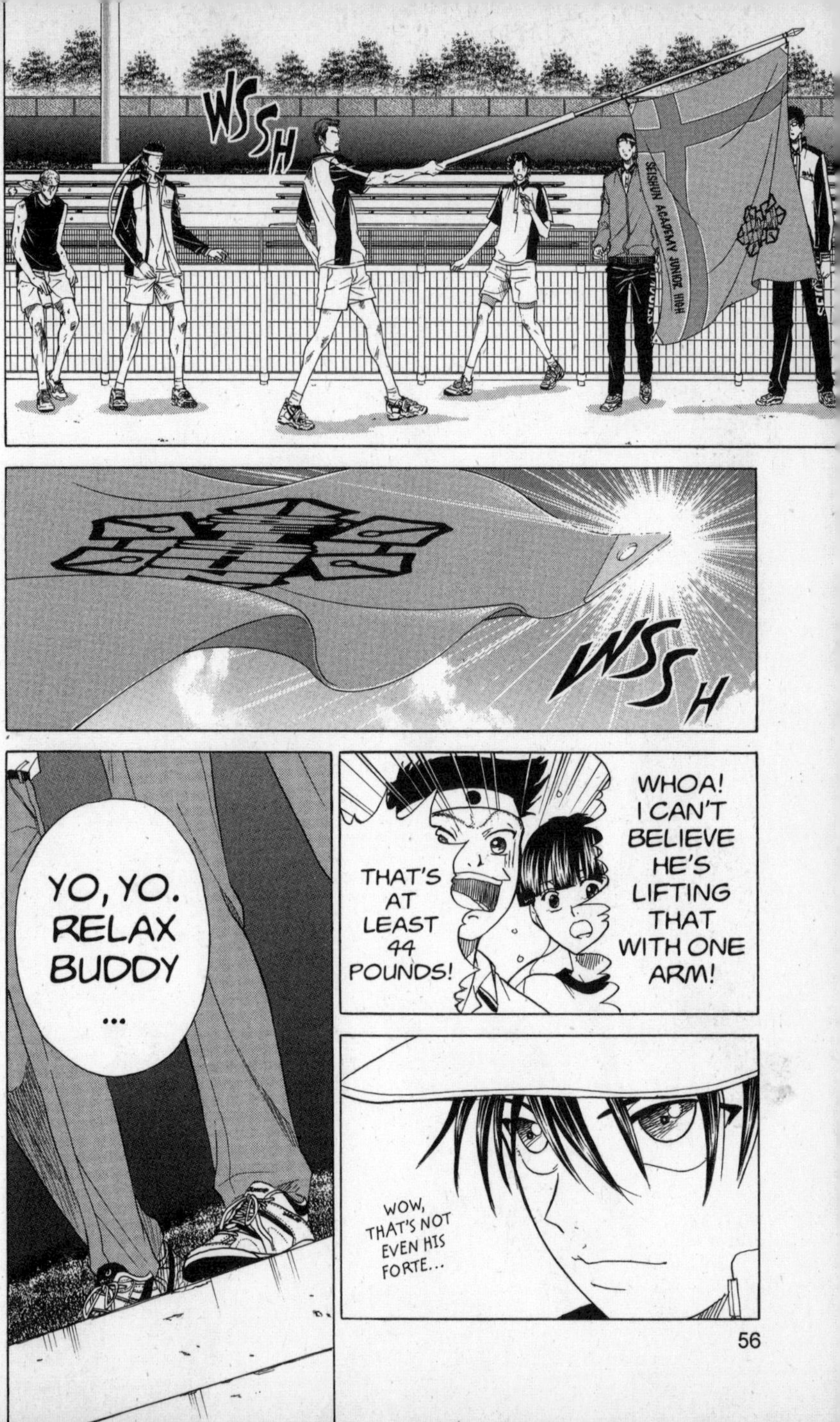
WSSH
SEISHUN ACADEMY JUNIOR HIGH
WSSH
WHOA! I CAN'T BELIEVE HE'S LIFTING THAT WITH ONE ARM!
THAT'S AT LEAST 44 POUNDS!
WOW, THAT'S NOT EVEN HIS FORTE...
YO, YO. RELAX BUDDY ...

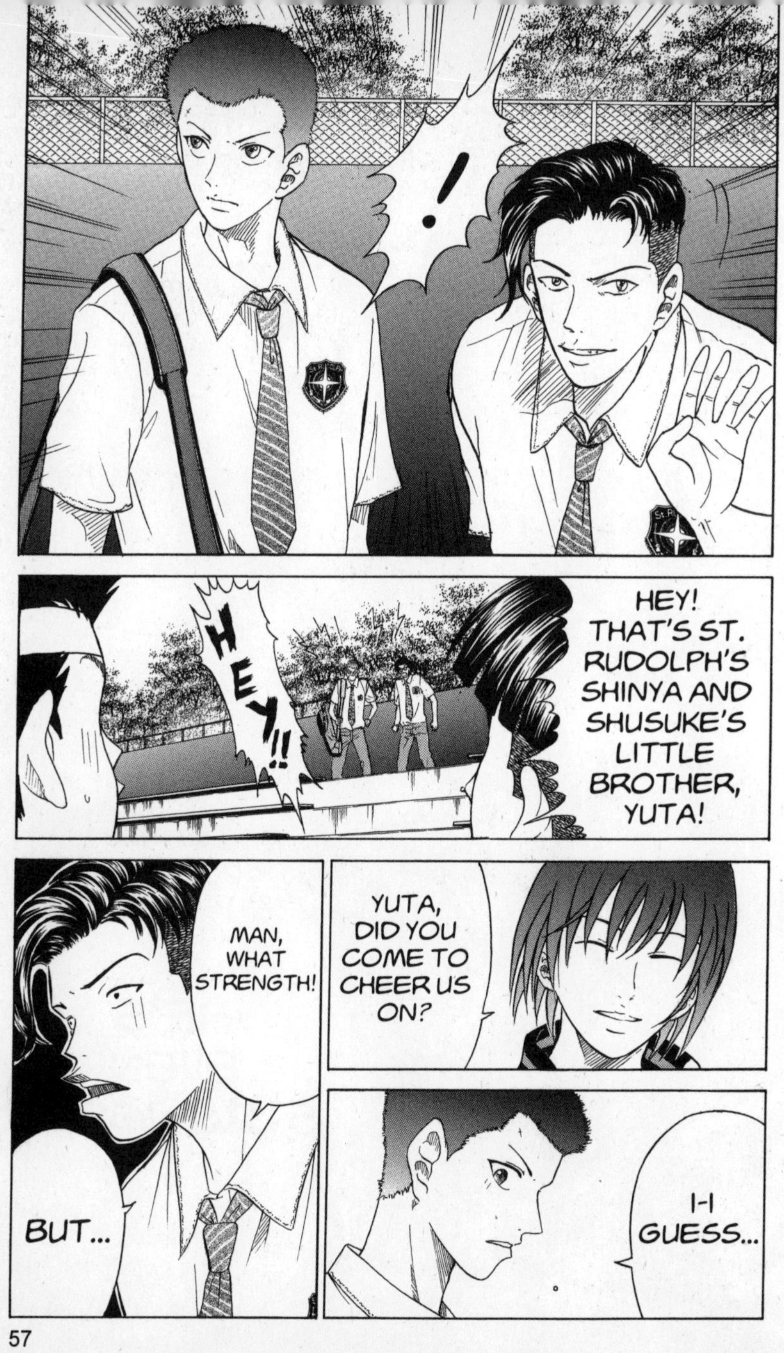
!
HEY! THAT'S ST. RUDOLPH'S SHINYA AND SHUSUKE'S LITTLE BROTHER, YUTA!
HEY!!
YUTA, DID YOU COME TO CHEER US ON?
I-I GUESS...
MAN, WHAT STRENGTH!
BUT...

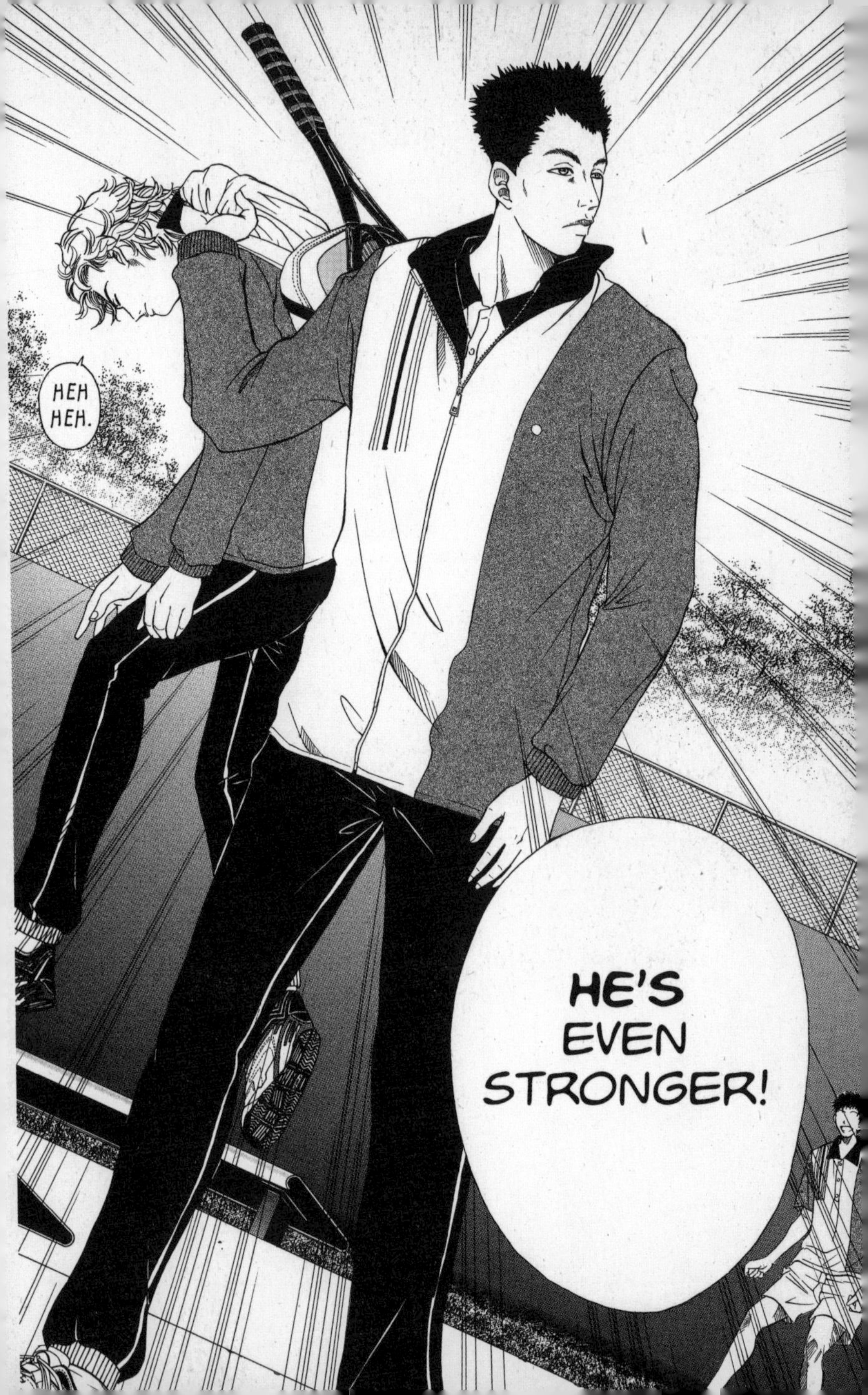
HE'S EVEN STRONGER!
HEH HEH.

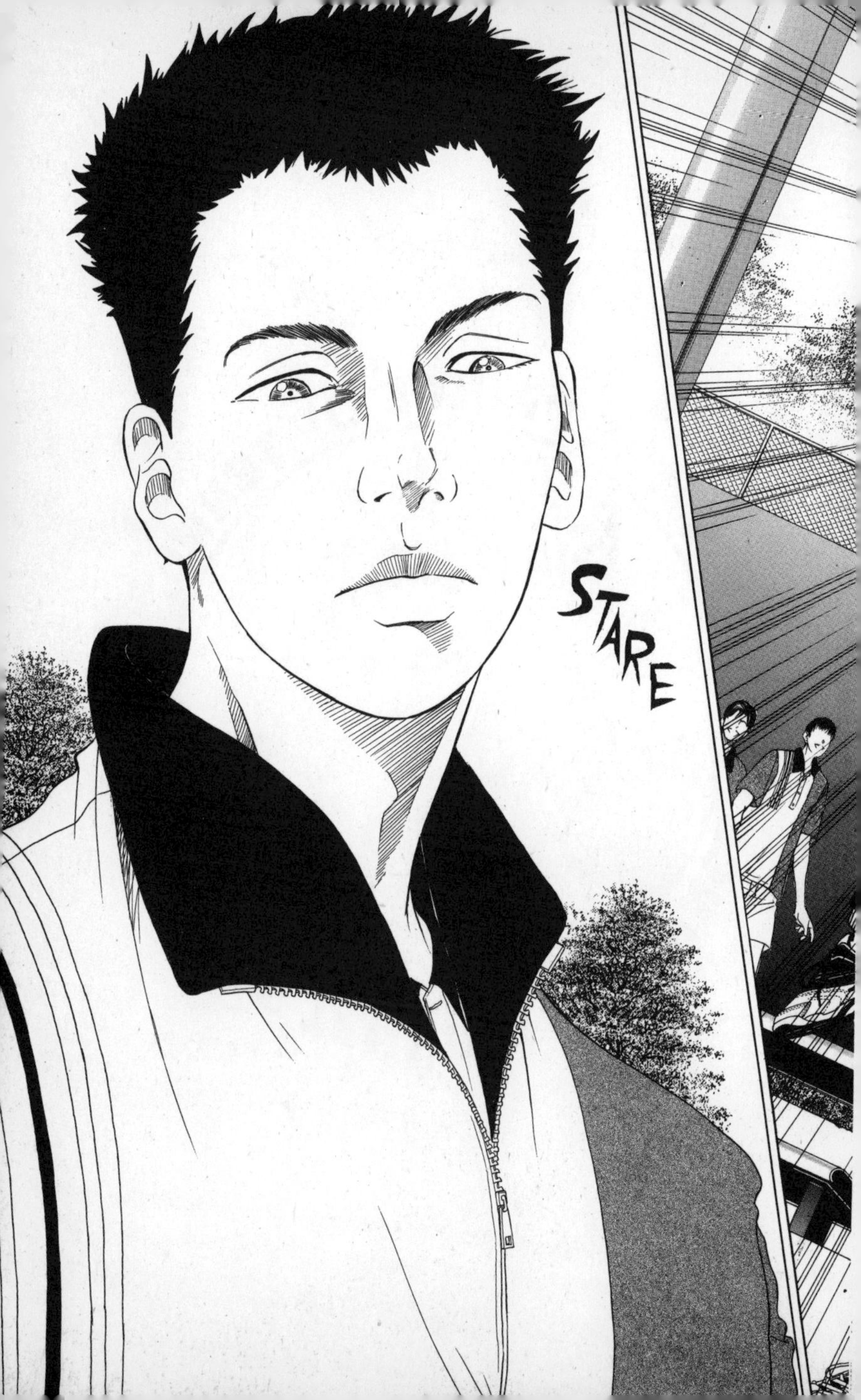
STARE

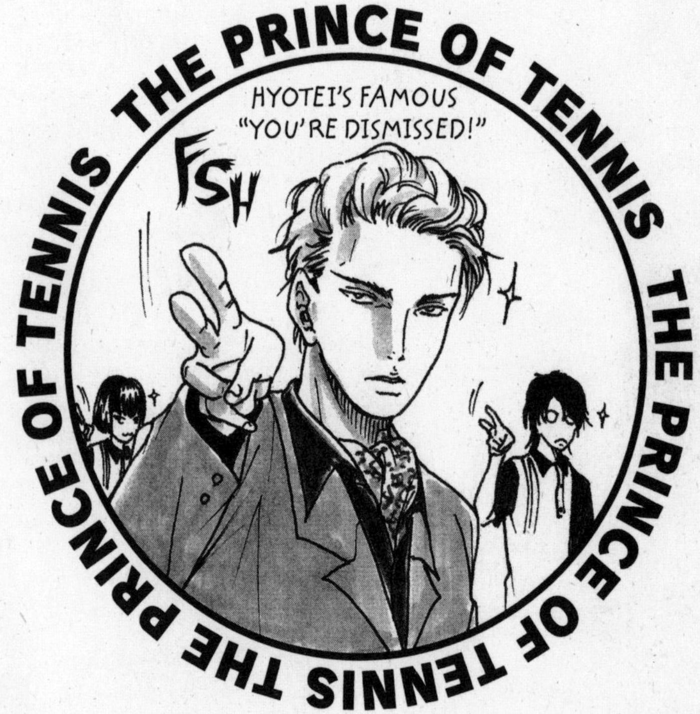
THE PRINCE OF TENNIS THE PRINCE OF TENNIS THE PRINCE OF TENNIS
HYOTEI'S FAMOUS
"YOU'RE DISMISSED!"
FSH

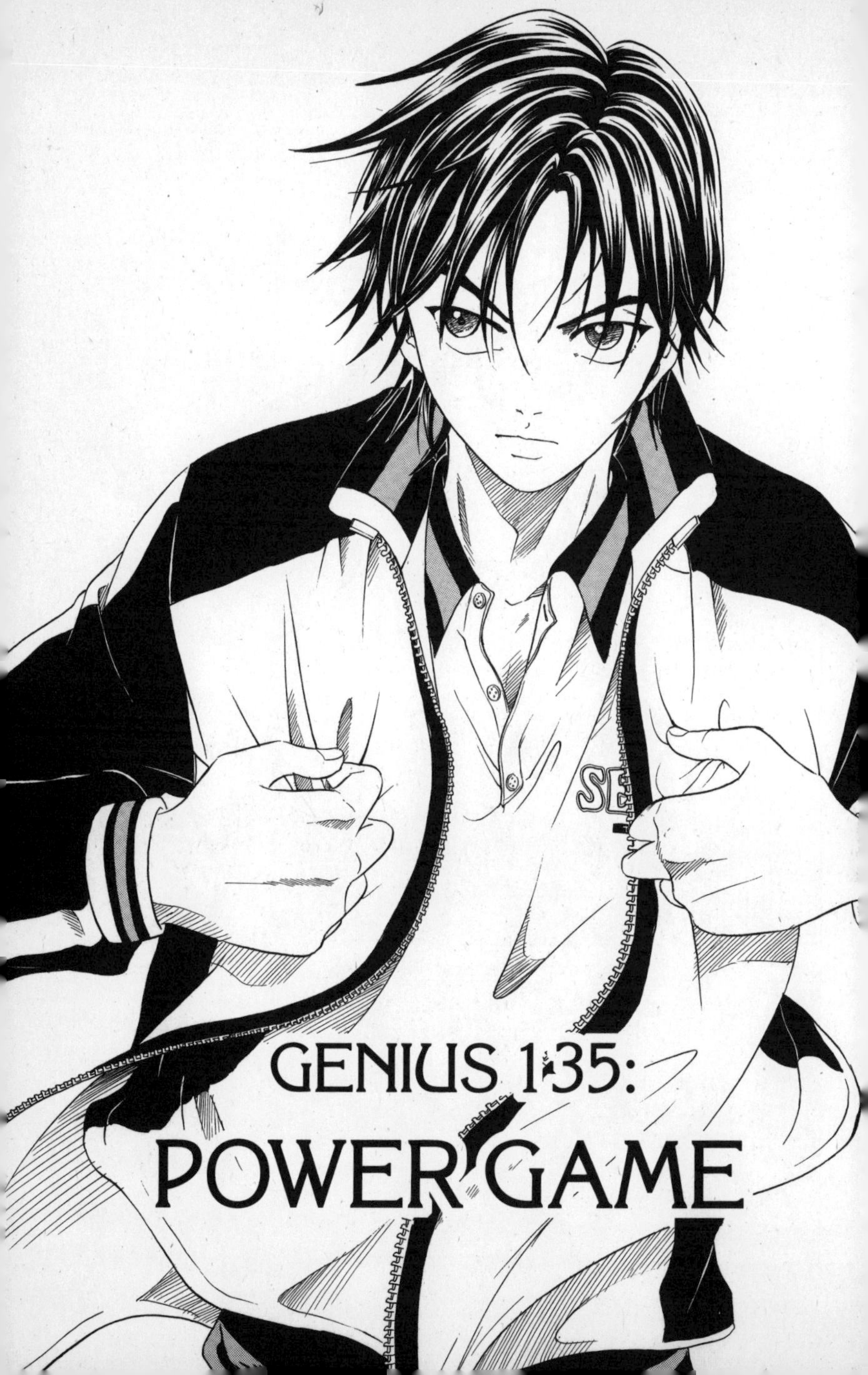
GENIUS 135:
POWER GAME

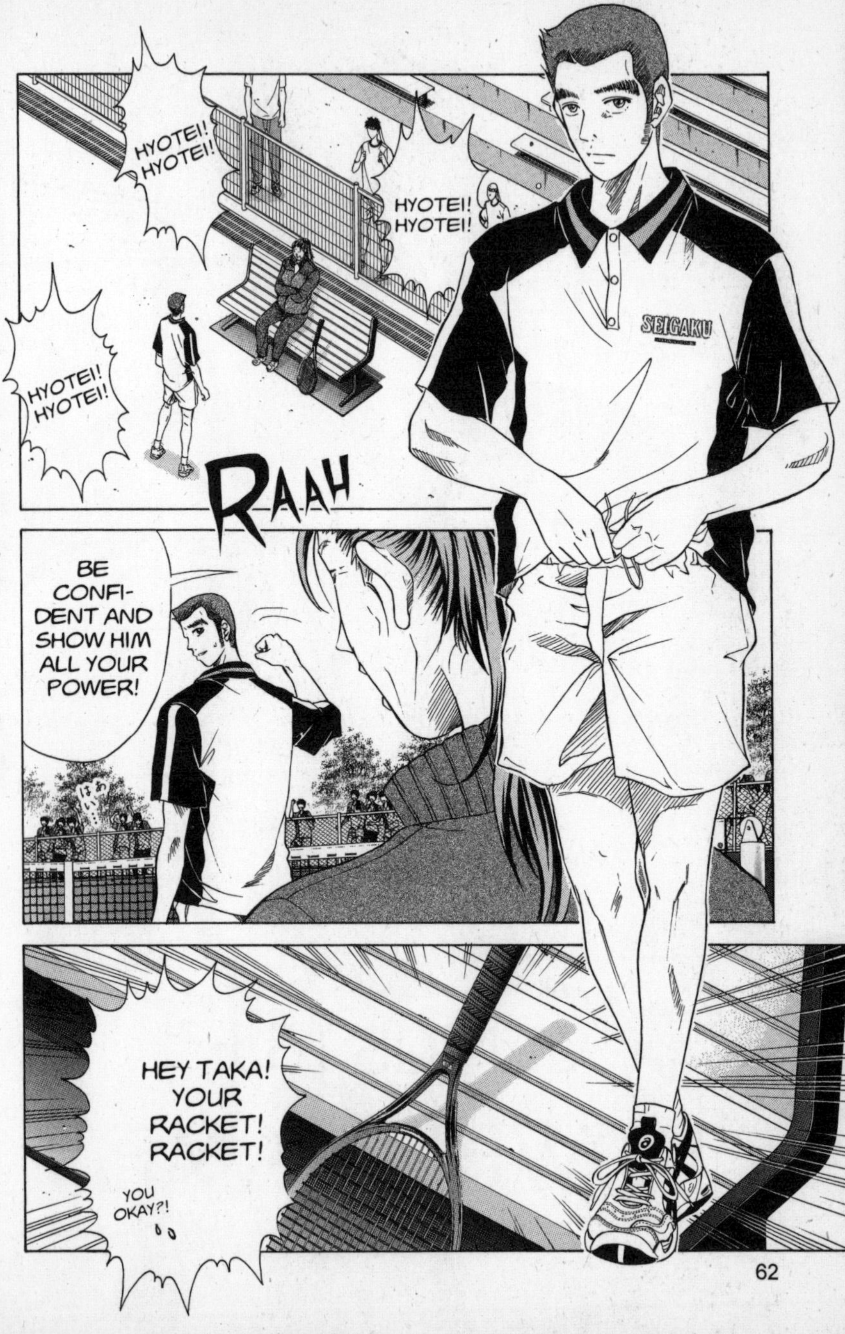
HYOTEI! HYOTEI!
HYOTEI! HYOTEI!
HYOTEI! HYOTEI!
RAAH
BE CONFIDENT AND SHOW HIM ALL YOUR POWER!
HEY TAKA! YOUR RACKET! RACKET!
YOU OKAY?!

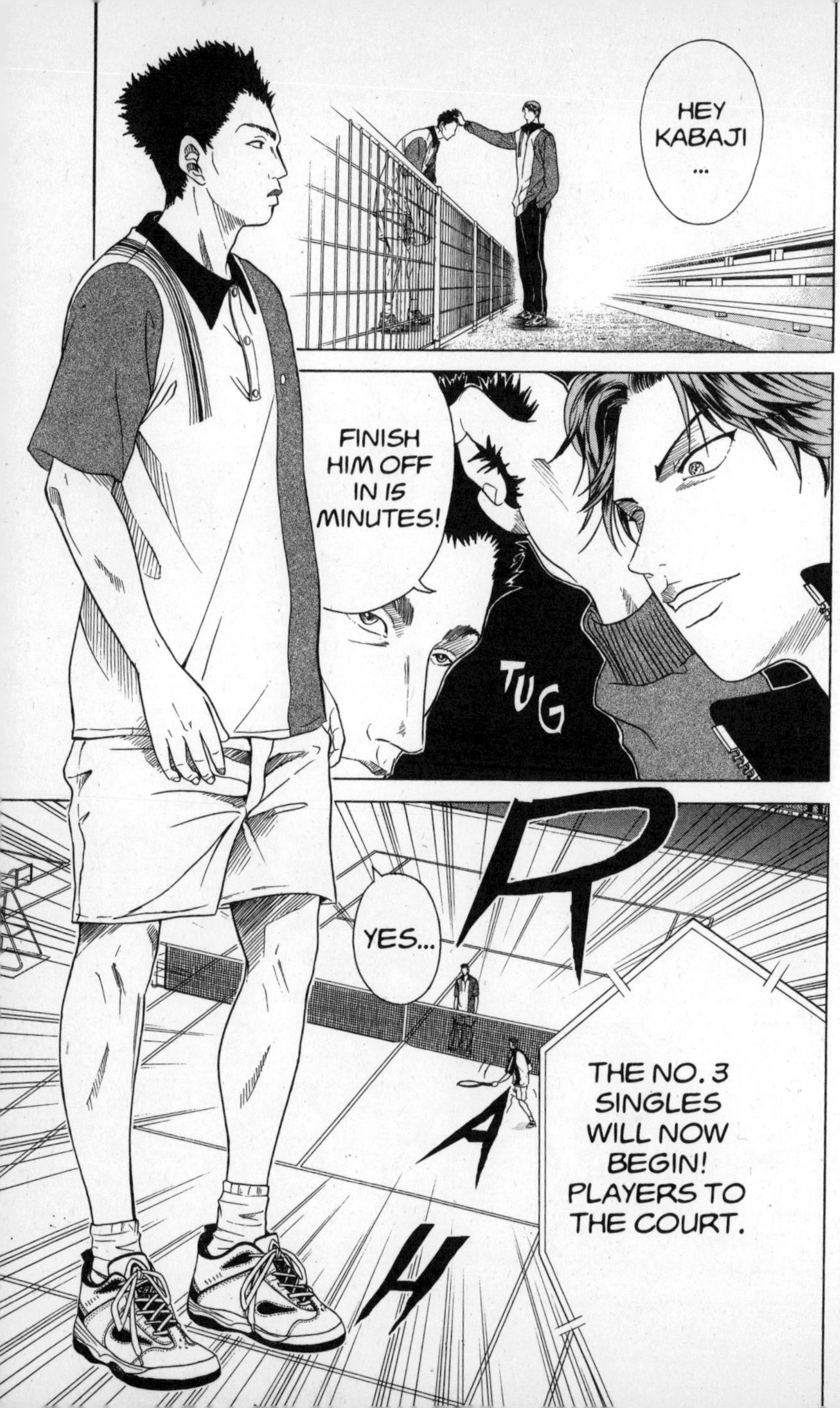
HEY KABAJI ...
FINISH HIM OFF IN 15 MINUTES!
TUG
YES...
RAH
THE NO. 3 SINGLES WILL NOW BEGIN! PLAYERS TO THE COURT.

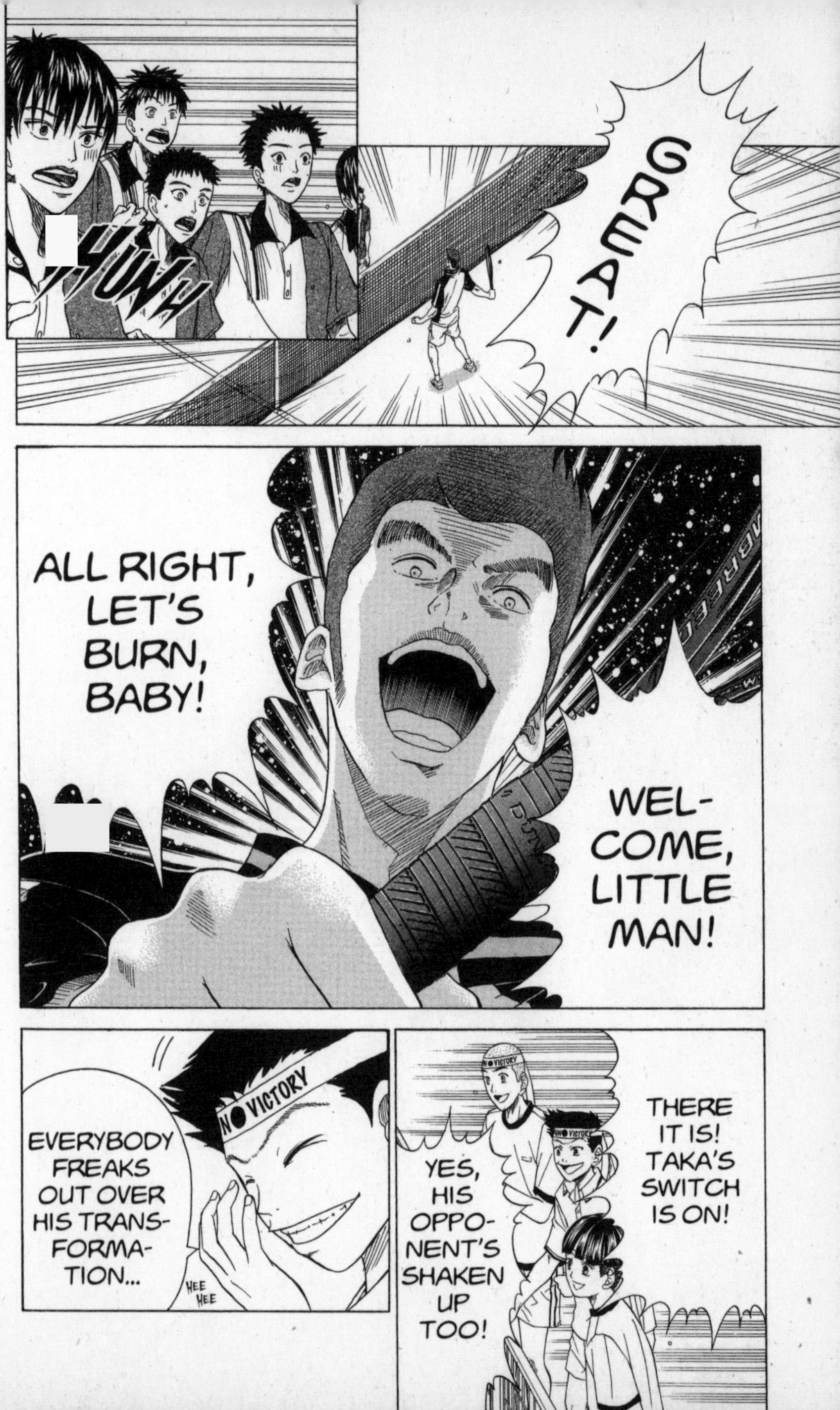
GREAT!
HUNH
WEL-COME, LITTLE MAN!
ALL RIGHT, LET'S BURN, BABY!
THERE IT IS! TAKA'S SWITCH IS ON!
YES, HIS OPPO-NENT'S SHAKEN UP TOO!
EVERYBODY FREAKS OUT OVER HIS TRANS-FORMA-TION...
HEE HEE

READ THIS WAY

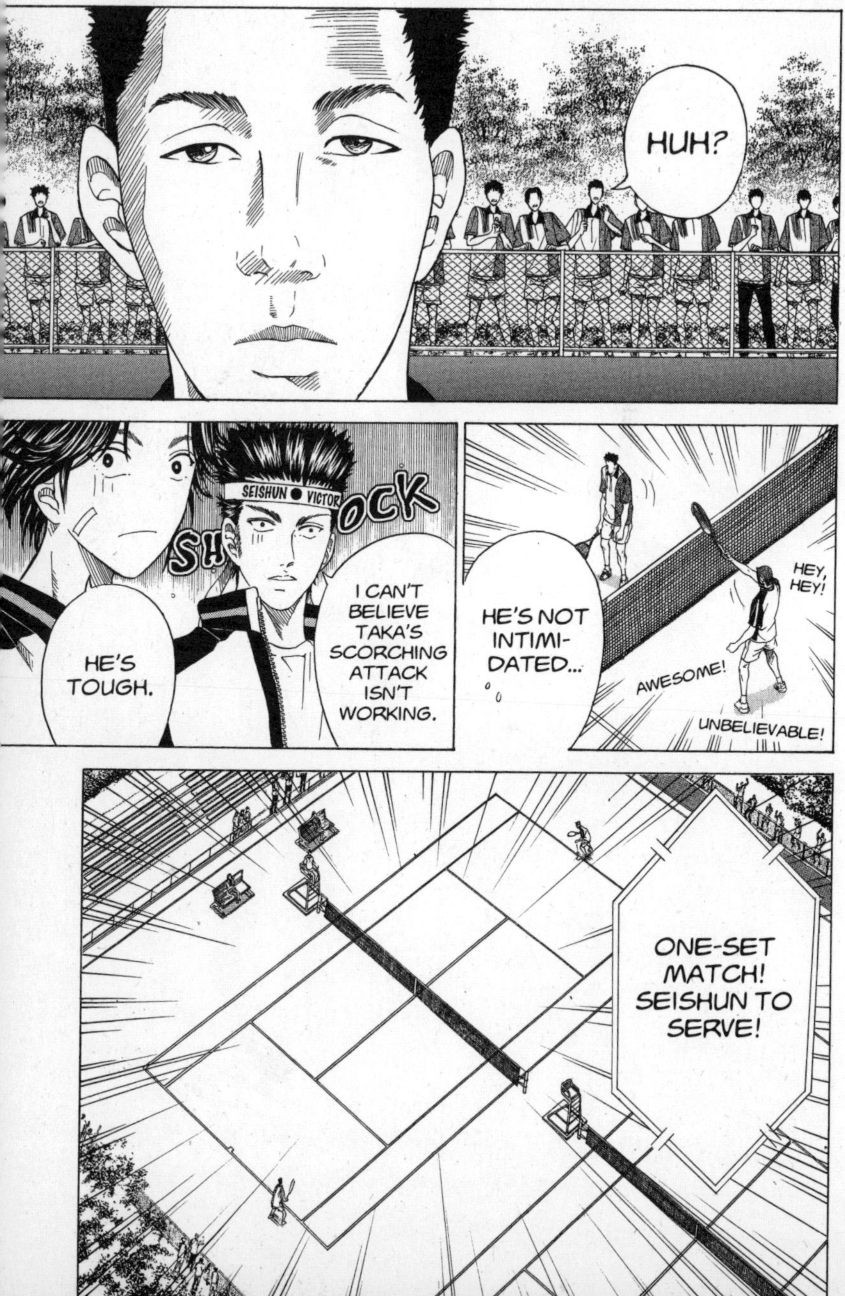
HUH?
HEY, HEY!
HE'S NOT INTIMIDATED...
AWESOME!
UNBELIEVABLE!
I CAN'T BELIEVE TAKA'S SCORCHING ATTACK ISN'T WORKING.
HE'S TOUGH.
ONE-SET MATCH! SEISHUN TO SERVE!

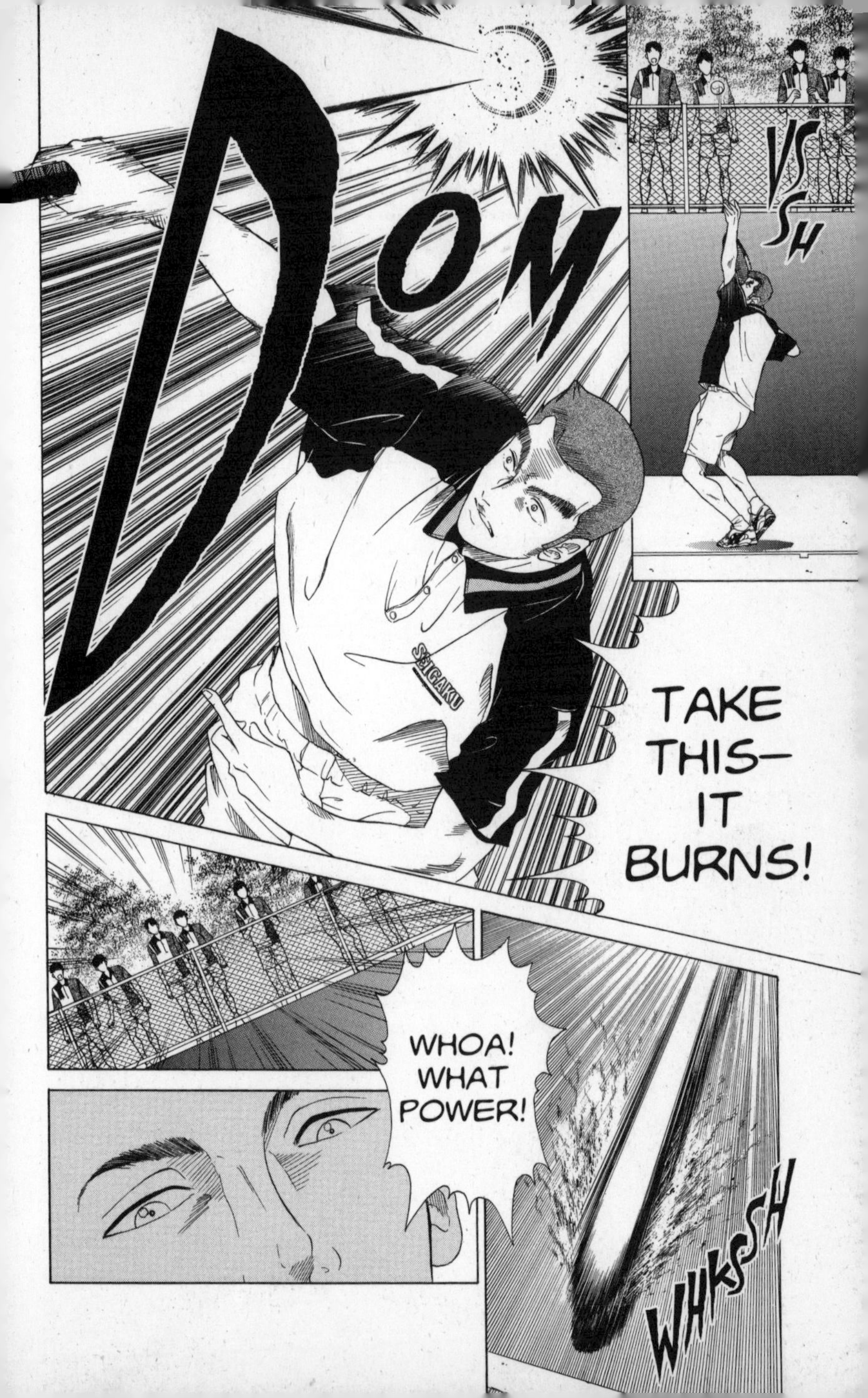
VSSH
DOM
TAKE THIS— IT BURNS!
WHKSSH
WHOA! WHAT POWER!

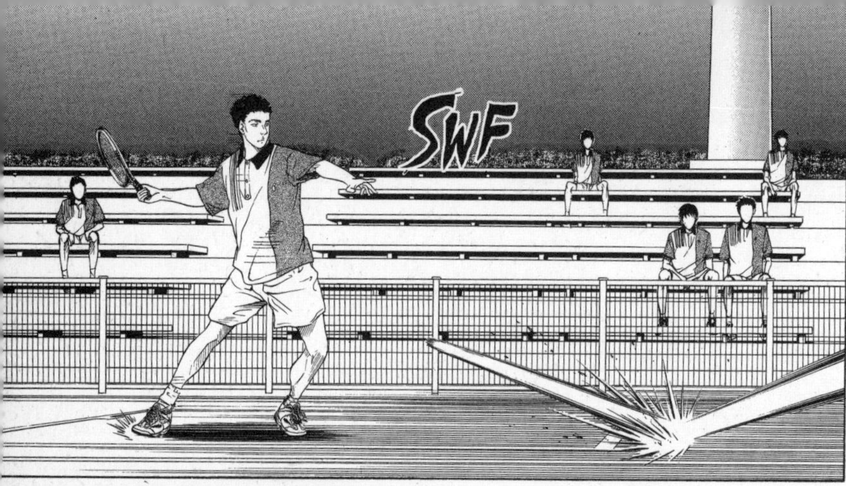
SWF
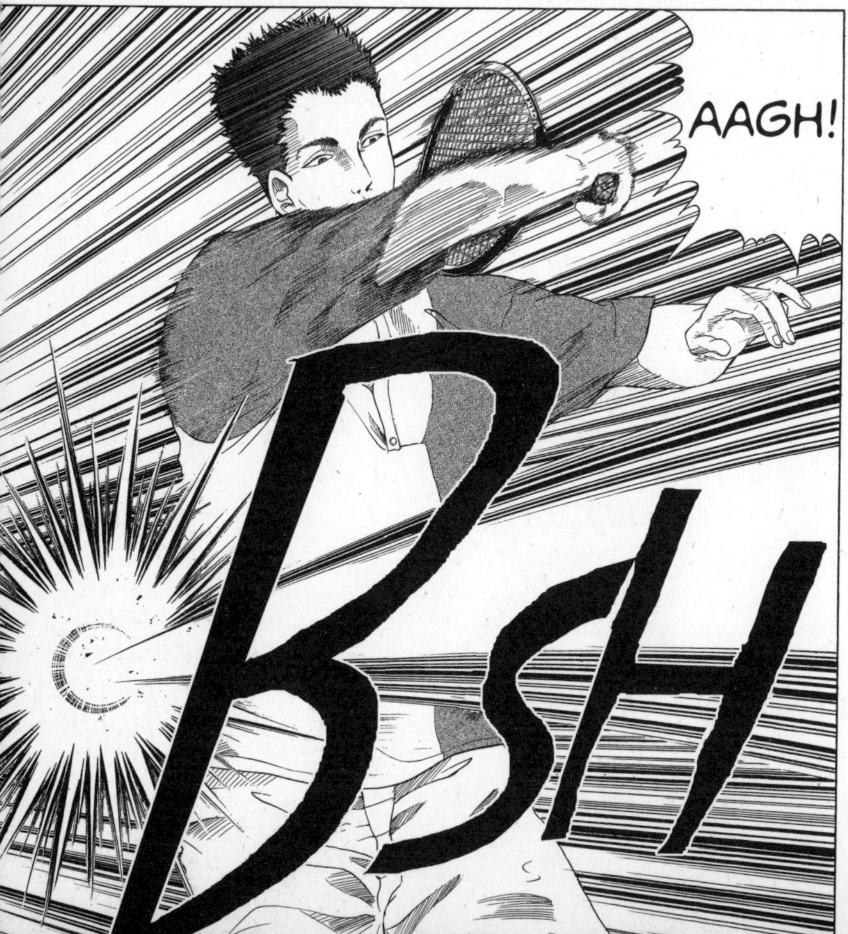
AAGH!
BSH

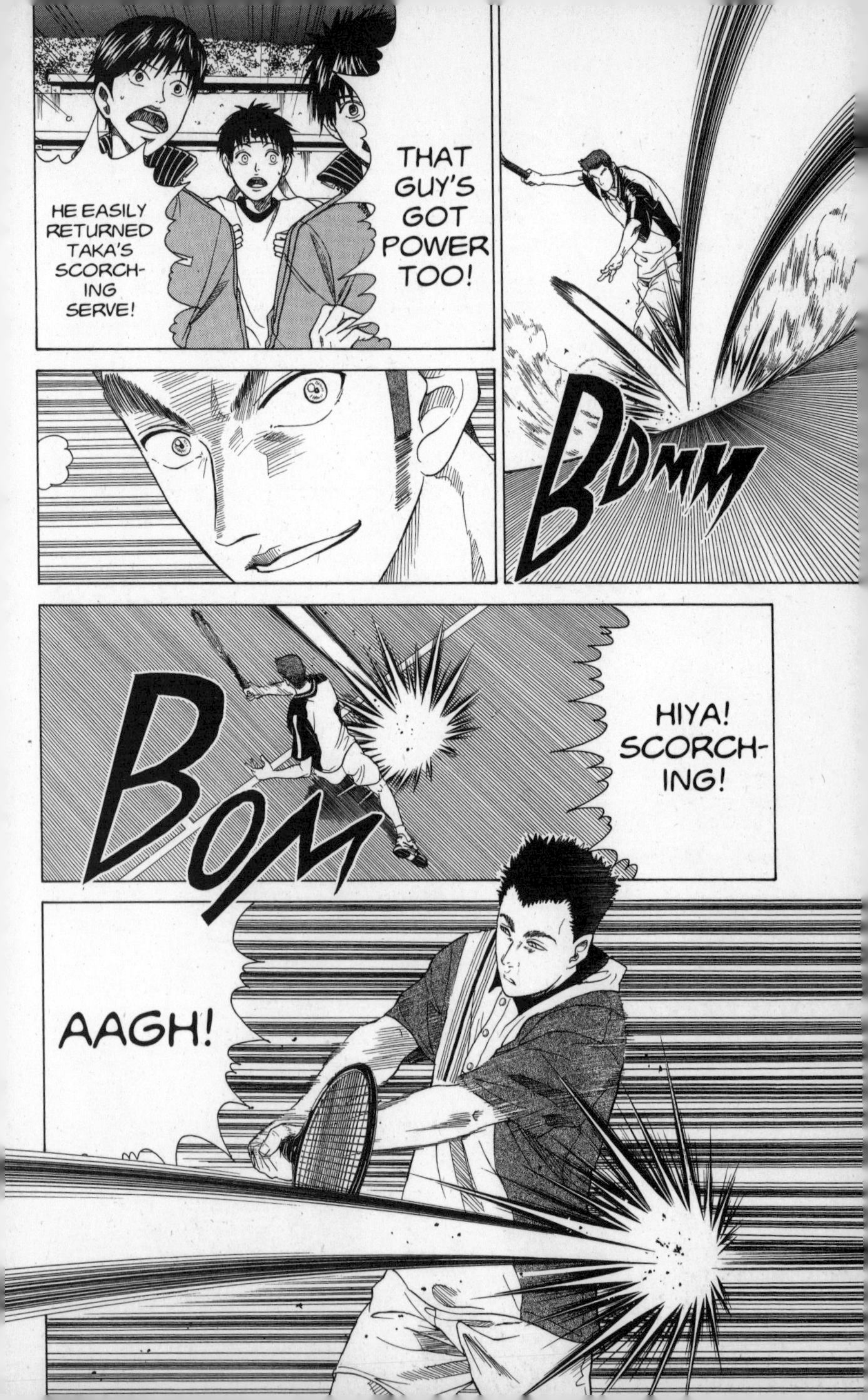
BDMM
THAT GUY'S GOT POWER TOO!
HE EASILY RETURNED TAKA'S SCORCHING SERVE!
HIYA! SCORCHING!
BOM
AAGH!

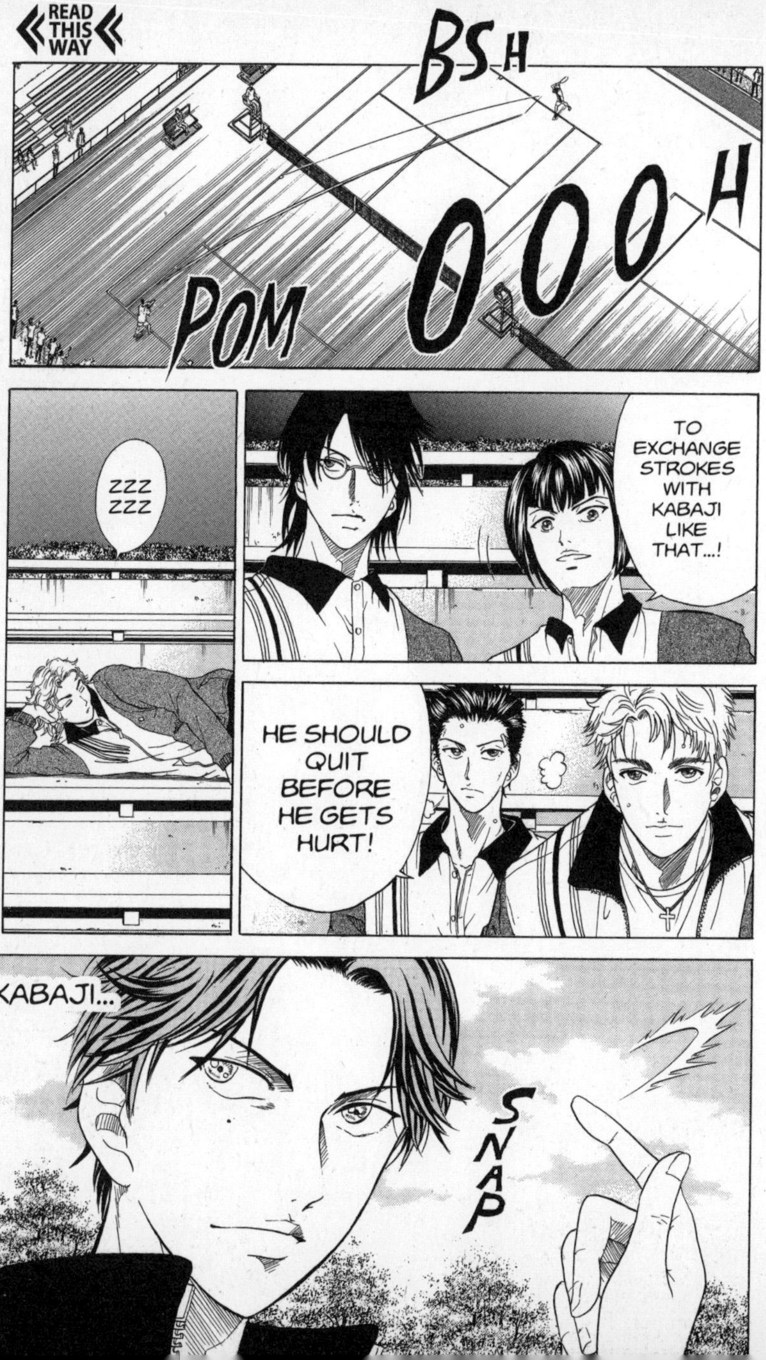
READ THIS WAY
BSH
POMOOOOH
TO EXCHANGE STROKES WITH KABAJI LIKE THAT...!
HE SHOULD QUIT BEFORE HE GETS HURT!
ZZZ ZZZ
KABAJI...
SNAP

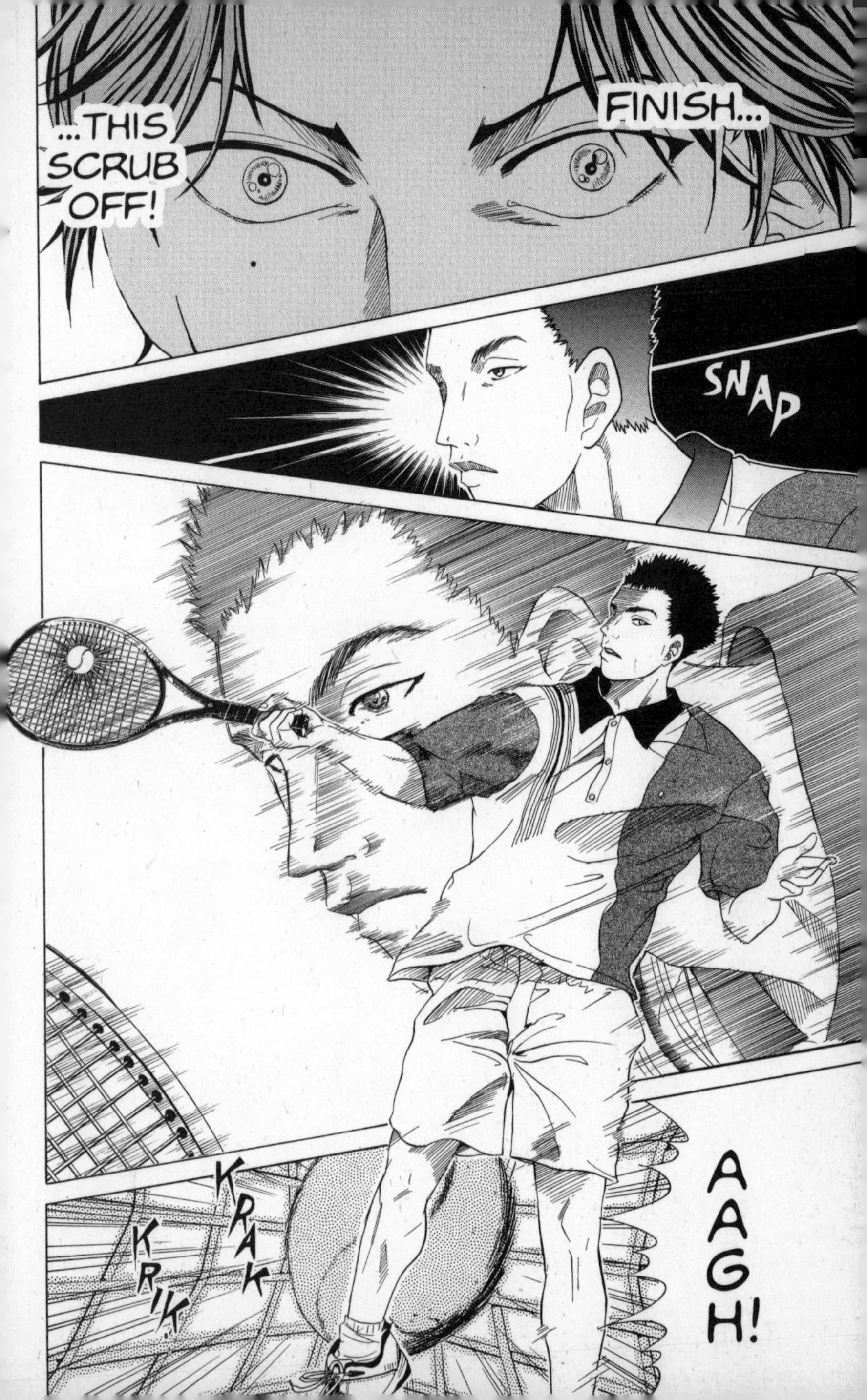
FINISH...
...THIS SCRUB OFF!
SNAP
AAGH!
KRAK
KRIK

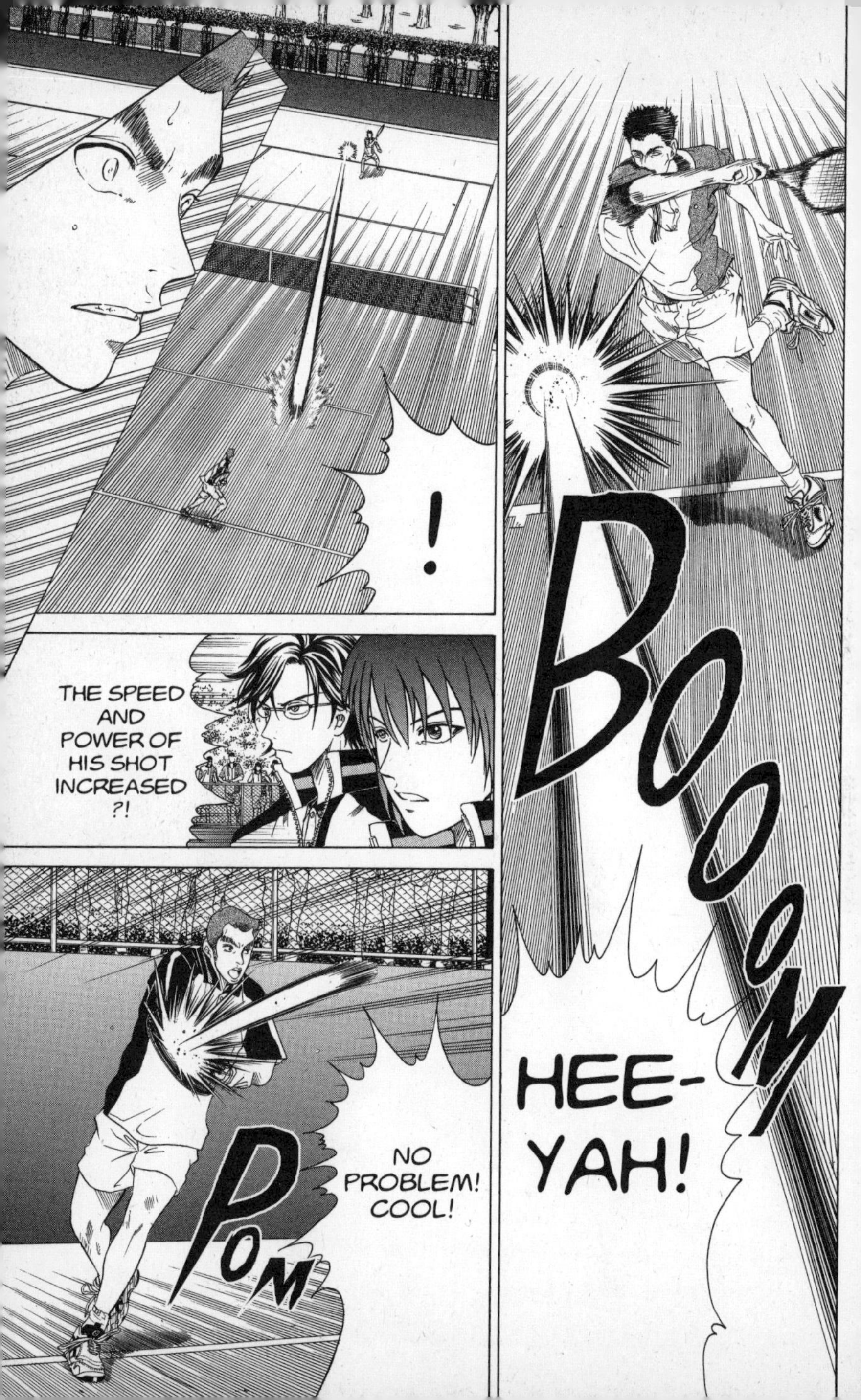
BOOOOM
HEE-YAH!
!
THE SPEED AND POWER OF HIS SHOT INCREASED ?!
NO PROBLEM! COOL!
POM

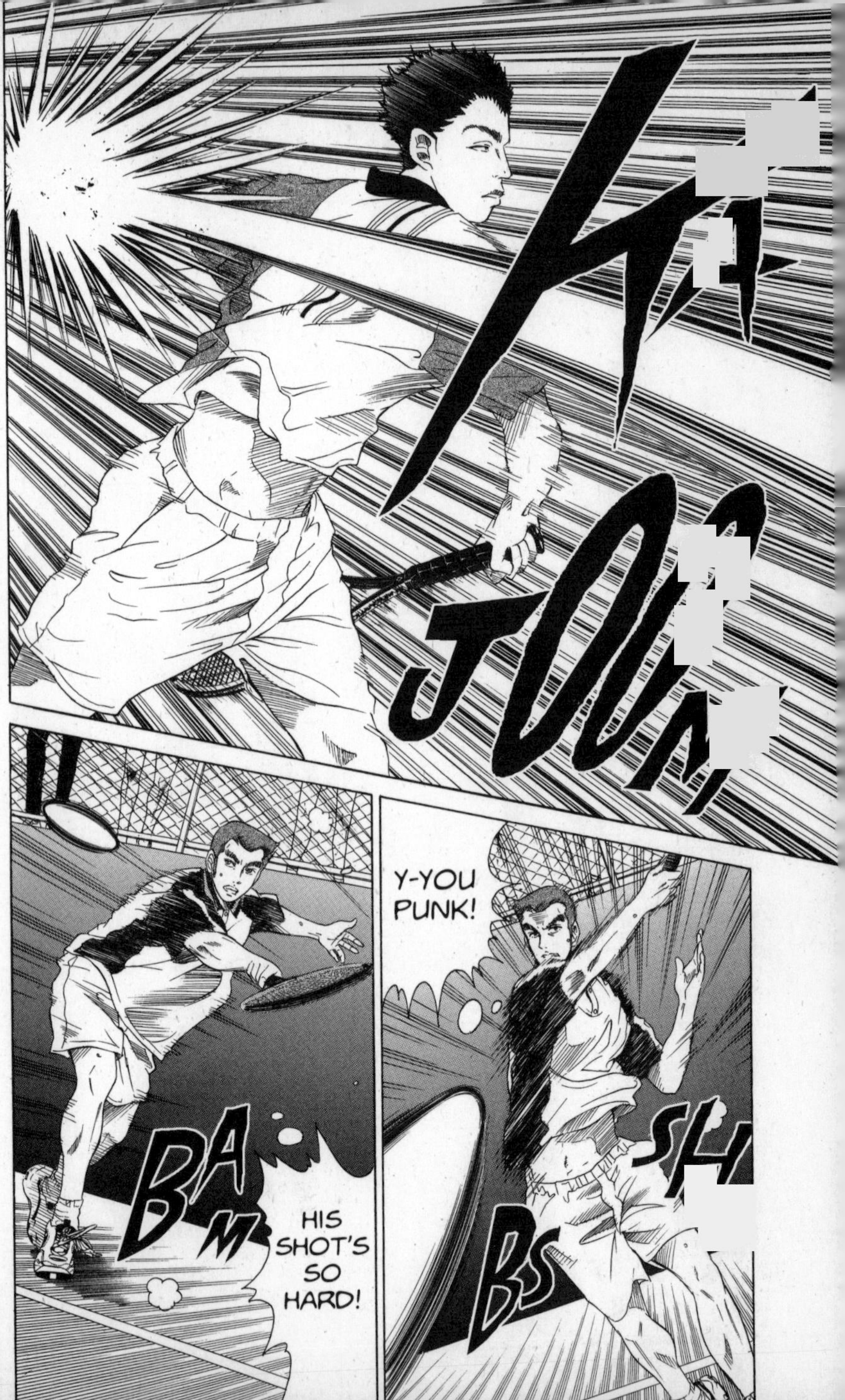
Y-YOU PUNK!
BAM
HIS SHOT'S SO HARD!

READ THIS WAY

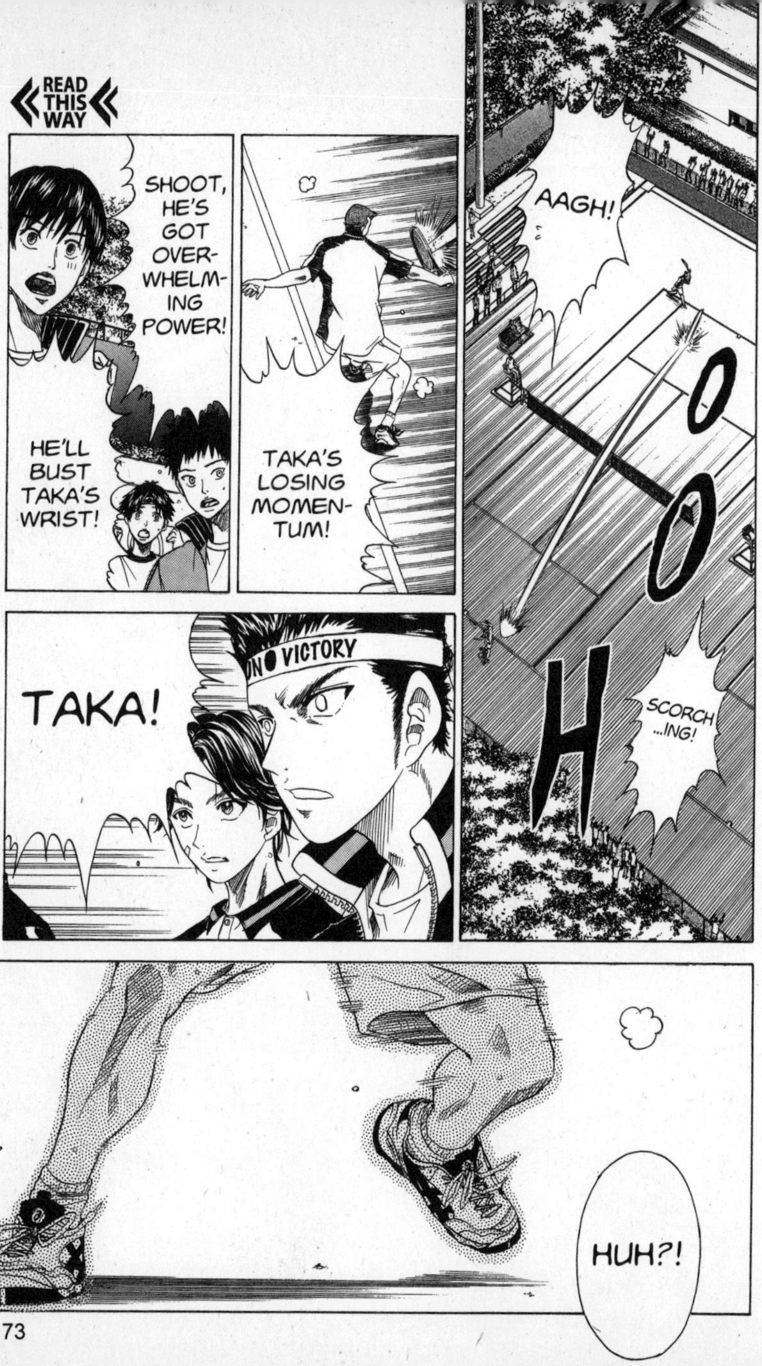

AAGH!
SCORCH ...ING!
TAKA'S LOSING MOMEN-TUM!
SHOOT, HE'S GOT OVER-WHELM-ING POWER!
HE'LL BUST TAKA'S WRIST!
TAKA!
HUH?!

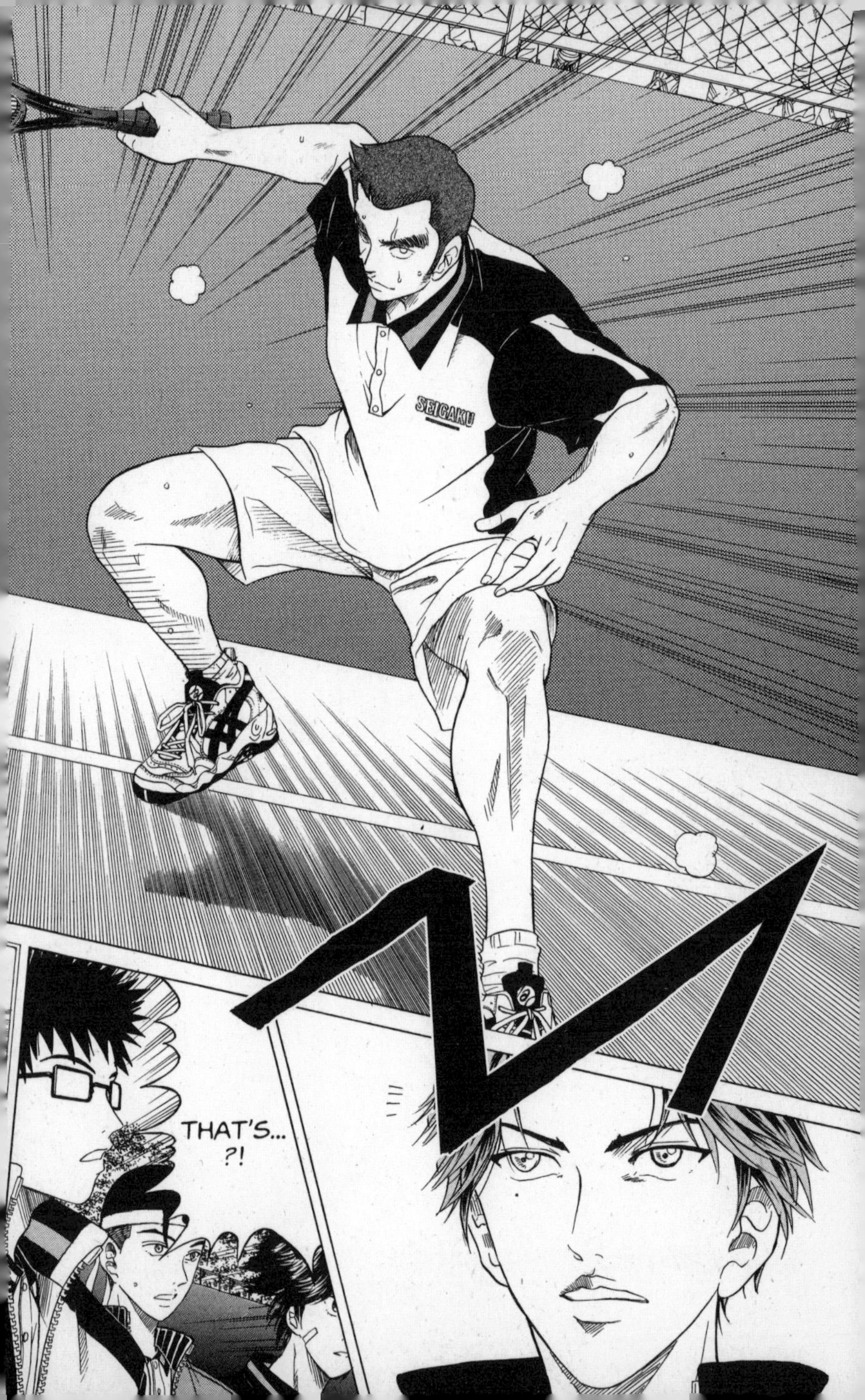
SEIGAKU
THAT'S... ?!

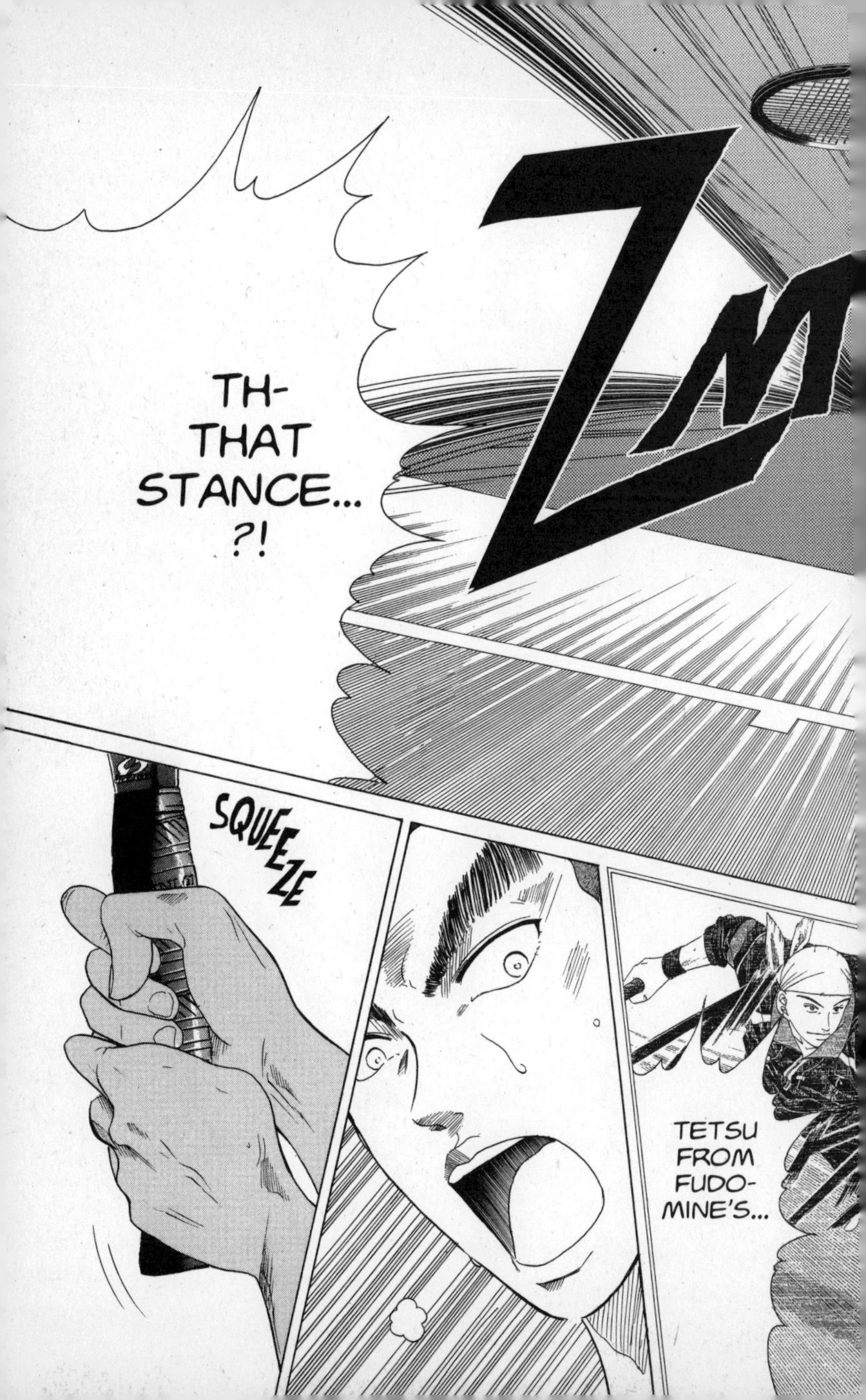
ZM
TH- THAT STANCE... ?!
TETSU FROM FUDO- MINE'S...
SQUEEZE

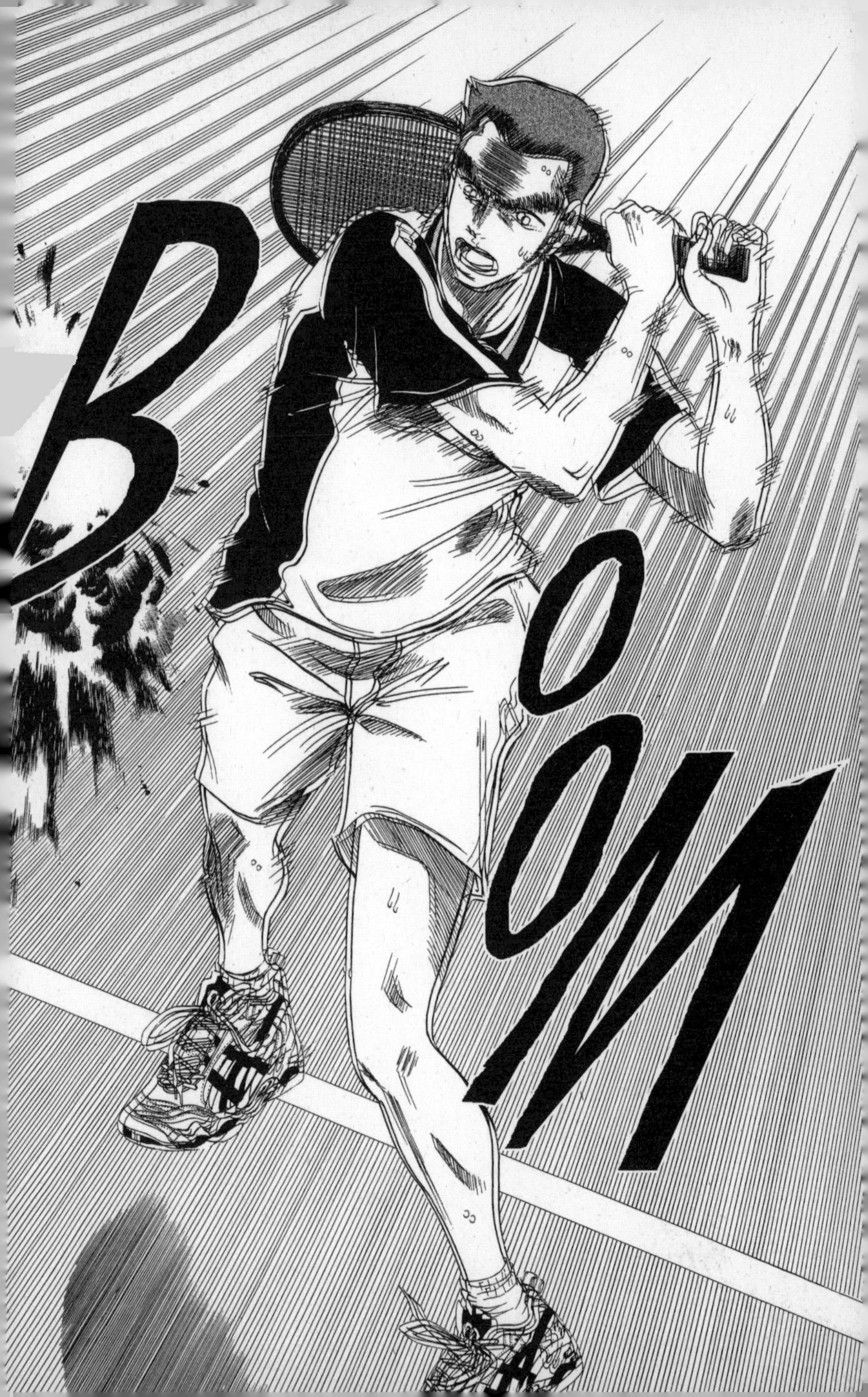
BOOM

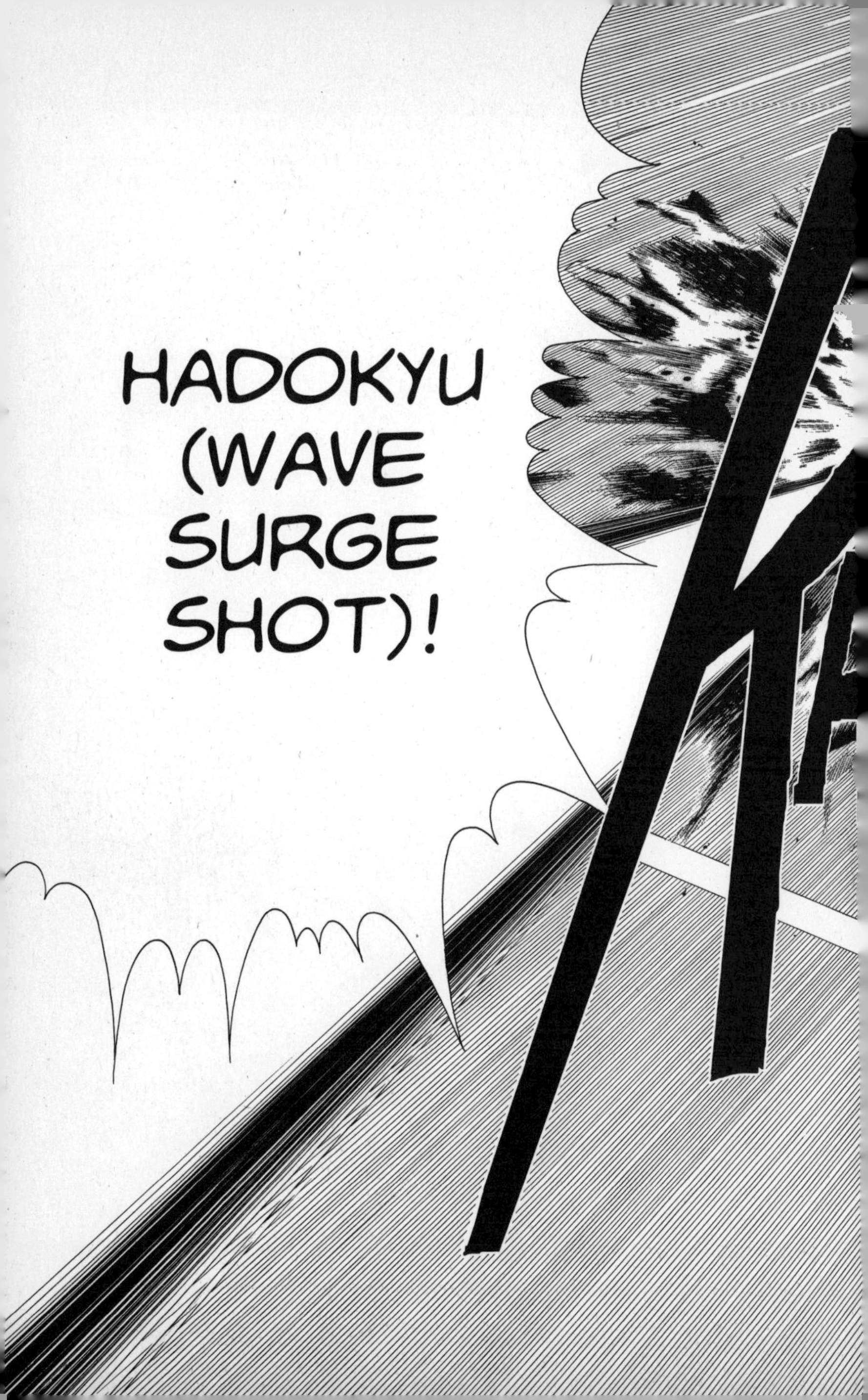
HADOKYU (WAVE SURGE SHOT)!

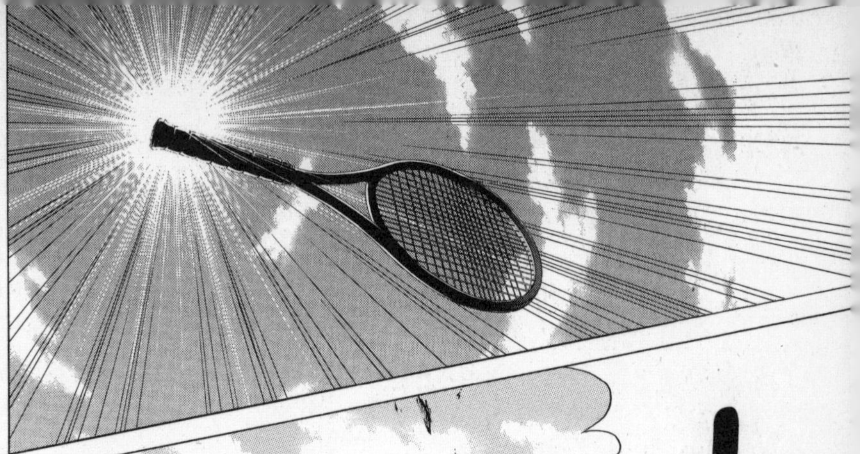

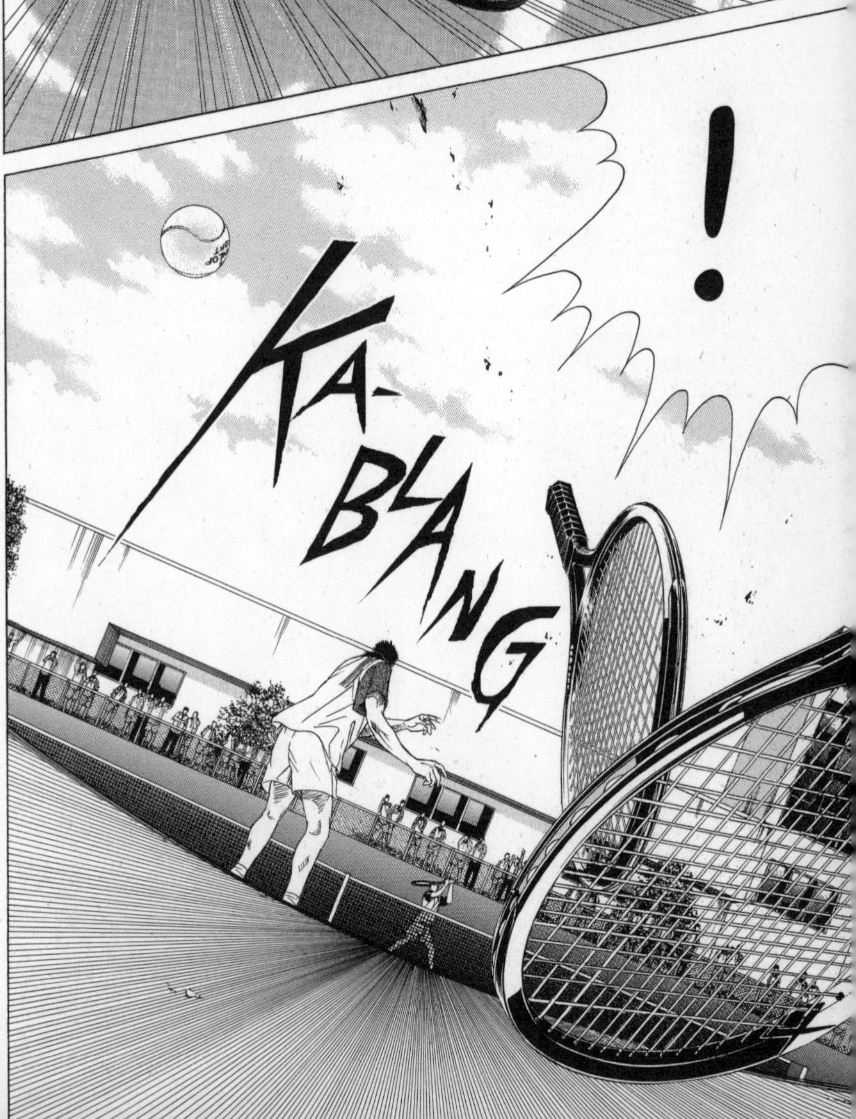
!
KA-BLANG

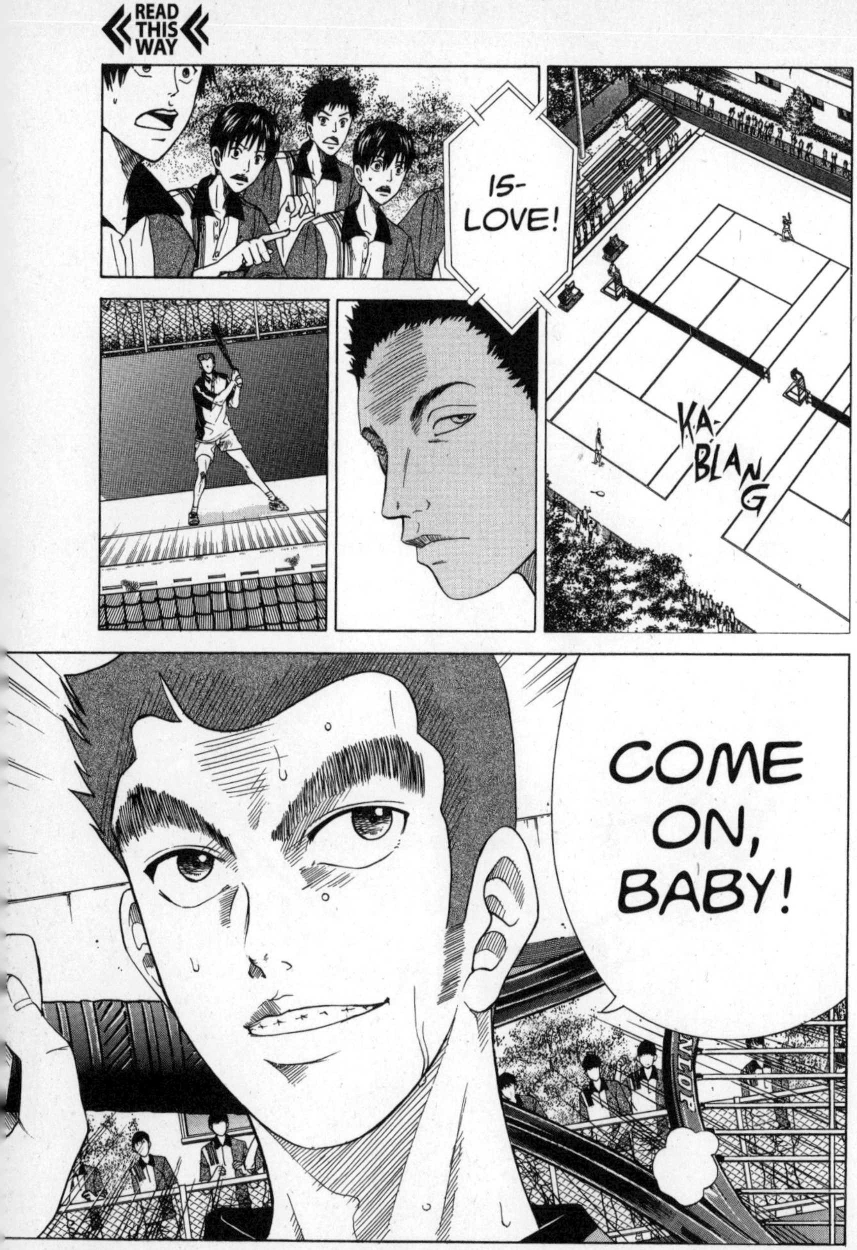
READ THIS WAY
15-LOVE!
KA-BLANG
COME ON, BABY!

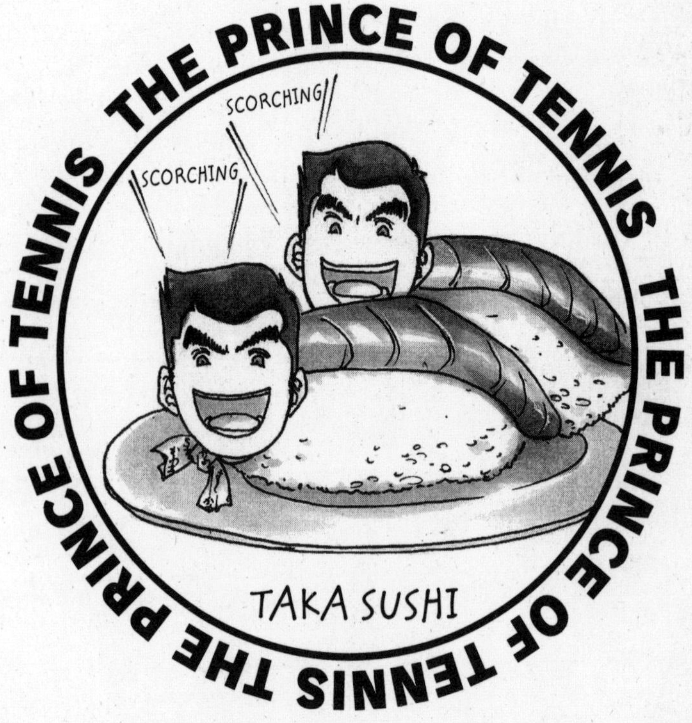
THE PRINCE OF TENNIS THE PRINCE OF TENNIS THE PRINCE OF TENNIS
SCORCHING
SCORCHING
TAKA SUSHI

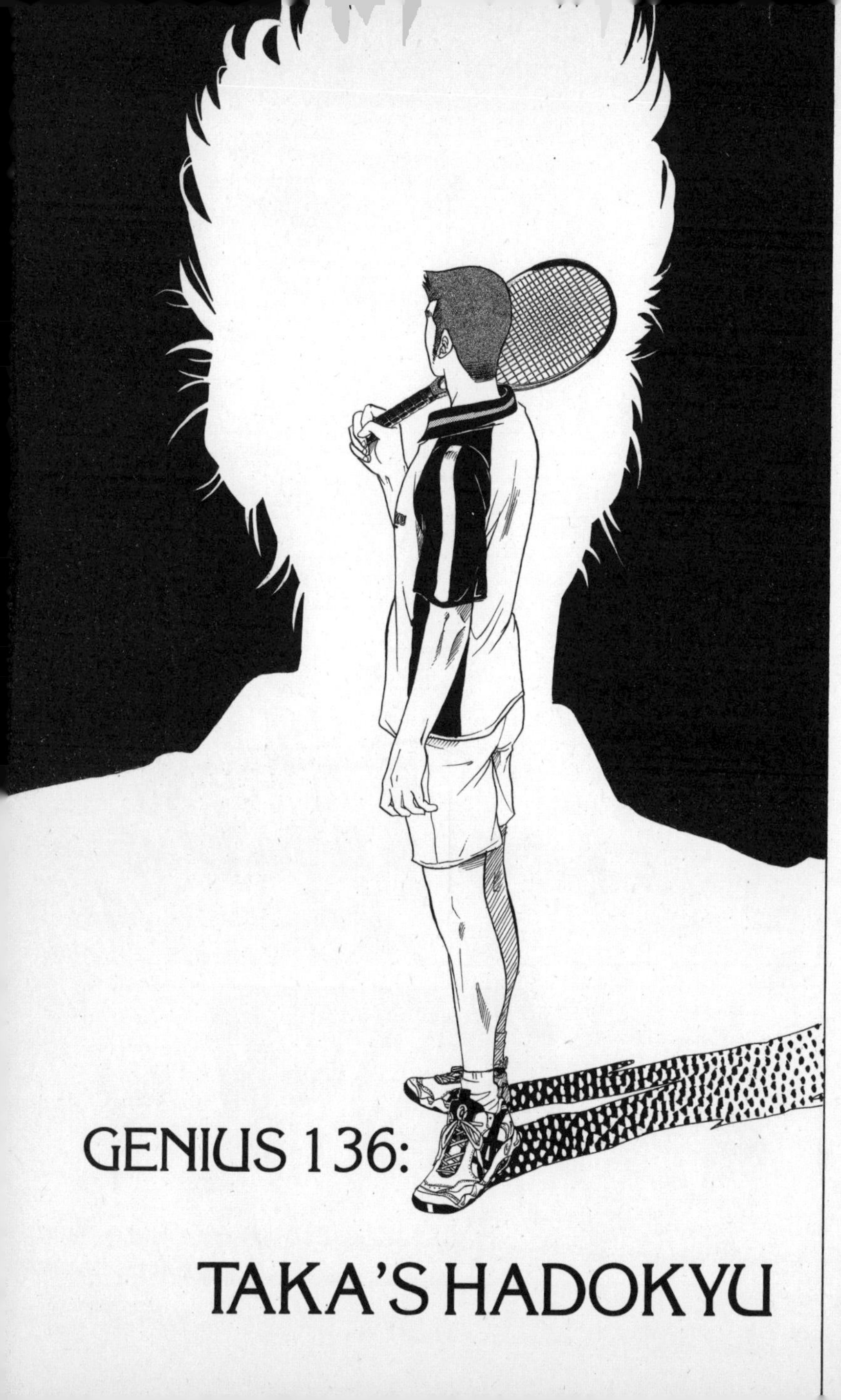
GENIUS 136:
TAKA'S HADOKYU

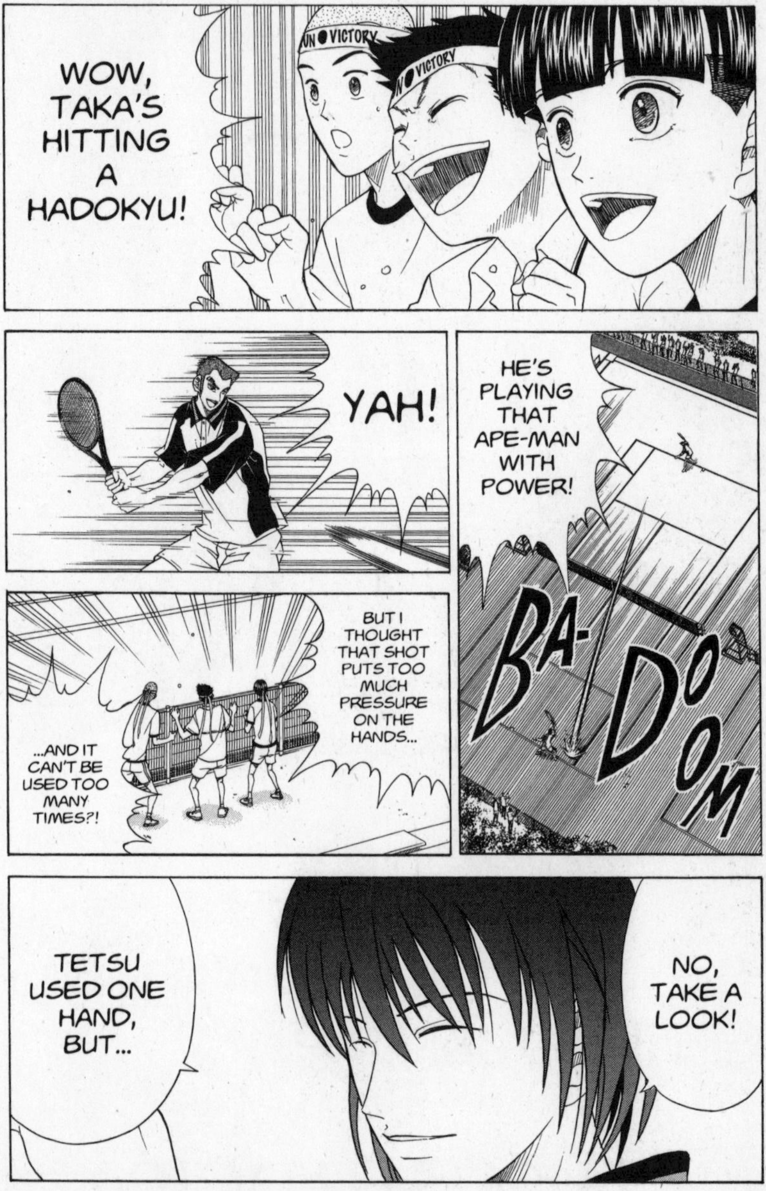
WOW, TAKA'S HITTING A HADOKYU!
HE'S PLAYING THAT APE-MAN WITH POWER!
BA-DOOM
YAH!
BUT I THOUGHT THAT SHOT PUTS TOO MUCH PRESSURE ON THE HANDS...
...AND IT CAN'T BE USED TOO MANY TIMES?!
NO, TAKE A LOOK!
TETSU USED ONE HAND, BUT...

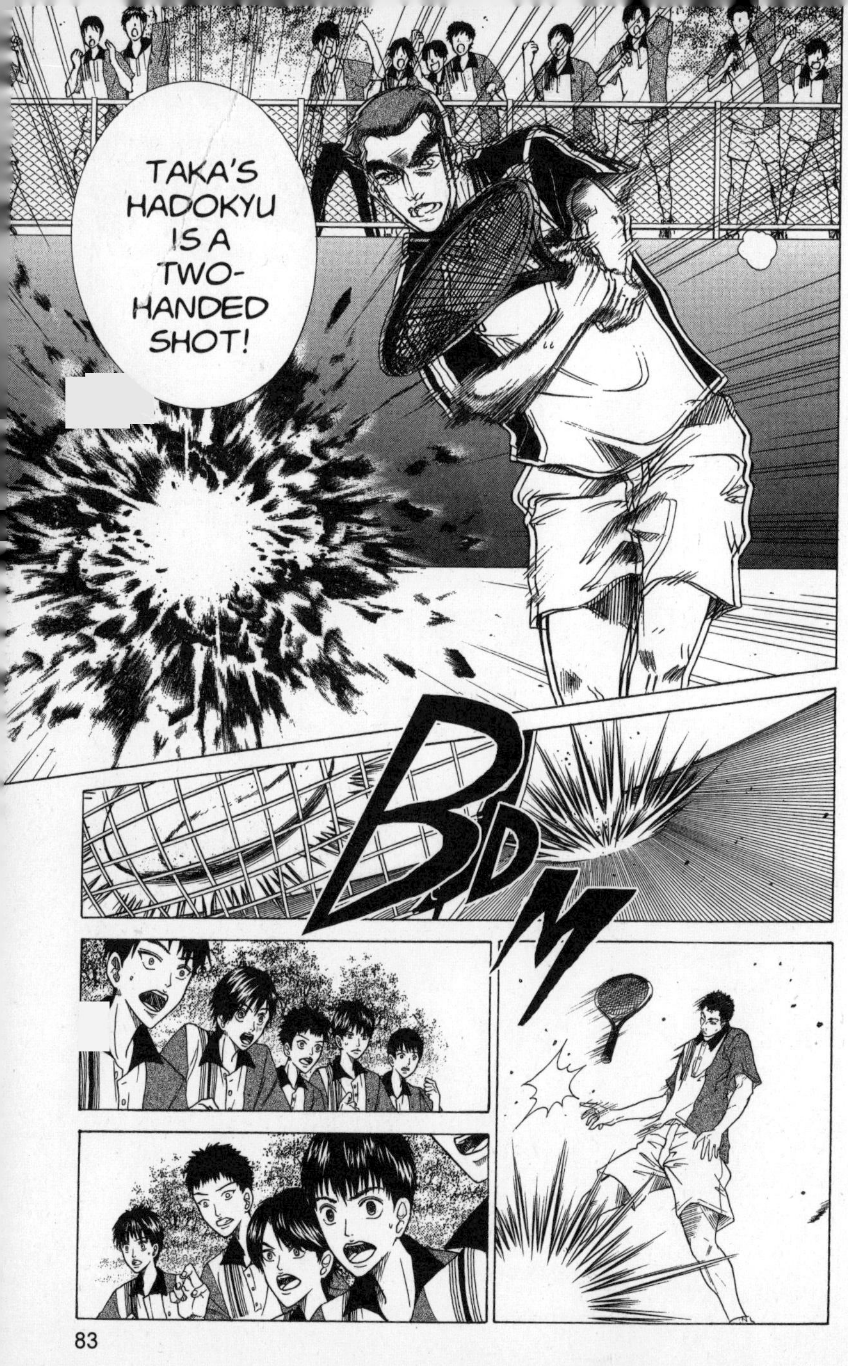
TAKA'S HADOKYU IS A TWO-HANDED SHOT!
BDM

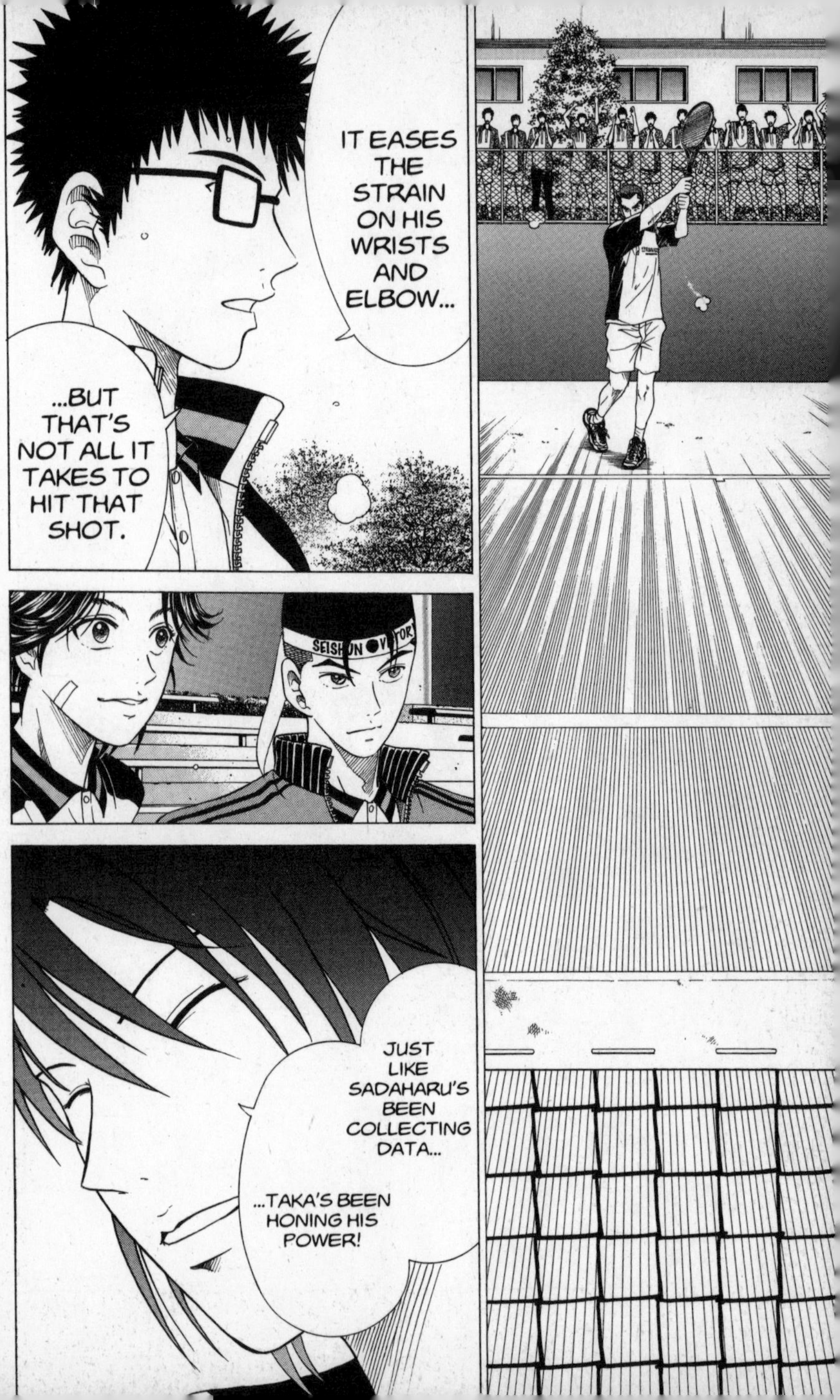
IT EASES THE STRAIN ON HIS WRISTS AND ELBOW...
...BUT THAT'S NOT ALL IT TAKES TO HIT THAT SHOT.
SEISHUN VICTORY
JUST LIKE SADAHARU'S BEEN COLLECTING DATA...
...TAKA'S BEEN HONING HIS POWER!

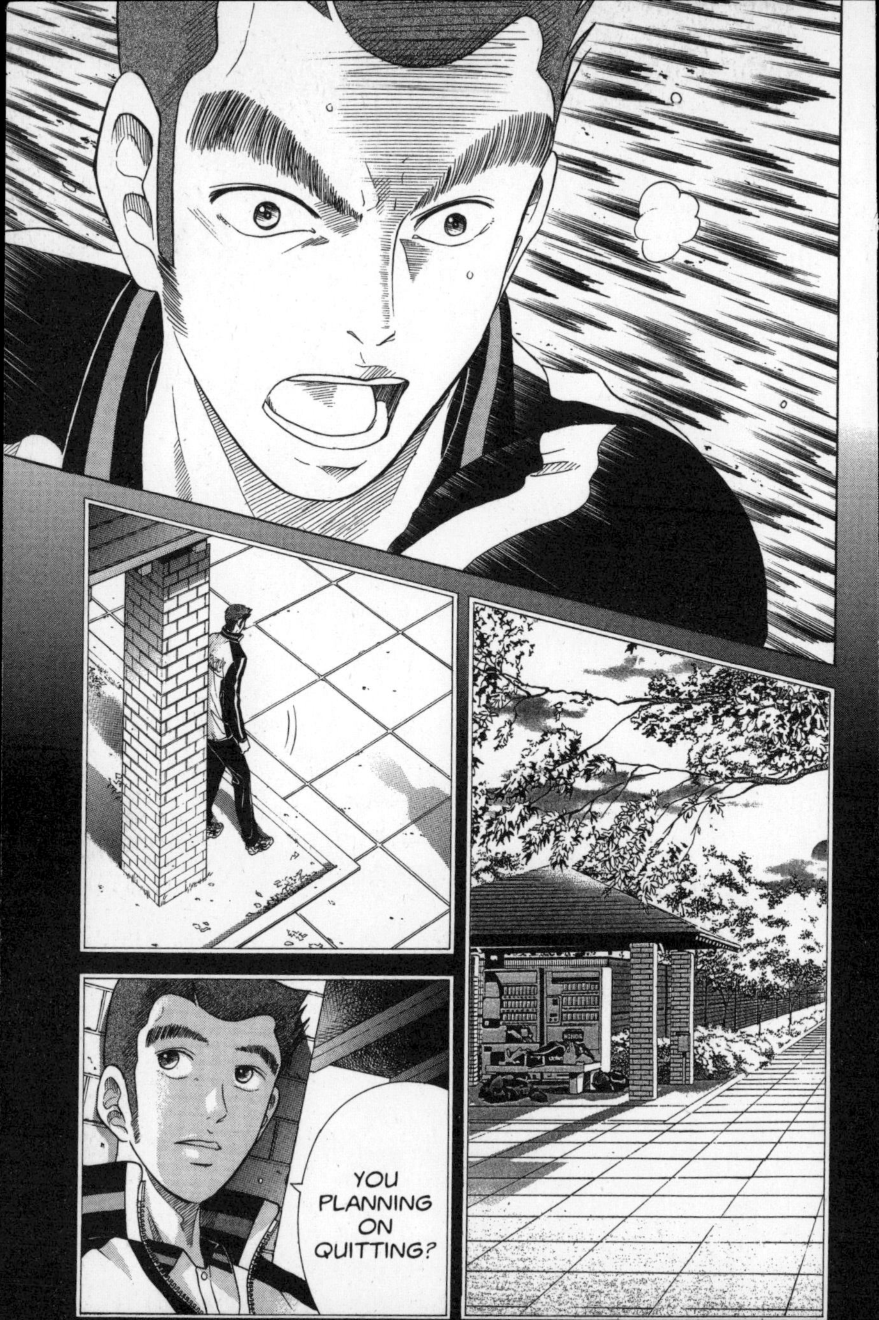
YOU PLANNING ON QUITTING?

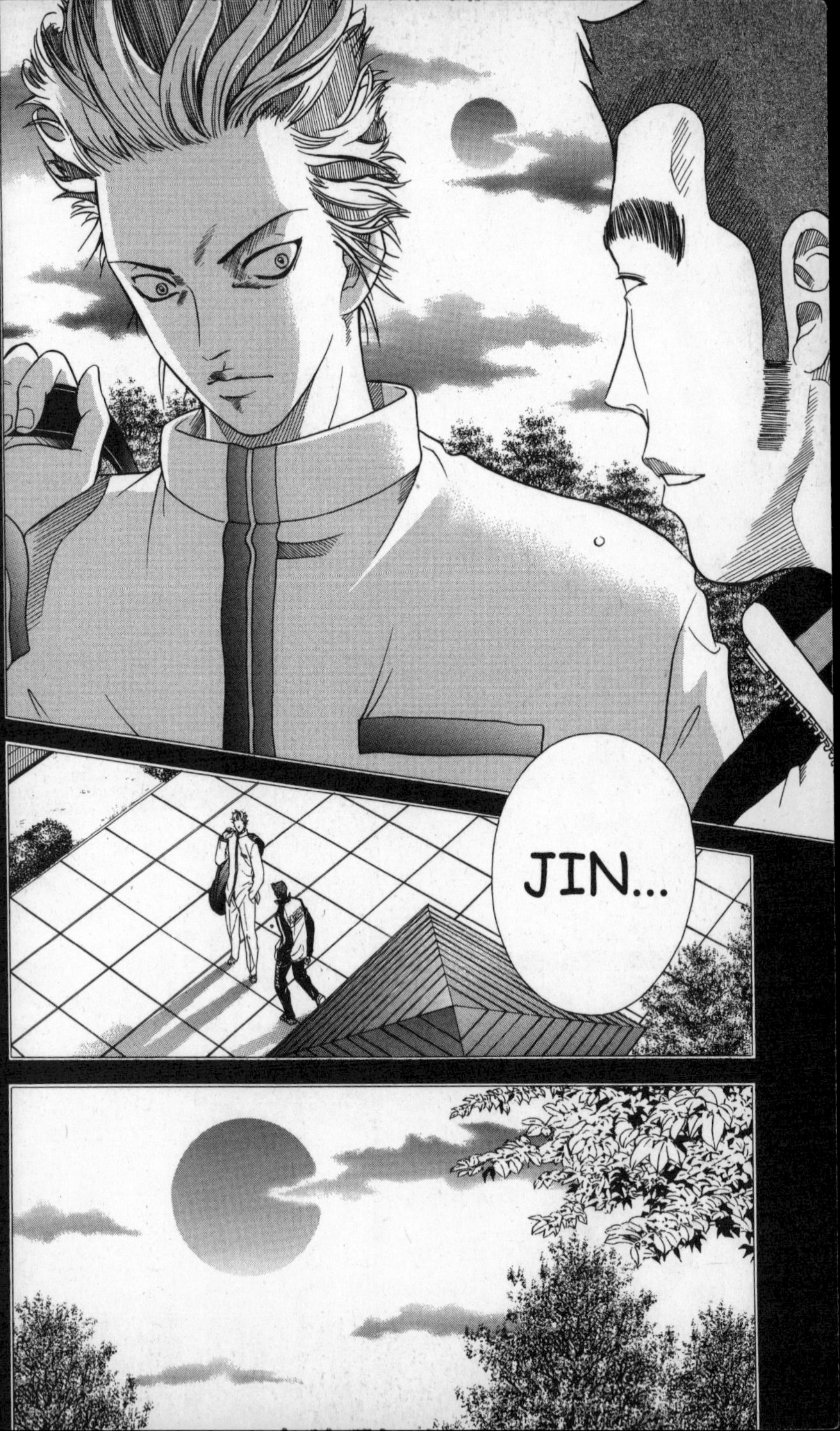
JIN...

READ THIS WAY

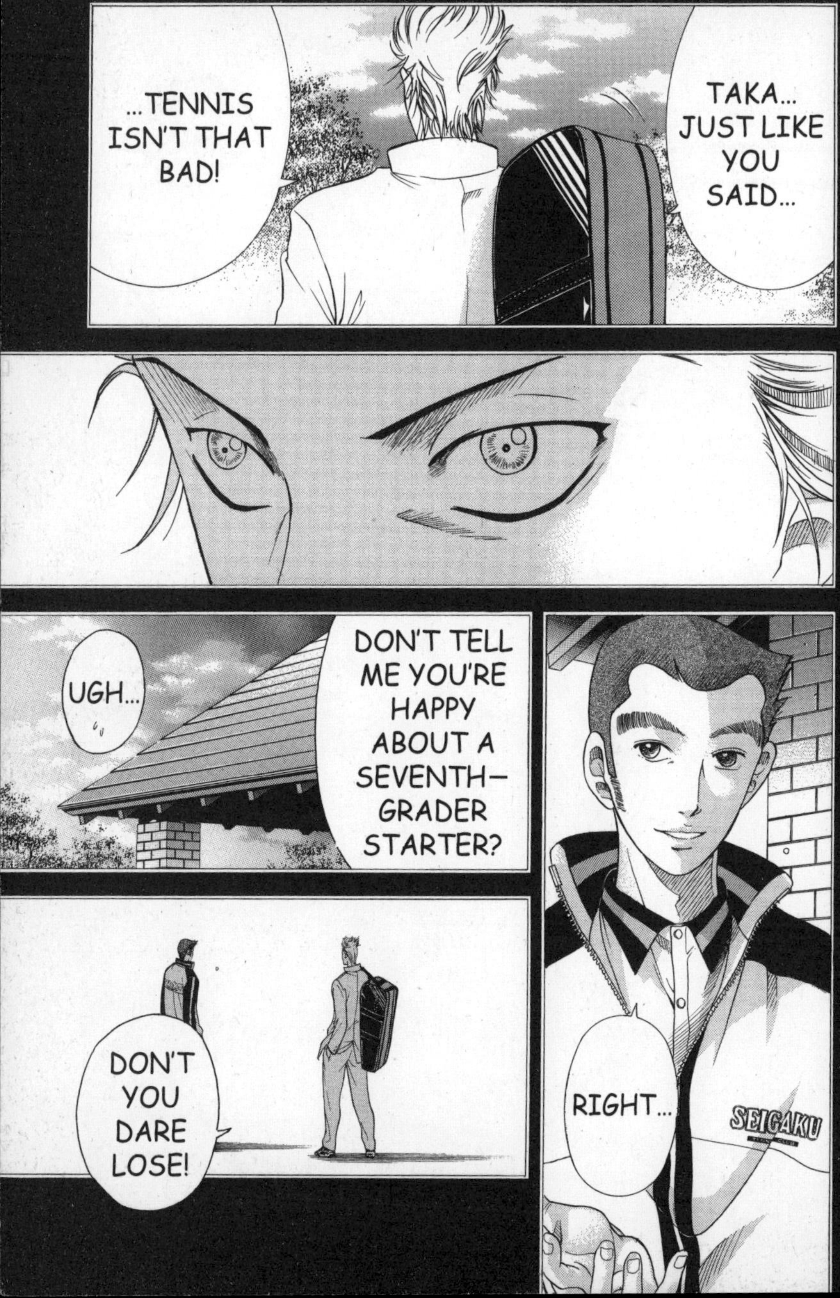
TAKA... JUST LIKE YOU SAID...
...TENNIS ISN'T THAT BAD!
DON'T TELL ME YOU'RE HAPPY ABOUT A SEVENTH-GRADER STARTER?
UGH...
DON'T YOU DARE LOSE!
RIGHT...
SEIGAKU

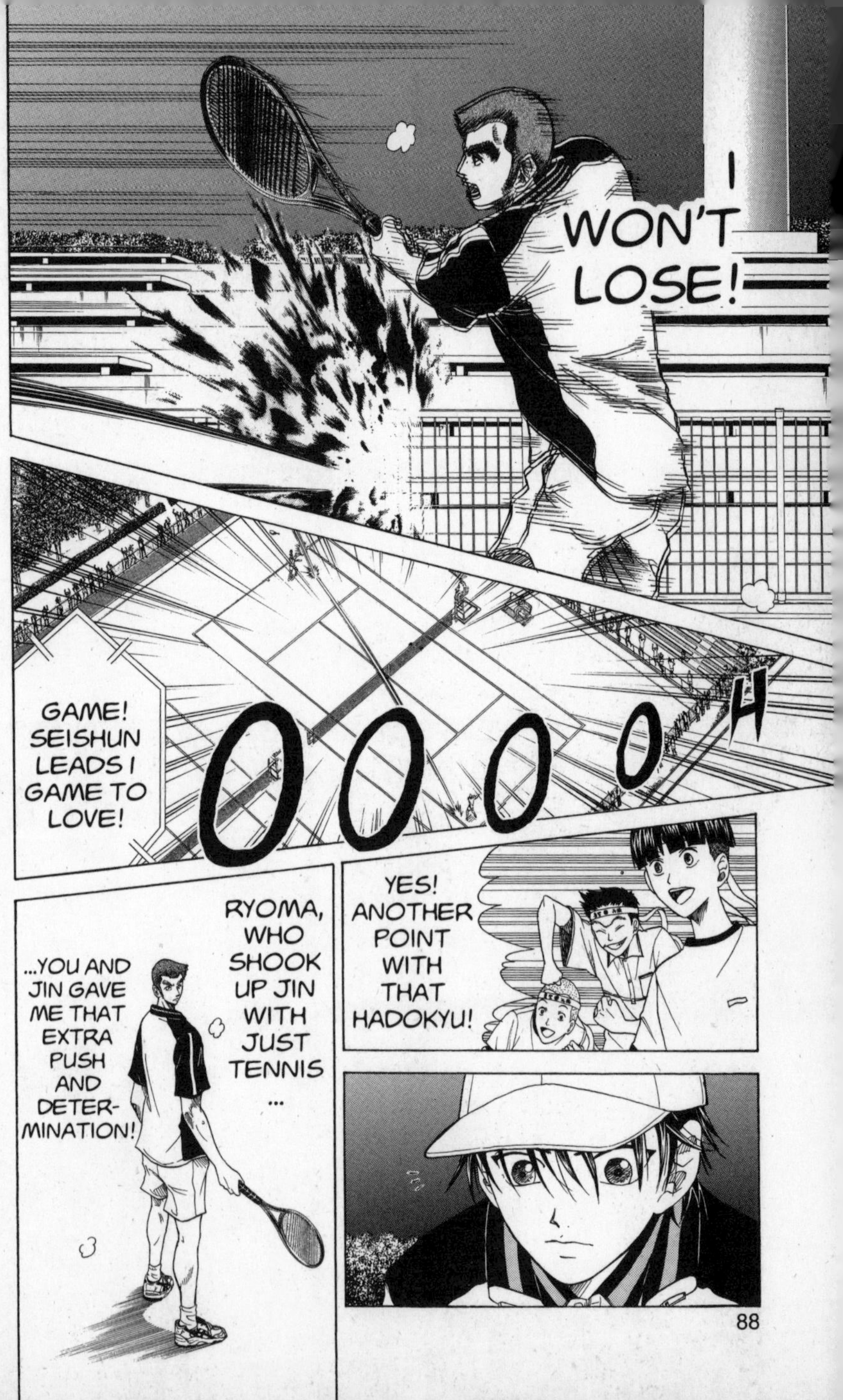
I WON'T LOSE!
OOOOH
GAME! SEISHUN LEADS 1 GAME TO LOVE!
YES! ANOTHER POINT WITH THAT HADOKYU!
RYOMA, WHO SHOOK UP JIN WITH JUST TENNIS...
...YOU AND JIN GAVE ME THAT EXTRA PUSH AND DETERMINATION!

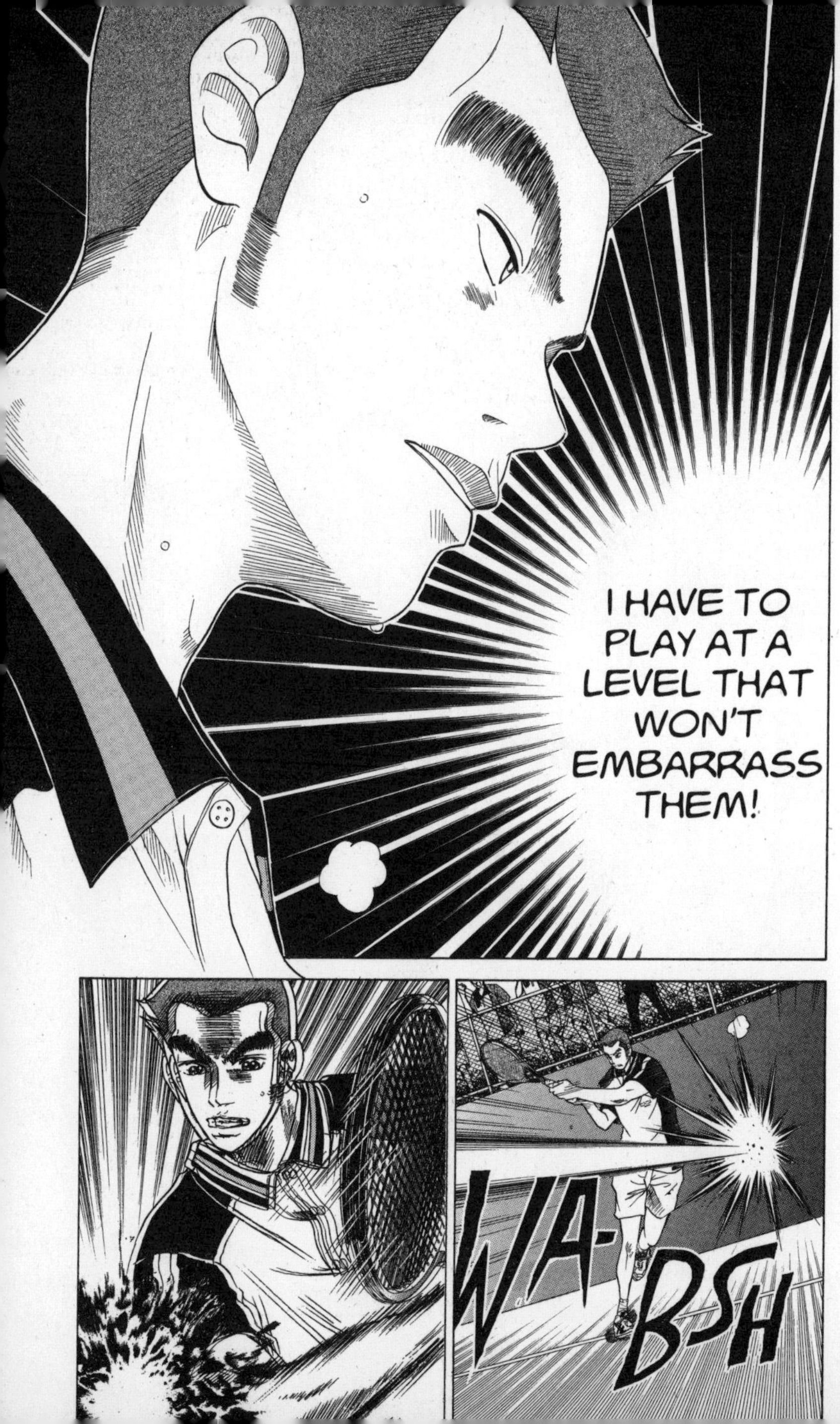
I HAVE TO PLAY AT A LEVEL THAT WON'T EMBARRASS THEM!
WA-BSH

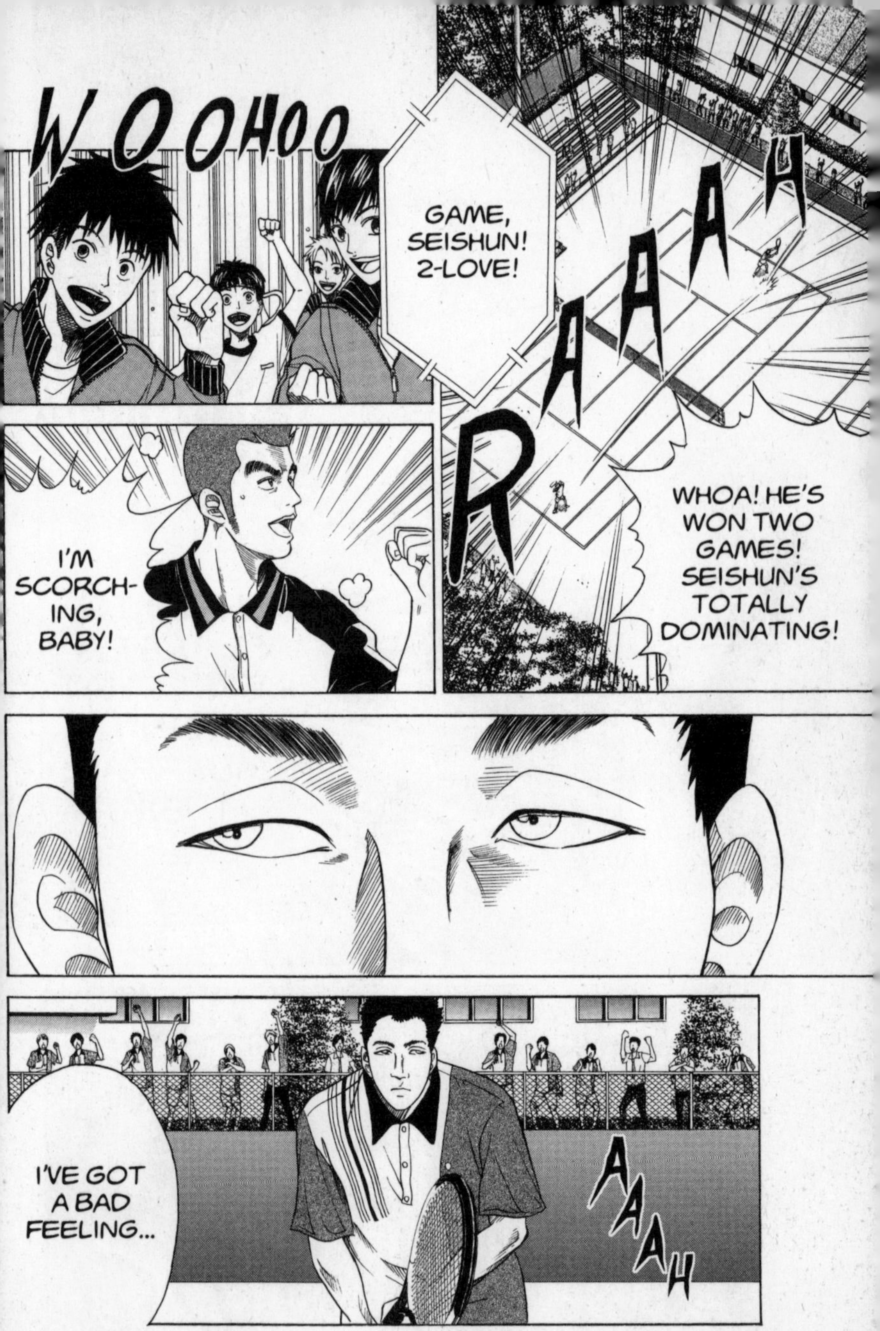
GAME, SEISHUN! 2-LOVE!
RAAAAH
WHOA! HE'S WON TWO GAMES! SEISHUN'S TOTALLY DOMINATING!
WOOHOO
I'M SCORCH-ING, BABY!
I'VE GOT A BAD FEELING...
AAAAH

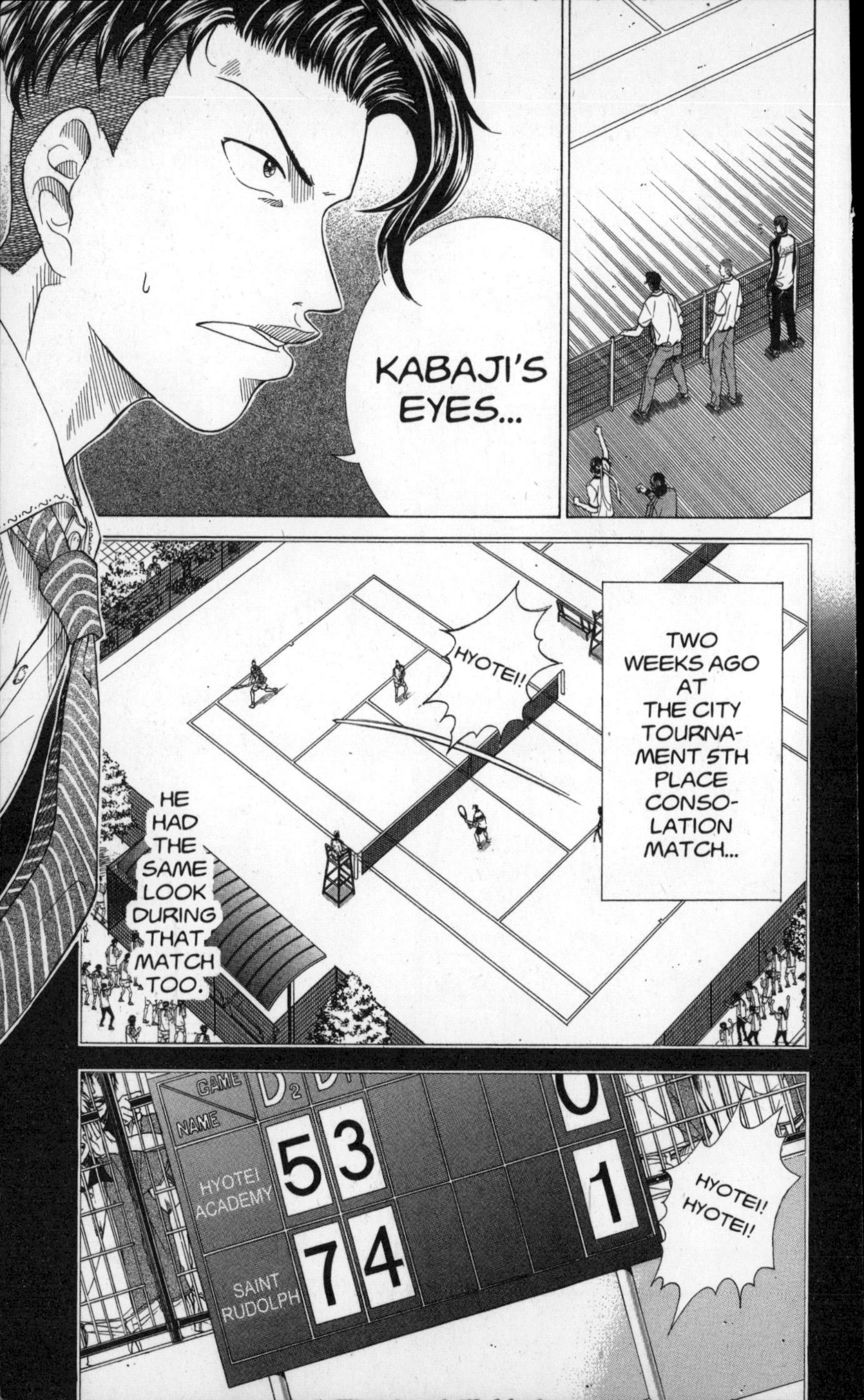
KABAJI'S EYES...
TWO WEEKS AGO AT THE CITY TOURNAMENT 5TH PLACE CONSOLATION MATCH...
HYOTEI!!
HE HAD THE SAME LOOK DURING THAT MATCH TOO.
HYOTEI!! HYOTEI!!
GAME
NAME
HYOTEI ACADEMY
53
SAINT RUDOLPH
74
0
1

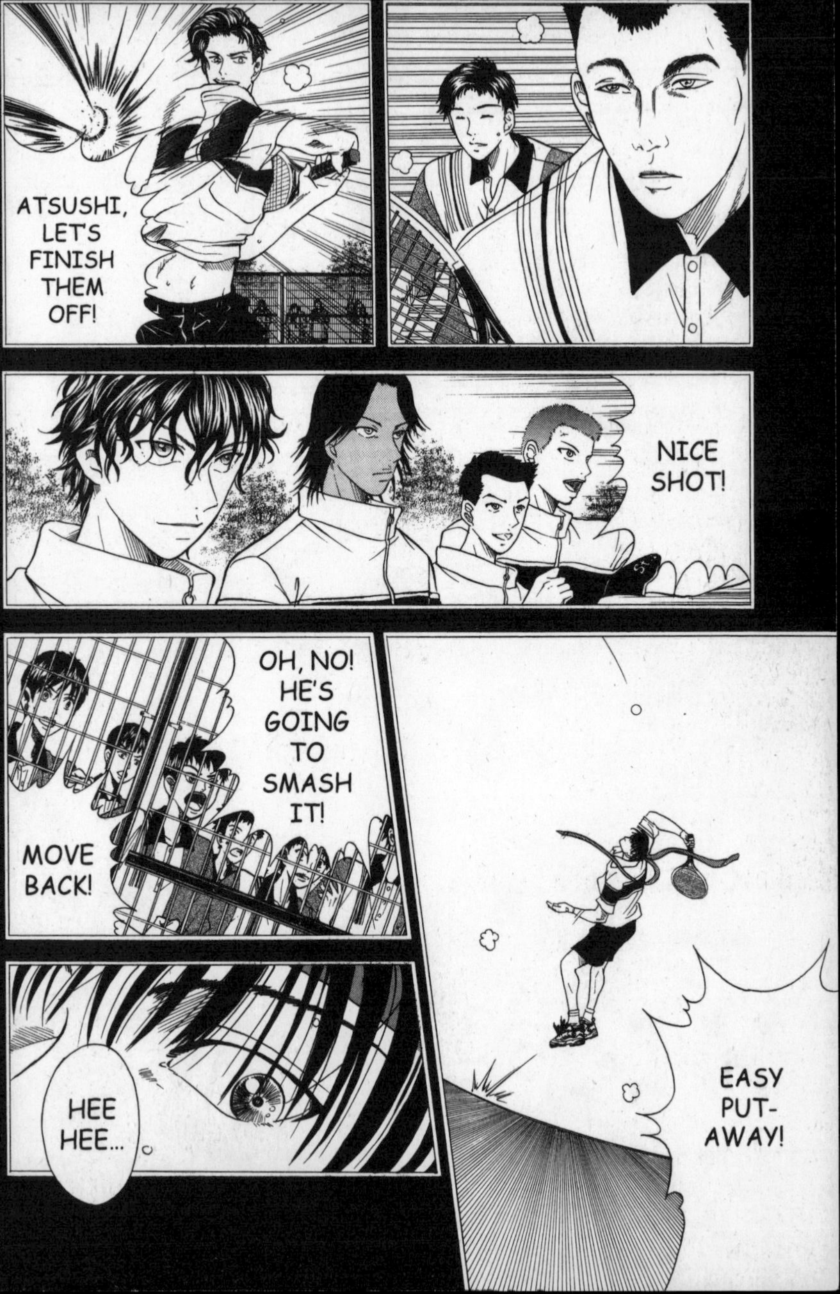
ATSUSHI, LET'S FINISH THEM OFF!
NICE SHOT!
EASY PUT-AWAY!
OH, NO! HE'S GOING TO SMASH IT!
MOVE BACK!
HEE HEE...

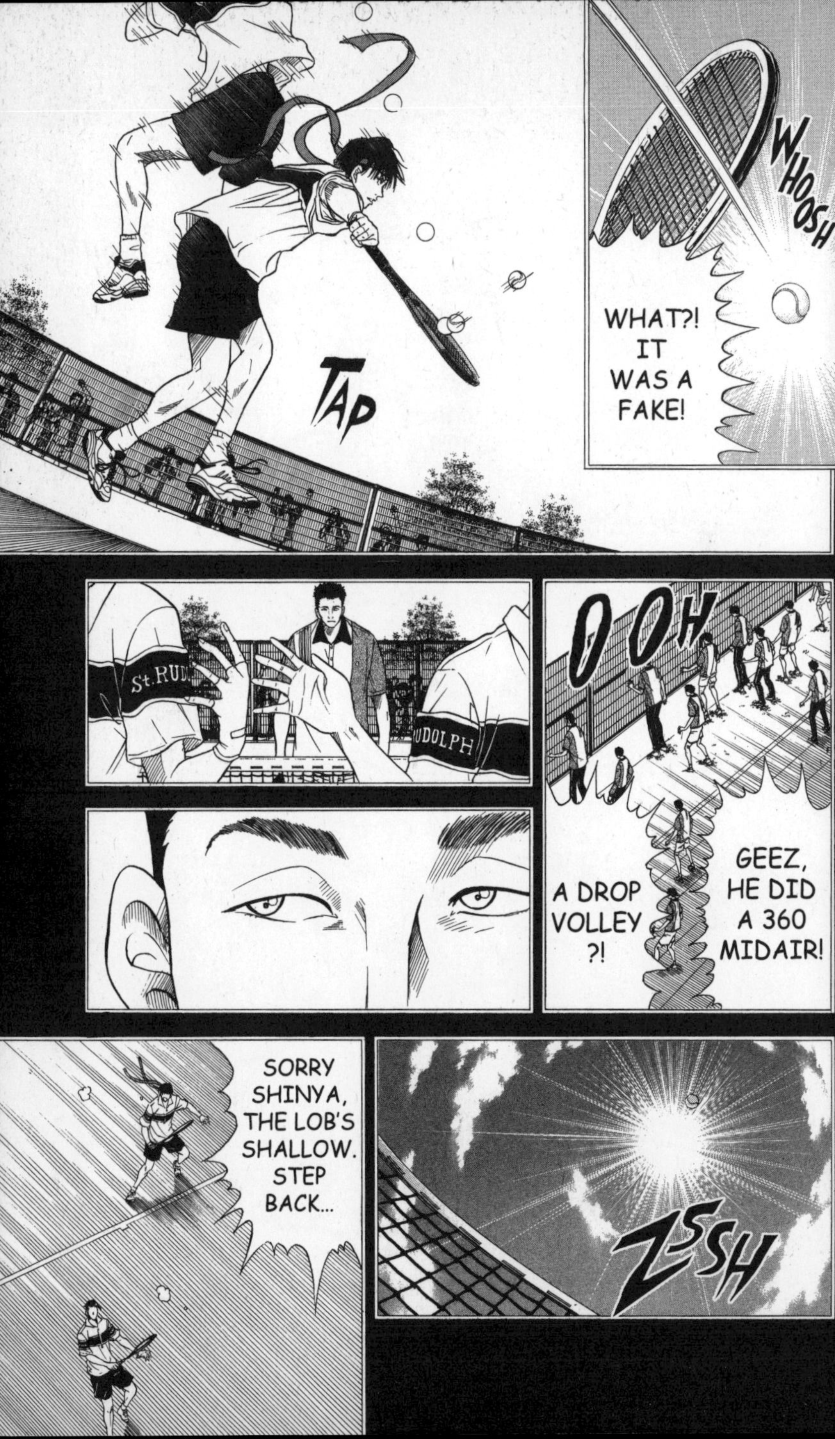
WHOOSH
WHAT?! IT WAS A FAKE!
TAP
OOOH
GEEZ, HE DID A 360 MIDAIR!
A DROP VOLLEY ?!
St.RUD
RUDOLPH
ZSSH
SORRY SHINYA, THE LOB'S SHALLOW. STEP BACK...

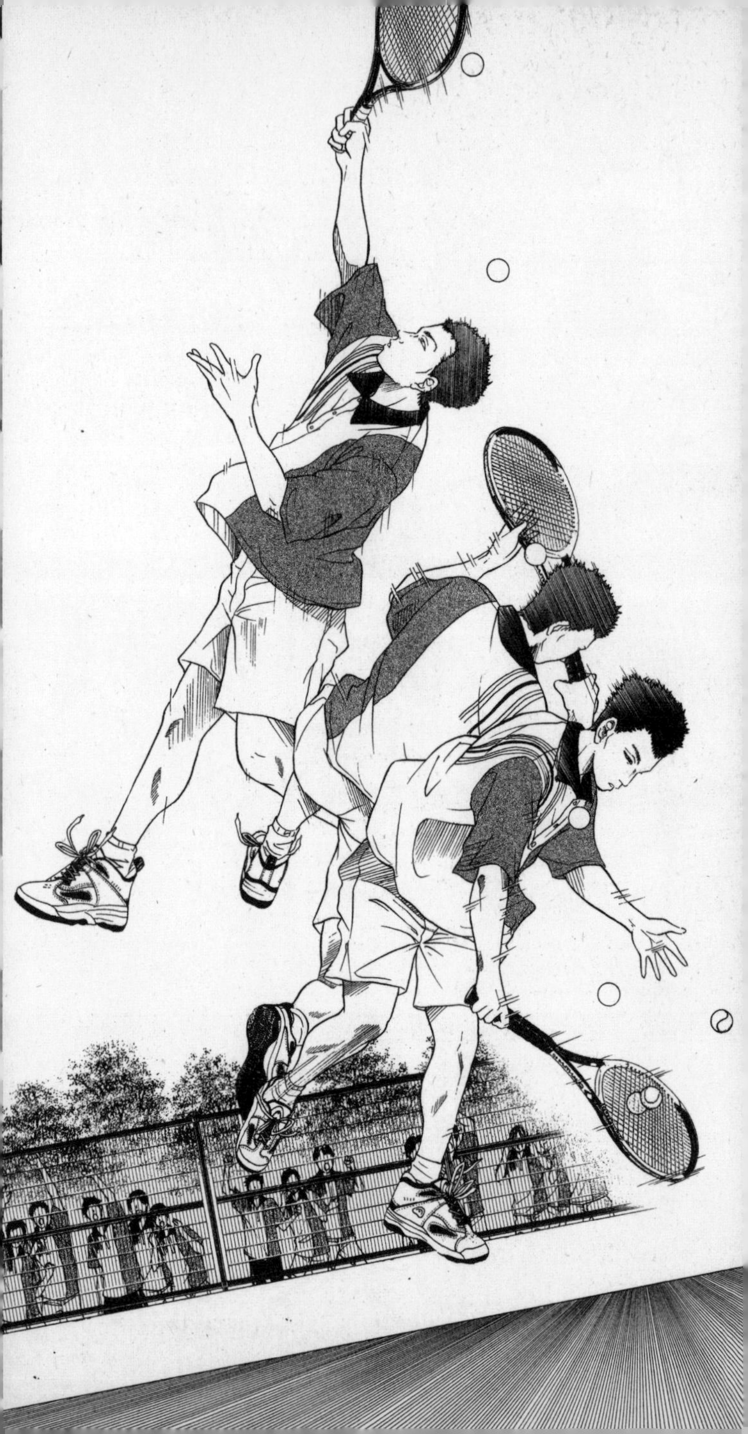

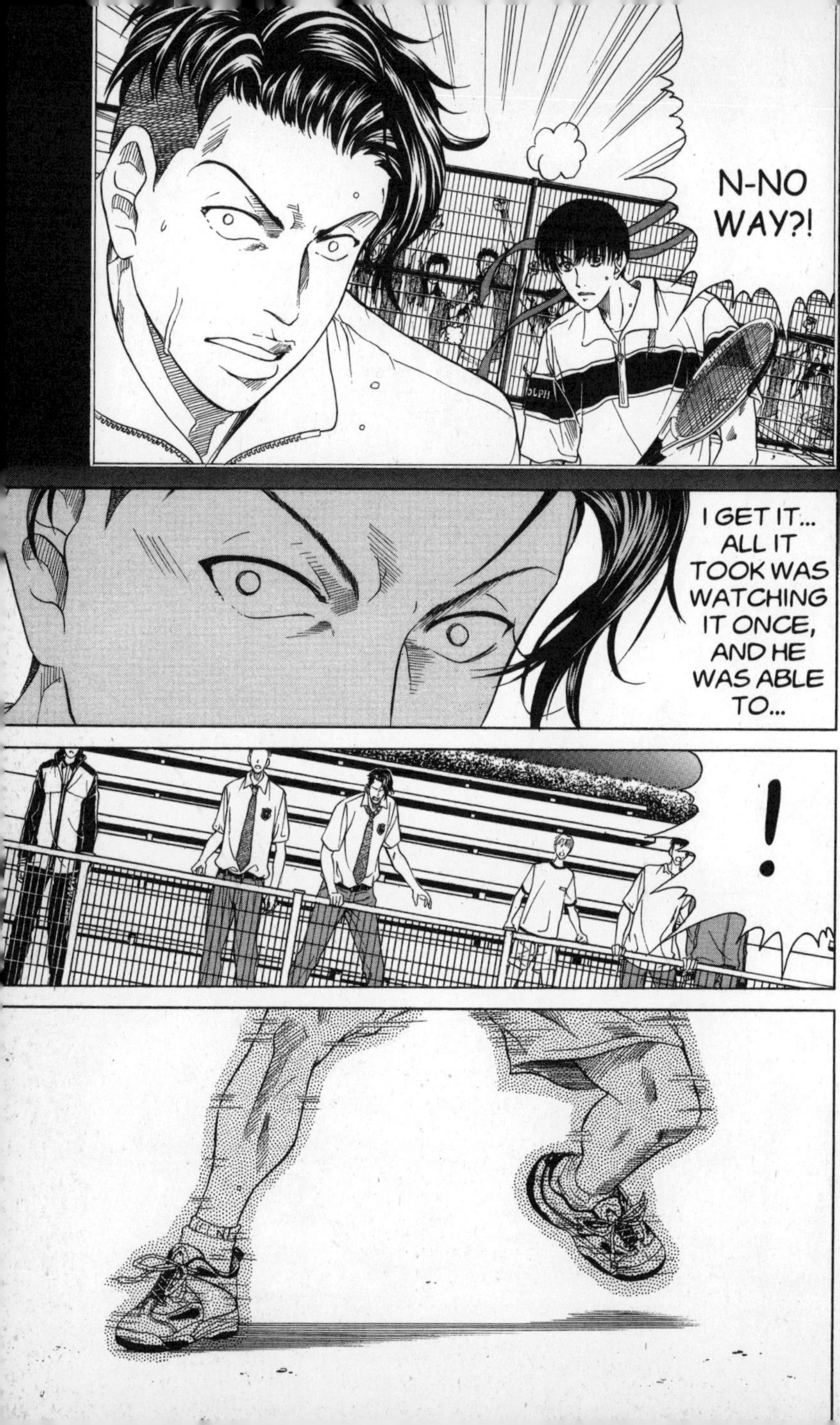
N-NO WAY?!
I GET IT... ALL IT TOOK WAS WATCHING IT ONCE, AND HE WAS ABLE TO...
!

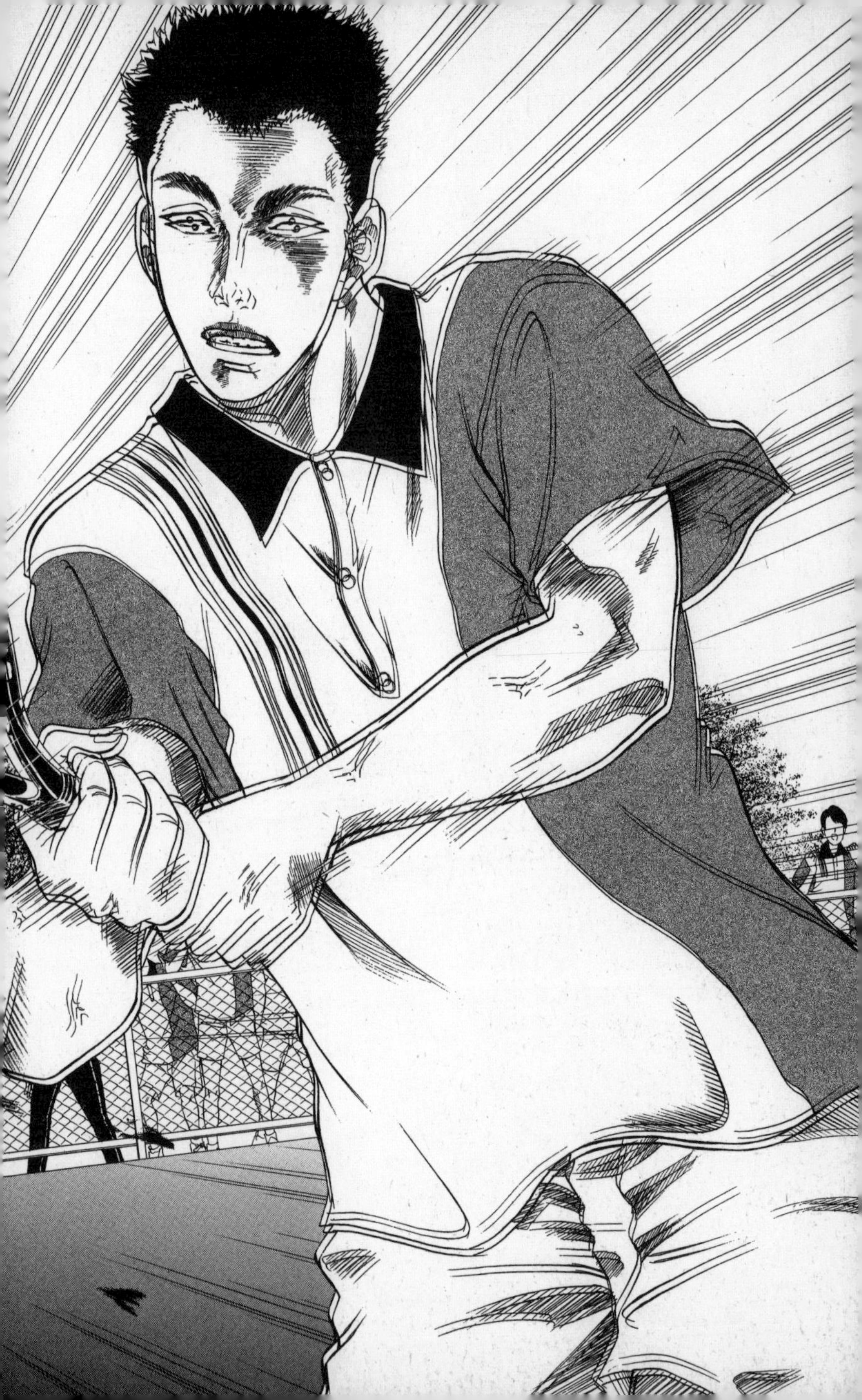

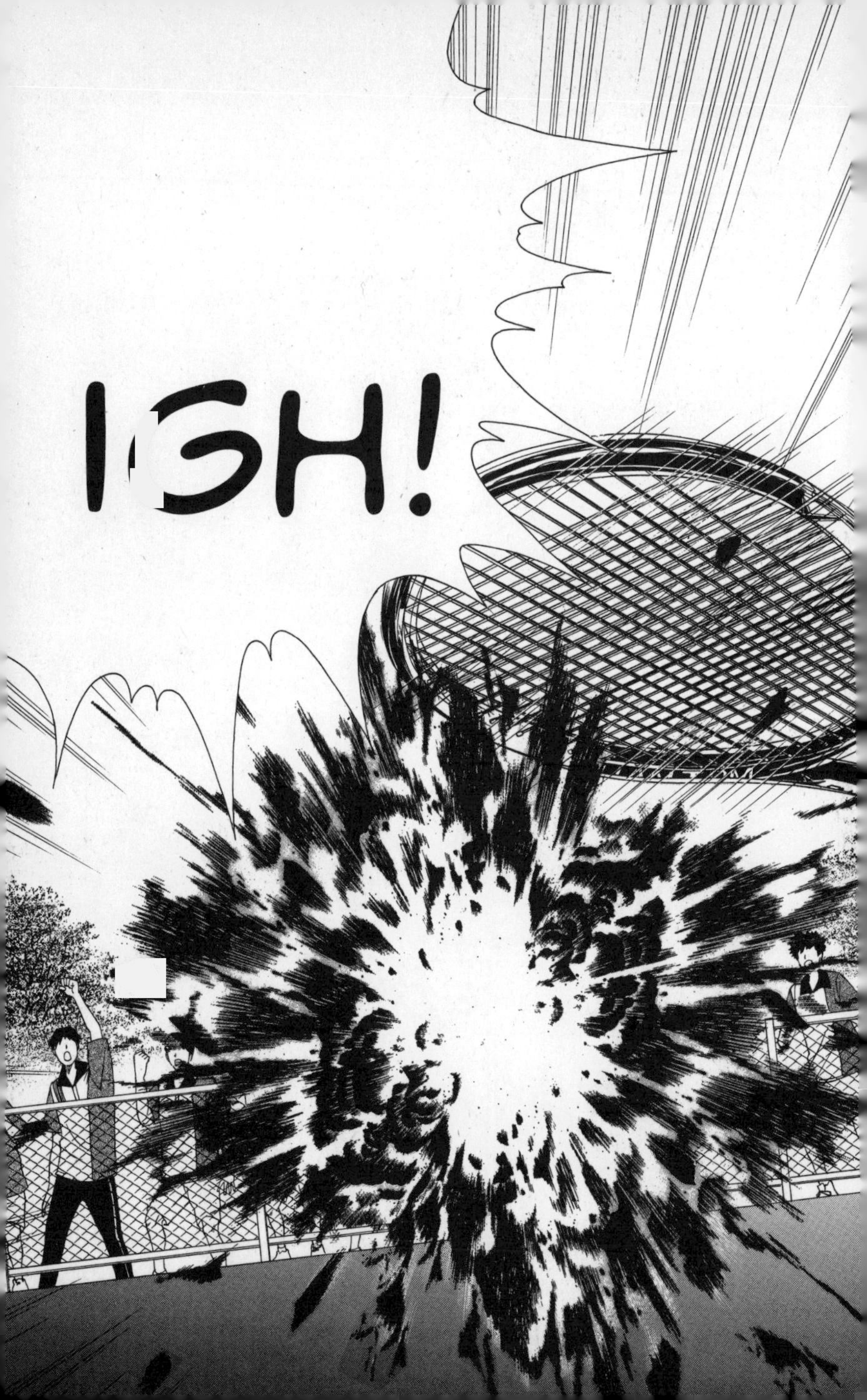
IGH!

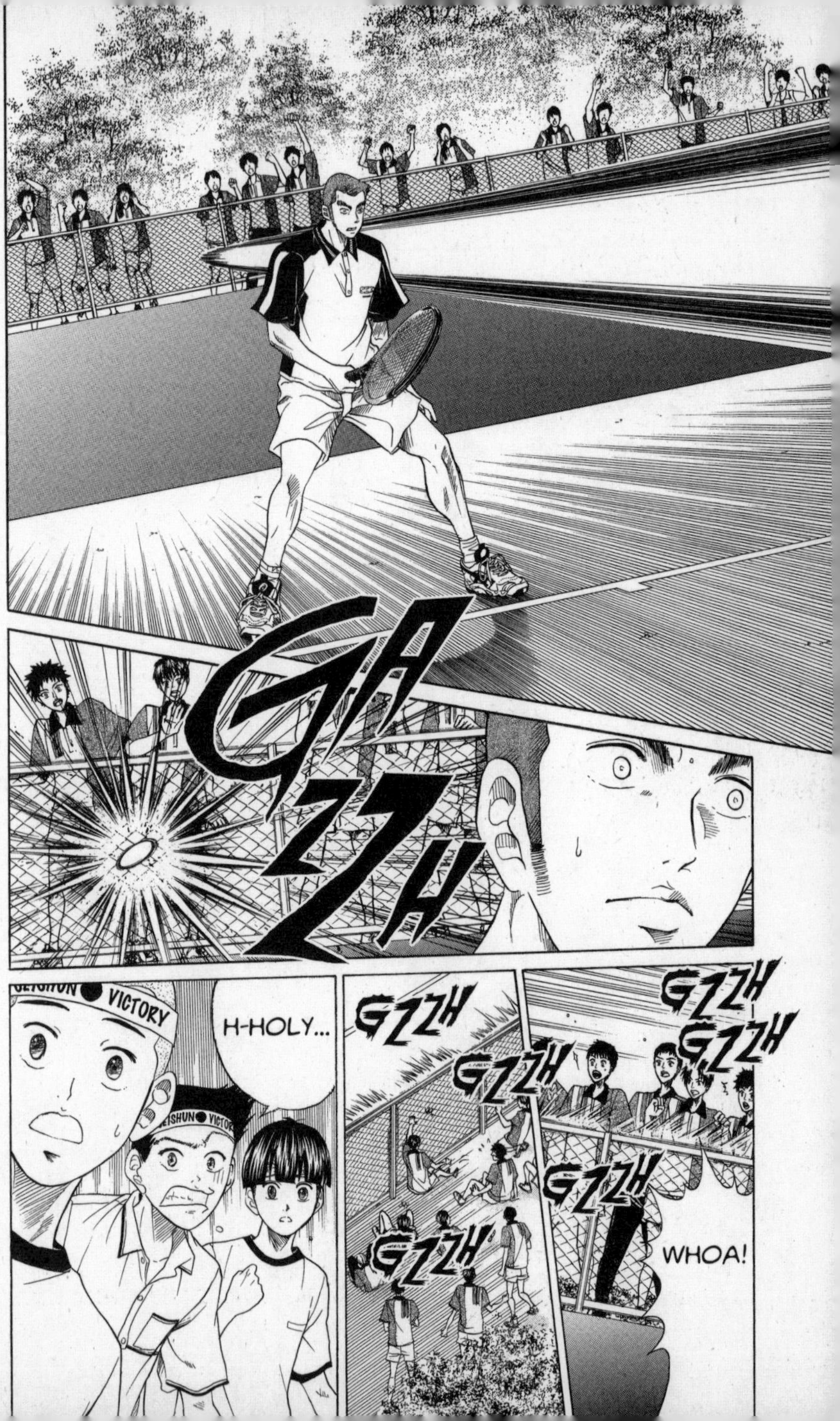
GAZZH
GZZH
GZZH
GZZH
WHOA!
GZZH
GZZH
GZZH
H-HOLY...

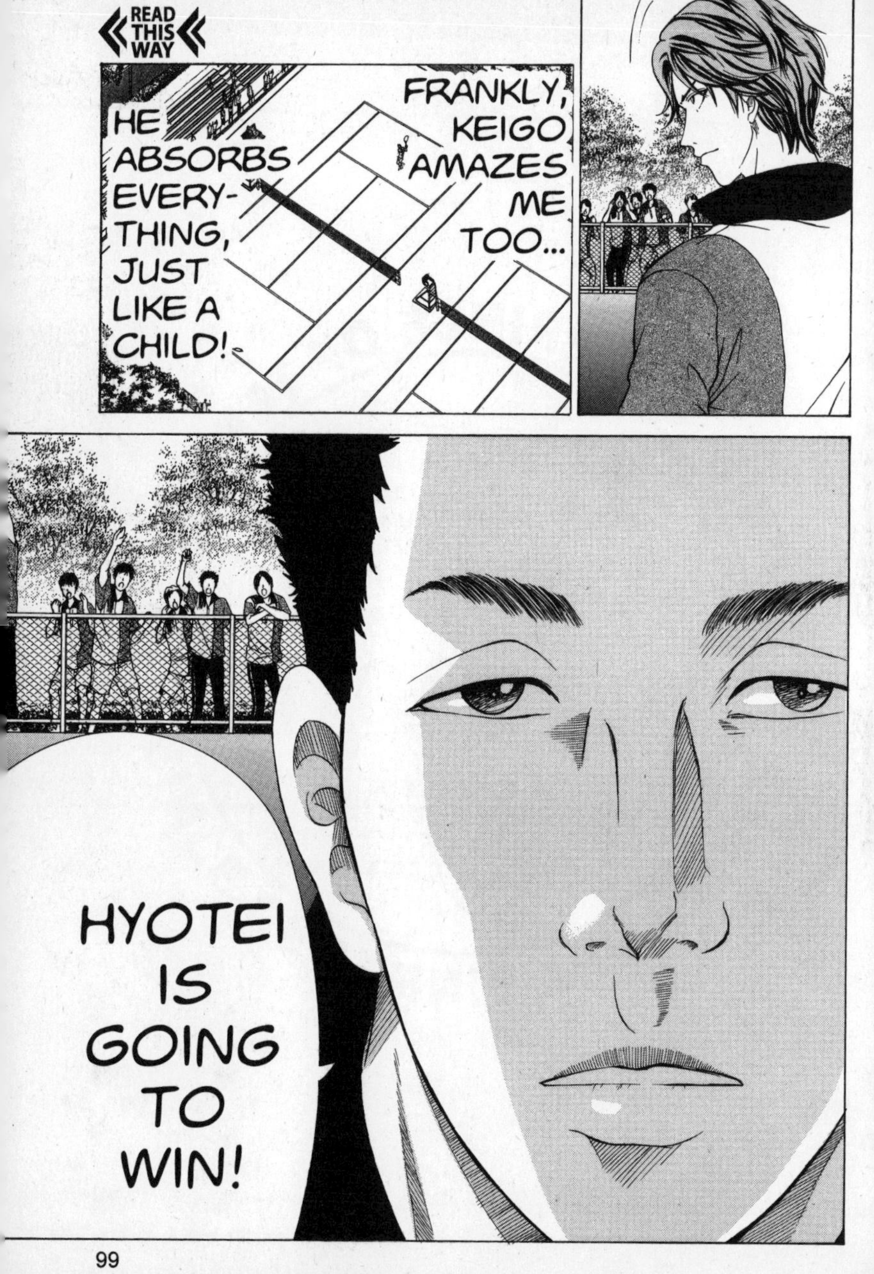
READ THIS WAY
FRANKLY, KEIGO AMAZES ME TOO...
HE ABSORBS EVERY-THING, JUST LIKE A CHILD!
HYOTEI IS GOING TO WIN!

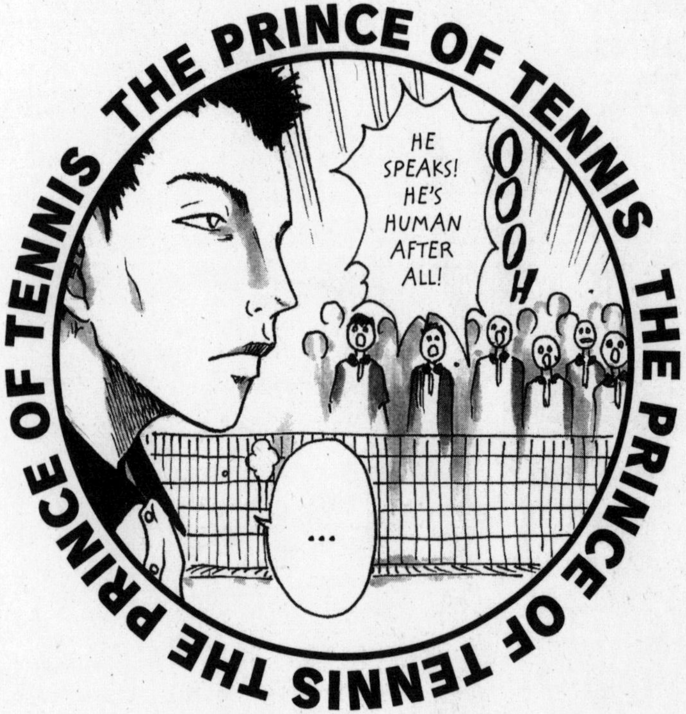
THE PRINCE OF TENNIS THE PRINCE OF TENNIS THE PRINCE OF TENNIS
OOOOH
HE SPEAKS! HE'S HUMAN AFTER ALL!
...

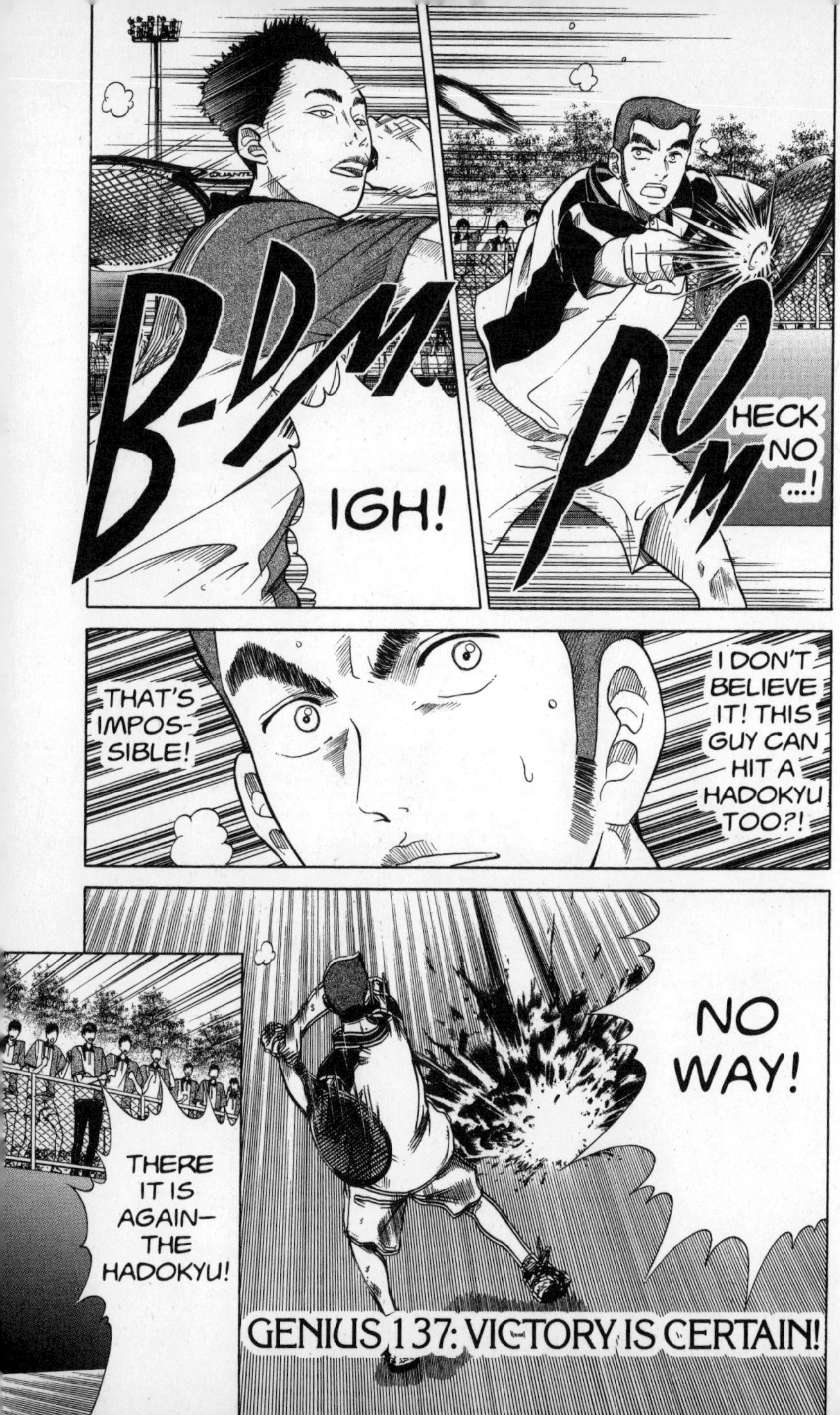
DOM
HECK NO ...!
B-DM
IGH!
I DON'T BELIEVE IT! THIS GUY CAN HIT A HADOKYU TOO?!
THAT'S IMPOSSIBLE!
NO WAY!
THERE IT IS AGAIN—THE HADOKYU!

GENIUS 137: VICTORY IS CERTAIN!

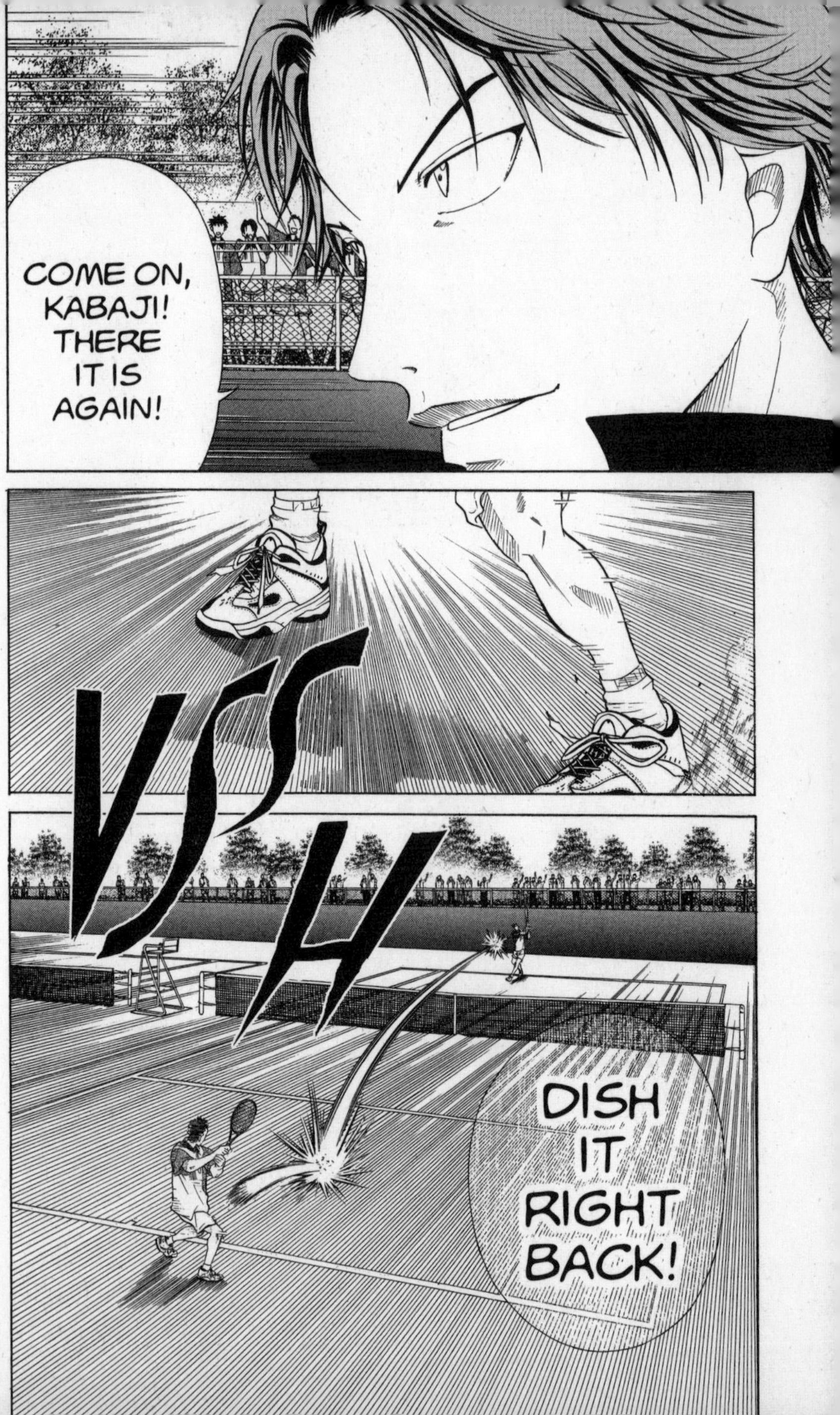
COME ON, KABAJI! THERE IT IS AGAIN!
VSSH
DISH IT RIGHT BACK!

GENIUS 137: VICTORY IS CERTAIN!

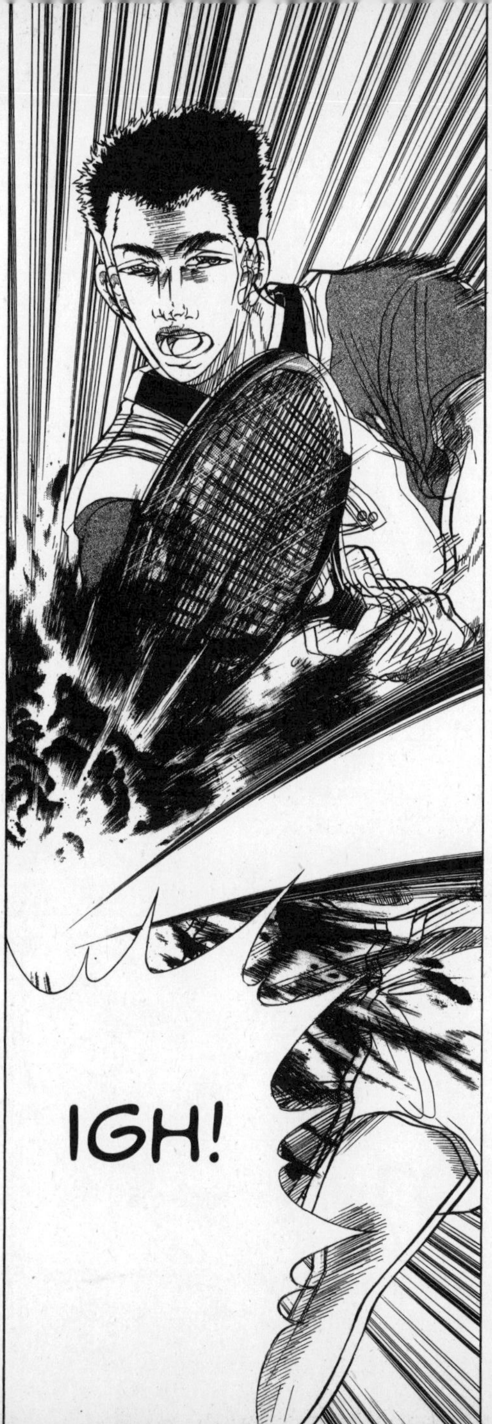
IGH!

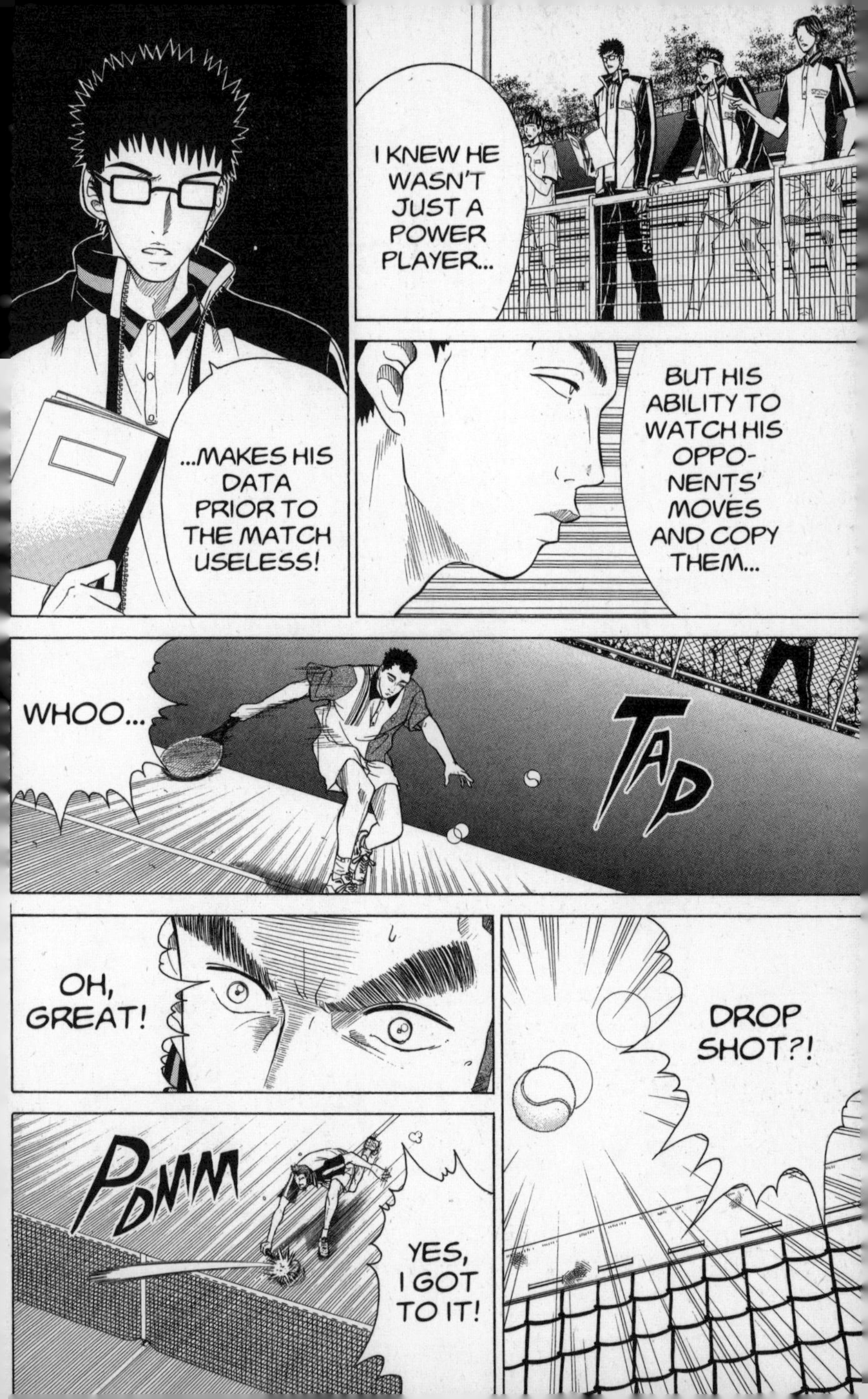
I KNEW HE WASN'T JUST A POWER PLAYER...
BUT HIS ABILITY TO WATCH HIS OPPO-NENTS' MOVES AND COPY THEM...
...MAKES HIS DATA PRIOR TO THE MATCH USELESS!
TAP
WHOO...
DROP SHOT?!
OH, GREAT!
PDMM
YES, I GOT TO IT!

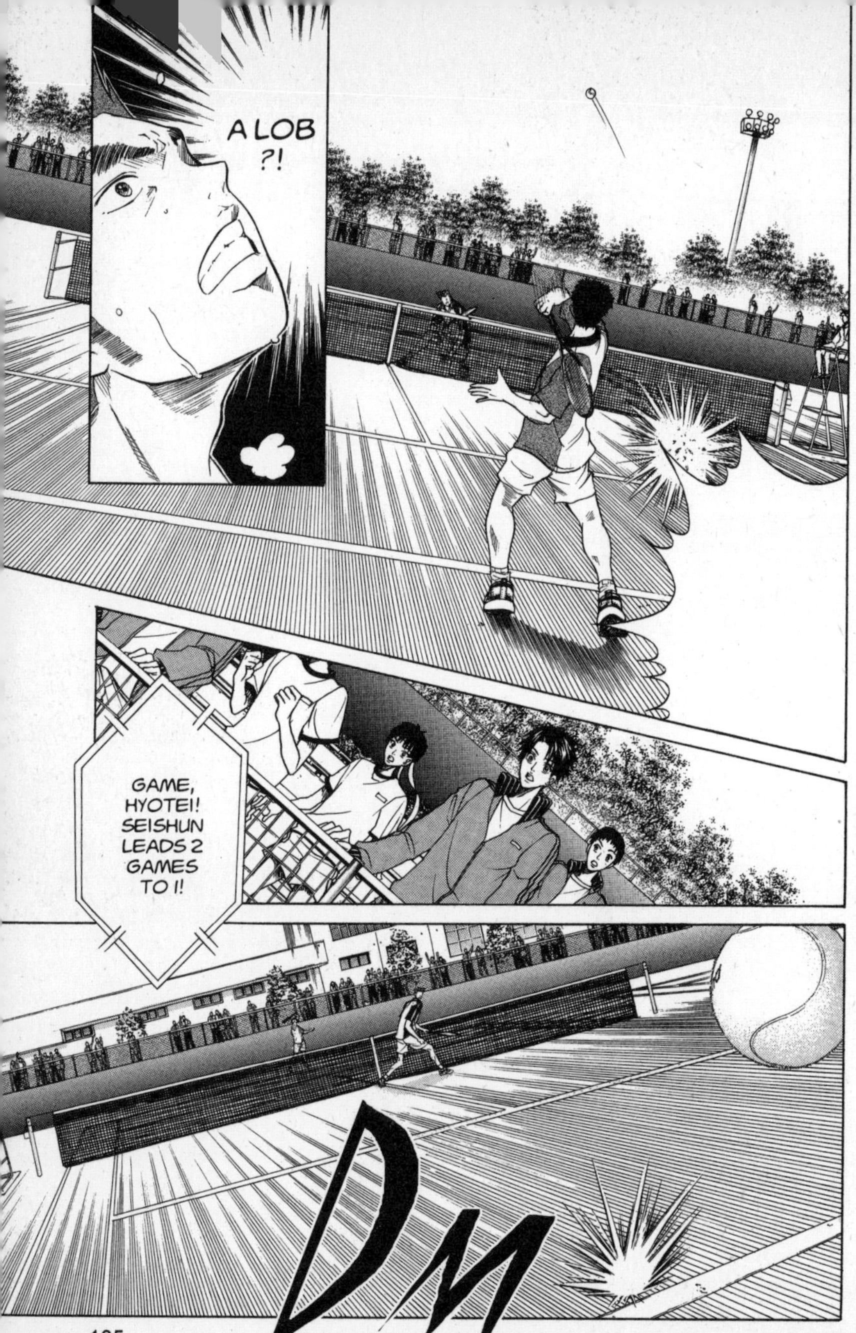
A LOB ?!
GAME, HYOTEI! SEISHUN LEADS 2 GAMES TO 1!
DM

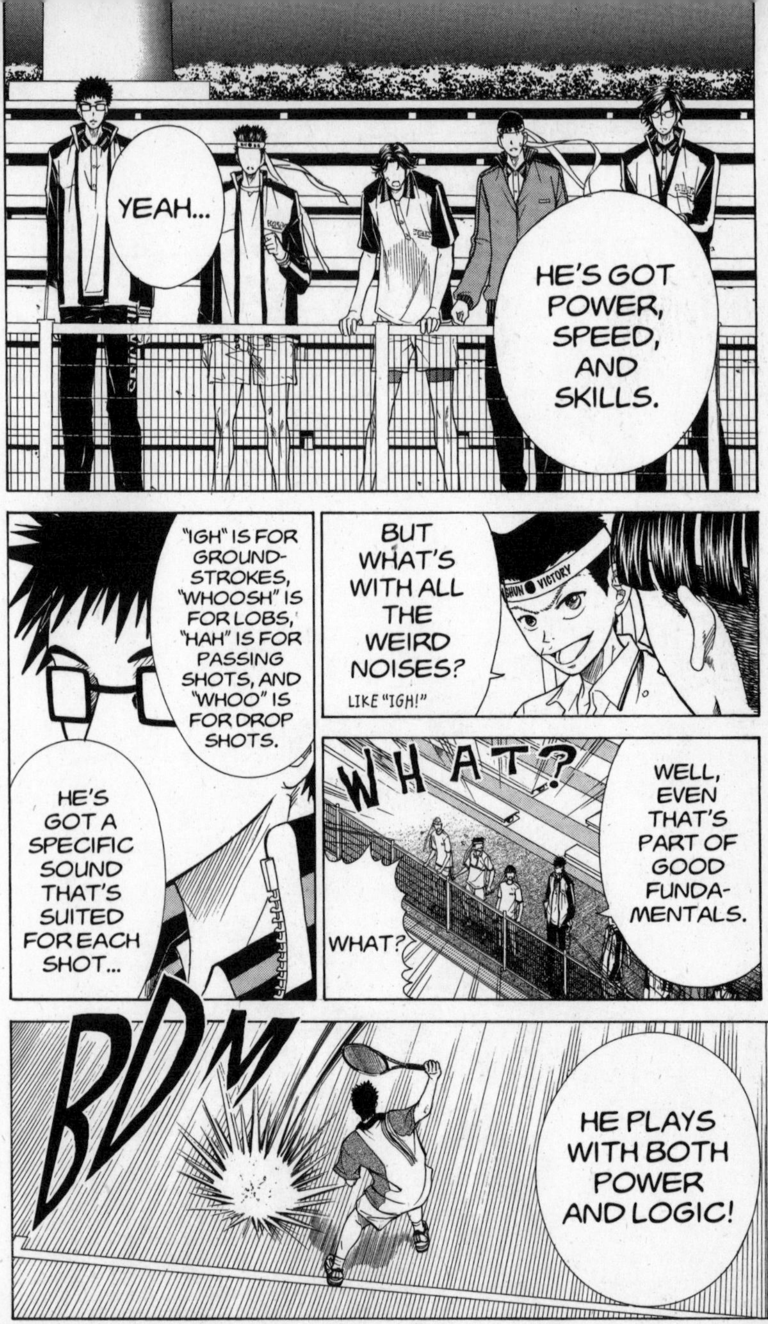
HE'S GOT POWER, SPEED, AND SKILLS.
YEAH...
BUT WHAT'S WITH ALL THE WEIRD NOISES?
LIKE "IGH!"
"IGH" IS FOR GROUND-STROKES, "WHOOSH" IS FOR LOBS, "HAH" IS FOR PASSING SHOTS, AND "WHOO" IS FOR DROP SHOTS.
HE'S GOT A SPECIFIC SOUND THAT'S SUITED FOR EACH SHOT...
WHAT?
WHAT?
WELL, EVEN THAT'S PART OF GOOD FUNDA-MENTALS.
BDM
HE PLAYS WITH BOTH POWER AND LOGIC!

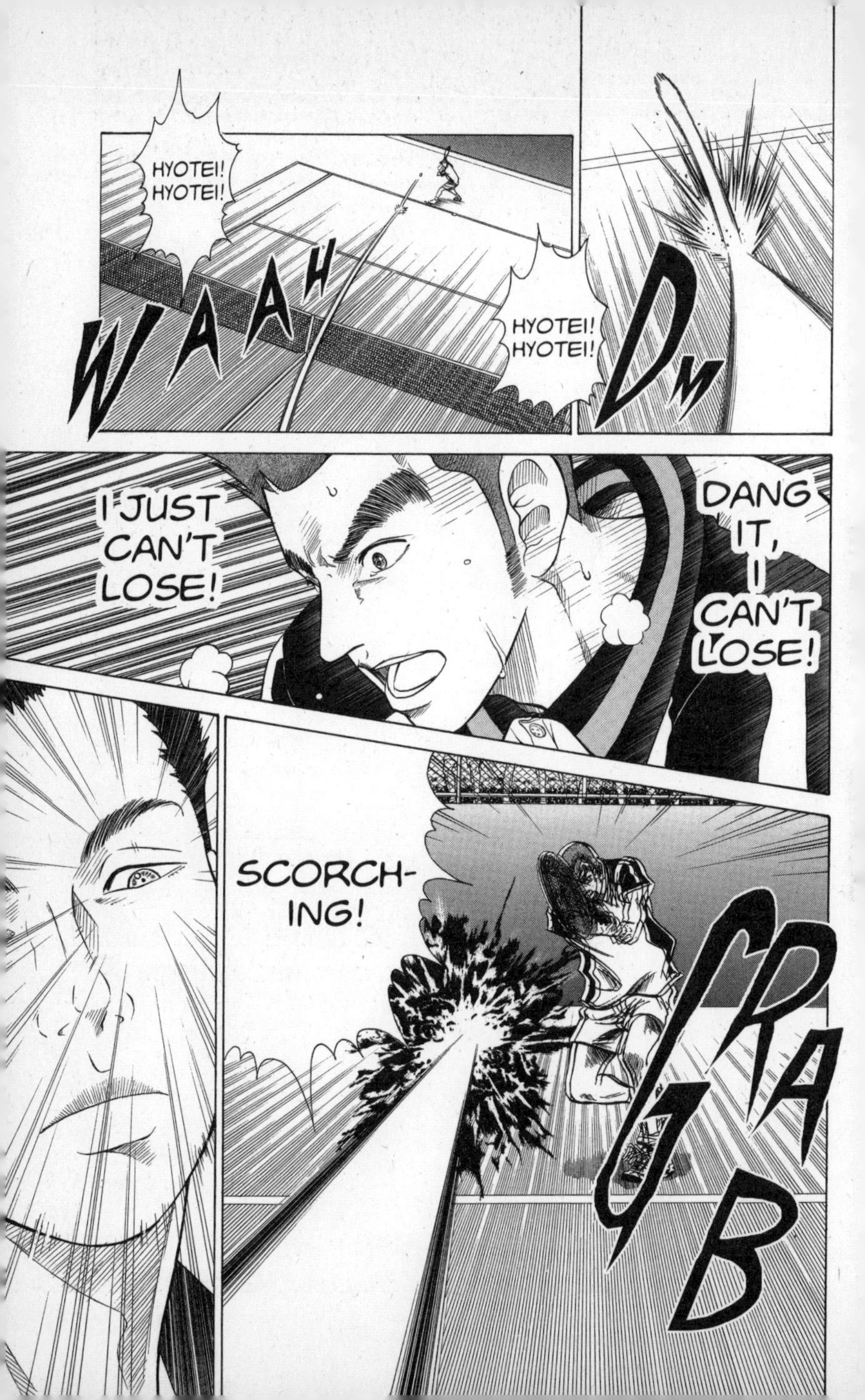

Dm
HYOTEI! HYOTEI!
HYOTEI! HYOTEI!
WAAH
DANG IT, I CAN'T LOSE!
I JUST CAN'T LOSE!
SCORCH-ING!
CRAAB

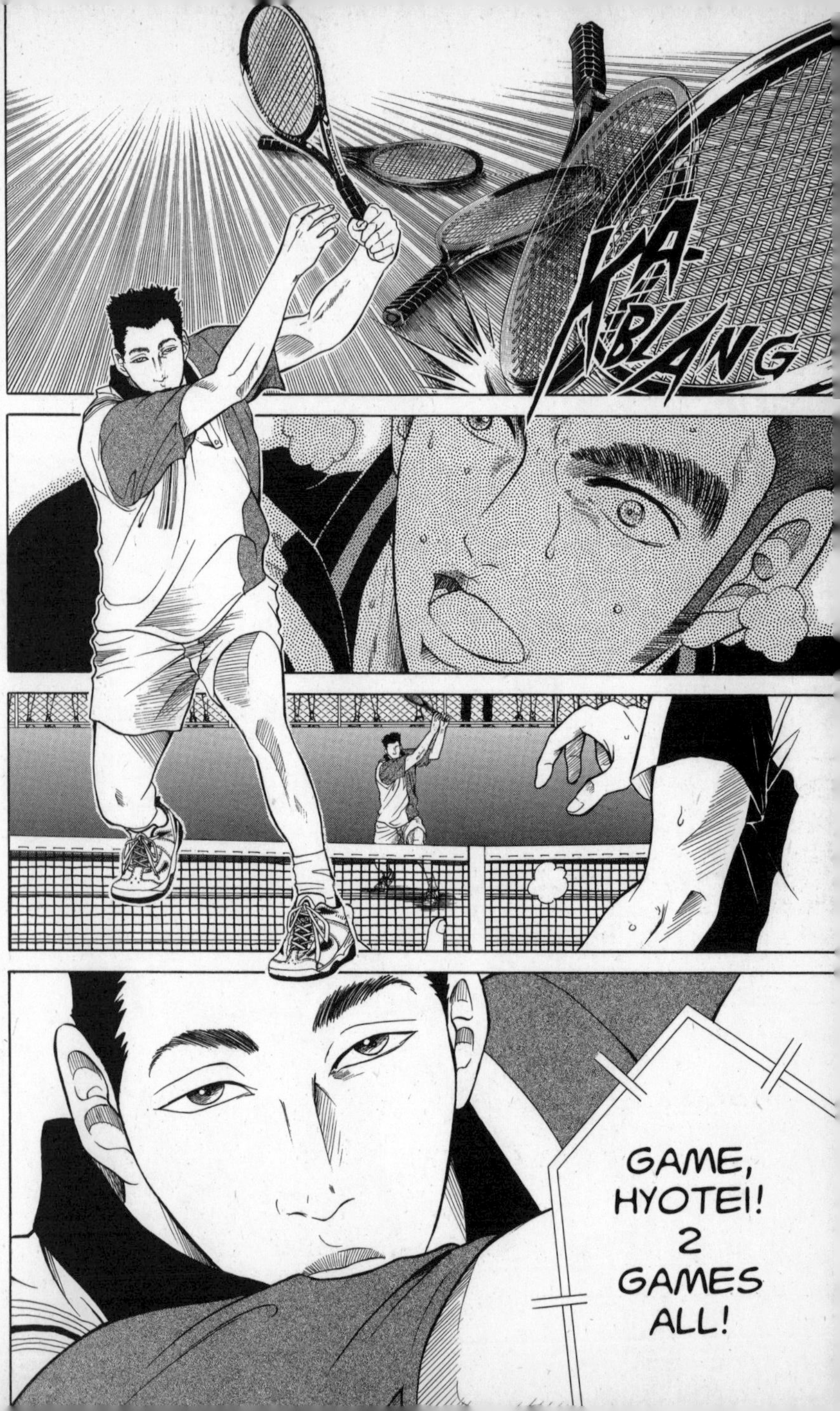
KA-BLANG
GAME, HYOTEI! 2 GAMES ALL!

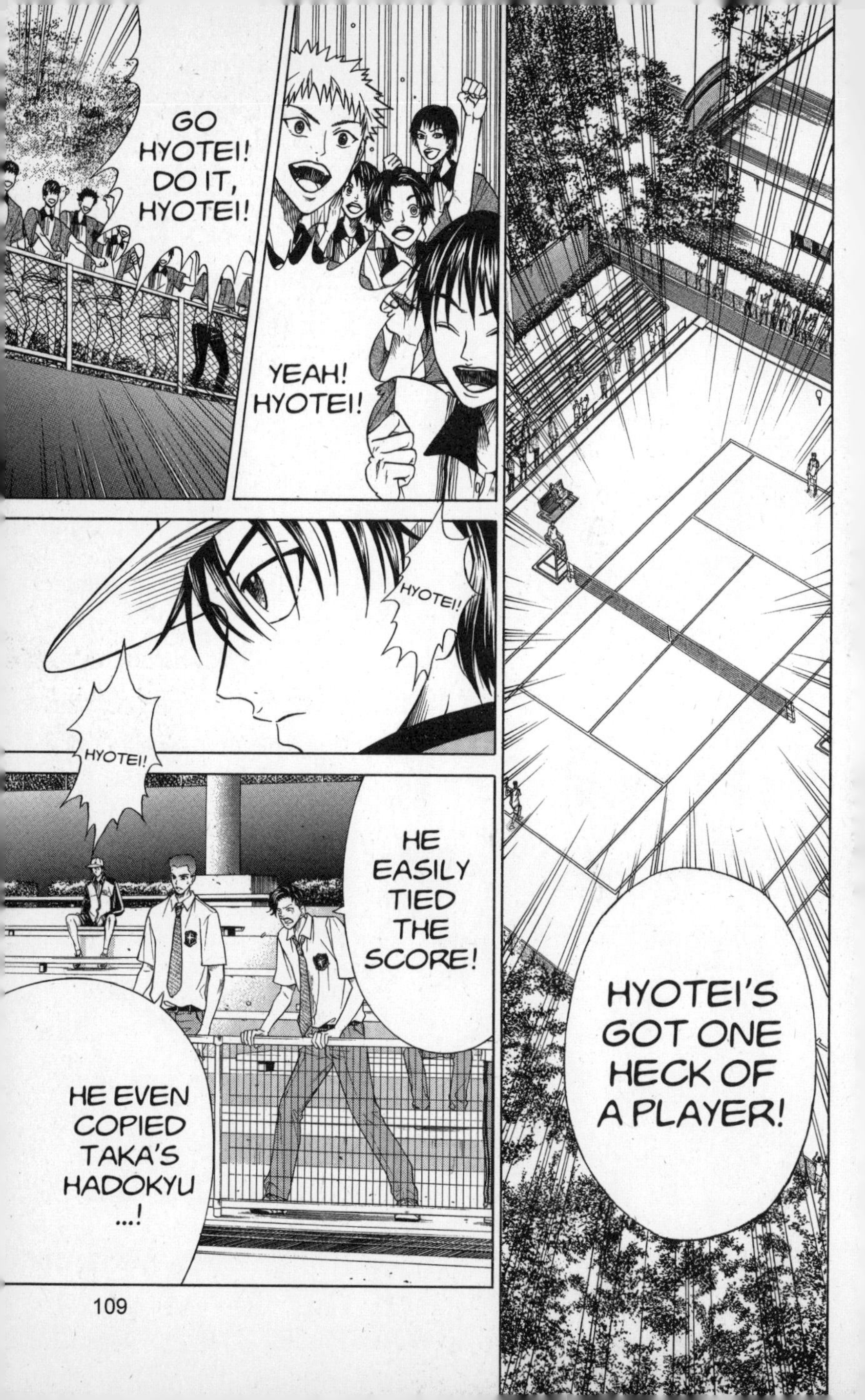
HYOTEI'S GOT ONE HECK OF A PLAYER!
YEAH! HYOTEI!
GO HYOTEI! DO IT, HYOTEI!
HYOTEI!
HYOTEI!
HE EASILY TIED THE SCORE!
HE EVEN COPIED TAKA'S HADOKYU ...!

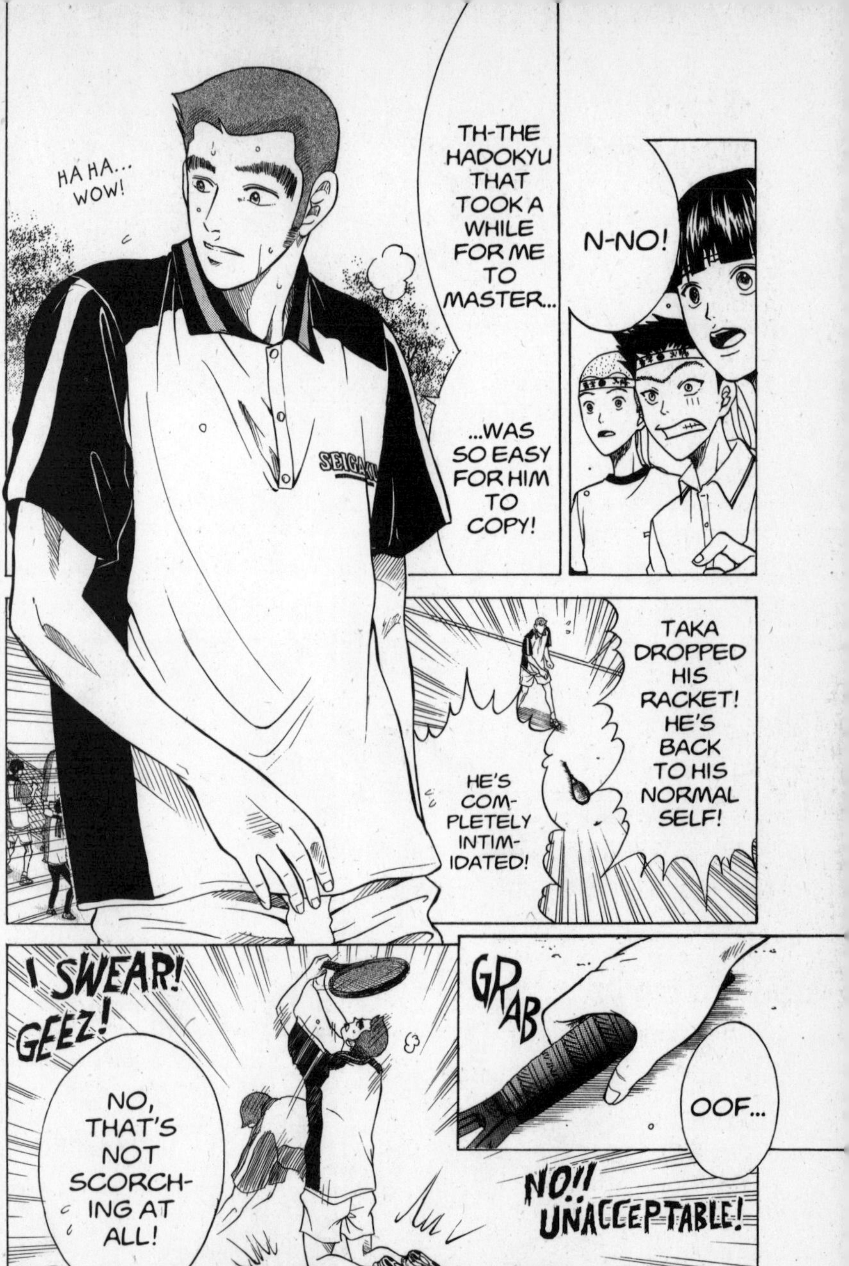
N-NO!
TH-THE HADOKYU THAT TOOK A WHILE FOR ME TO MASTER...
...WAS SO EASY FOR HIM TO COPY!
TAKA DROPPED HIS RACKET! HE'S BACK TO HIS NORMAL SELF!
HE'S COMPLETELY INTIMIDATED!
HA HA... WOW!
GRAB
OOF...
NO!! UNACCEPTABLE!
I SWEAR! GEEZ!
NO, THAT'S NOT SCORCHING AT ALL!

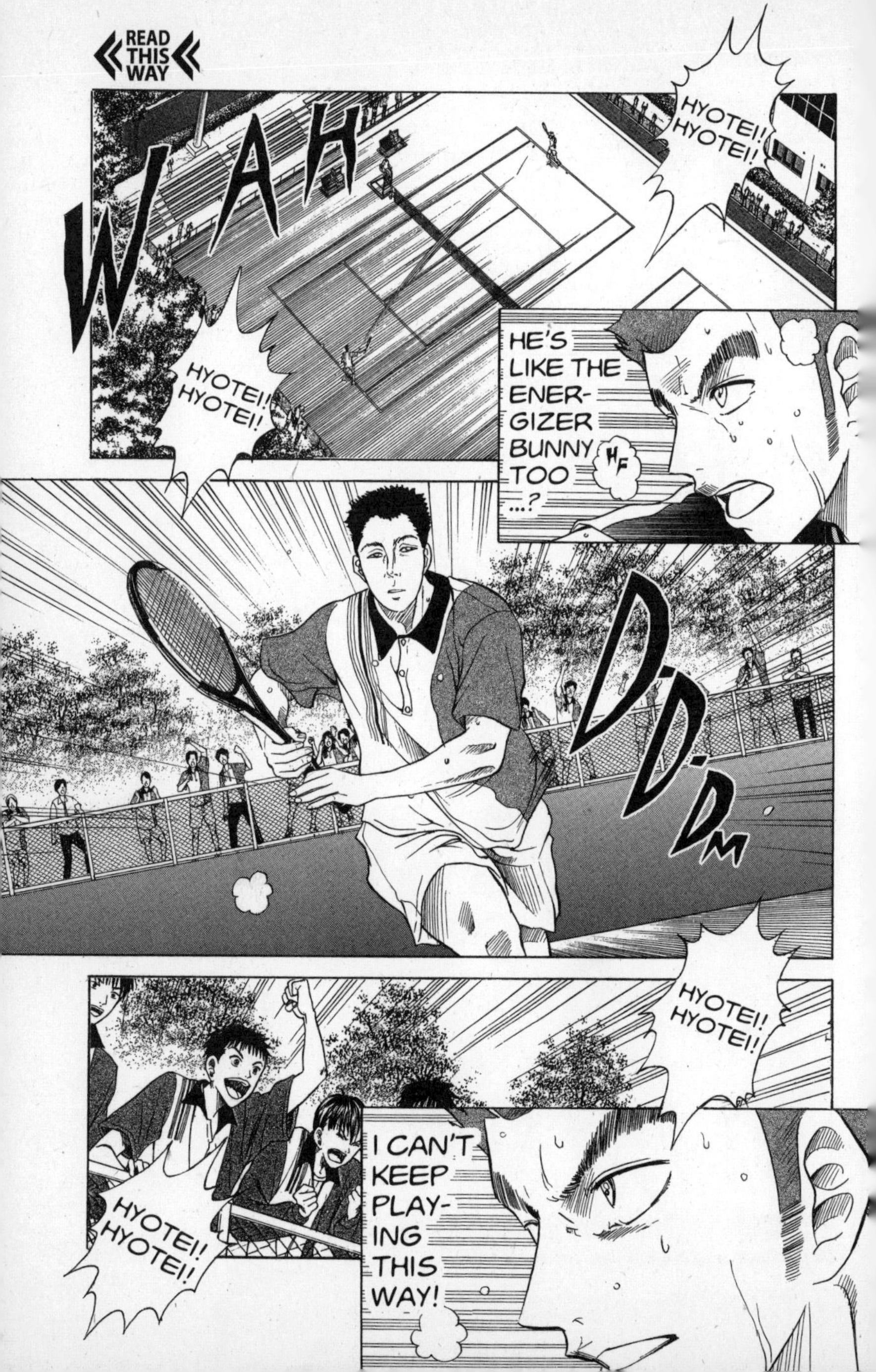
READ THIS WAY
HYOTEI!! HYOTEI!!
WAH
HYOTEI!! HYOTEI!!
HE'S LIKE THE ENER-GIZER BUNNY TOO ...?
HF
D-D-DM
HYOTEI!! HYOTEI!!
I CAN'T KEEP PLAY-ING THIS WAY!
HYOTEI!! HYOTEI!!

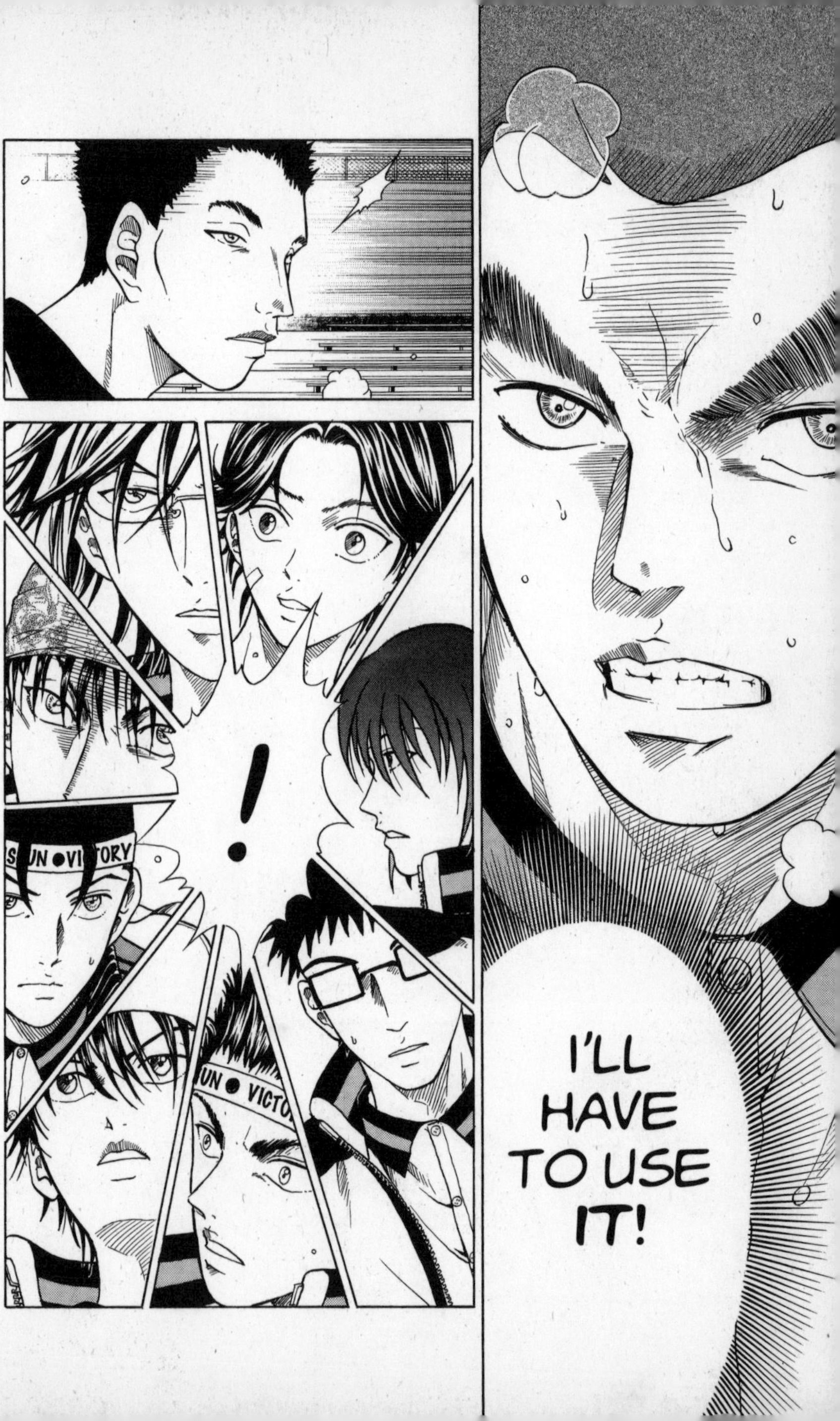
I'LL HAVE TO USE IT!
!

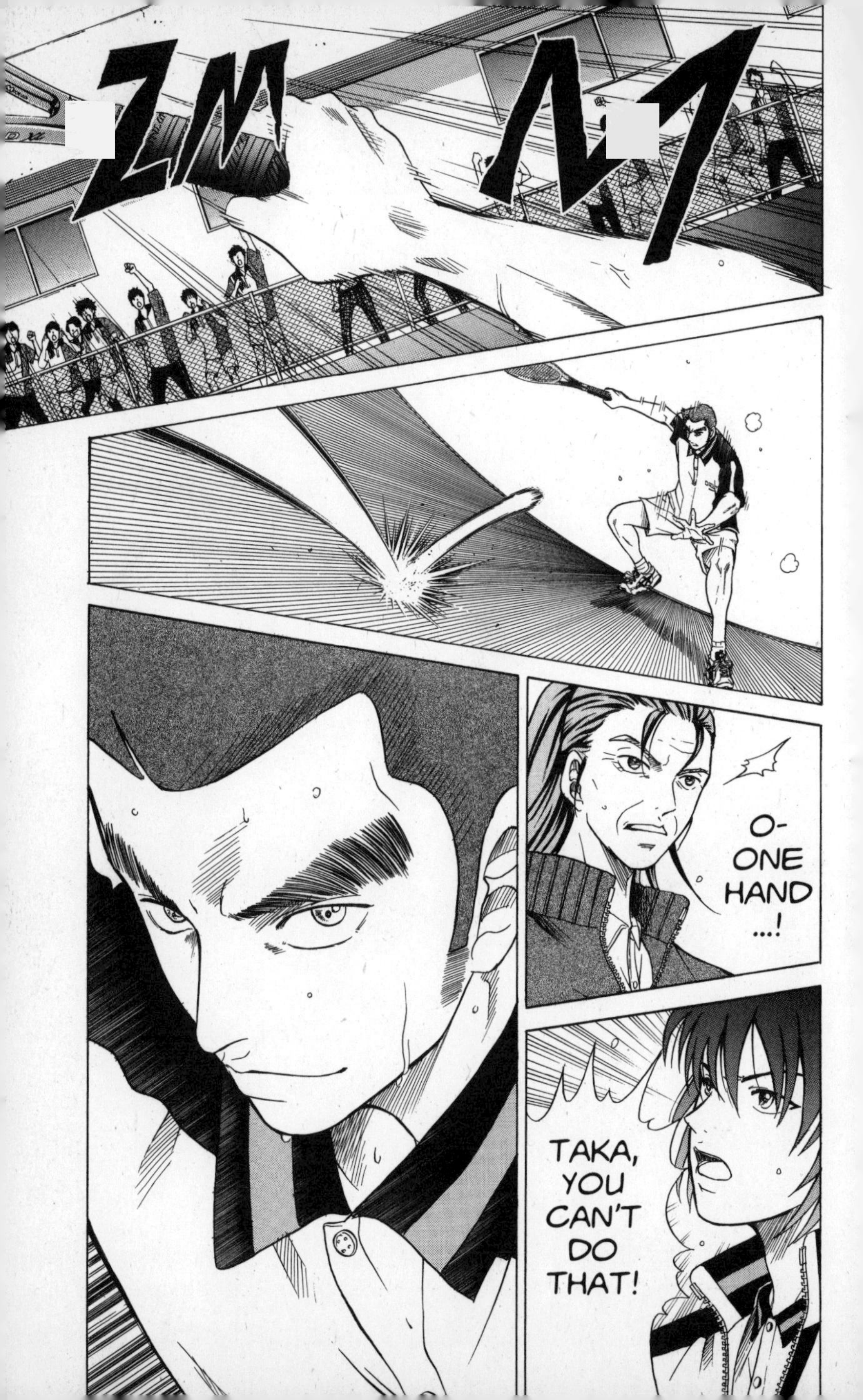
O-ONE HAND ...!
TAKA, YOU CAN'T DO THAT!

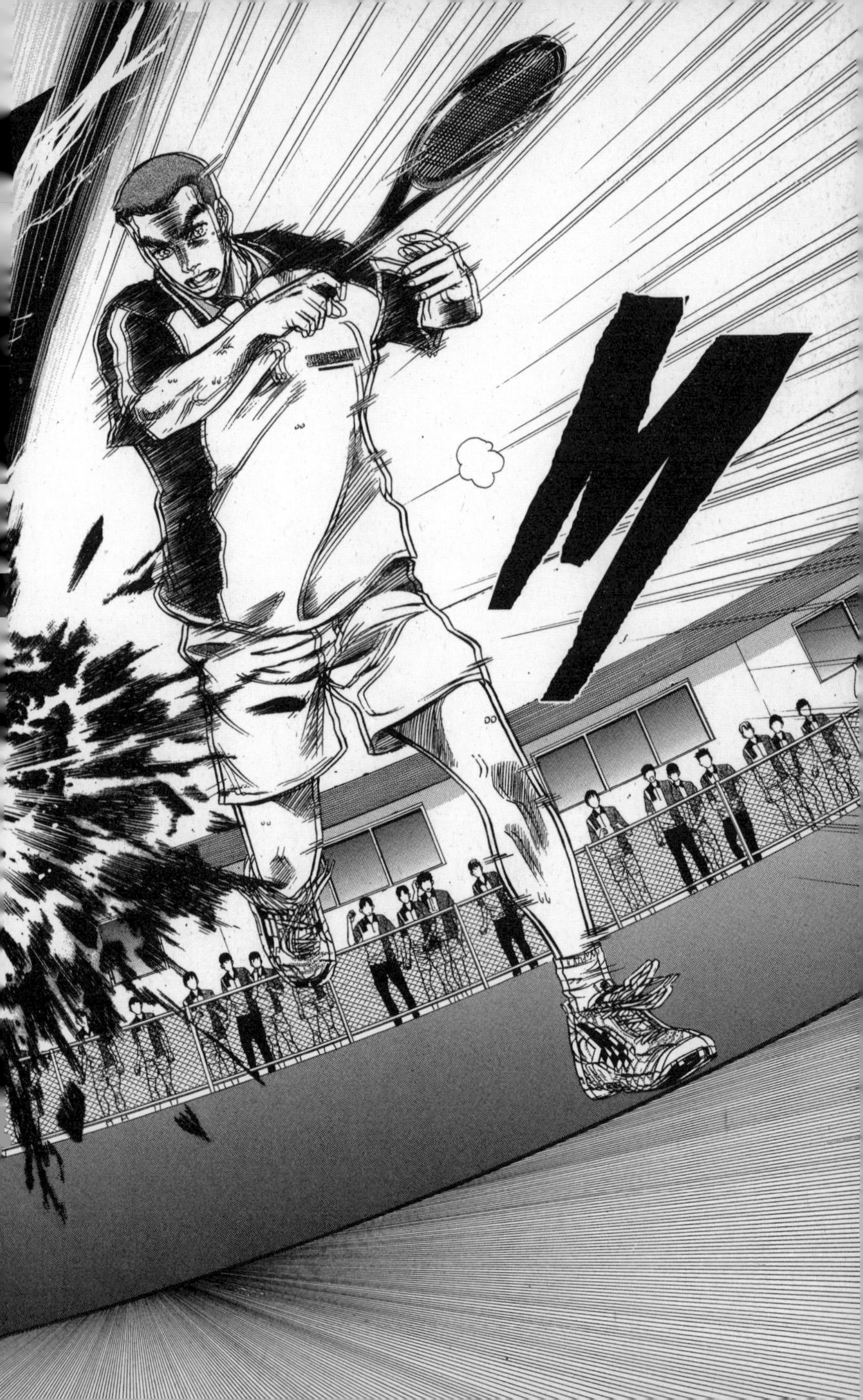

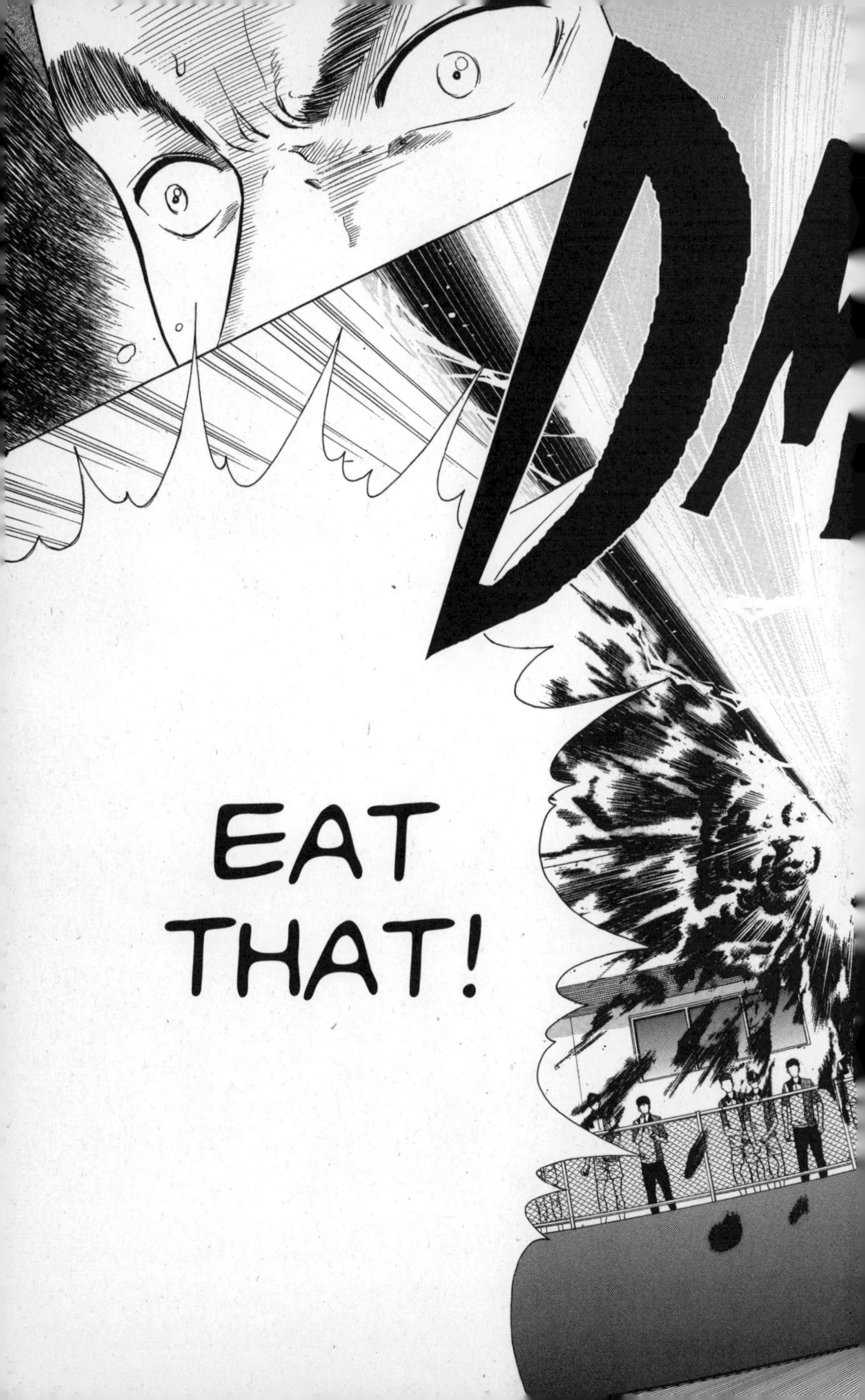
EAT THAT!

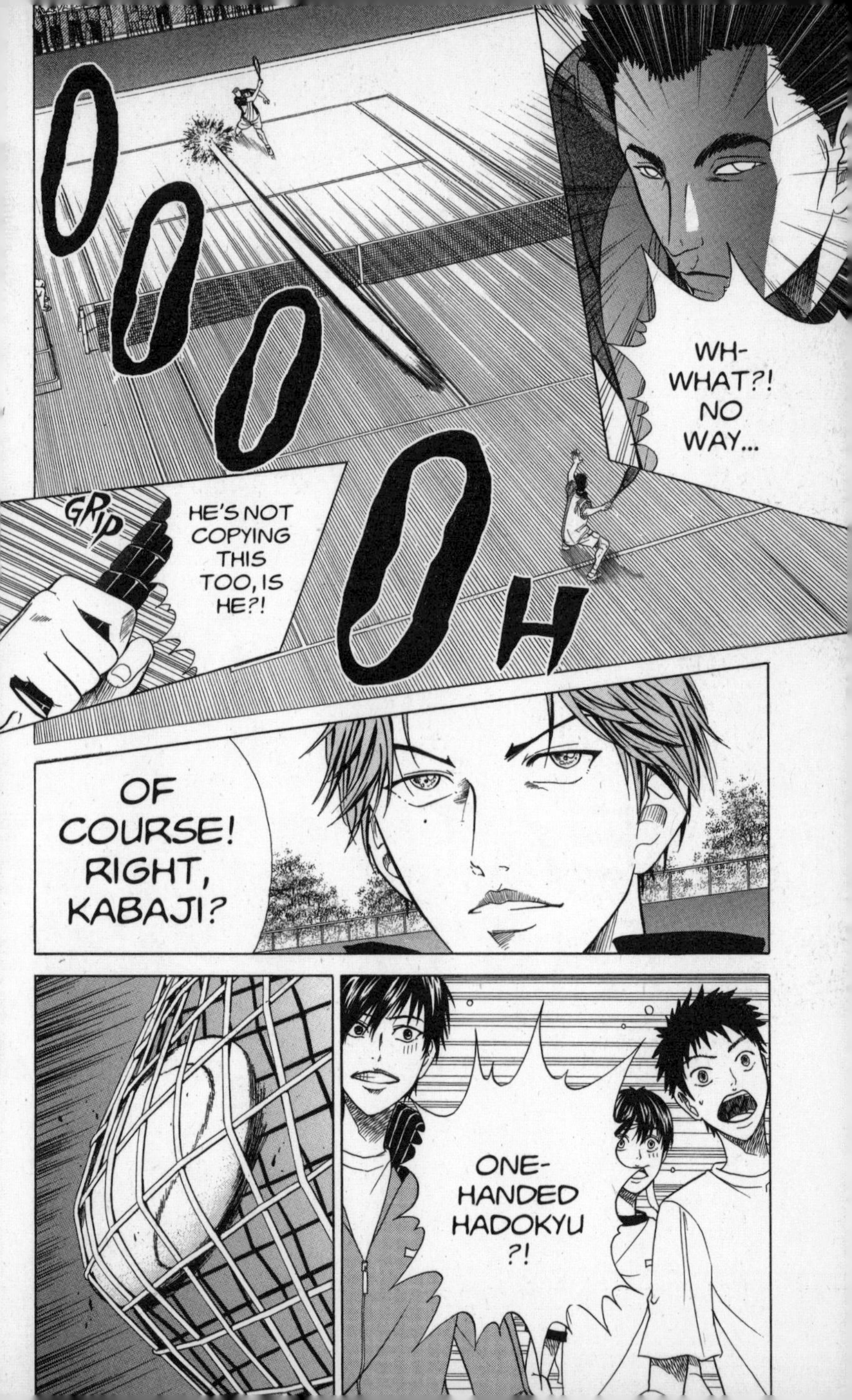
WH-WHAT?! NO WAY...
OOOOOH
HE'S NOT COPYING THIS TOO, IS HE?!
GRIP
OF COURSE! RIGHT, KABAJI?
ONE-HANDED HADOKYU ?!

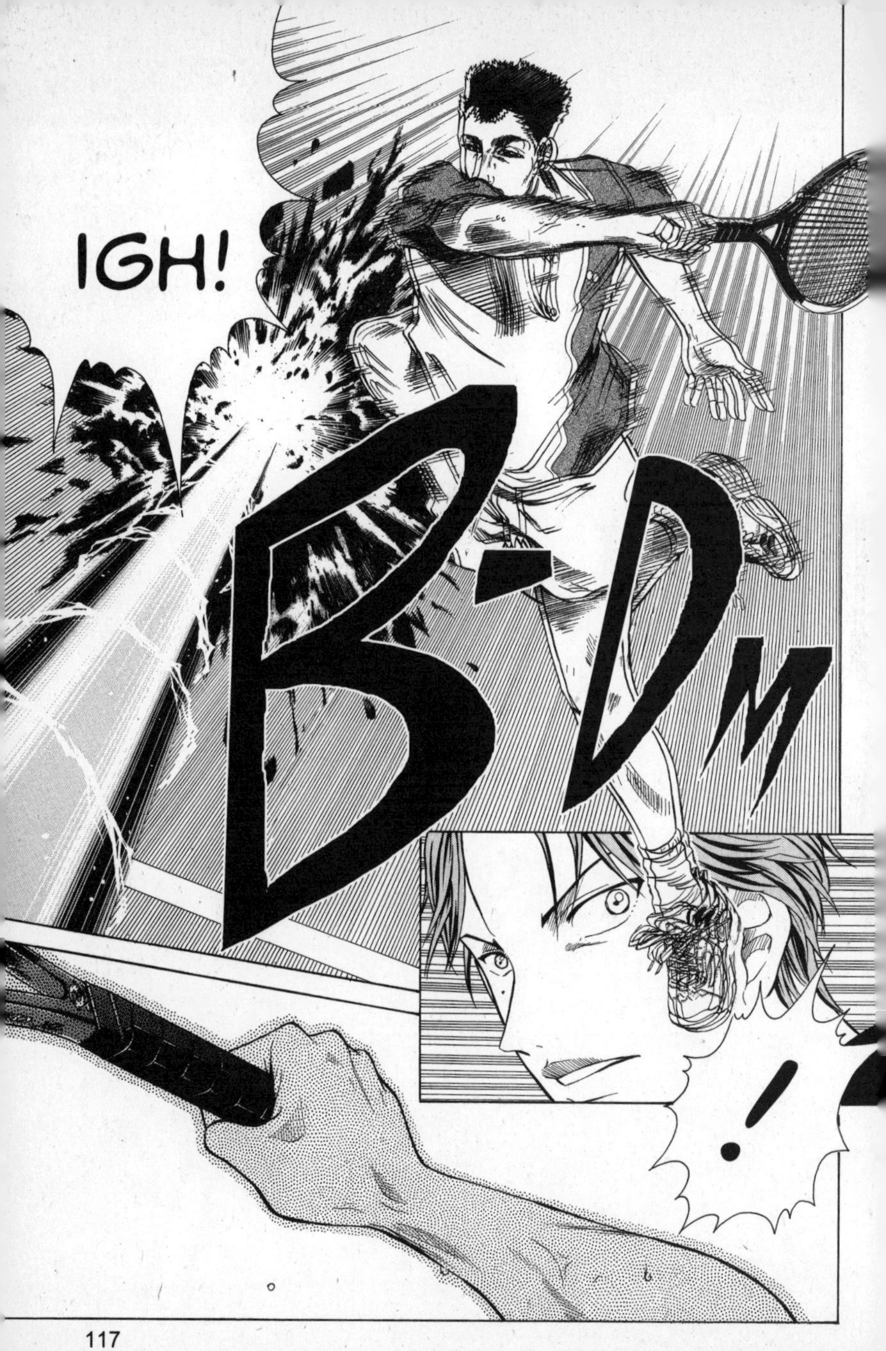
IGH!
B-DM
!

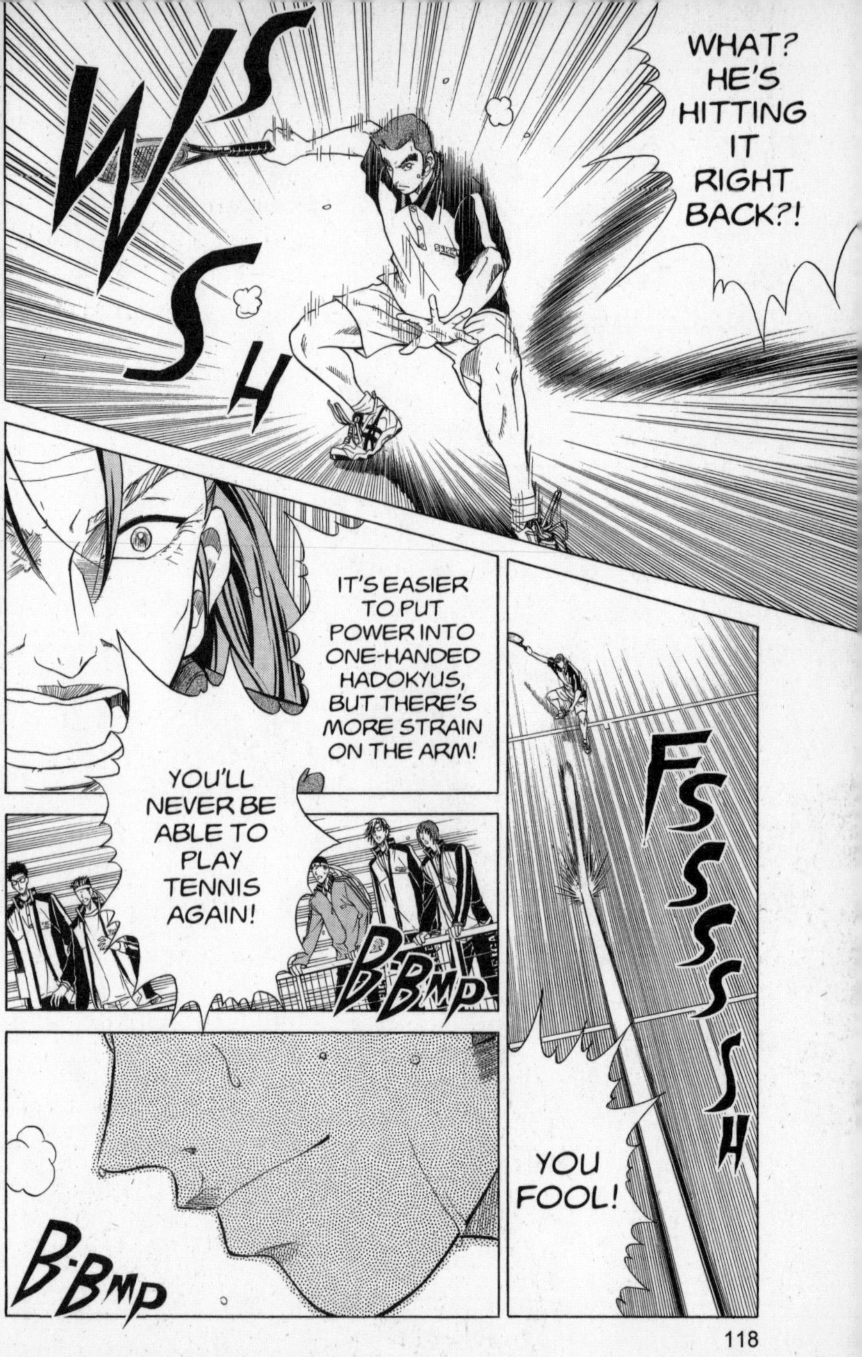
WHAT? HE'S HITTING IT RIGHT BACK?!
WSSH
FSSSSH
YOU FOOL!
IT'S EASIER TO PUT POWER INTO ONE-HANDED HADOKYUS, BUT THERE'S MORE STRAIN ON THE ARM!
YOU'LL NEVER BE ABLE TO PLAY TENNIS AGAIN!
B-BMP
B-BMP

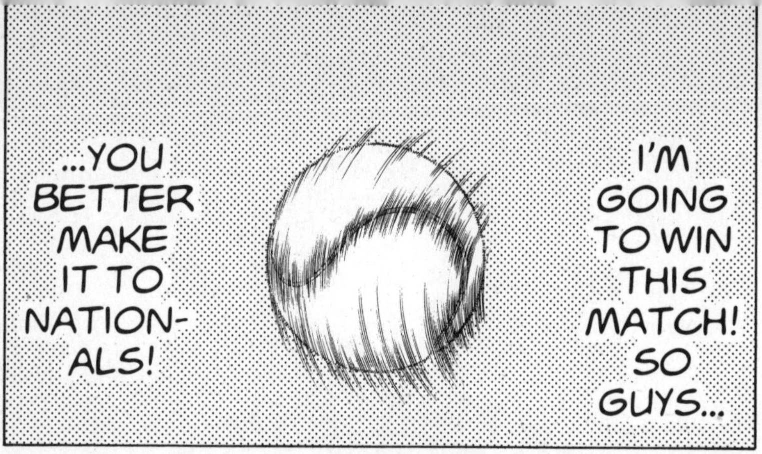
I'M GOING TO WIN THIS MATCH! SO GUYS...
...YOU BETTER MAKE IT TO NATION-ALS!
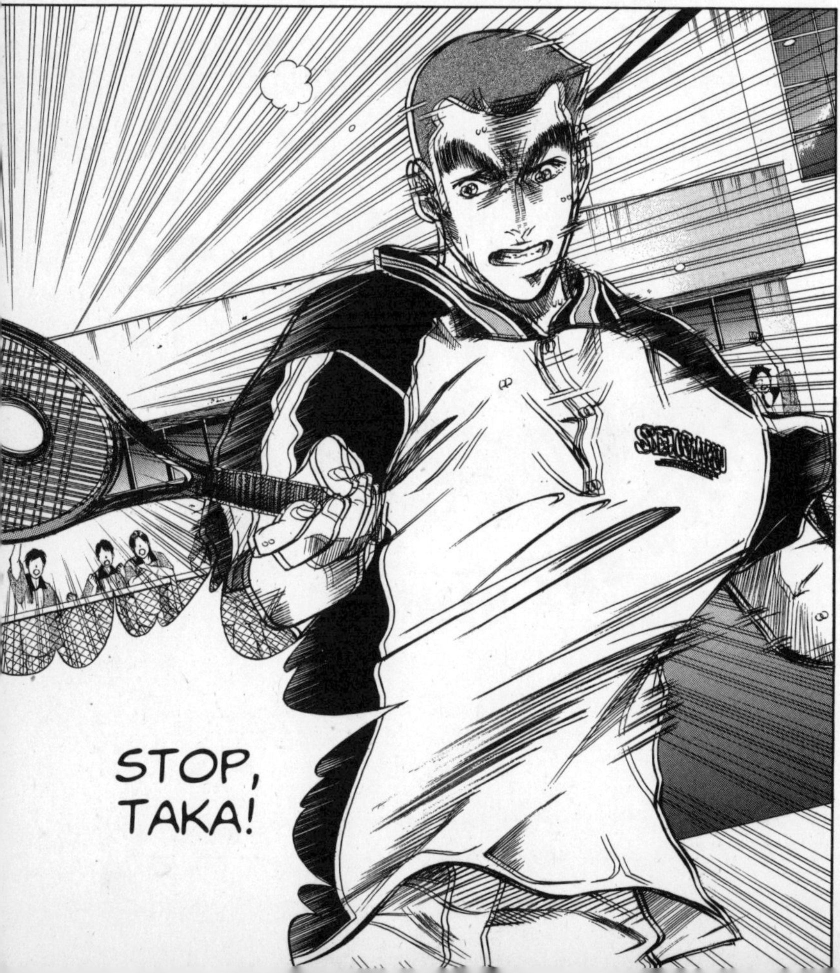
STOP, TAKA!

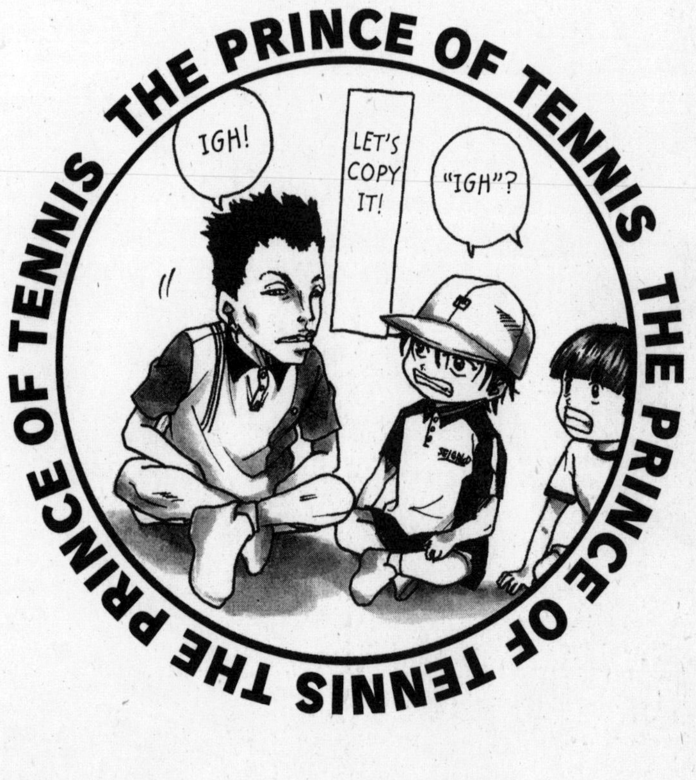
THE PRINCE OF TENNIS THE PRINCE OF TENNIS THE PRINCE OF TENNIS
IGH!
LET'S COPY IT!
"IGH"?

GENIUS 138: HADOKYU VS. HADOKYU

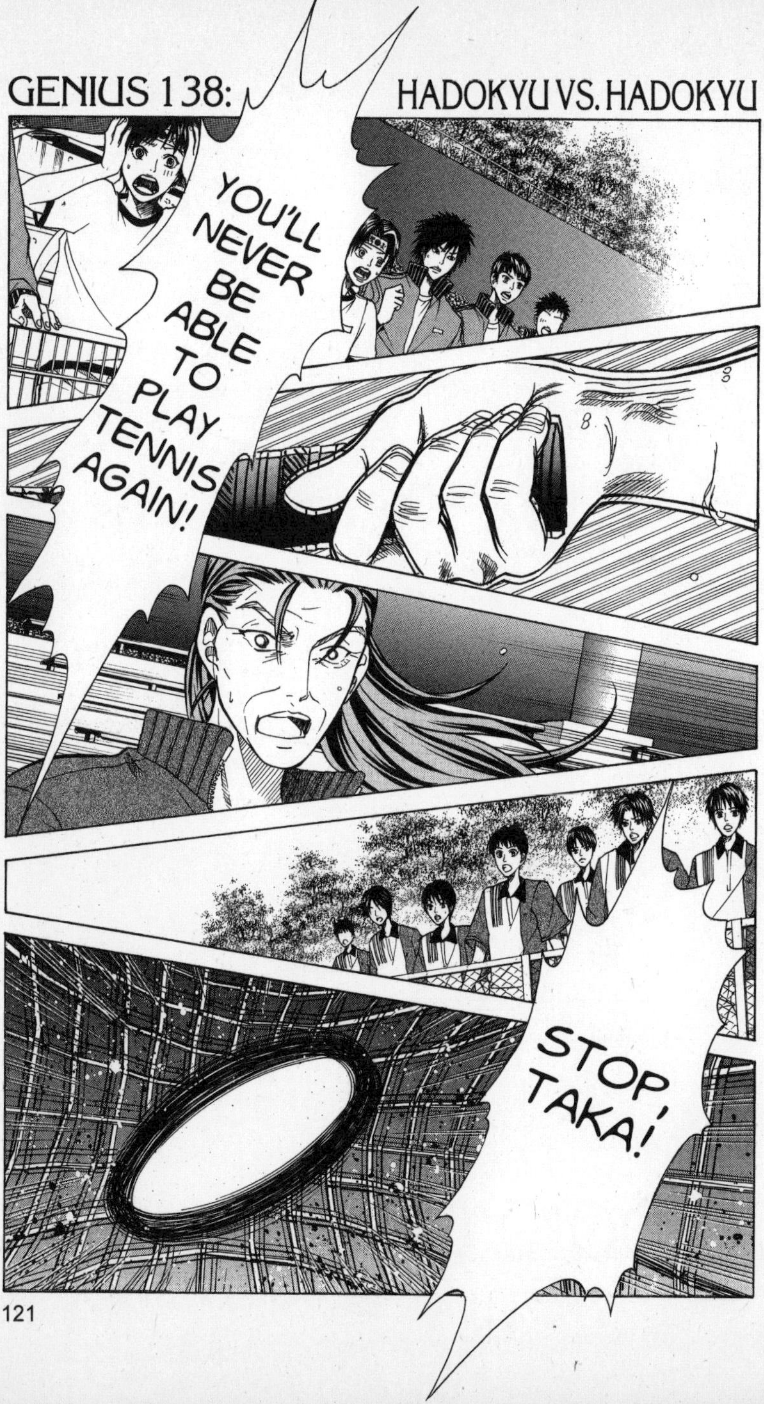
YOU'LL NEVER BE ABLE TO PLAY TENNIS AGAIN!
STOP, TAKA!

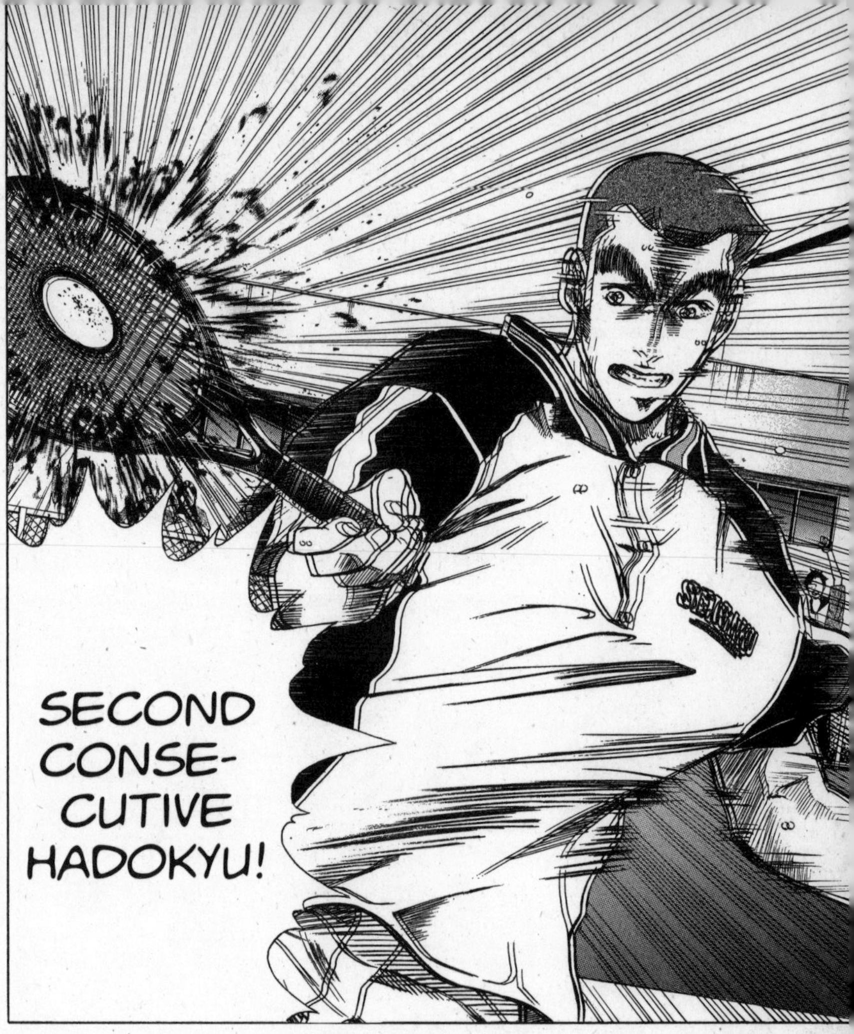
SECOND CONSE-CUTIVE HADOKYU!

GENIUS 138:

HADOKYU VS. HADOKYU

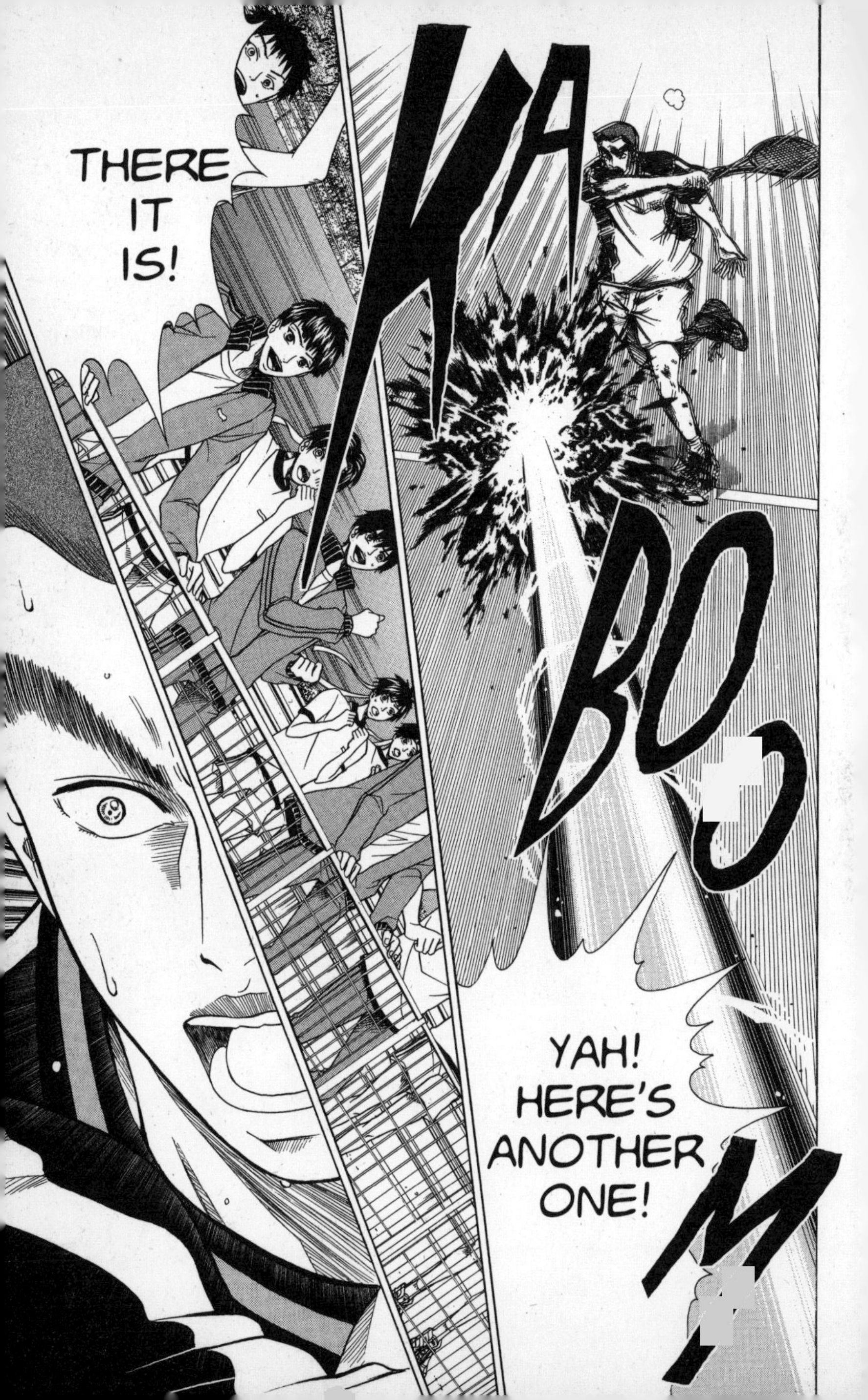
KA BO M
YAH! HERE'S ANOTHER ONE!
THERE IT IS!

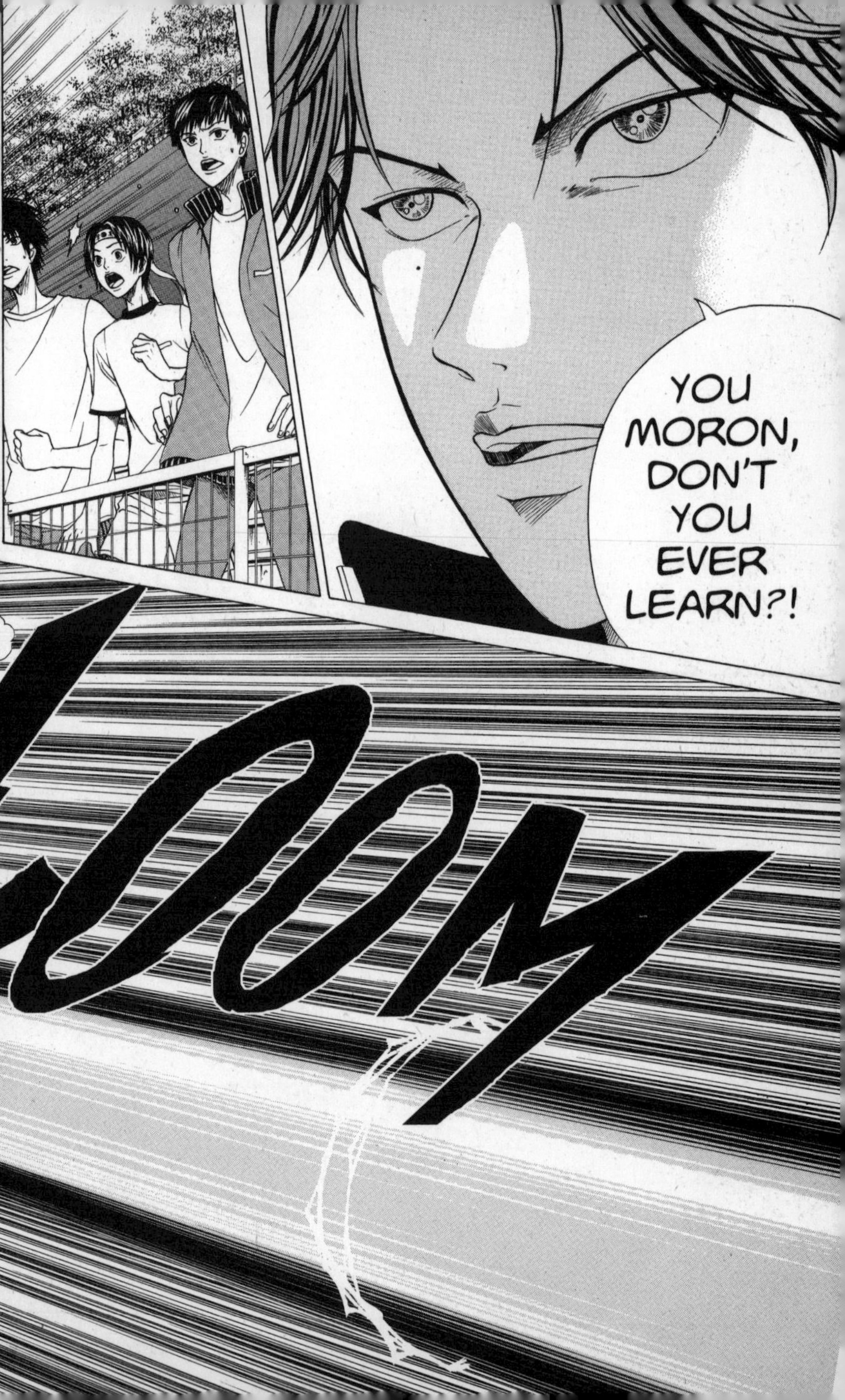
YOU MORON, DON'T YOU EVER LEARN?!

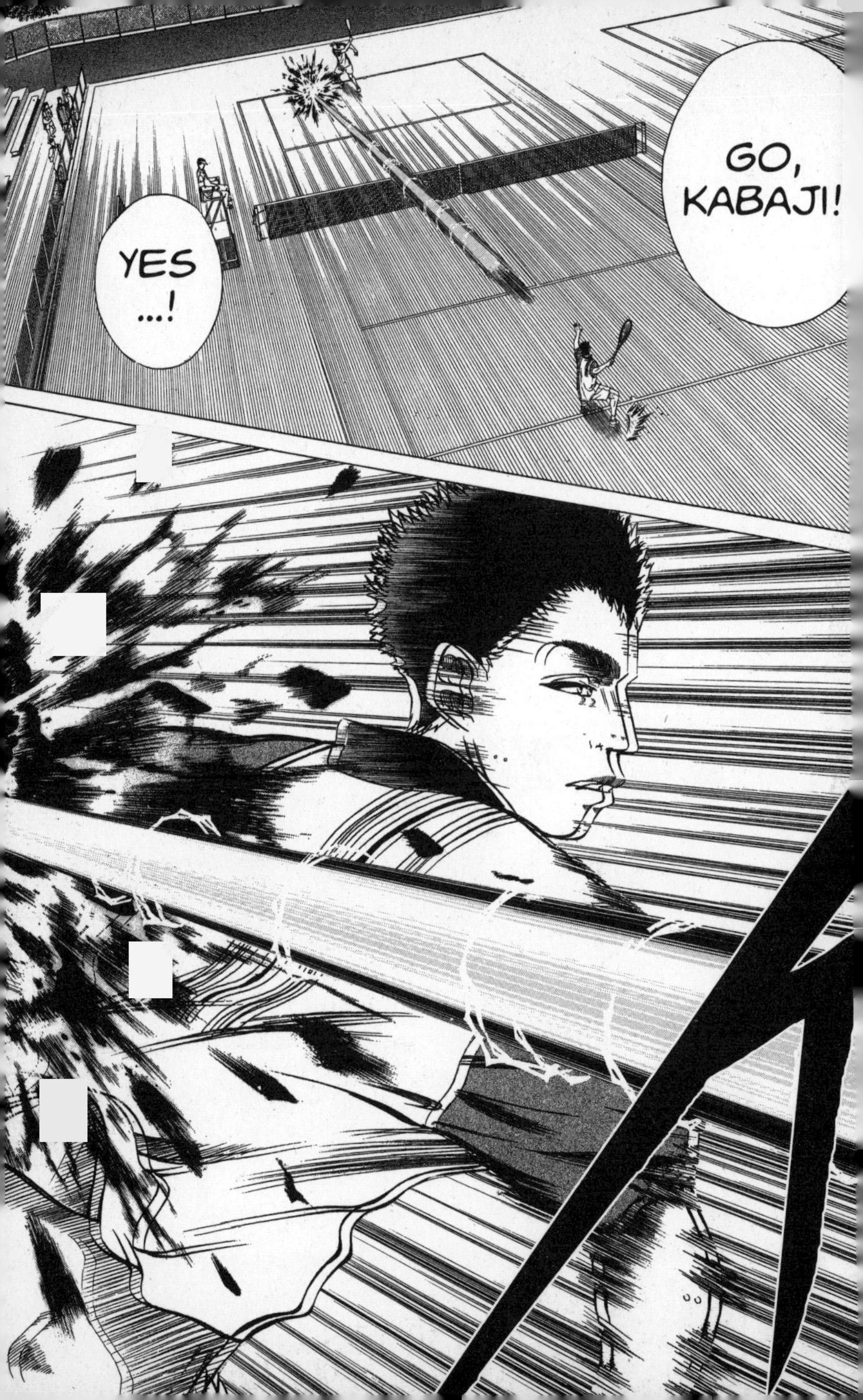
GO, KABAJI!
YES ...!

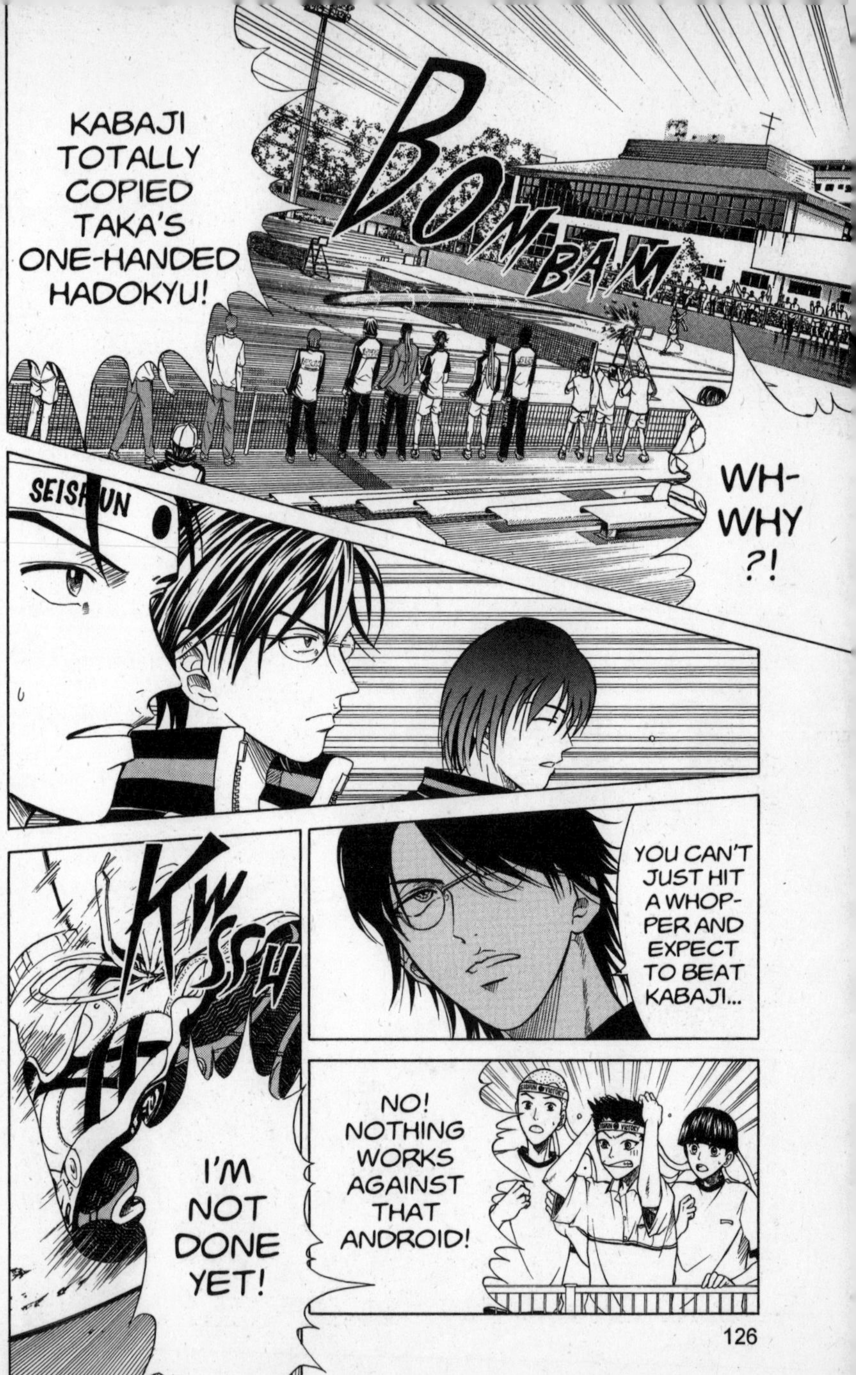
BOMBAM
KABAJI TOTALLY COPIED TAKA'S ONE-HANDED HADOKYU!
WH-WHY?!
SEISHUN
YOU CAN'T JUST HIT A WHOPPER AND EXPECT TO BEAT KABAJI...
NO! NOTHING WORKS AGAINST THAT ANDROID!
KWSSH
I'M NOT DONE YET!

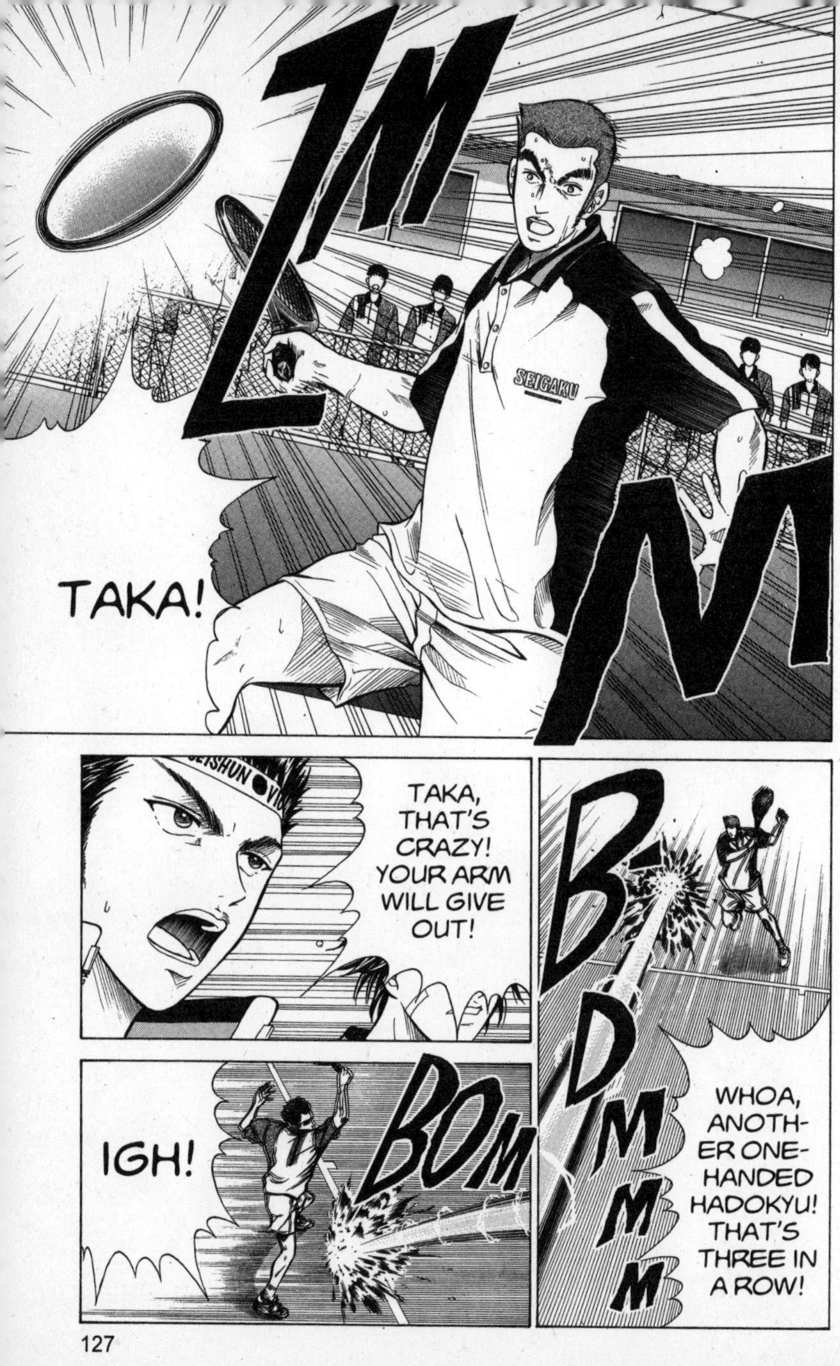
ZMM
TAKA!
BDMMM
WHOA, ANOTH-ER ONE-HANDED HADOKYU! THAT'S THREE IN A ROW!
TAKA, THAT'S CRAZY! YOUR ARM WILL GIVE OUT!
BOM
IGH!

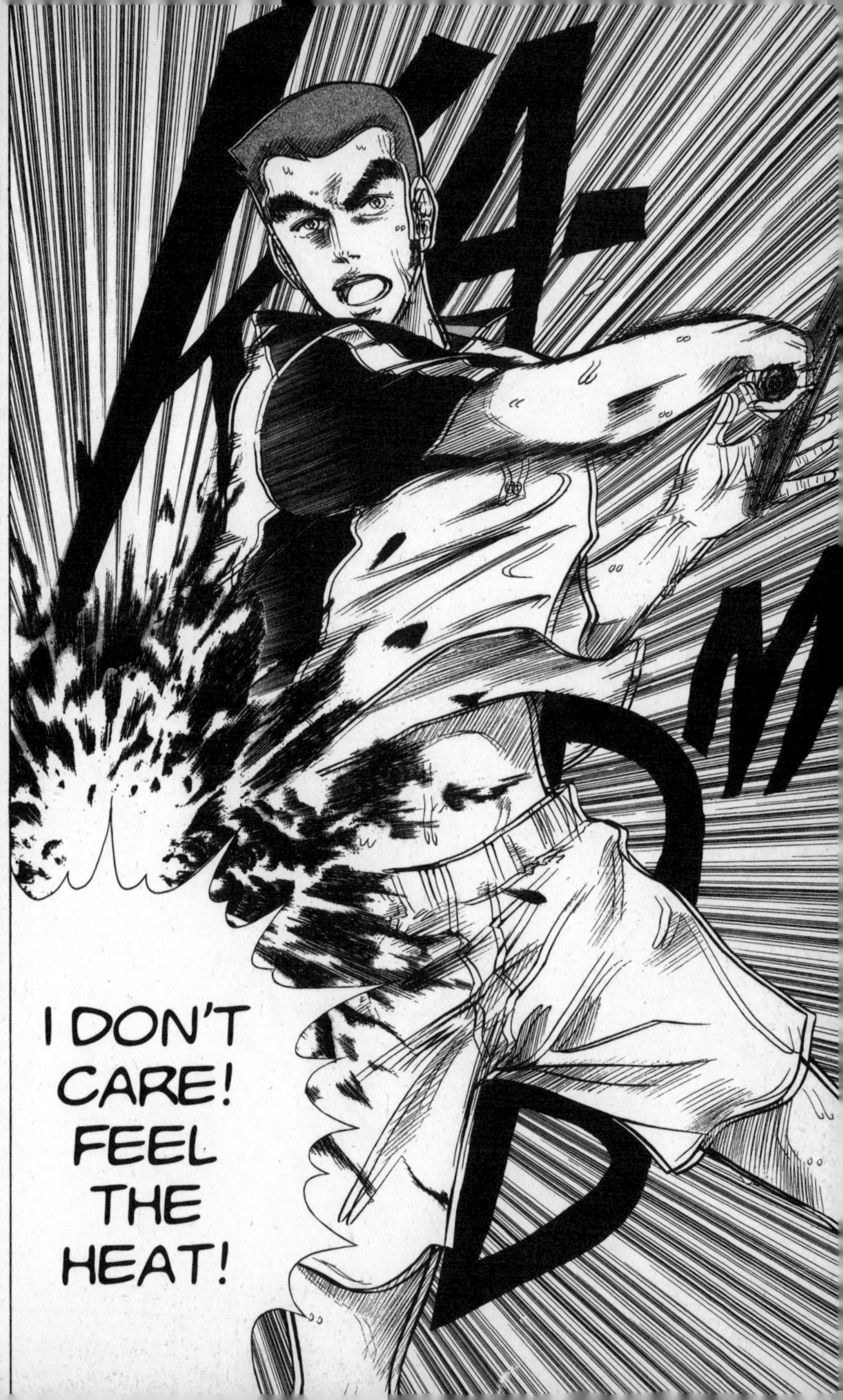
I DON'T CARE! FEEL THE HEAT!

READ THIS WAY

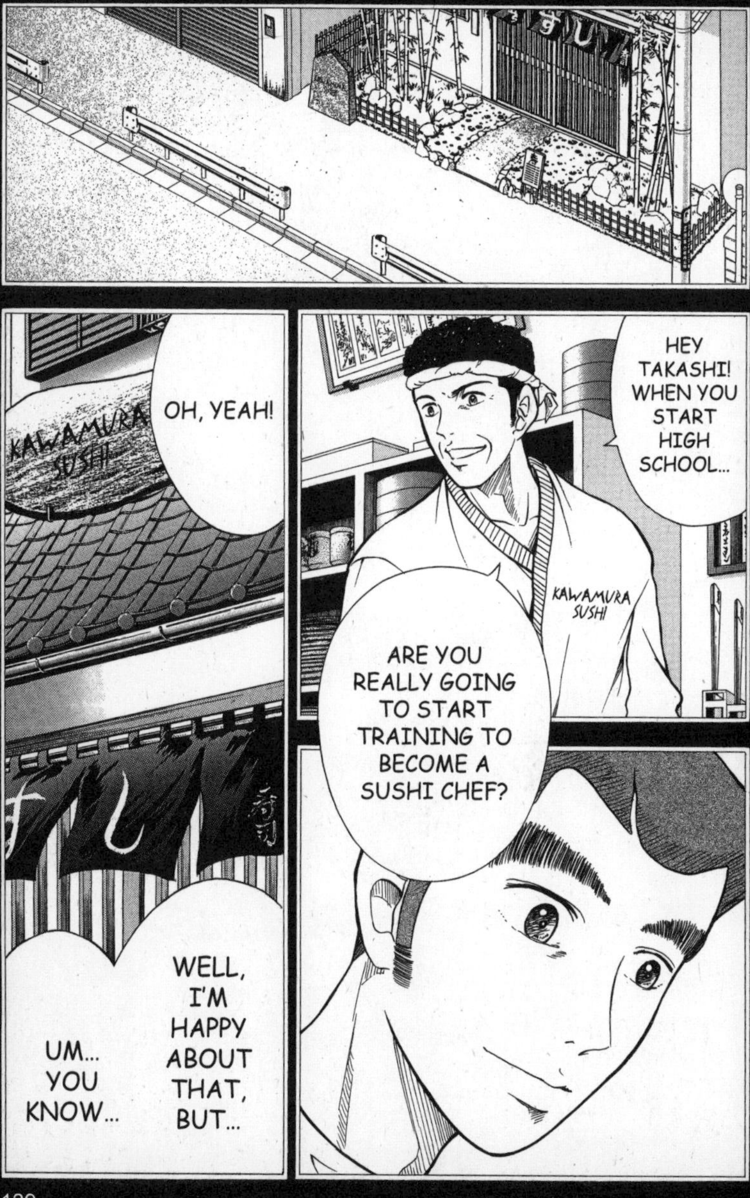

HEY TAKASHI! WHEN YOU START HIGH SCHOOL...
KAWAMURA SUSHI
ARE YOU REALLY GOING TO START TRAINING TO BECOME A SUSHI CHEF?
OH, YEAH!
KAWAMURA SUSHI
WELL, I'M HAPPY ABOUT THAT, BUT...
UM... YOU KNOW...

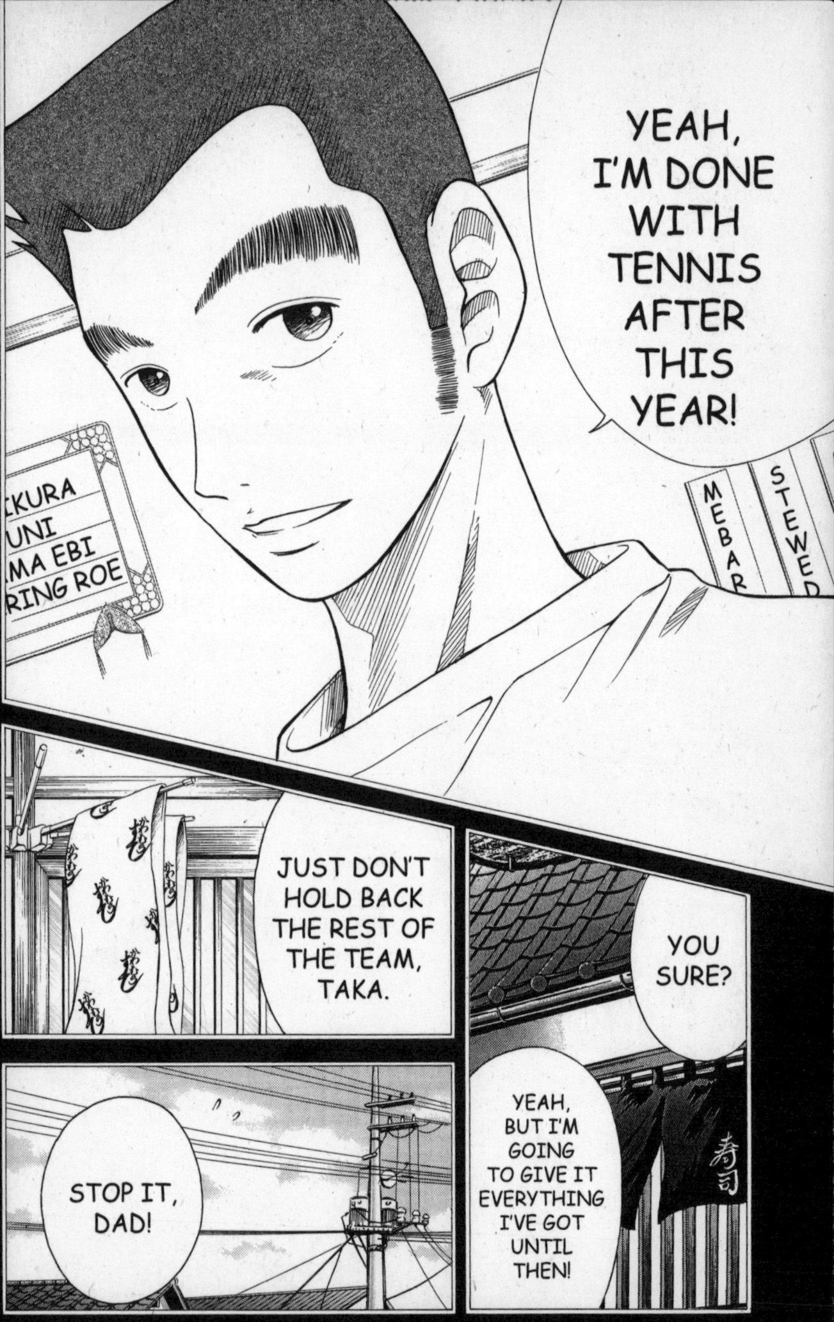
YEAH, I'M DONE WITH TENNIS AFTER THIS YEAR!
KURA
UNI
MA EBI
RING ROE
MEBAR
STEWED
YOU SURE?
YEAH, BUT I'M GOING TO GIVE IT EVERYTHING I'VE GOT UNTIL THEN!
JUST DON'T HOLD BACK THE REST OF THE TEAM, TAKA.
STOP IT, DAD!

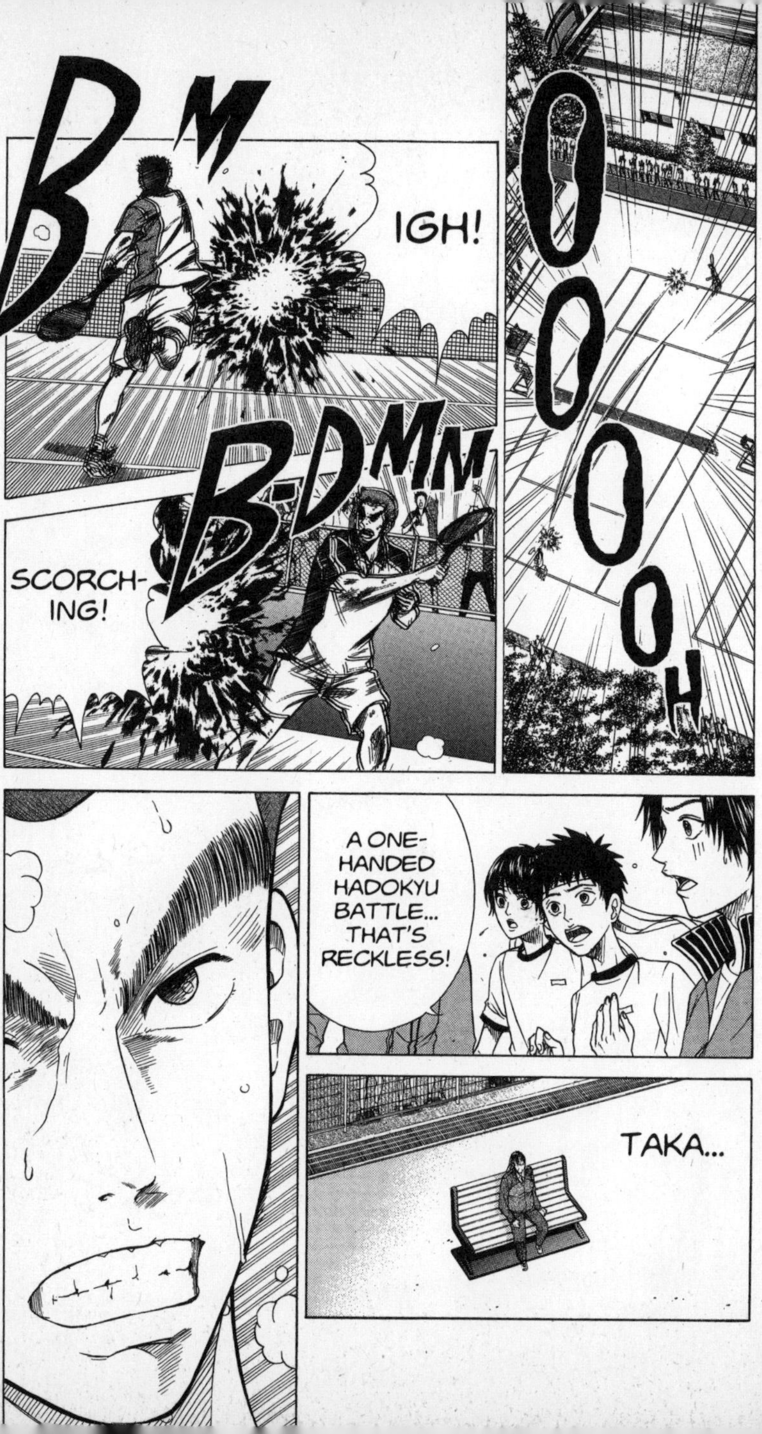
OOOOOOH
BM
IGH!
BDMM
SCORCHING!
A ONE-HANDED HADOKYU BATTLE... THAT'S RECKLESS!
TAKA...

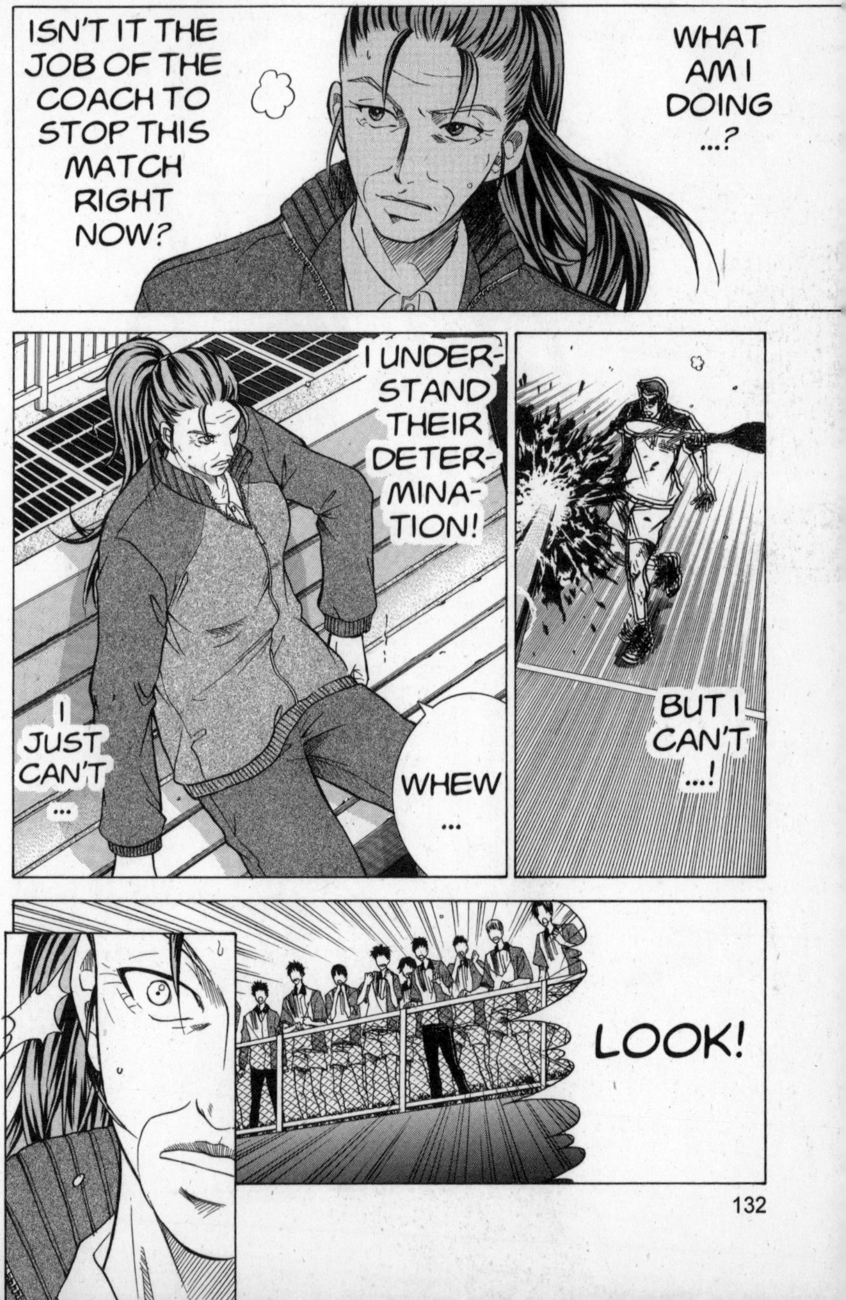
ISN'T IT THE JOB OF THE COACH TO STOP THIS MATCH RIGHT NOW?
WHAT AM I DOING ...?
I UNDER-STAND THEIR DETER-MINA-TION!
I JUST CAN'T ...
WHEW ...
BUT I CAN'T ...!
LOOK!

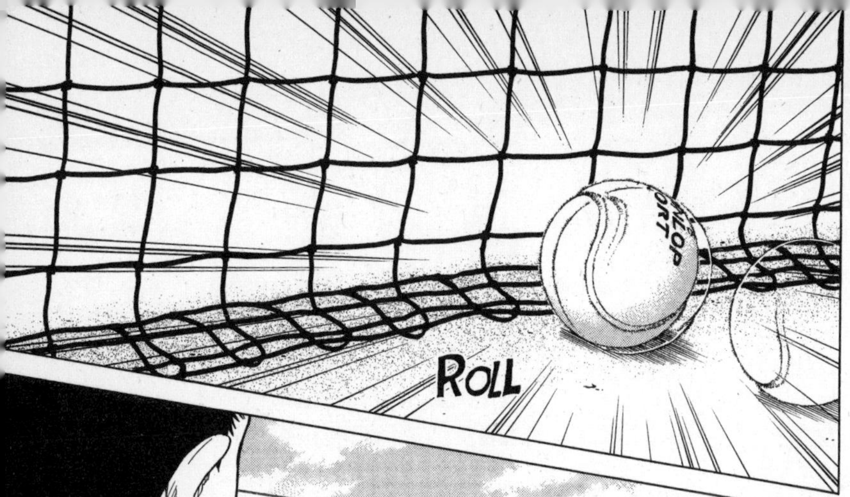
ROLL
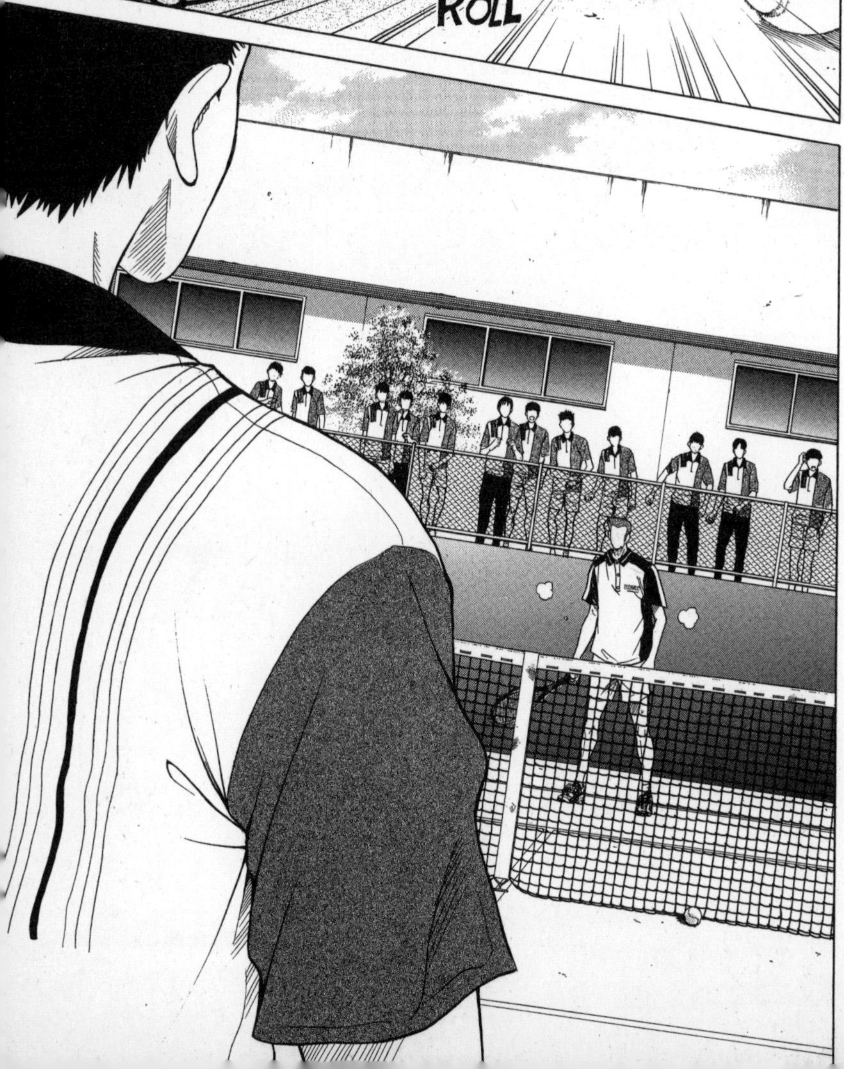

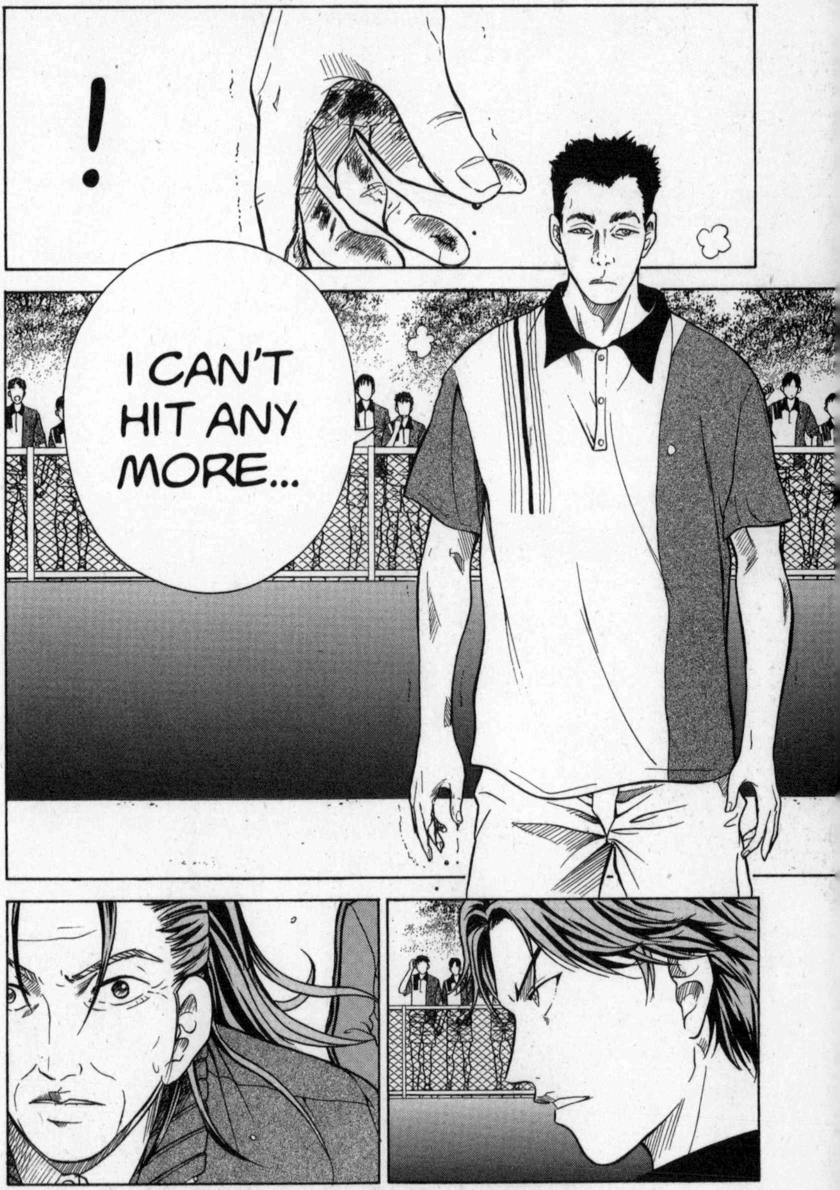
!
I CAN'T HIT ANY MORE...

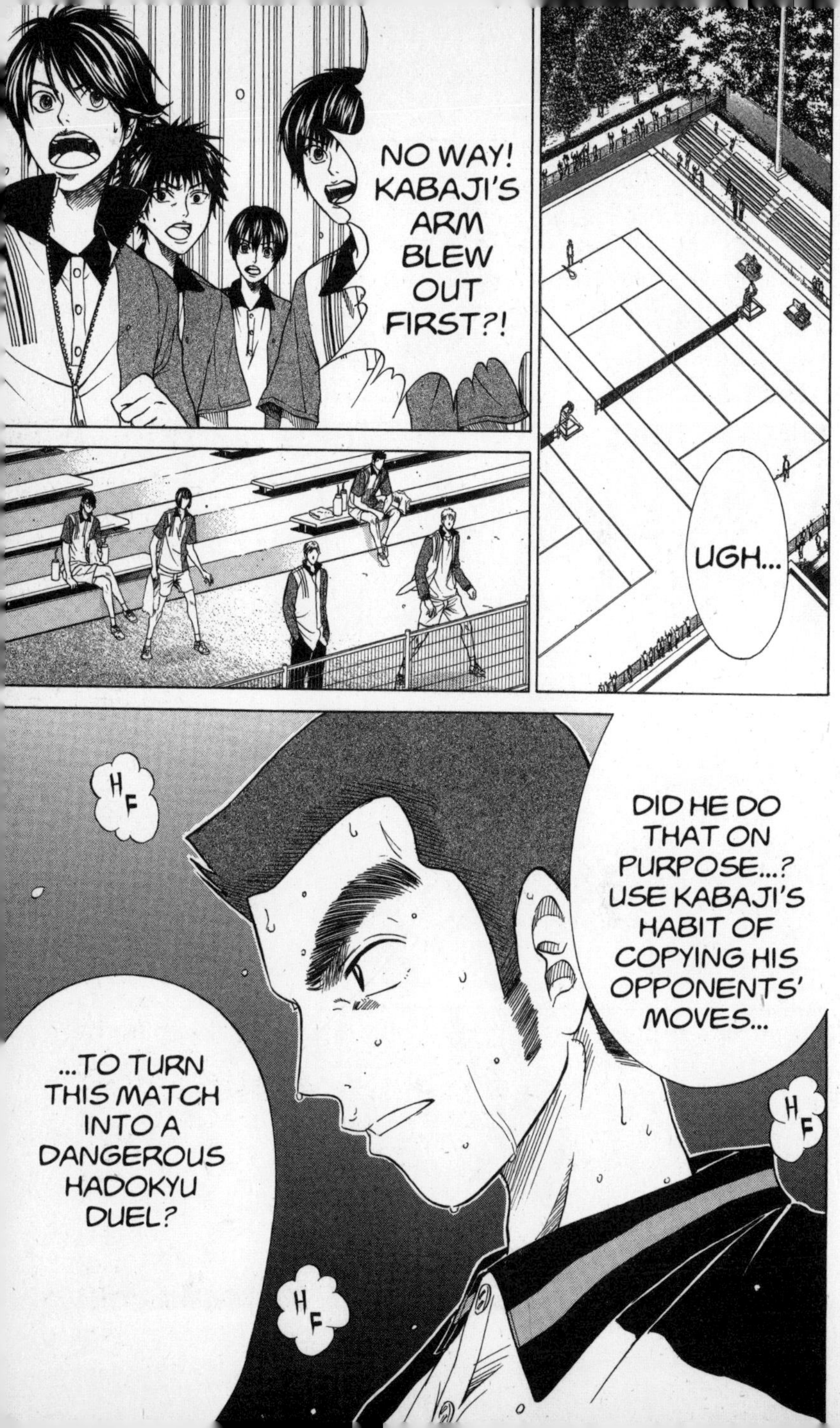
UGH...
NO WAY! KABAJI'S ARM BLEW OUT FIRST?!
DID HE DO THAT ON PURPOSE...? USE KABAJI'S HABIT OF COPYING HIS OPPONENTS' MOVES...
HF
HF
...TO TURN THIS MATCH INTO A DANGEROUS HADOKYU DUEL?
HF

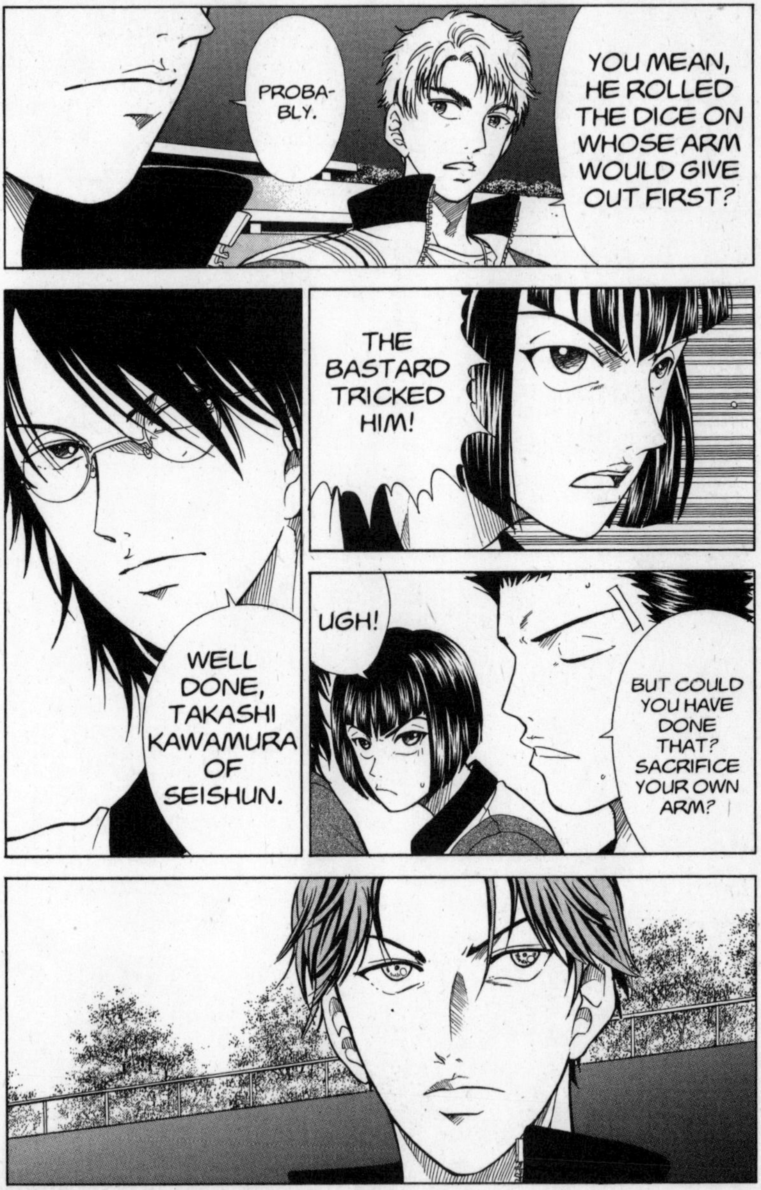
YOU MEAN, HE ROLLED THE DICE ON WHOSE ARM WOULD GIVE OUT FIRST?
PROBA-BLY.
THE BASTARD TRICKED HIM!
BUT COULD YOU HAVE DONE THAT? SACRIFICE YOUR OWN ARM?
UGH!
WELL DONE, TAKASHI KAWAMURA OF SEISHUN.

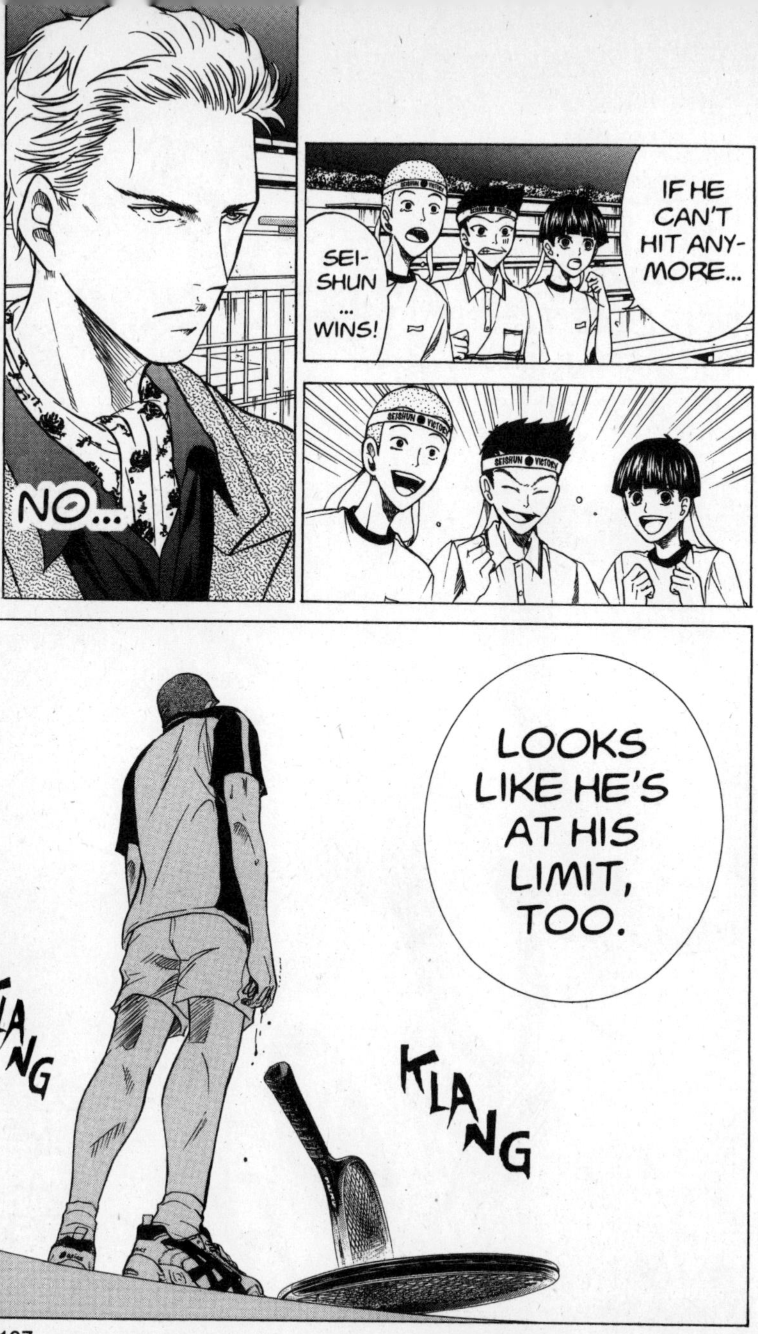
IF HE CAN'T HIT ANYMORE...
SEI-SHUN ... WINS!
NO...
LOOKS LIKE HE'S AT HIS LIMIT, TOO.
KLANG
KLANG

SINCE BOTH PLAYERS ARE UNABLE TO CONTINUE PLAYING...
NO. 3 SINGLES IS A FORFEIT!
OOOH

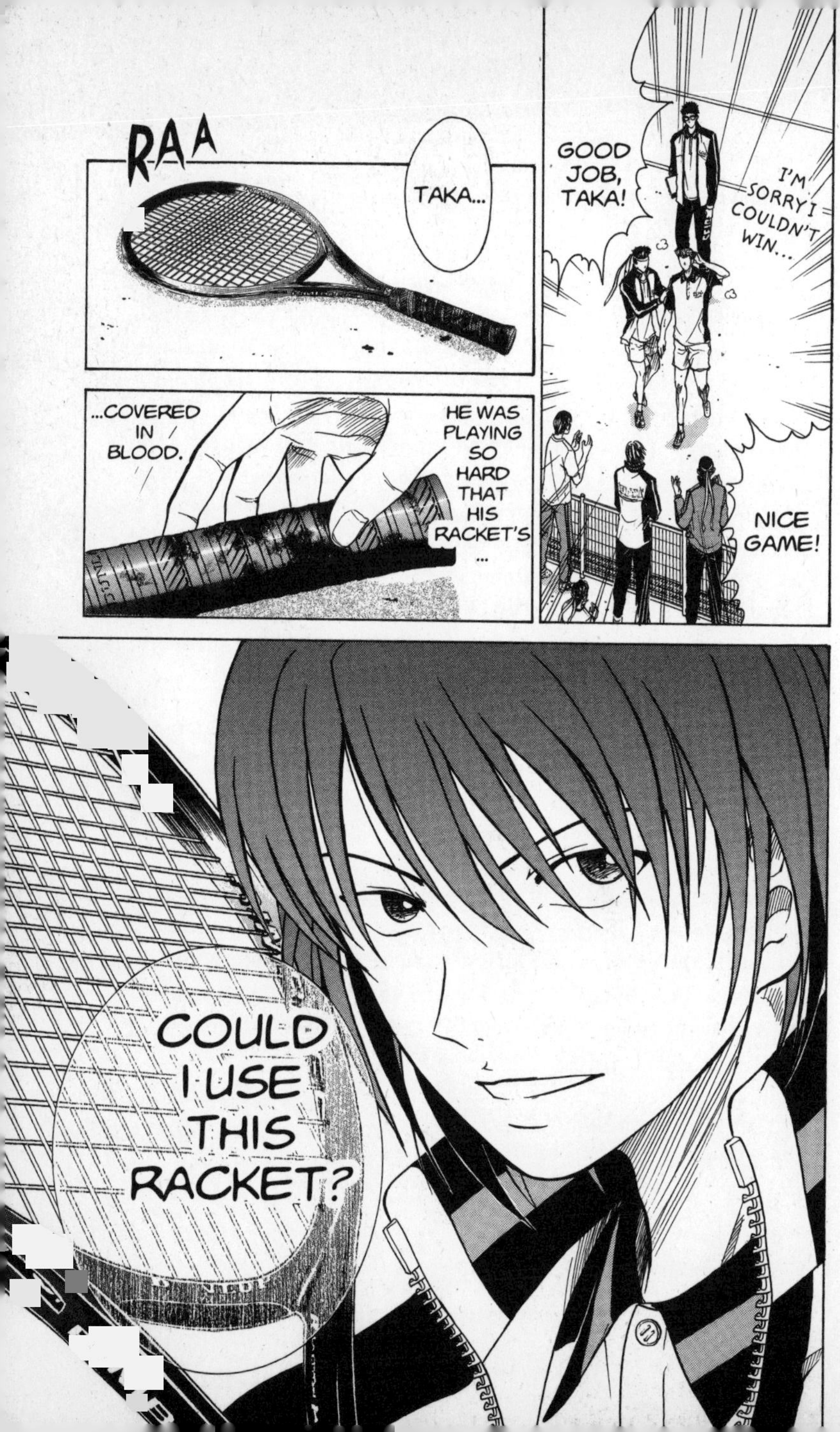
I'M SORRY I COULDN'T WIN...
GOOD JOB, TAKA!
NICE GAME!
RAA
TAKA...
HE WAS PLAYING SO HARD THAT HIS RACKET'S ...
...COVERED IN BLOOD.
COULD I USE THIS RACKET?

テニスの王子様 THE PRINCE OF TENNIS™

Thank you for reading The Prince of Tennis Vol. 16.

I had a very pleasant experience in late August and September of 2002—I was able to watch the U.S. Open! All I can say after watching the world's top pros play right in front of my eyes was "Wow!" I was so grateful for the opportunity. (I was shocked at the amount of food they serve in America too!) September 23rd is "Tennis Day." Many different events are held across Japan to help popularize tennis. I participated in a discussion panel with Shuzo Matsuoka and Naoko Sawamatsu at Ariake's Tennis Forest. (We didn't announce it in Jump, so many people were surprised.) What I enjoyed the most was learning about the growing popularity of tennis among kids. I would be so pleased if the animation and the added exposure of tennis from this manga would encourage kids to take up the sport!

2002 is almost over... I'm looking forward to 2003. Thank you for all the fan letters. I'm happy to read fan letters from new fans. I'm able to identify the hardcore fans by their envelopes now. It is my source of power! I read them all...while I take a bath. (Laugh)

Jump Festa in Tokyo will be held in 12/21 and 12/22. I'm looking forward to the opportunity to see you guys again. For those of you who are interested in going, please check out the details in Jump. (There will be a ton of The Prince of Tennis merchandise, an airing of an original animation, and a talk-show with me and the voice actors, etc.)

Well then, I'll see you in Vol. 17! Keep supporting Ryoma and The Prince of Tennis!

テニスの王子様

T. KONOMI

2002.10.23

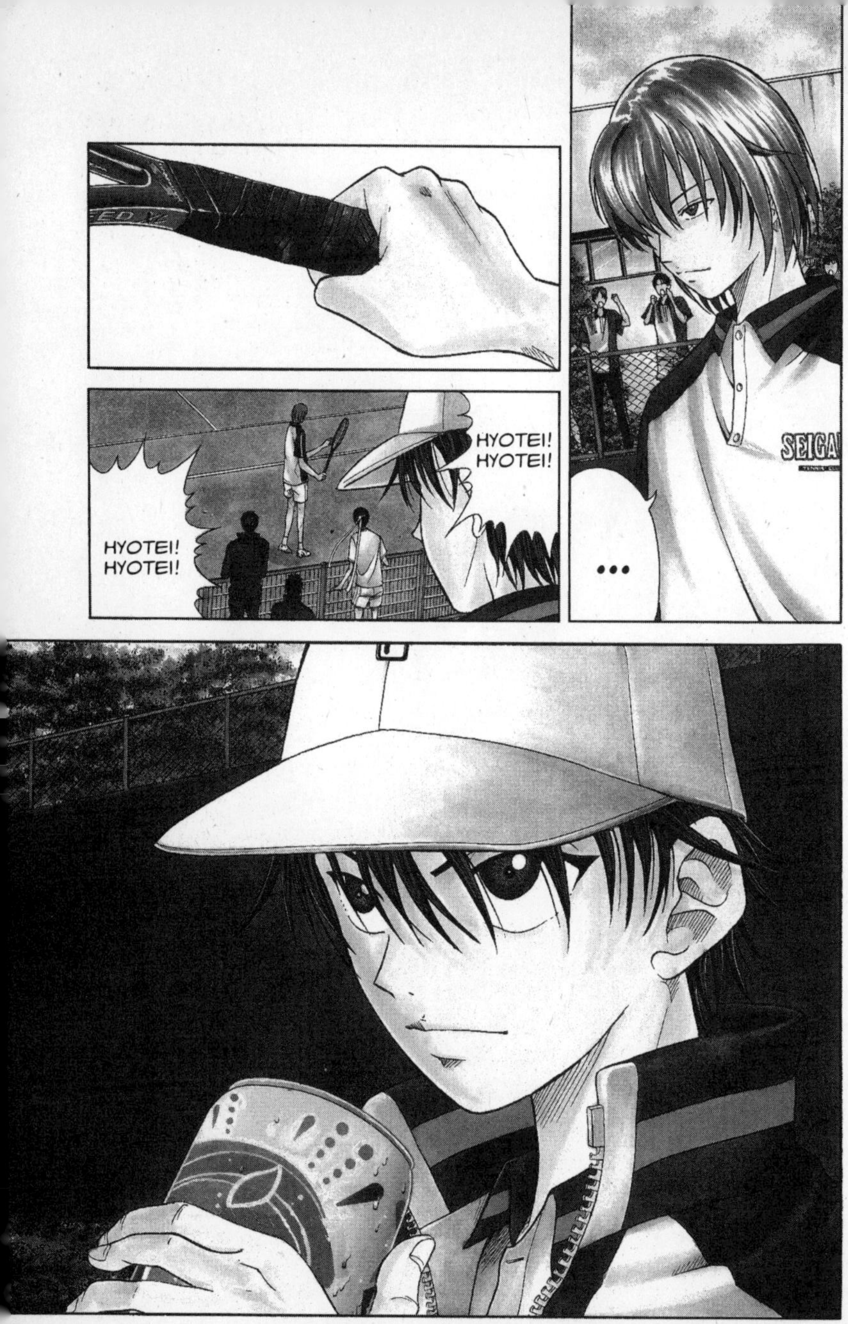
...
HYOTEI! HYOTEI!
HYOTEI! HYOTEI!

GENIUS 139: SHUSUKE FUJI

GENIUS 139: SHUSUKE FUJI

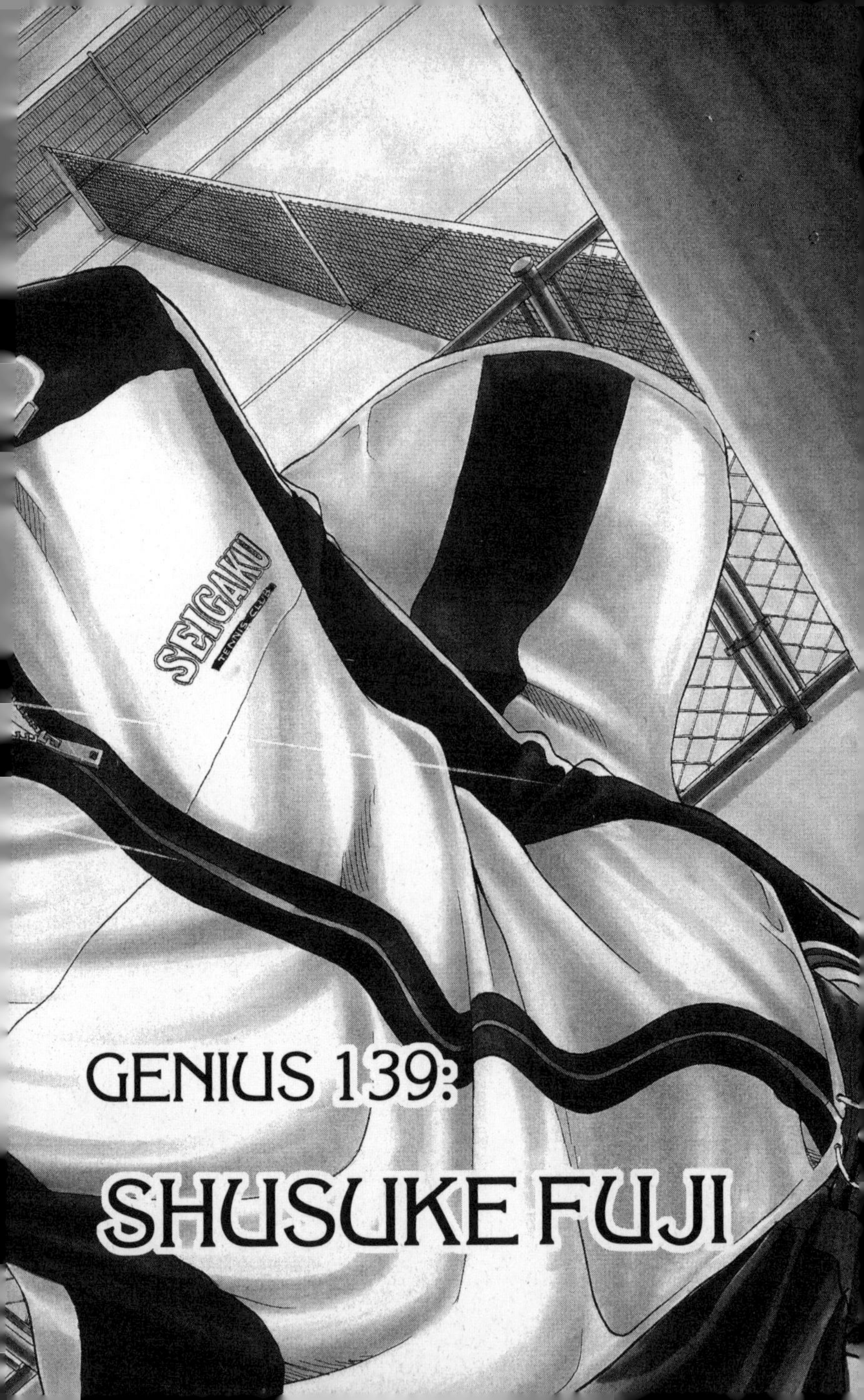
SEIGAKU
TENNIS CLUB

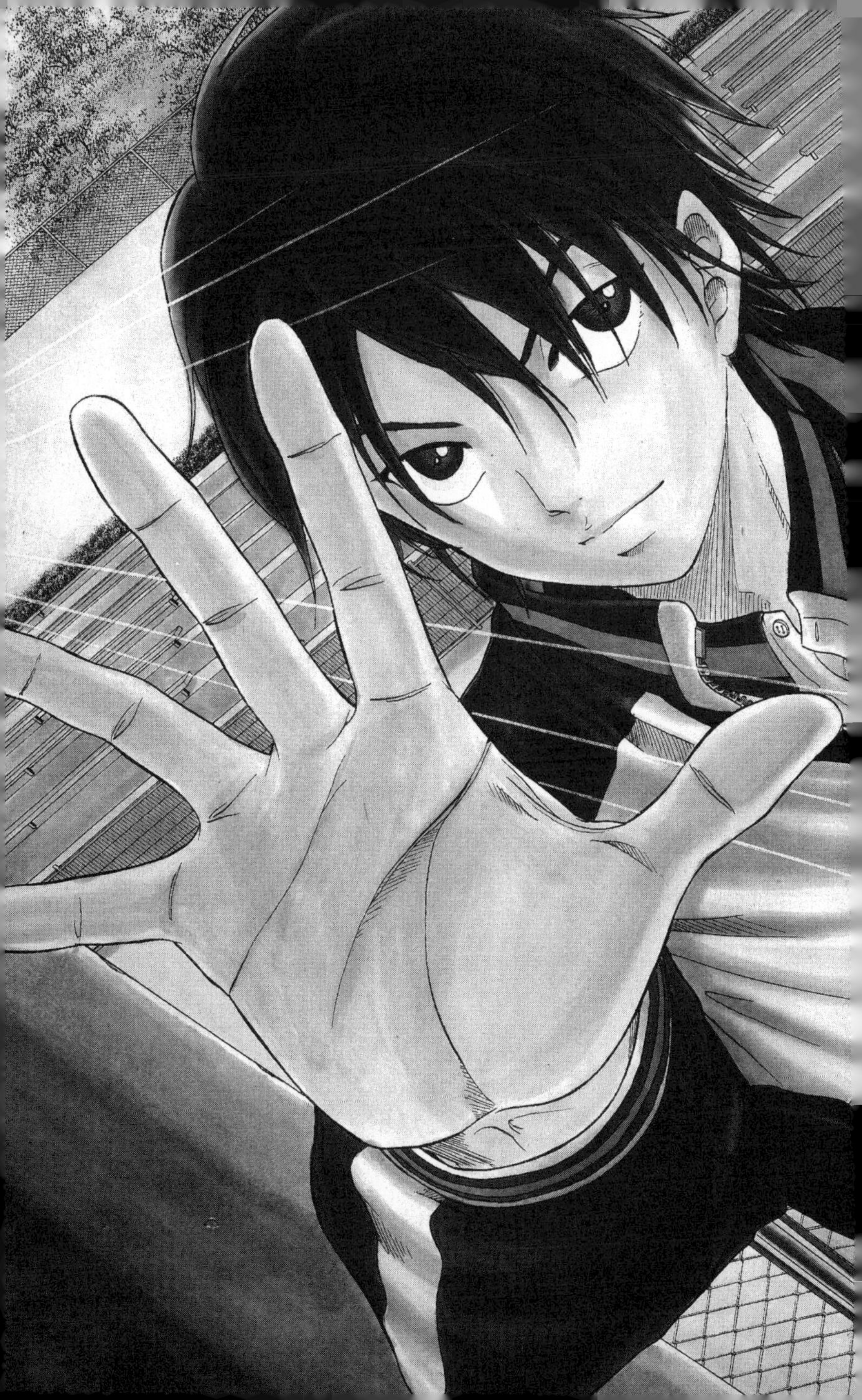

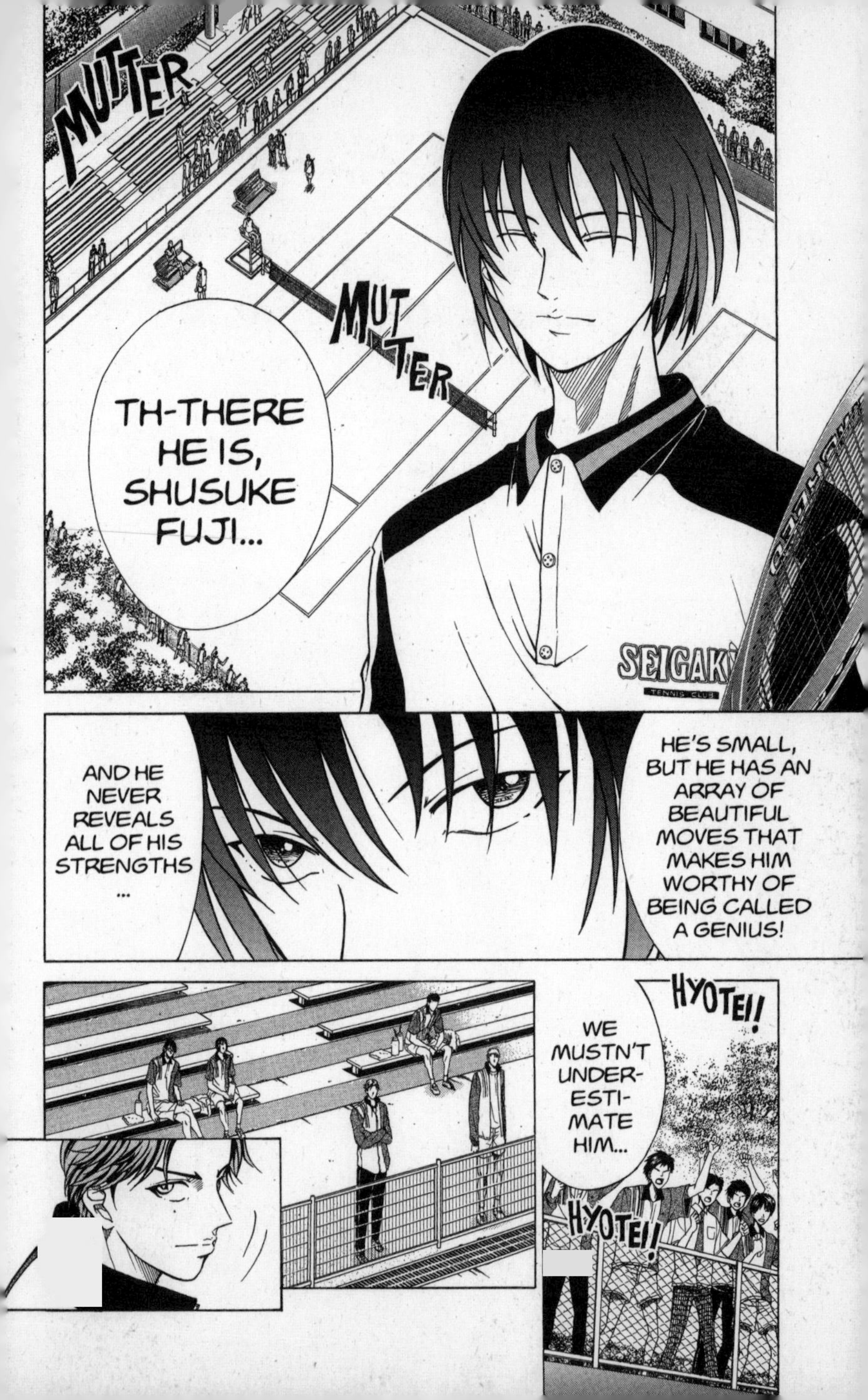
MUTTER
MUTTER
TH-THERE HE IS, SHUSUKE FUJI...
SEIGAKU
HE'S SMALL, BUT HE HAS AN ARRAY OF BEAUTIFUL MOVES THAT MAKES HIM WORTHY OF BEING CALLED A GENIUS!
AND HE NEVER REVEALS ALL OF HIS STRENGTHS ...
HYOTEI!
WE MUSTN'T UNDER-ESTI-MATE HIM...
HYOTEI!

READ THIS WAY

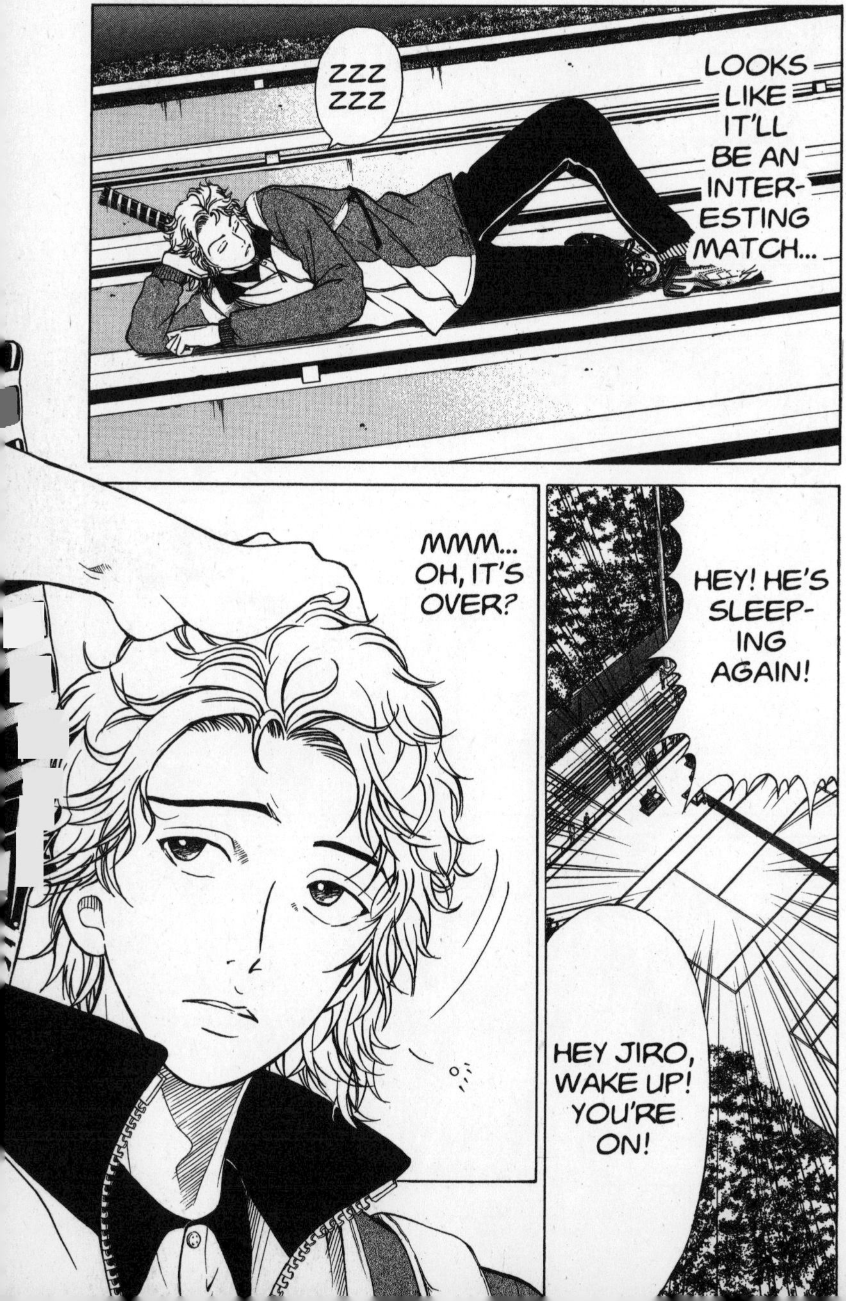
LOOKS LIKE IT'LL BE AN INTER-ESTING MATCH...
ZZZ ZZZ
HEY! HE'S SLEEP-ING AGAIN!
HEY JIRO, WAKE UP! YOU'RE ON!
MMM... OH, IT'S OVER?

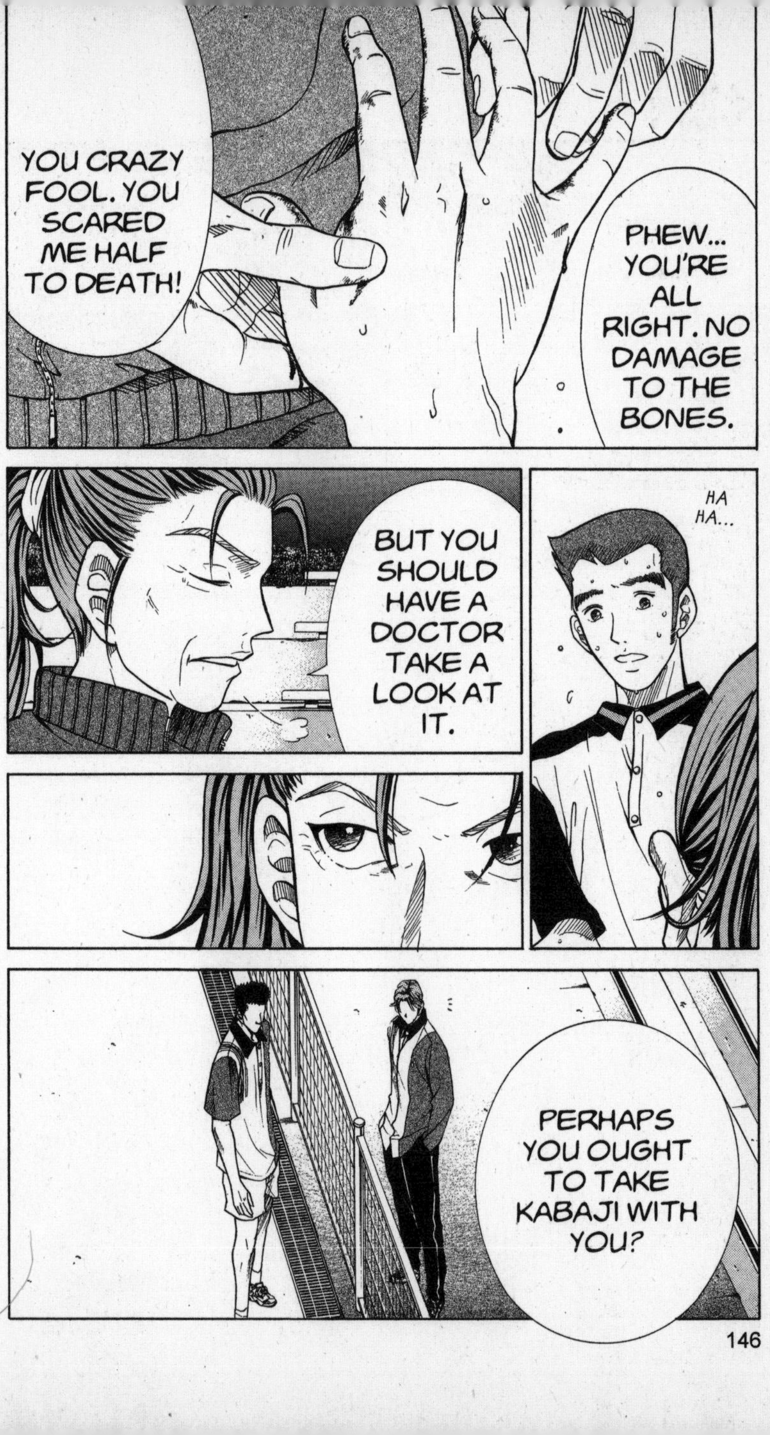
PHEW... YOU'RE ALL RIGHT. NO DAMAGE TO THE BONES.
YOU CRAZY FOOL. YOU SCARED ME HALF TO DEATH!
HA HA...
BUT YOU SHOULD HAVE A DOCTOR TAKE A LOOK AT IT.
PERHAPS YOU OUGHT TO TAKE KABAJI WITH YOU?

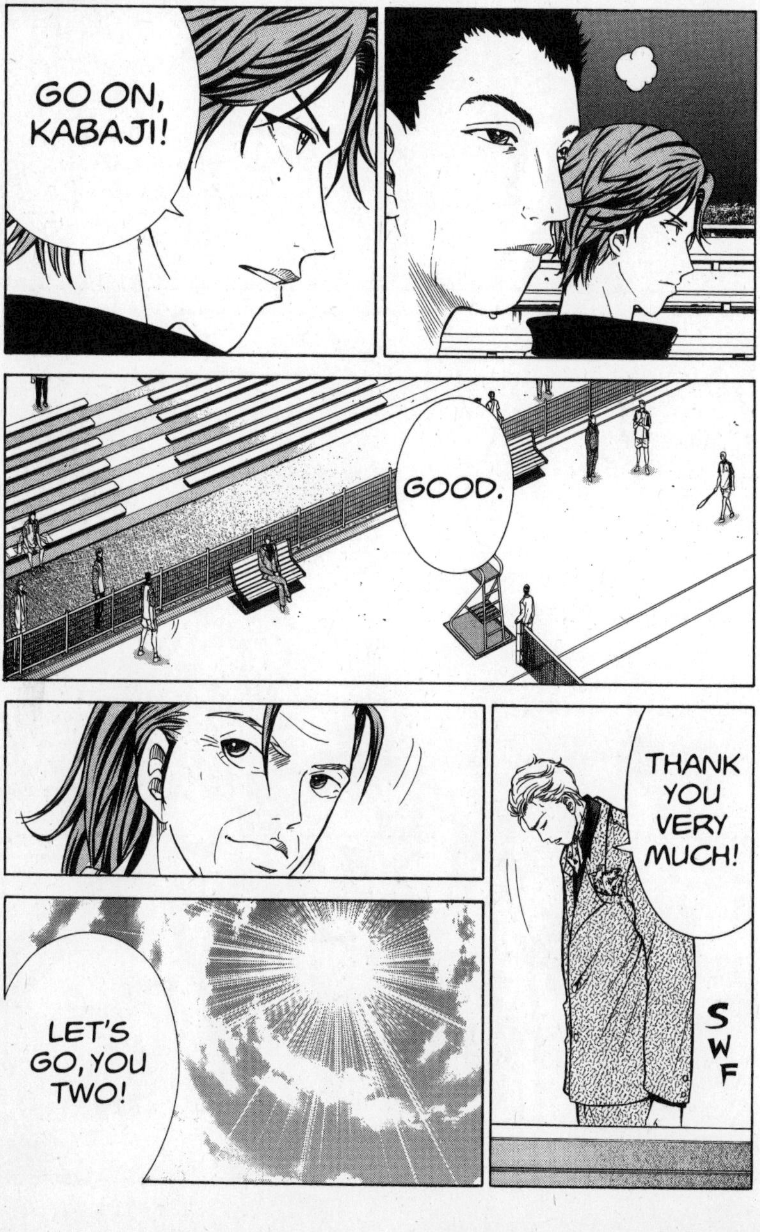
GO ON, KABAJI!
GOOD.
THANK YOU VERY MUCH!
SWF
LET'S GO, YOU TWO!

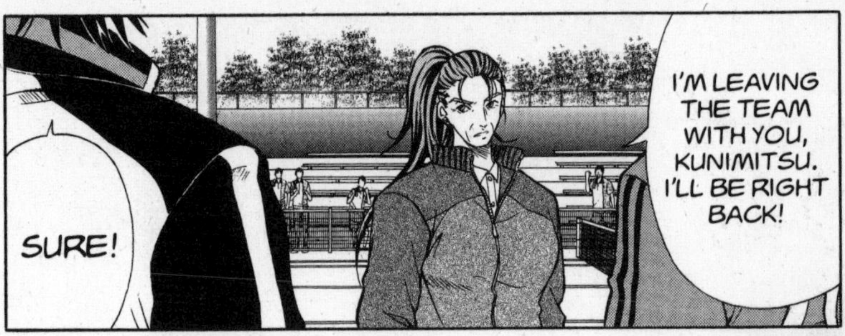
I'M LEAVING THE TEAM WITH YOU, KUNIMITSU. I'LL BE RIGHT BACK!
SURE!
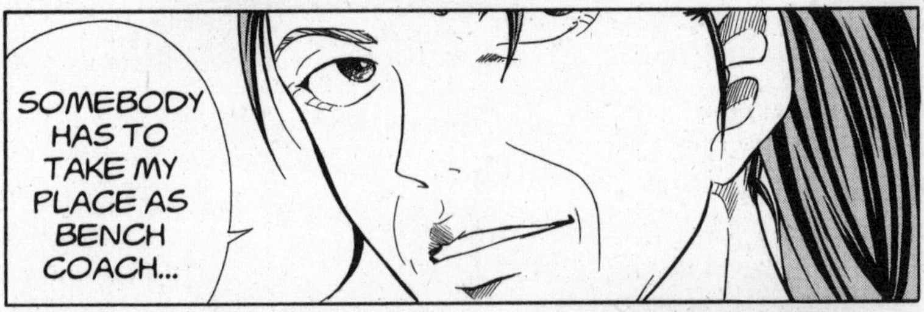
SOMEBODY HAS TO TAKE MY PLACE AS BENCH COACH...
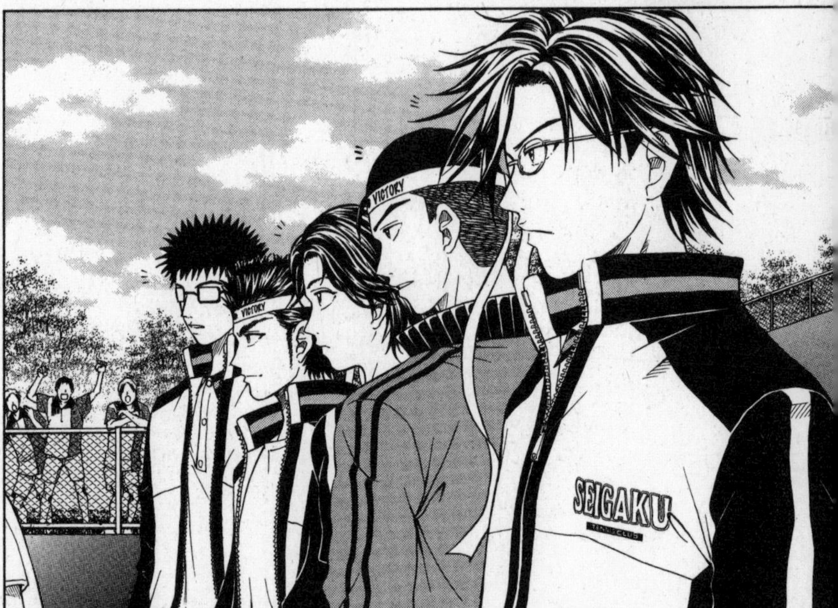
SEIGAKU

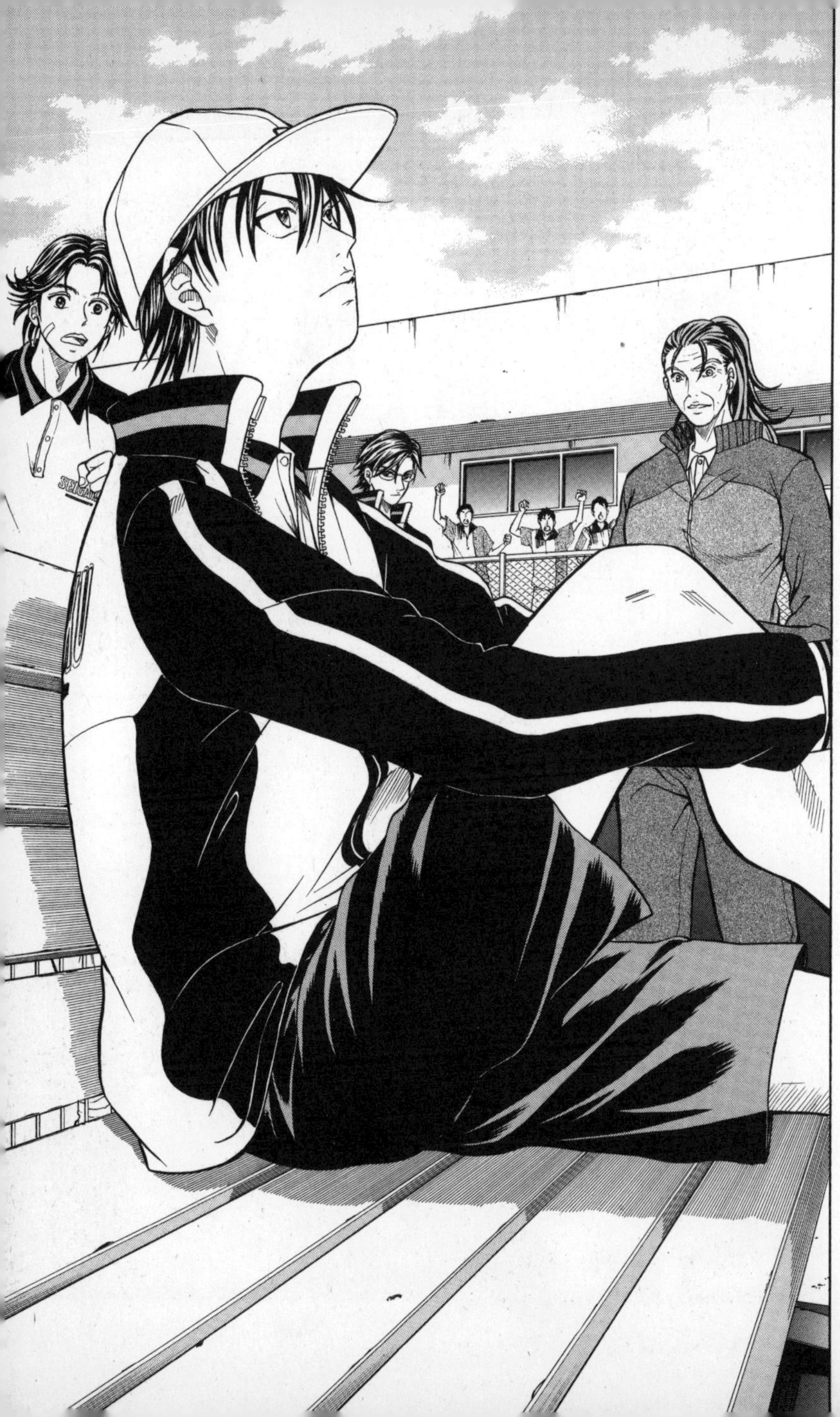

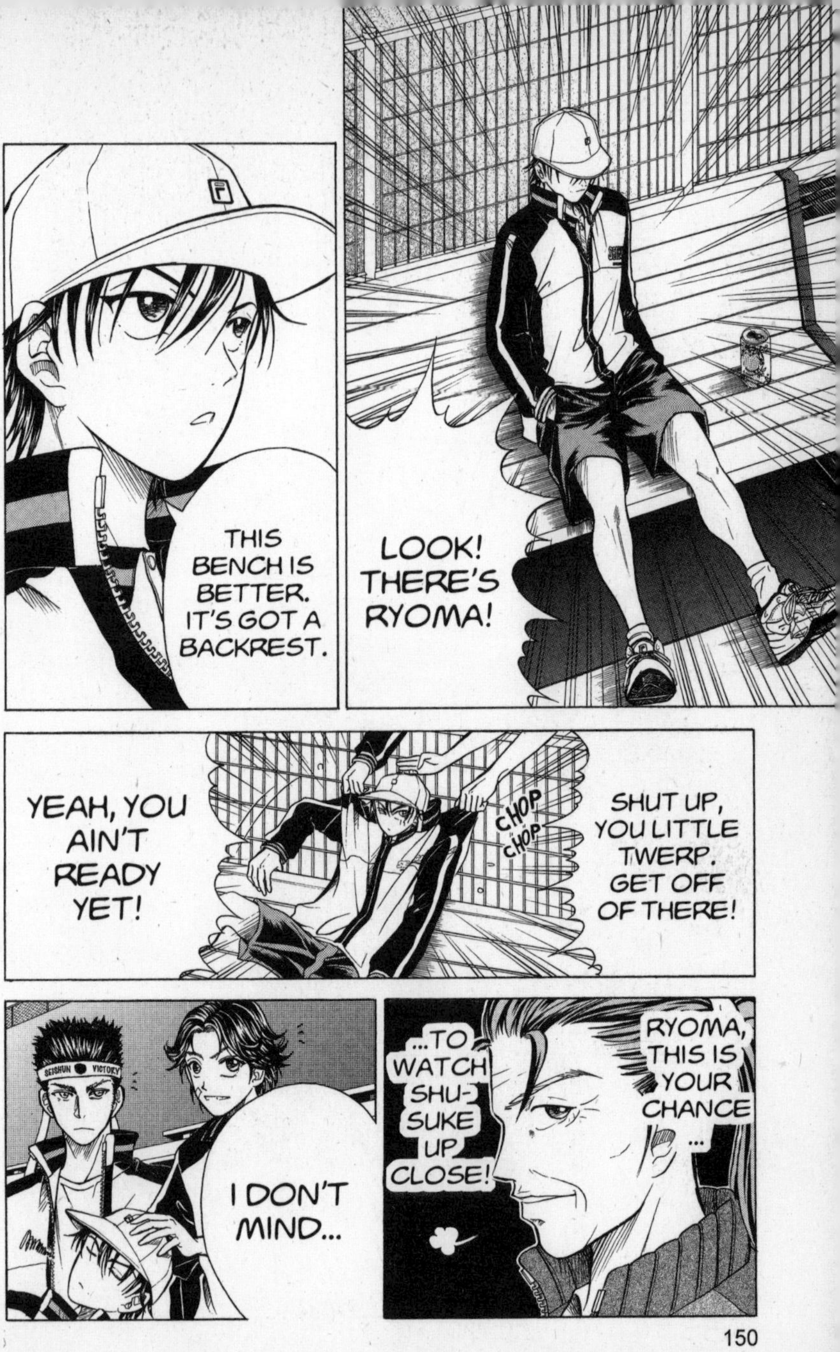
LOOK! THERE'S RYOMA!
THIS BENCH IS BETTER. IT'S GOT A BACKREST.
SHUT UP, YOU LITTLE TWERP. GET OFF OF THERE!
CHOP CHOP
YEAH, YOU AIN'T READY YET!
RYOMA, THIS IS YOUR CHANCE...
...TO WATCH SHU-SUKE UP CLOSE!
SEISHUN VICTORY
I DON'T MIND...

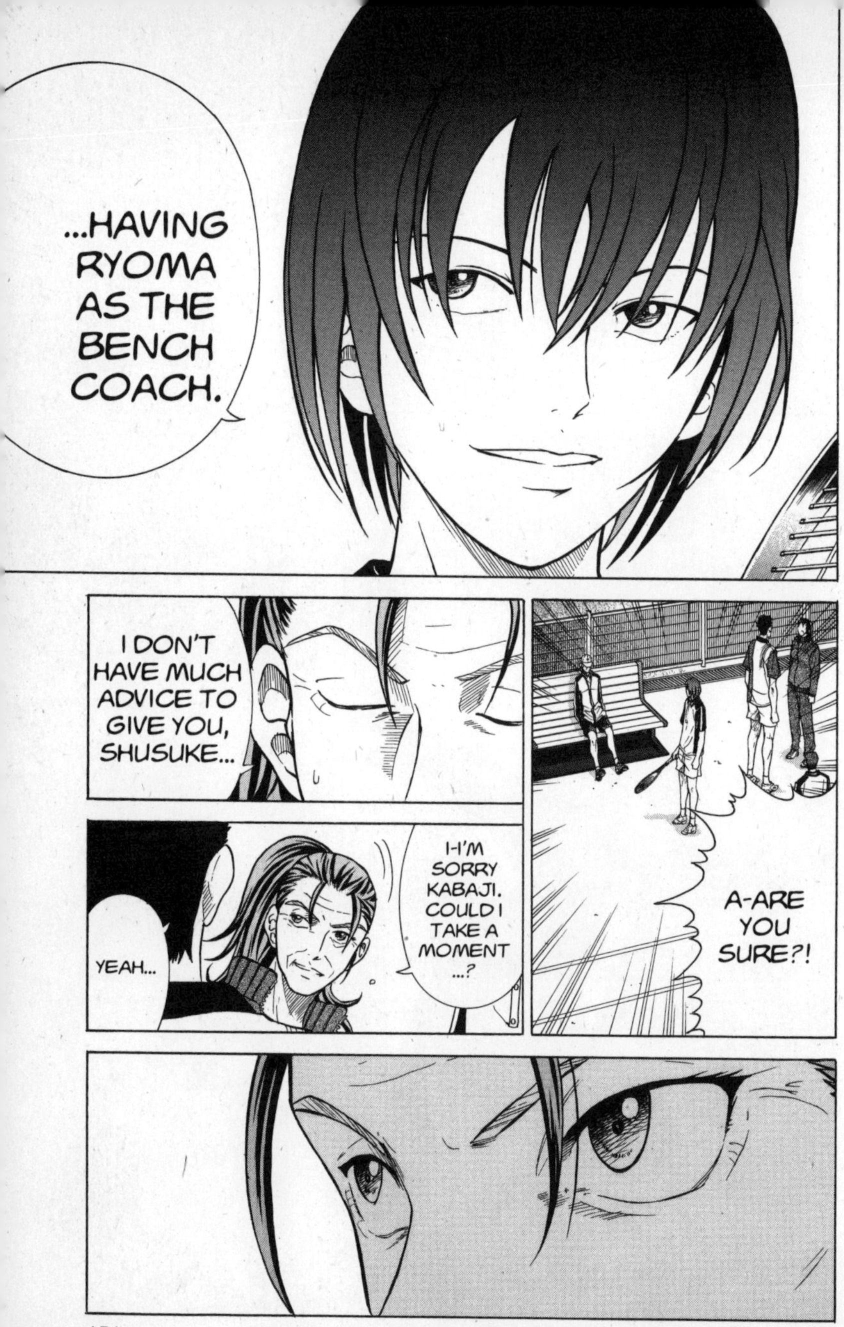
...HAVING RYOMA AS THE BENCH COACH.
A-ARE YOU SURE?!
I DON'T HAVE MUCH ADVICE TO GIVE YOU, SHUSUKE...
I-I'M SORRY KABAJI. COULD I TAKE A MOMENT ...?
YEAH...

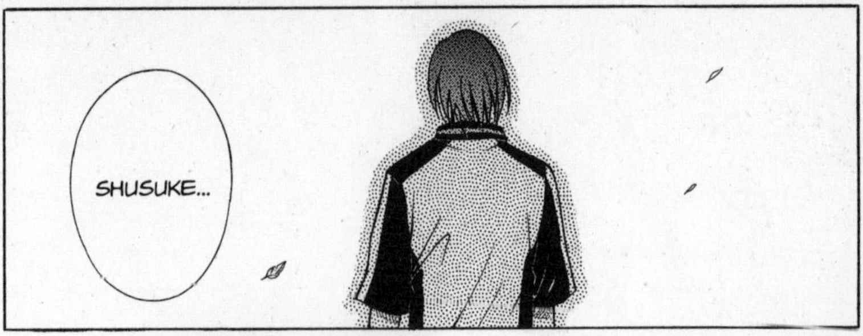
SHUSUKE...
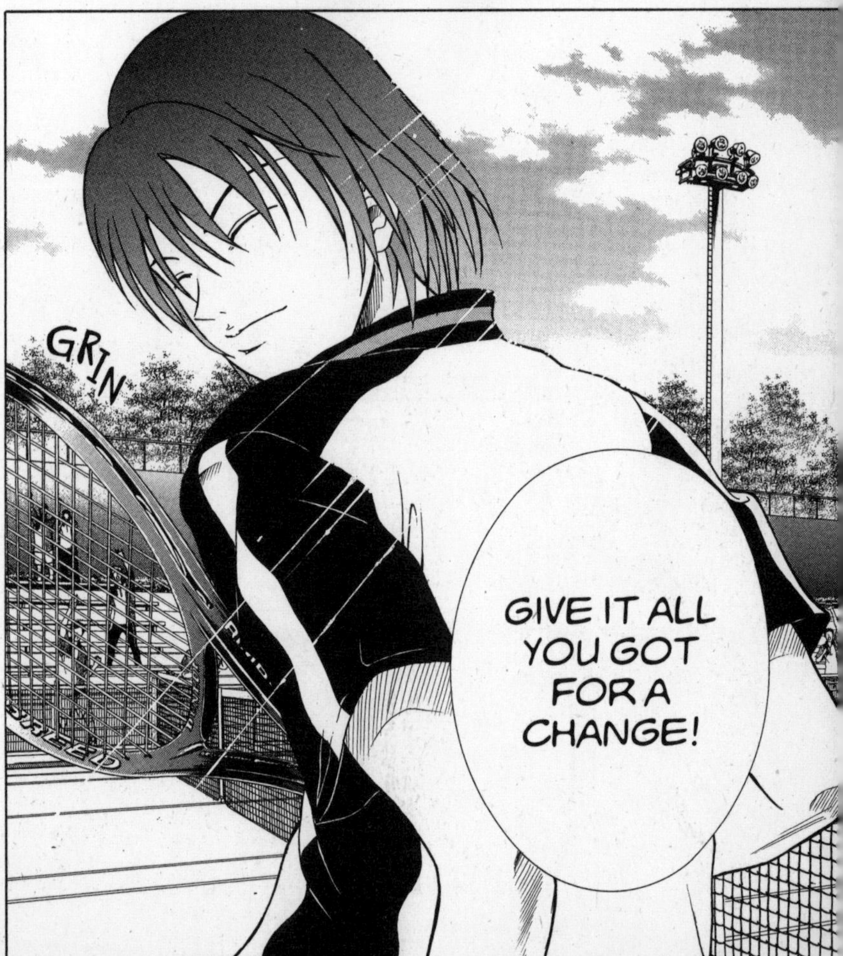
GRIN
GIVE IT ALL YOU GOT FOR A CHANGE!

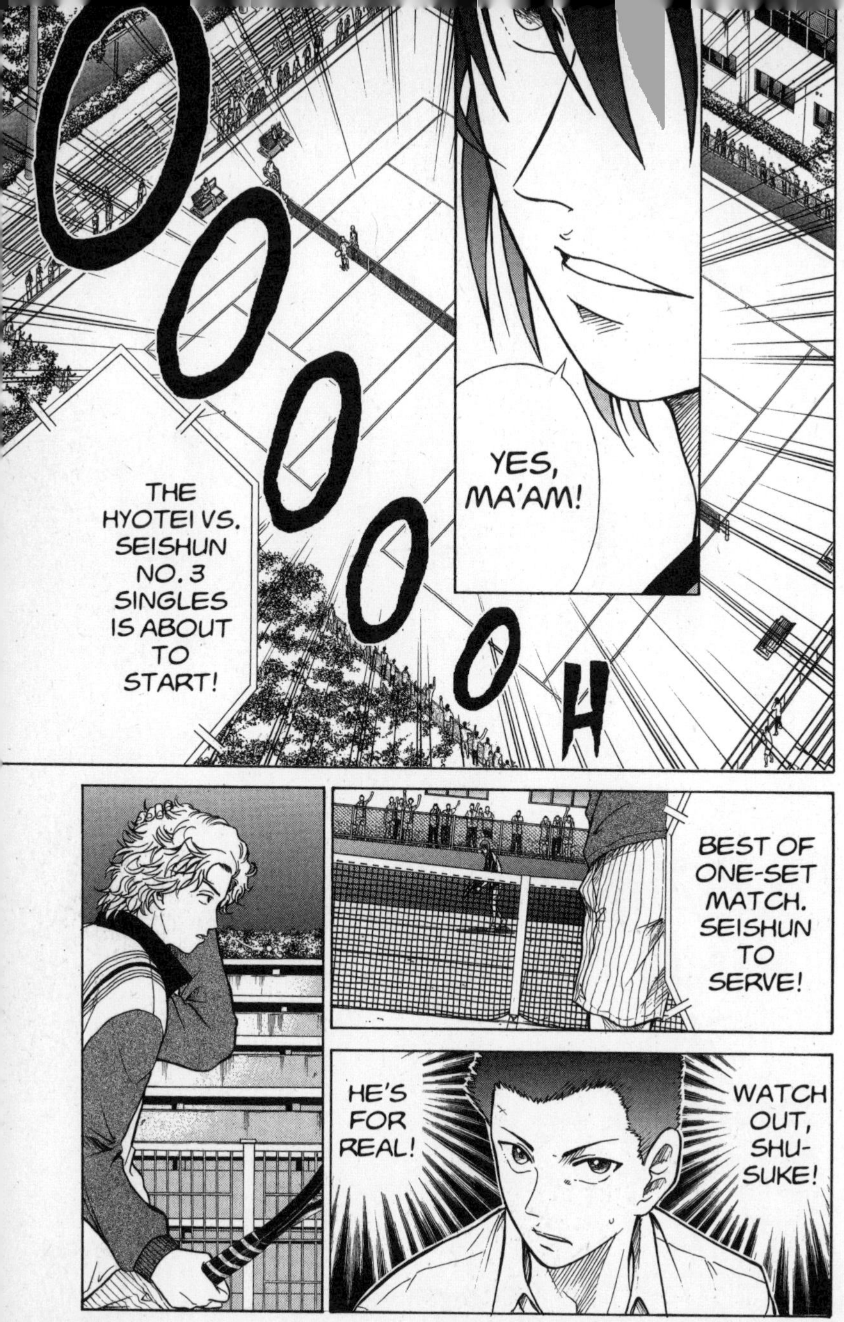
YES, MA'AM!
THE HYOTEI VS. SEISHUN NO. 3 SINGLES IS ABOUT TO START!
OOOOOOH
BEST OF ONE-SET MATCH. SEISHUN TO SERVE!
WATCH OUT, SHU-SUKE!
HE'S FOR REAL!

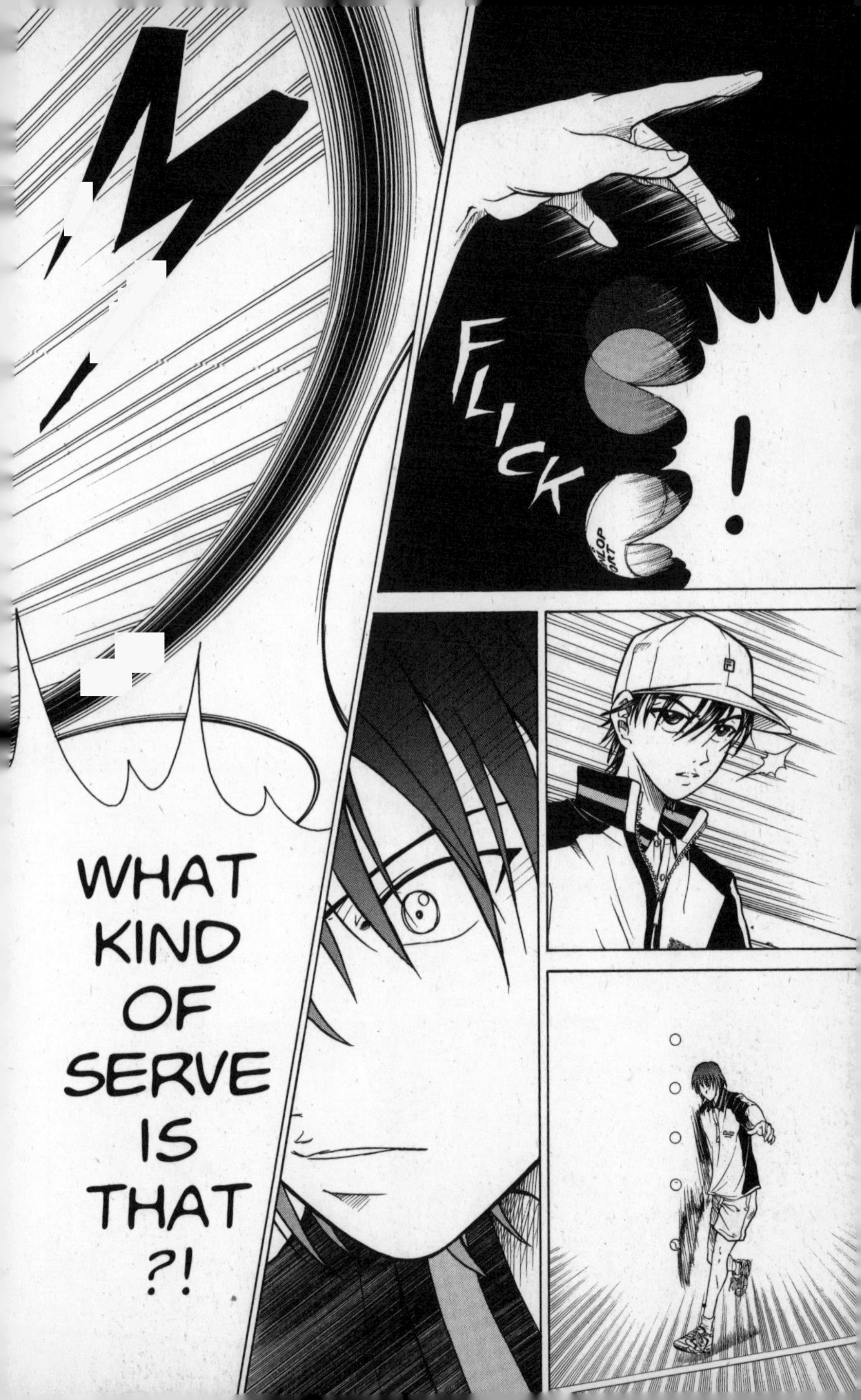
FLICK
!
WHAT KIND OF SERVE IS THAT?!

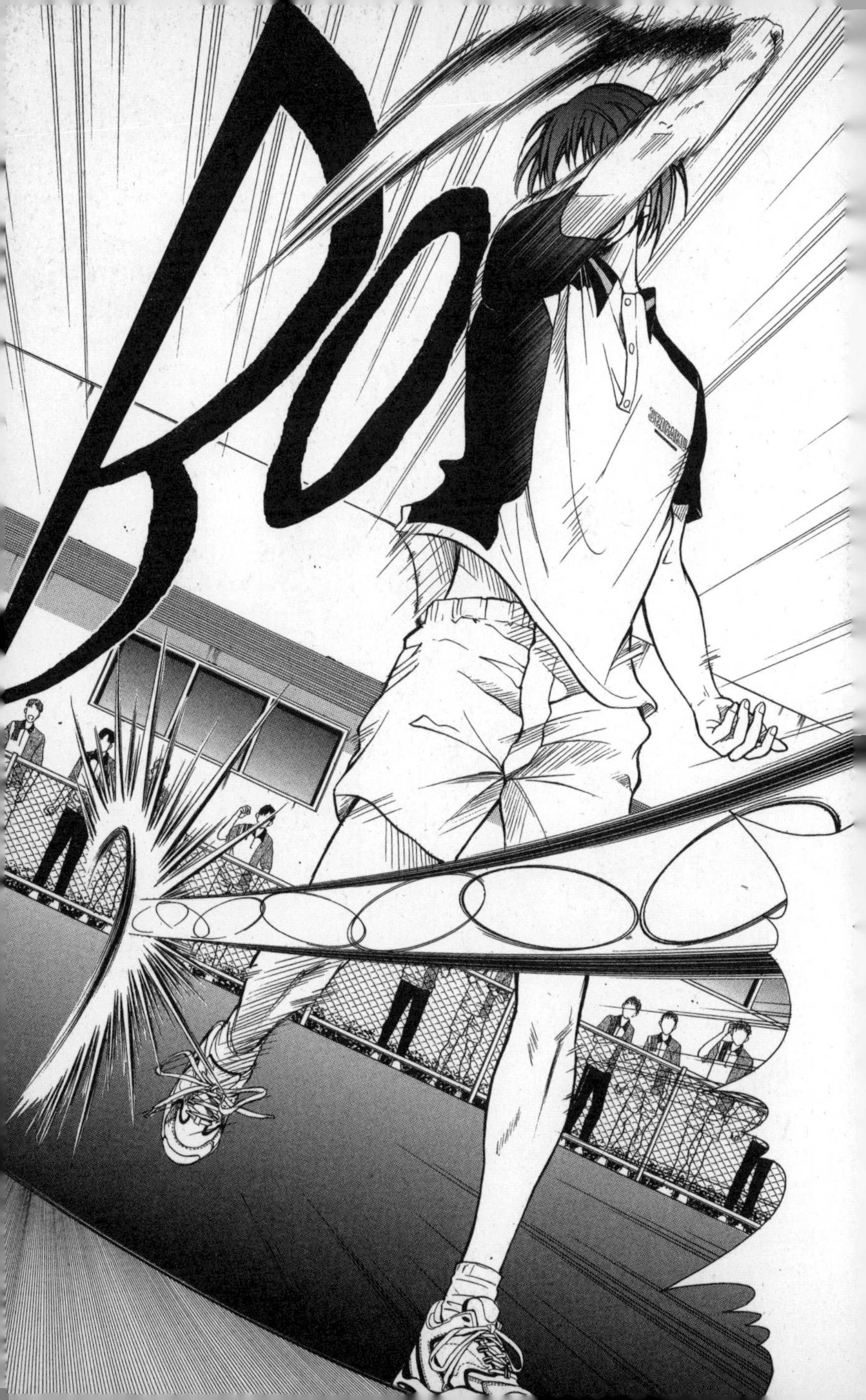
BA
SEIGAKU

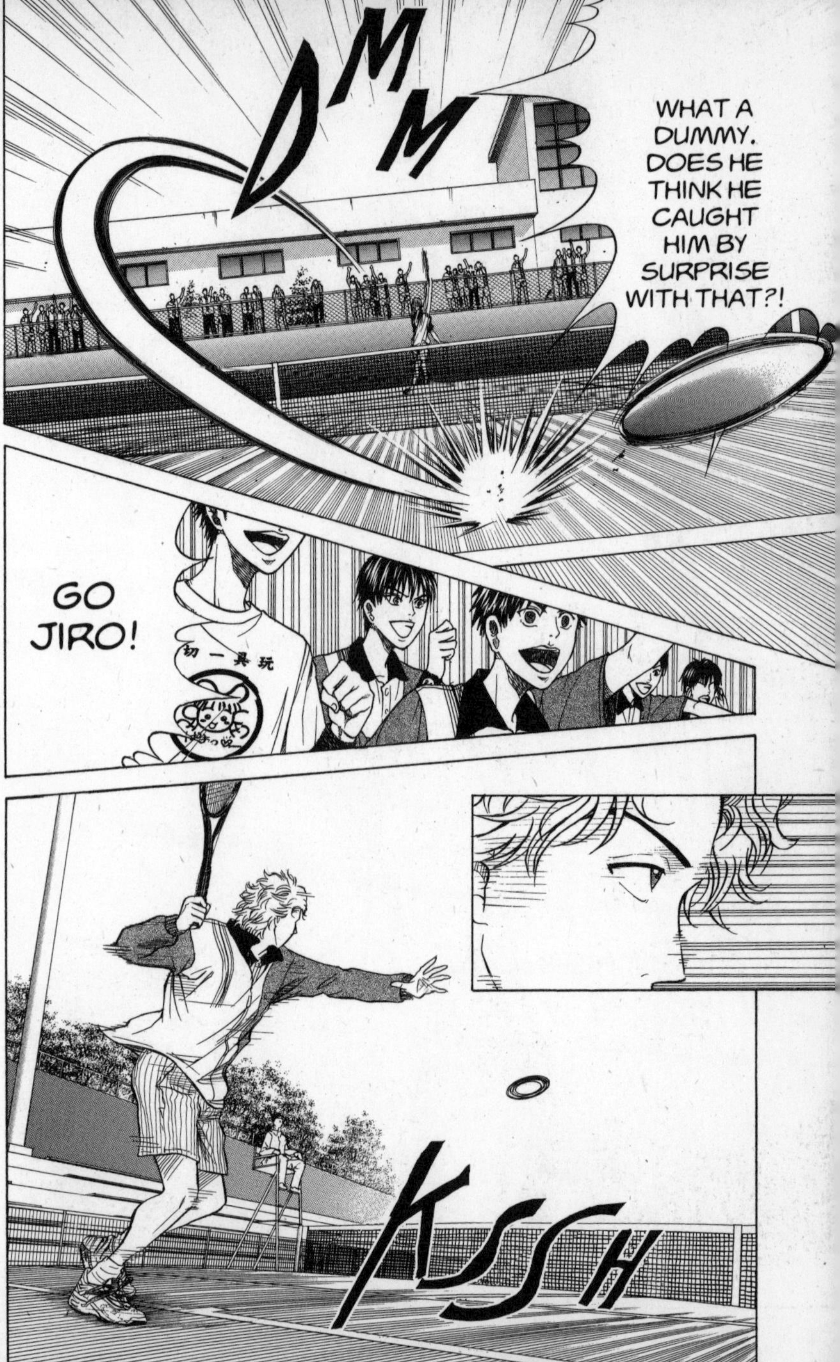
WHAT A DUMMY. DOES HE THINK HE CAUGHT HIM BY SURPRISE WITH THAT?!
DMM
GO JIRO!
KSSH

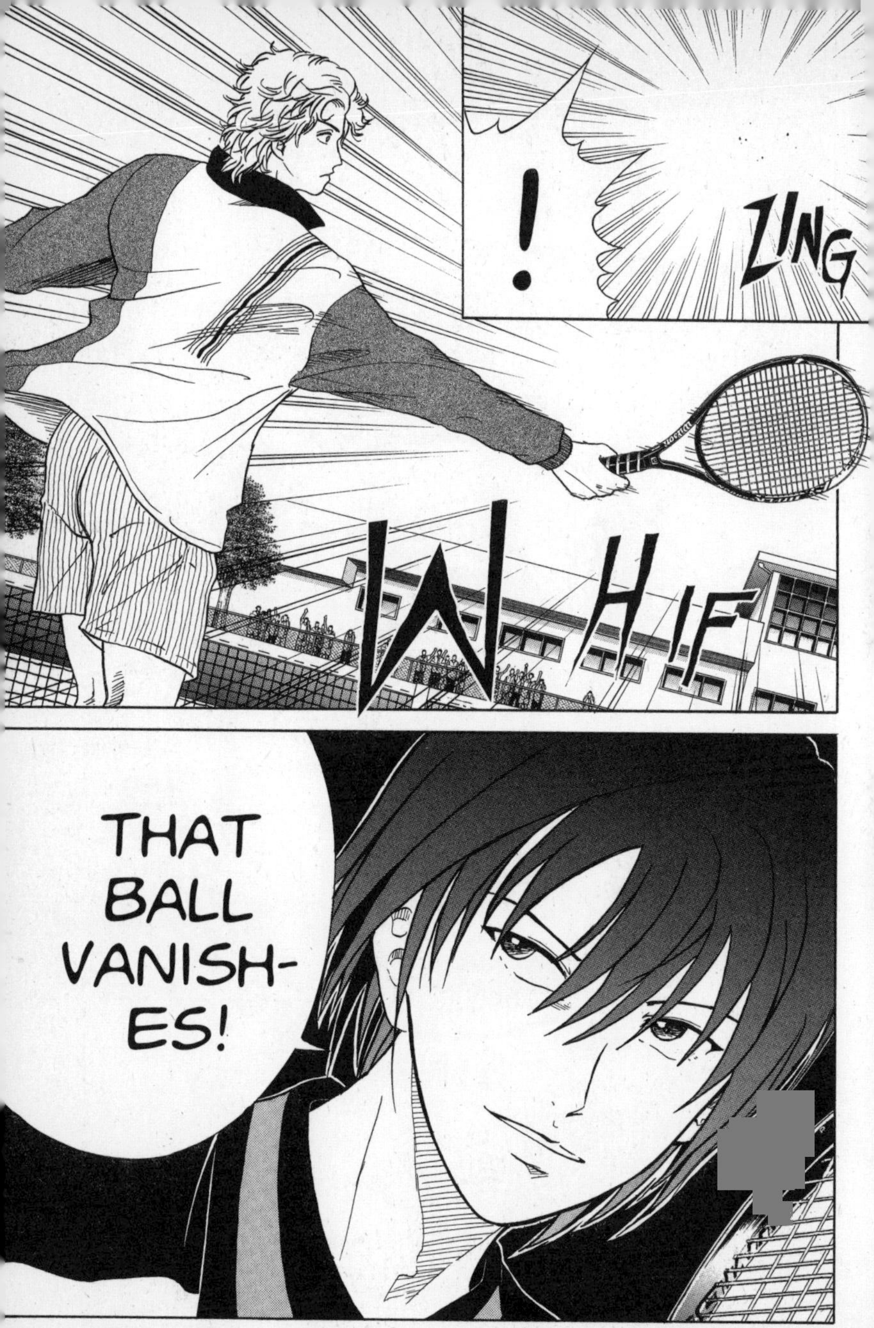
!
ZING
WHIF
THAT BALL VANISH-ES!

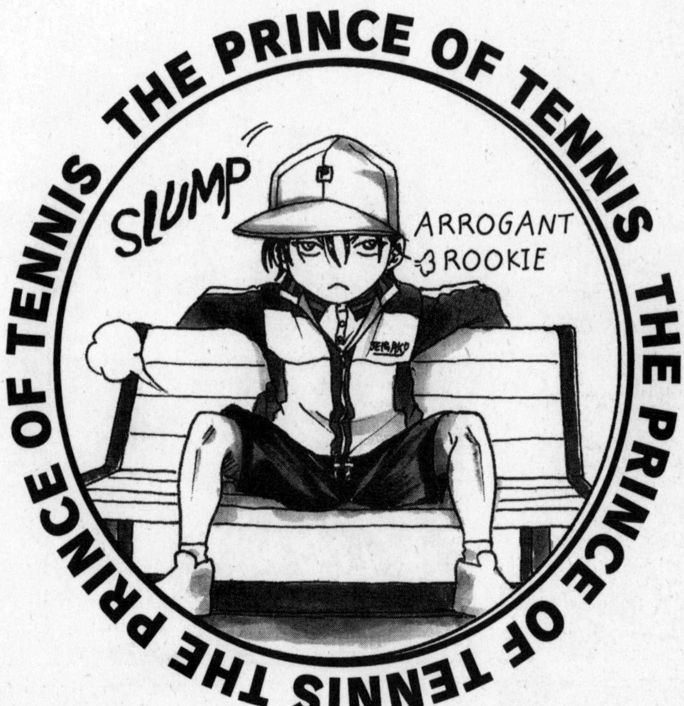
THE PRINCE OF TENNIS THE PRINCE OF TENNIS THE PRINCE OF TENNIS
SLUMP
ARROGANT ROOKIE
SEIGAKU

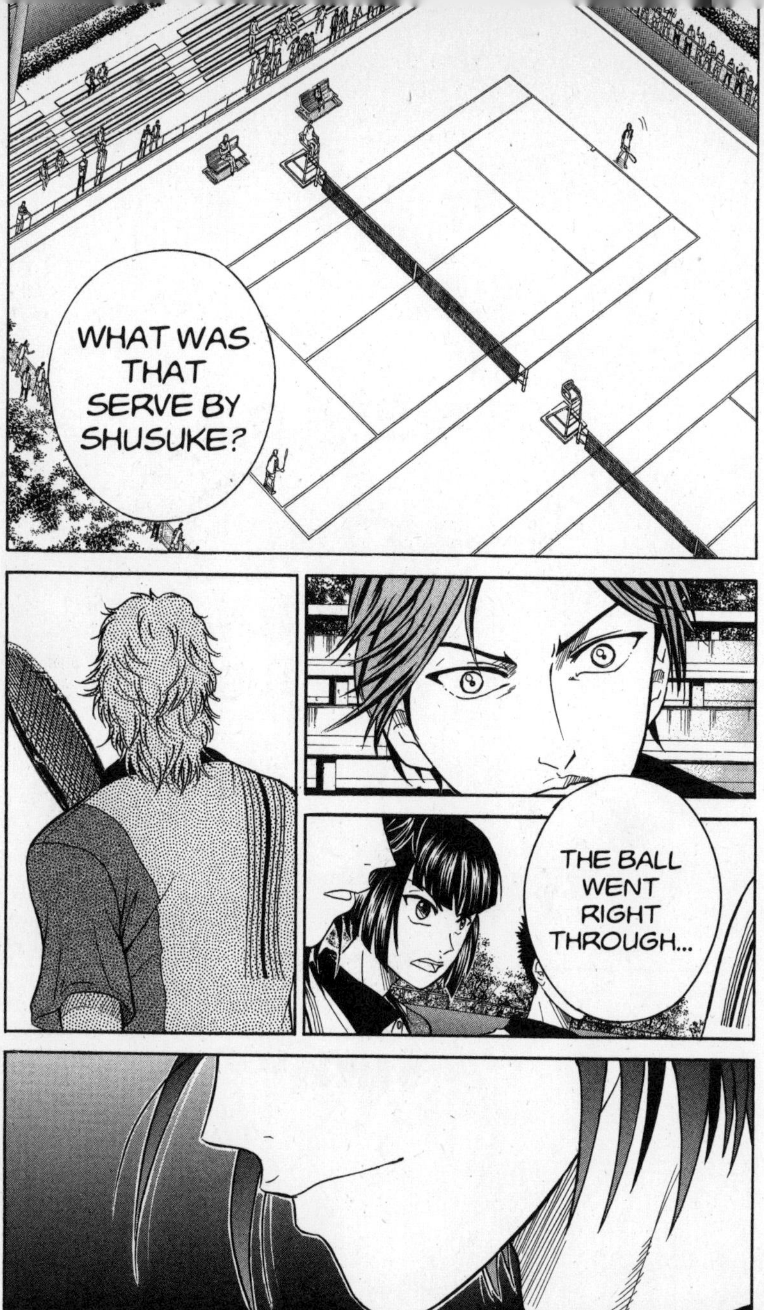
WHAT WAS THAT SERVE BY SHUSUKE?
THE BALL WENT RIGHT THROUGH...

GENIUS 140: JIRO WAKES UP

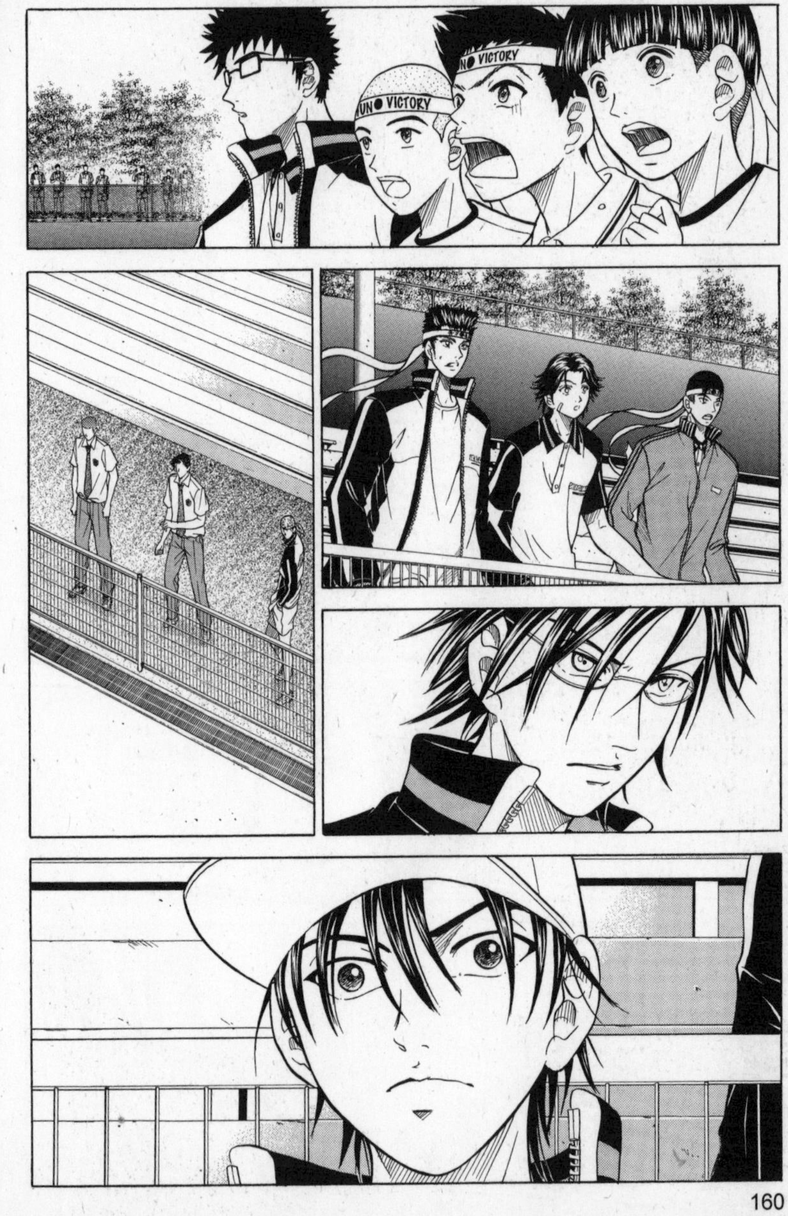
VICTORY
VICTORY
VICTORY

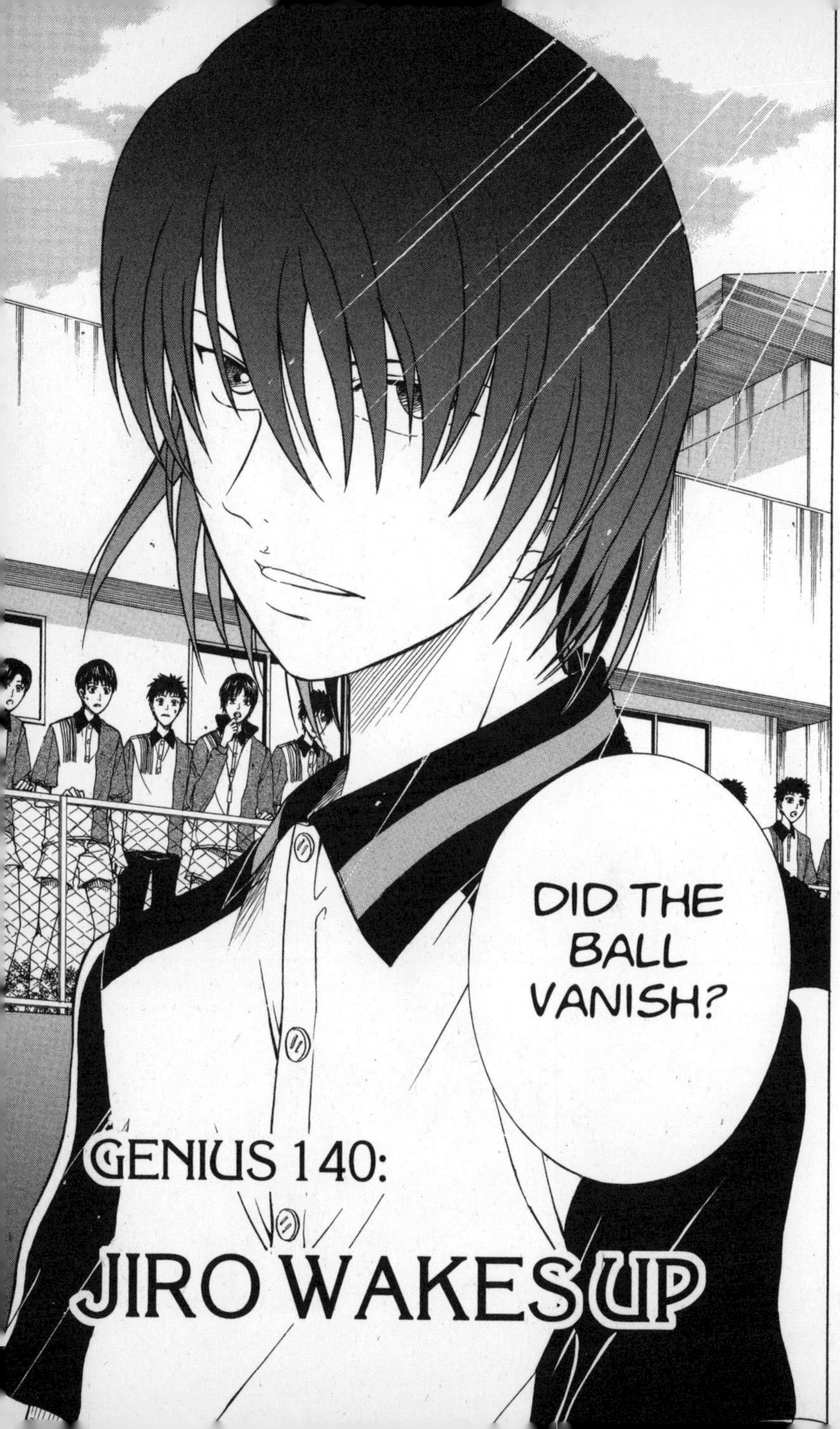
DID THE BALL VANISH?
GENIUS 140:
JIRO WAKES UP

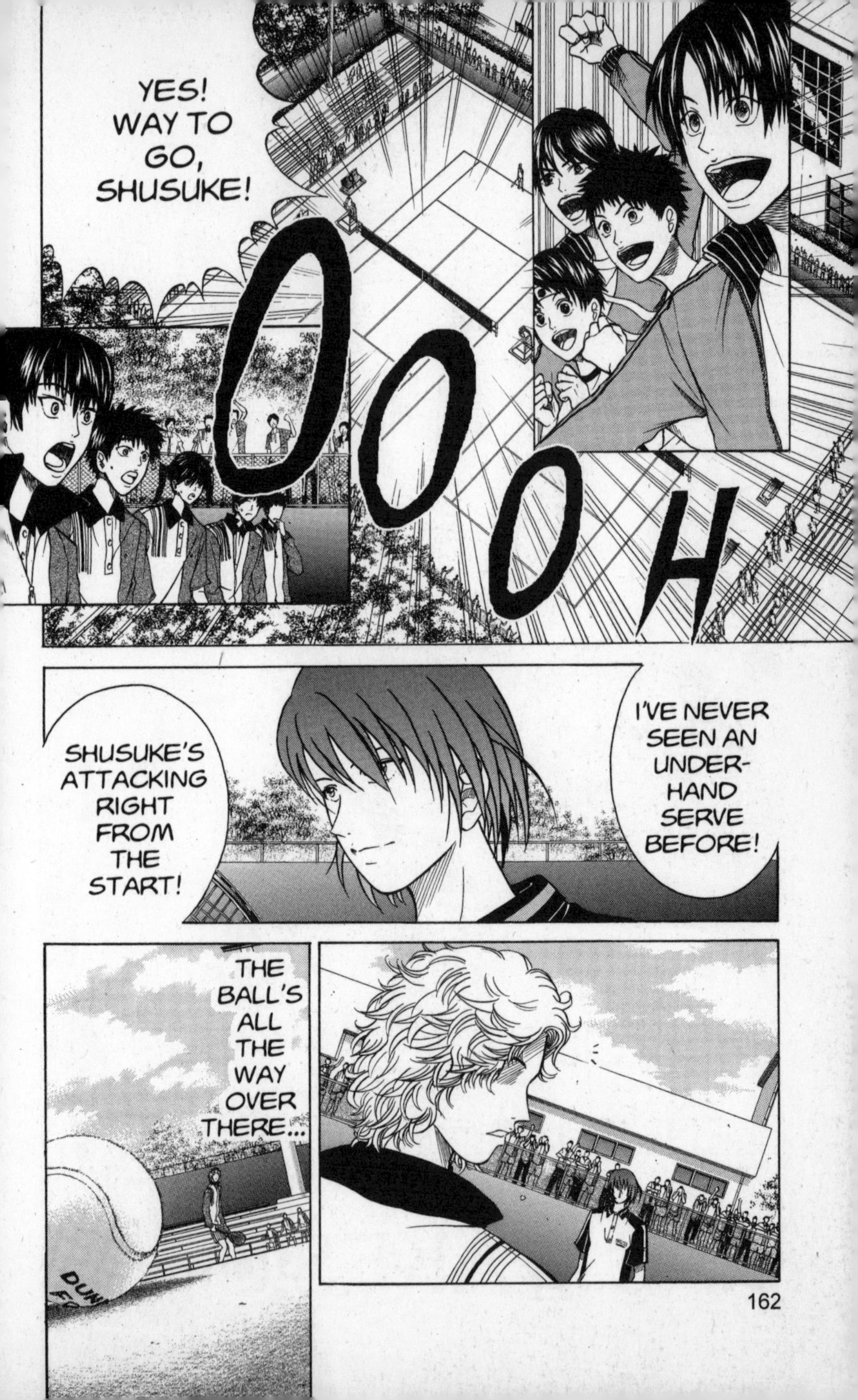
YES! WAY TO GO, SHUSUKE!
OOOOH
I'VE NEVER SEEN AN UNDER-HAND SERVE BEFORE!
SHUSUKE'S ATTACKING RIGHT FROM THE START!
THE BALL'S ALL THE WAY OVER THERE...

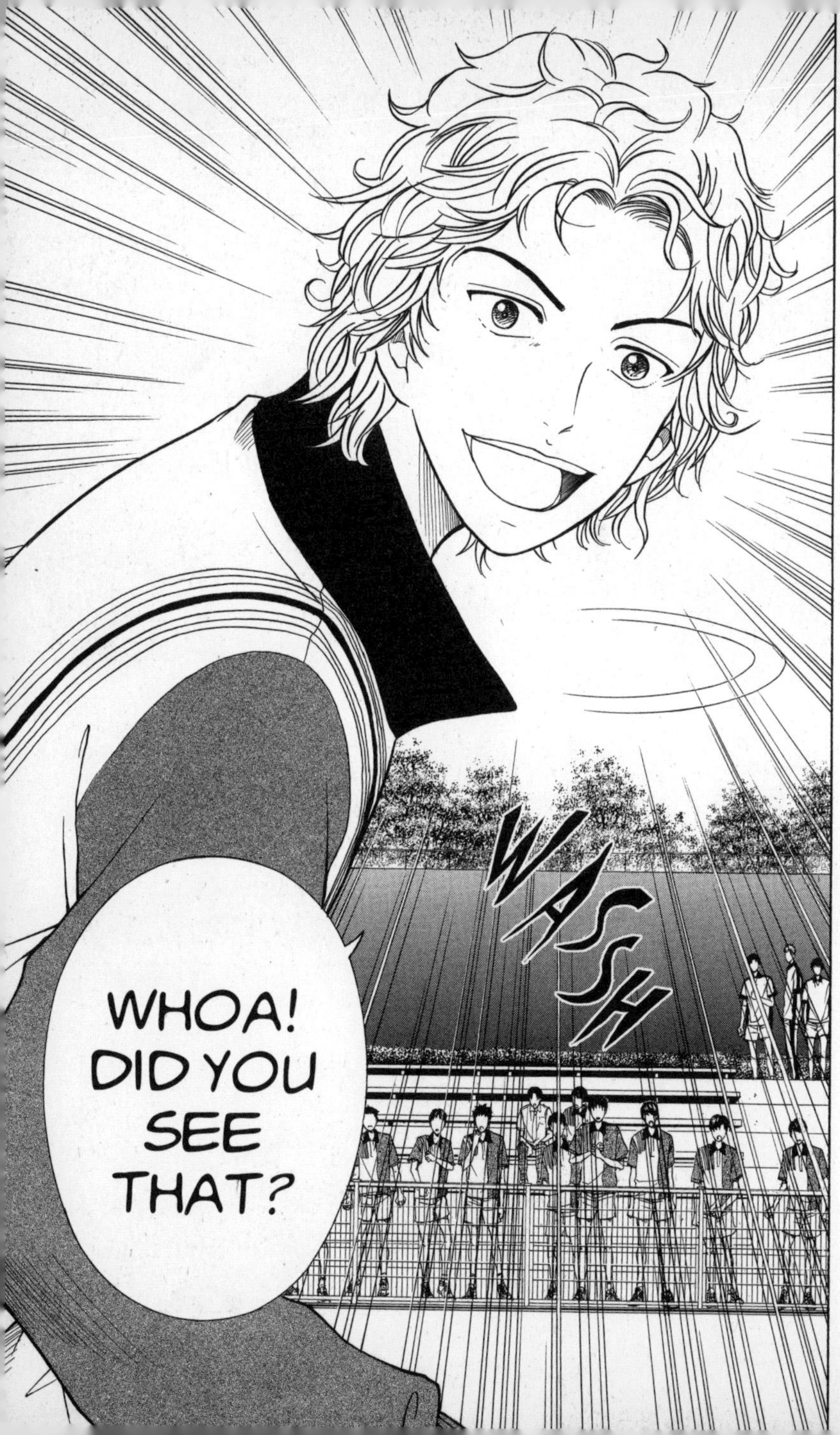
WASH
WHOA! DID YOU SEE THAT?

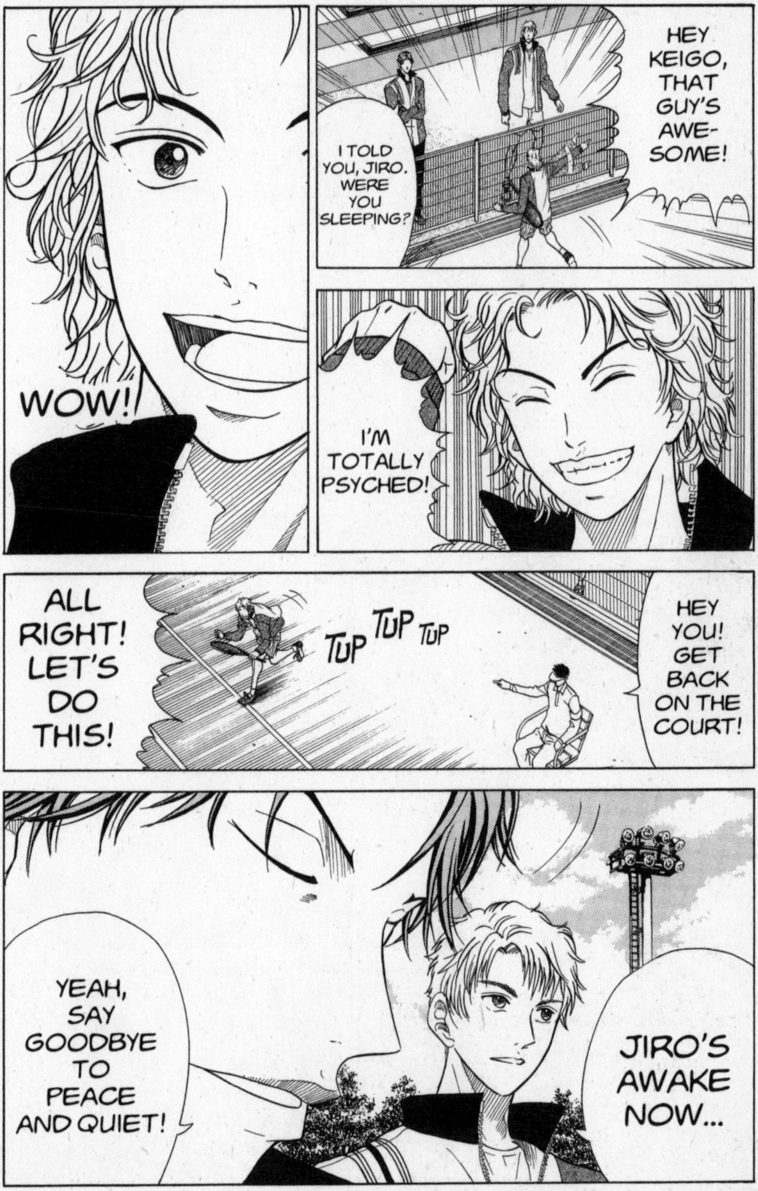
HEY KEIGO, THAT GUY'S AWE-SOME!
I TOLD YOU, JIRO. WERE YOU SLEEPING?
I'M TOTALLY PSYCHED!
WOW!
HEY YOU! GET BACK ON THE COURT!
TUP TUP TUP
ALL RIGHT! LET'S DO THIS!
JIRO'S AWAKE NOW...
YEAH, SAY GOODBYE TO PEACE AND QUIET!

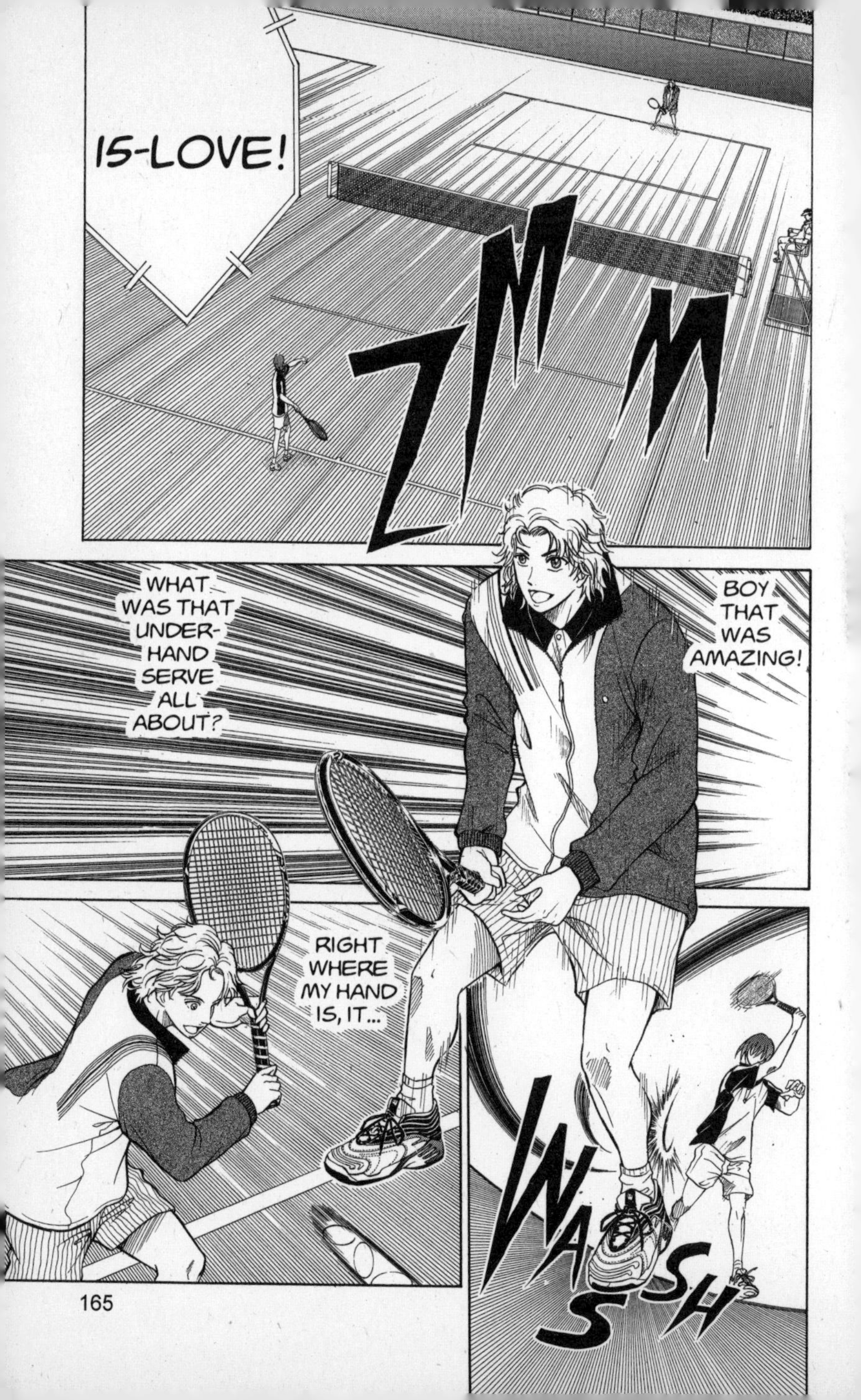
15-LOVE!
ZMM
BOY THAT WAS AMAZING!
WHAT WAS THAT UNDER-HAND SERVE ALL ABOUT?
WASSH
RIGHT WHERE MY HAND IS, IT...

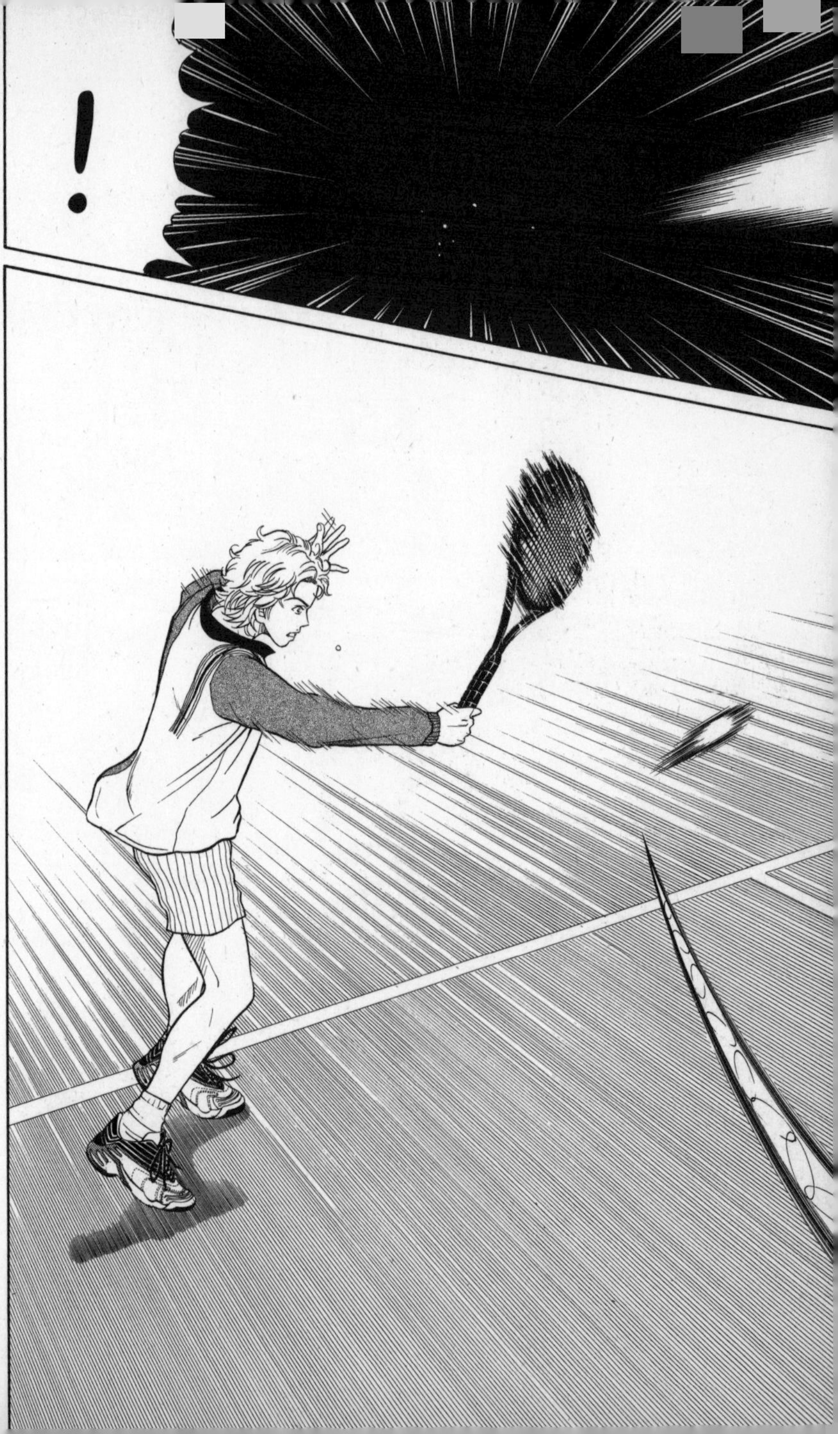
!

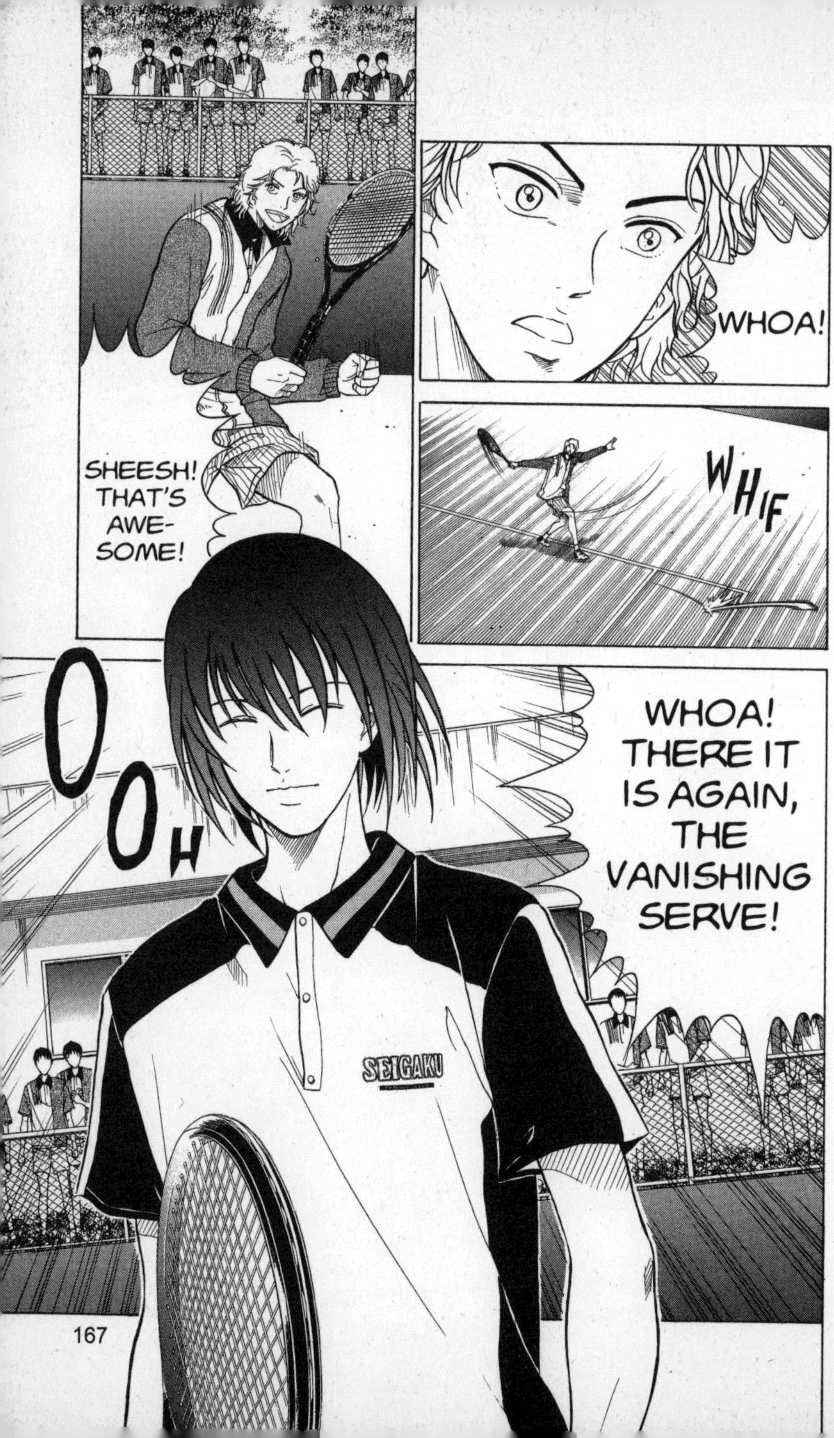
WHOA!
WHIF
SHEESH! THAT'S AWE-SOME!
WHOA! THERE IT IS AGAIN, THE VANISHING SERVE!
OOH

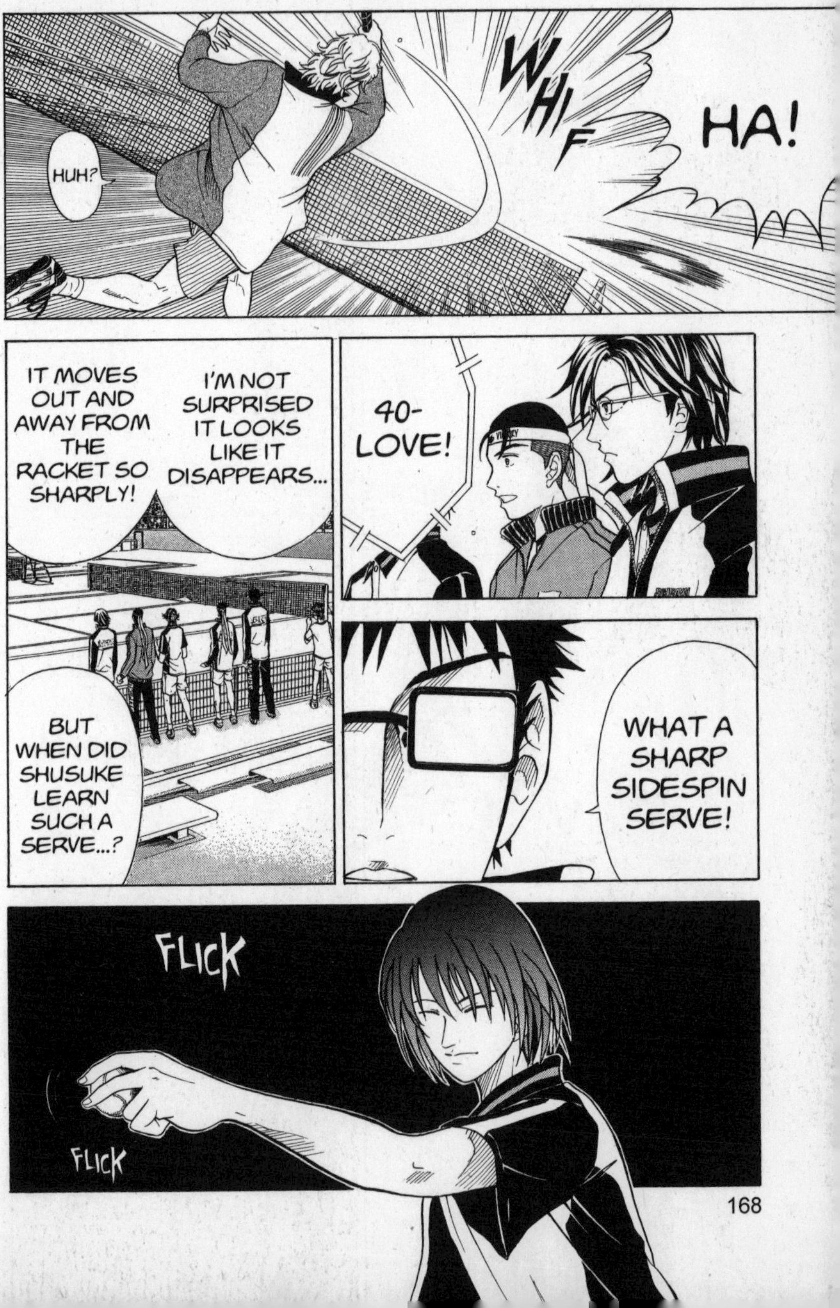
WHIFF
HA!
HUH?
40-LOVE!
WHAT A SHARP SIDESPIN SERVE!
I'M NOT SURPRISED IT LOOKS LIKE IT DISAPPEARS...
IT MOVES OUT AND AWAY FROM THE RACKET SO SHARPLY!
BUT WHEN DID SHUSUKE LEARN SUCH A SERVE...?
FLICK
FLICK

READ THIS WAY

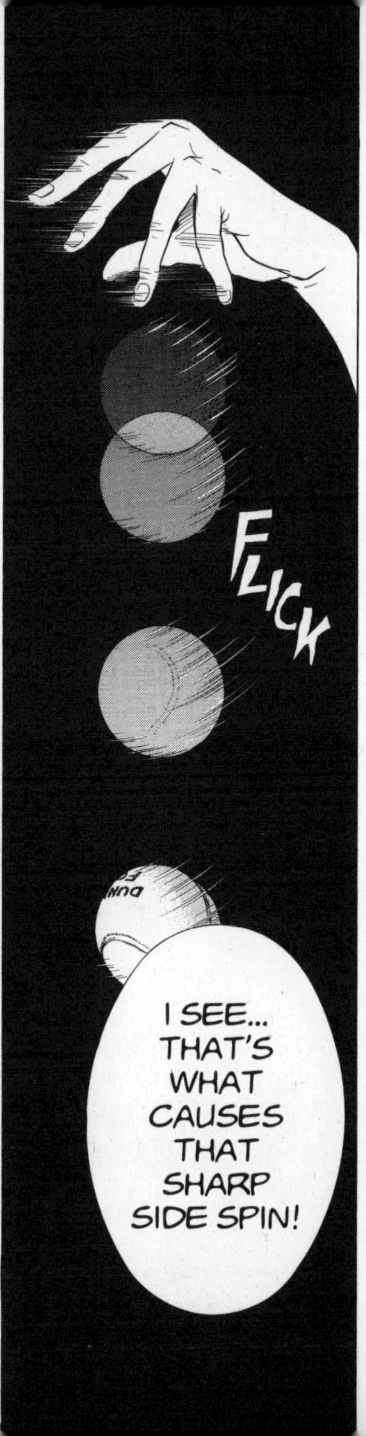
FLICK
I SEE... THAT'S WHAT CAUSES THAT SHARP SIDE SPIN!

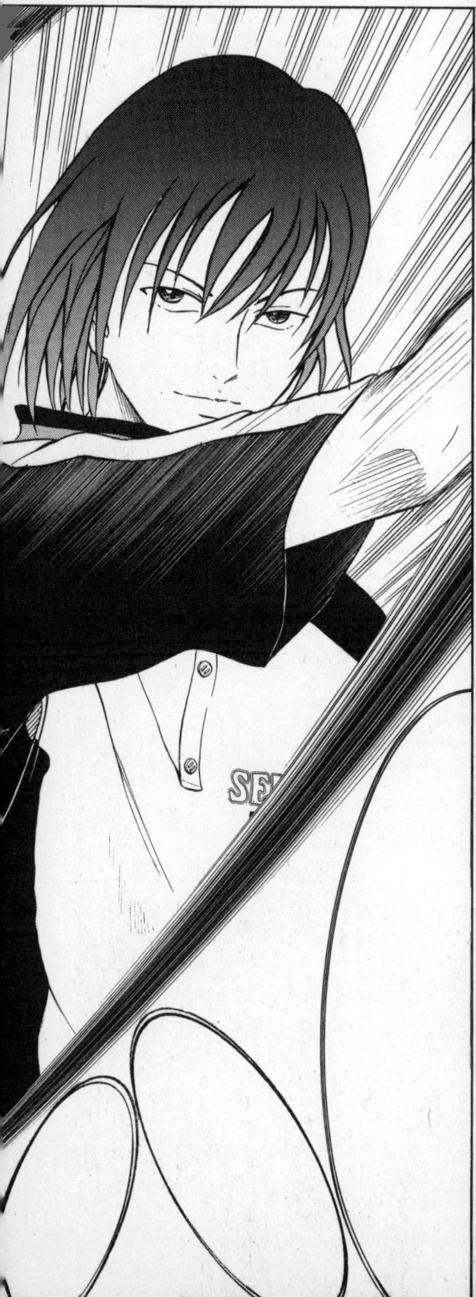

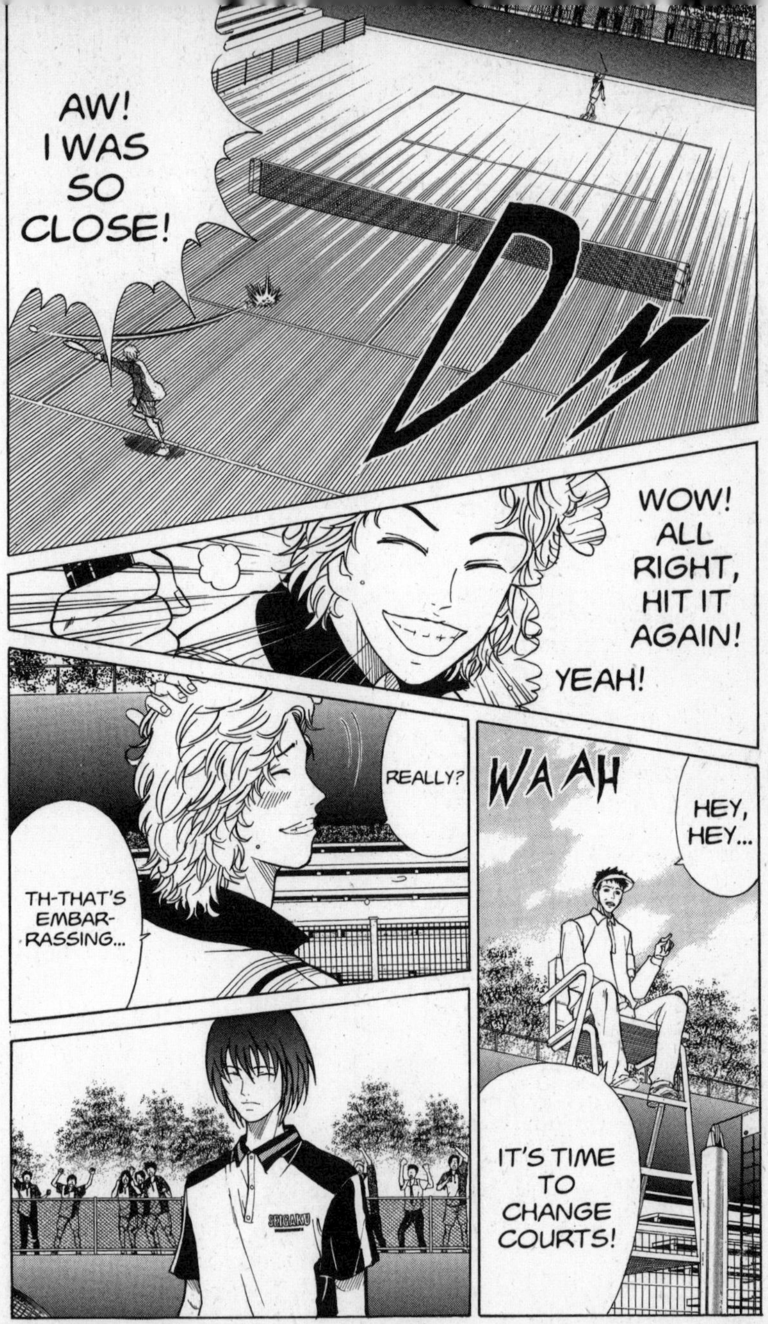
AW! I WAS SO CLOSE!
DM
WOW! ALL RIGHT, HIT IT AGAIN!
YEAH!
WAAH
HEY, HEY...
IT'S TIME TO CHANGE COURTS!
REALLY?
TH-THAT'S EMBAR-RASSING...
SEIGAKU

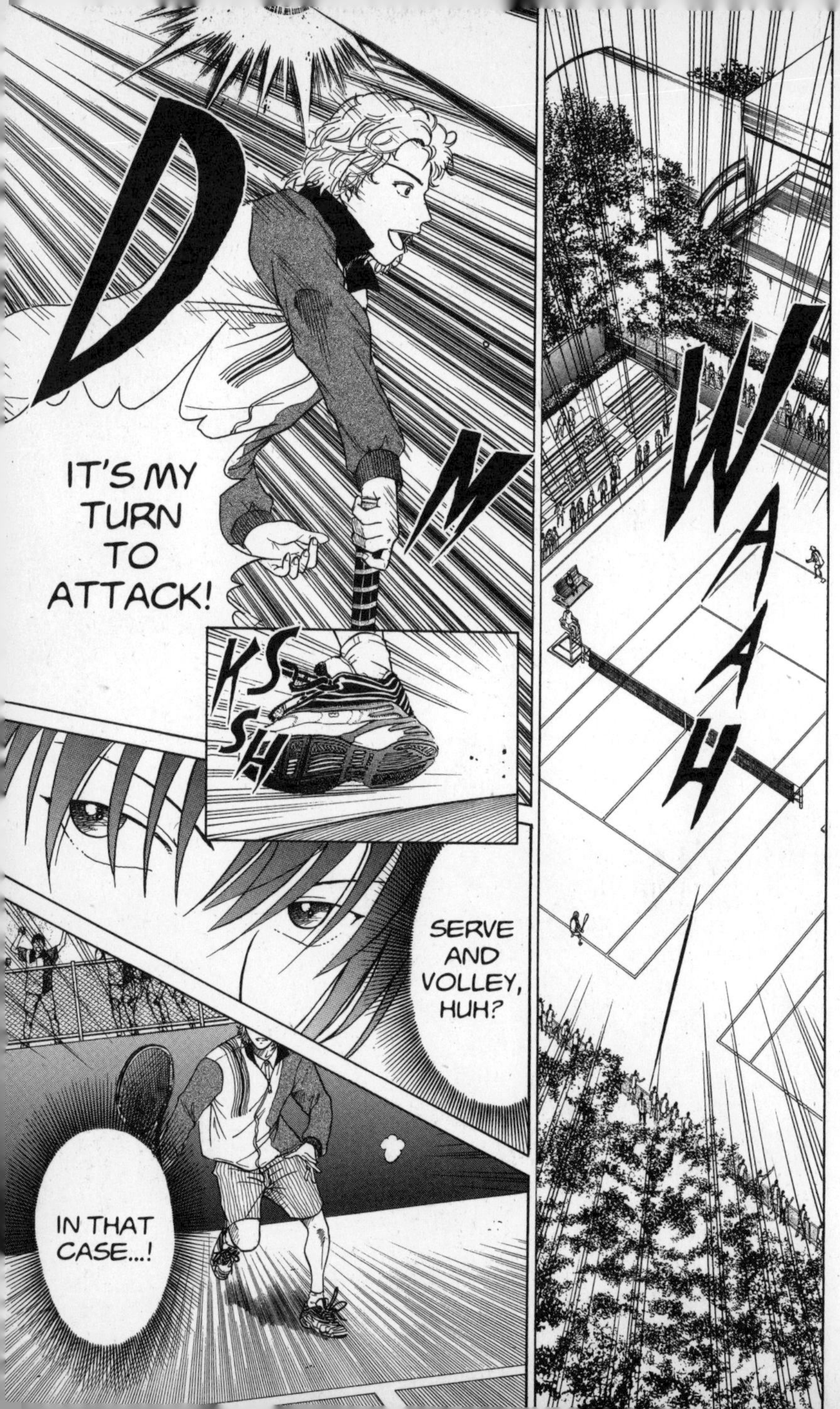
WAAAH
DM
IT'S MY TURN TO ATTACK!
KSSH
SERVE AND VOLLEY, HUH?
IN THAT CASE...!

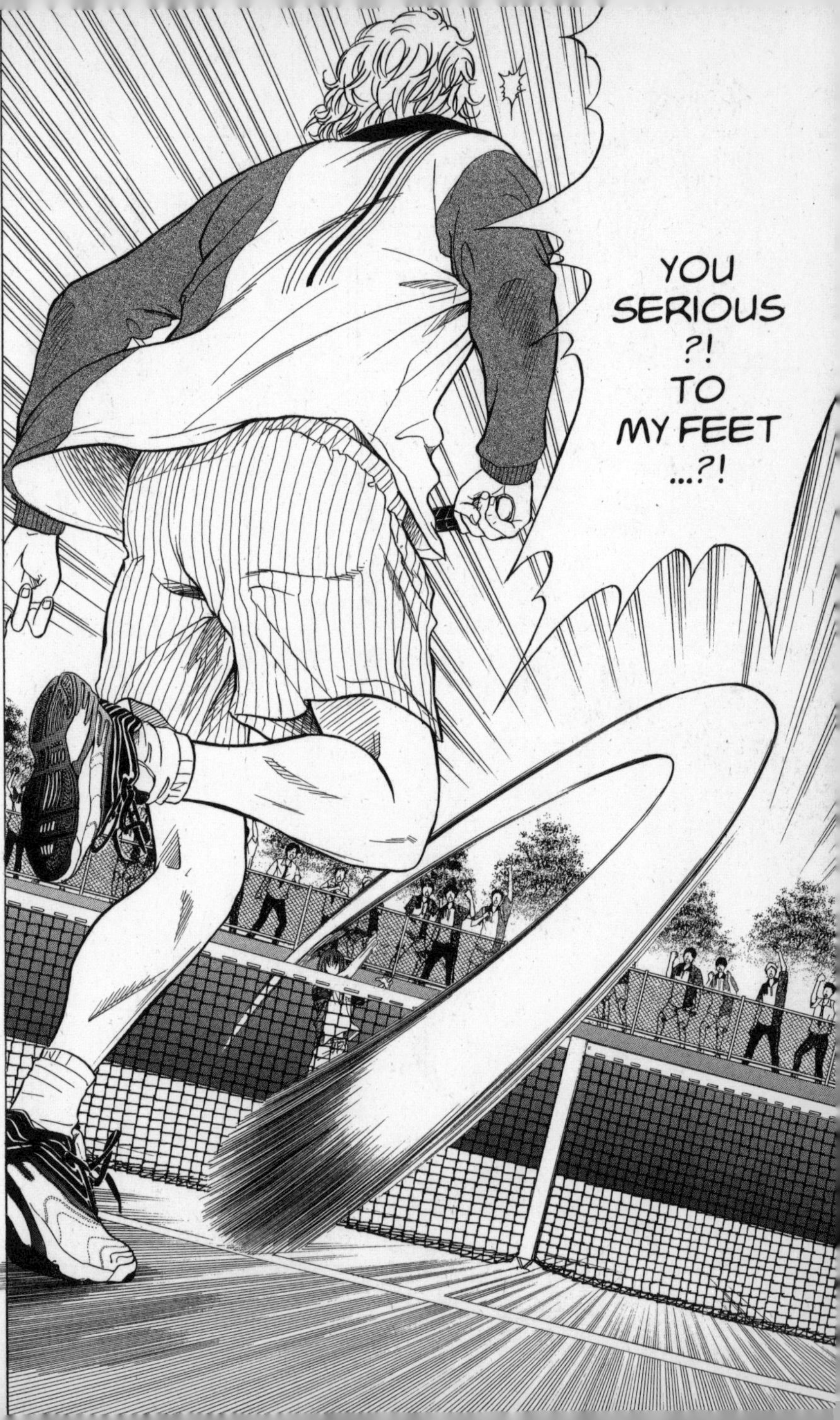
YOU SERIOUS ?! TO MY FEET ...?!

READ THIS WAY

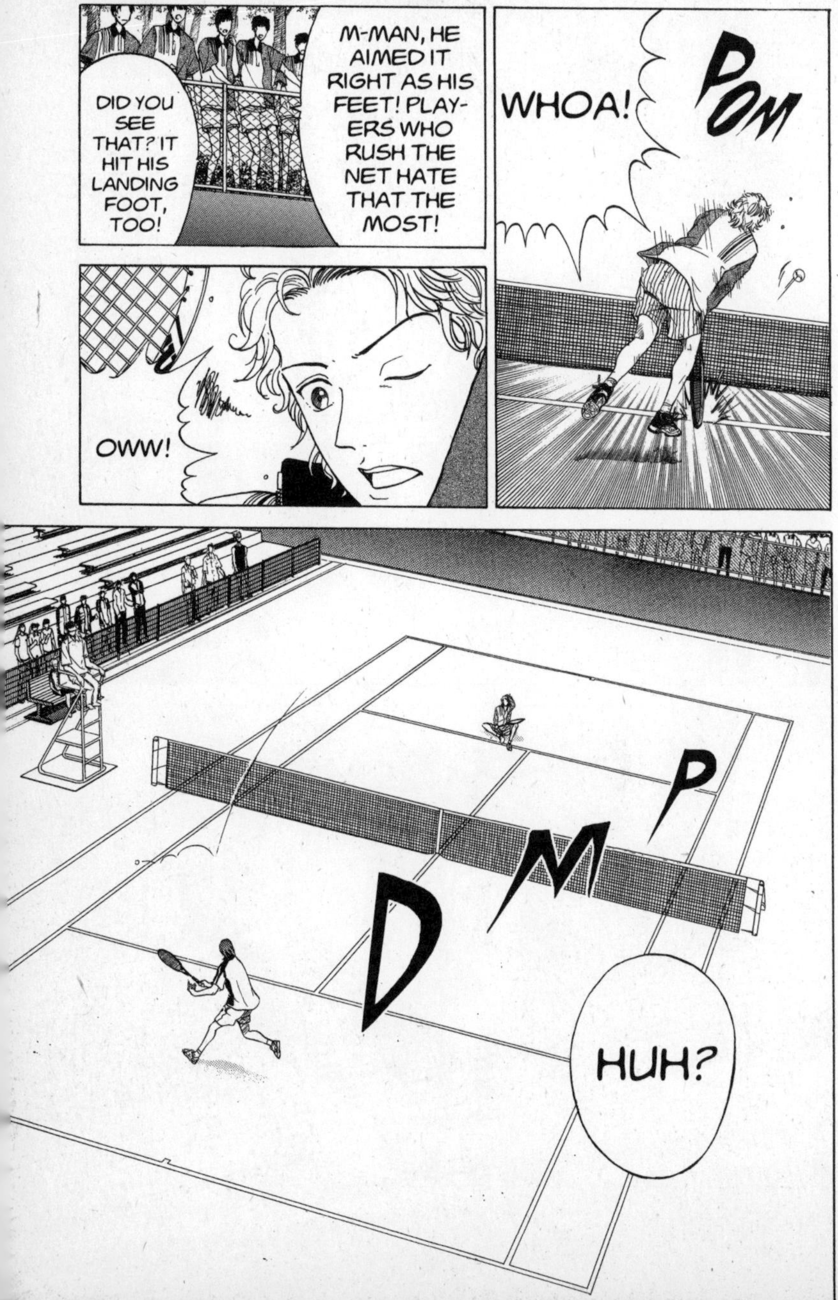
WHOA!
POM
M-MAN, HE AIMED IT RIGHT AS HIS FEET! PLAYERS WHO RUSH THE NET HATE THAT THE MOST!
DID YOU SEE THAT? IT HIT HIS LANDING FOOT, TOO!
OWW!
DMP
HUH?

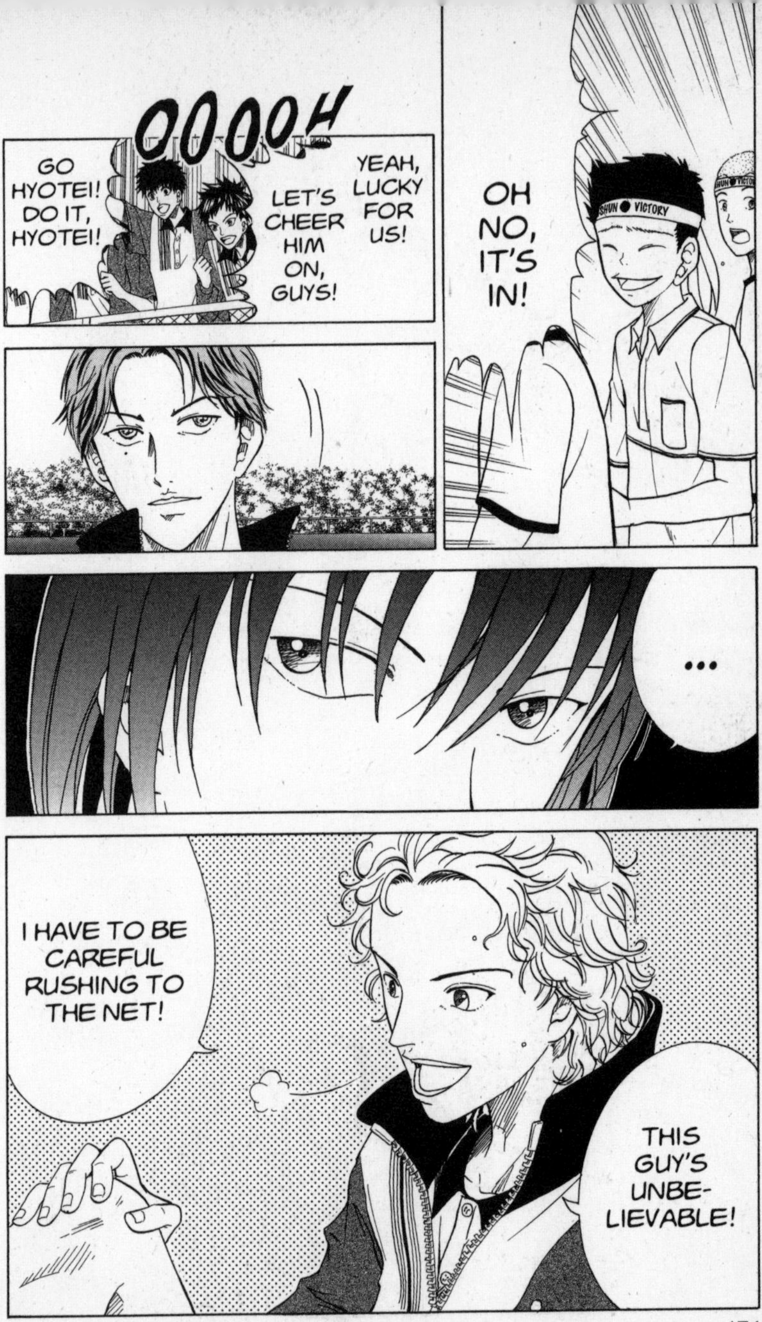
OH NO, IT'S IN!
OOOOH
YEAH, LUCKY FOR US!
LET'S CHEER HIM ON, GUYS!
GO HYOTEI! DO IT, HYOTEI!
...
THIS GUY'S UNBE-LIEVABLE!
I HAVE TO BE CAREFUL RUSHING TO THE NET!

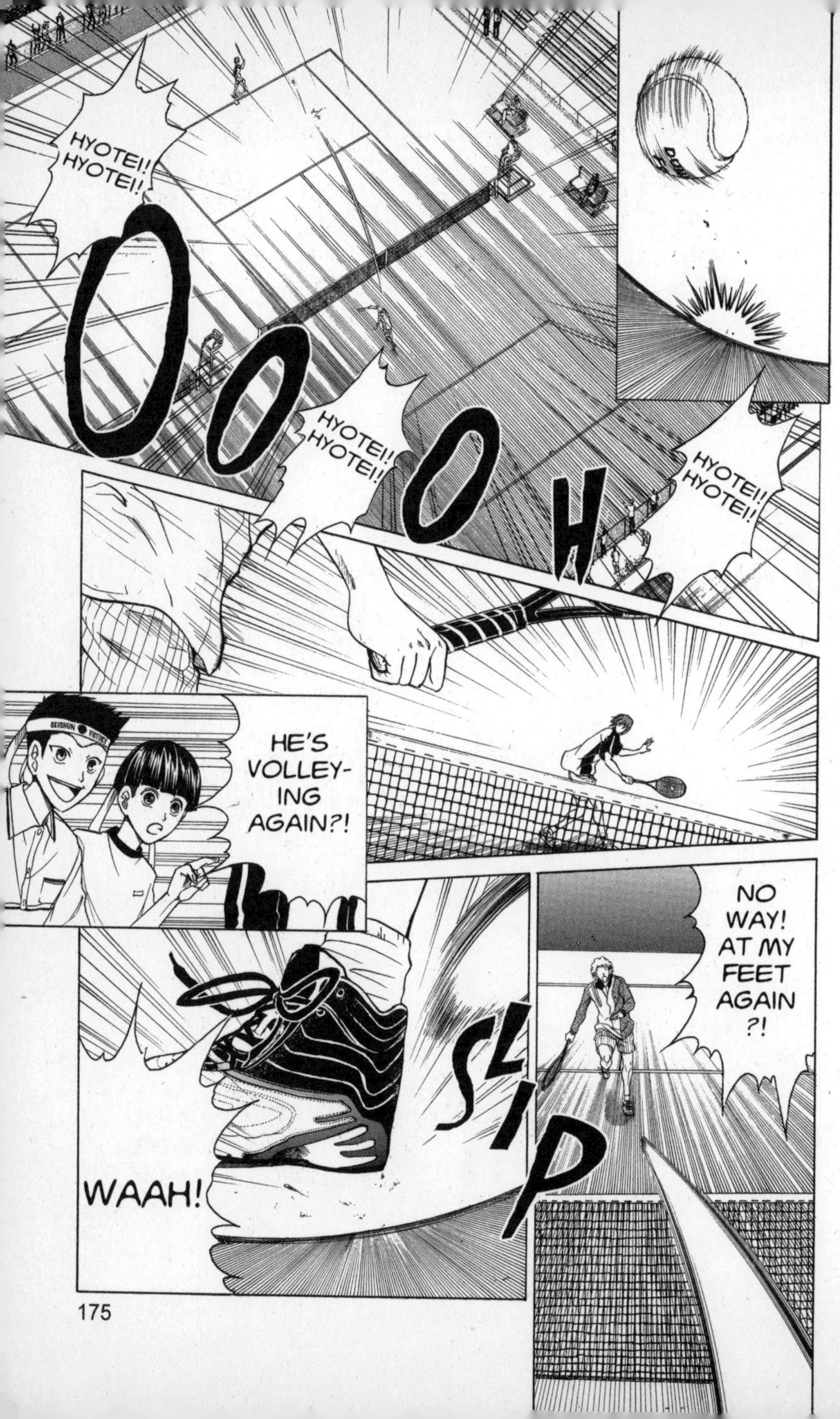
HYOTEI!! HYOTEI!!
HYOTEI!! HYOTEI!!
HYOTEI!! HYOTEI!!
OOOH
HE'S VOLLEY-ING AGAIN?!
NO WAY! AT MY FEET AGAIN ?!
SLIP
WAAH!

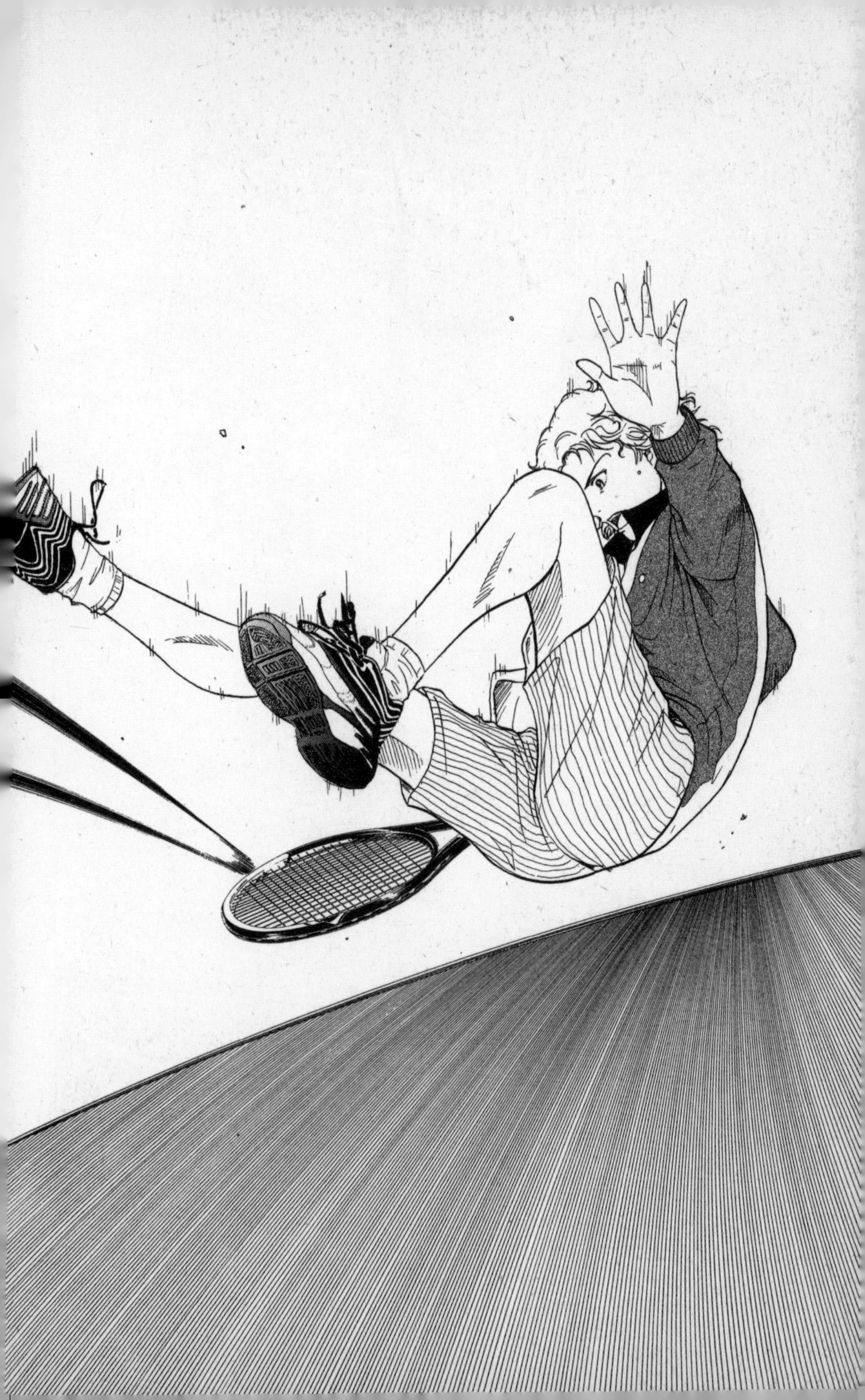

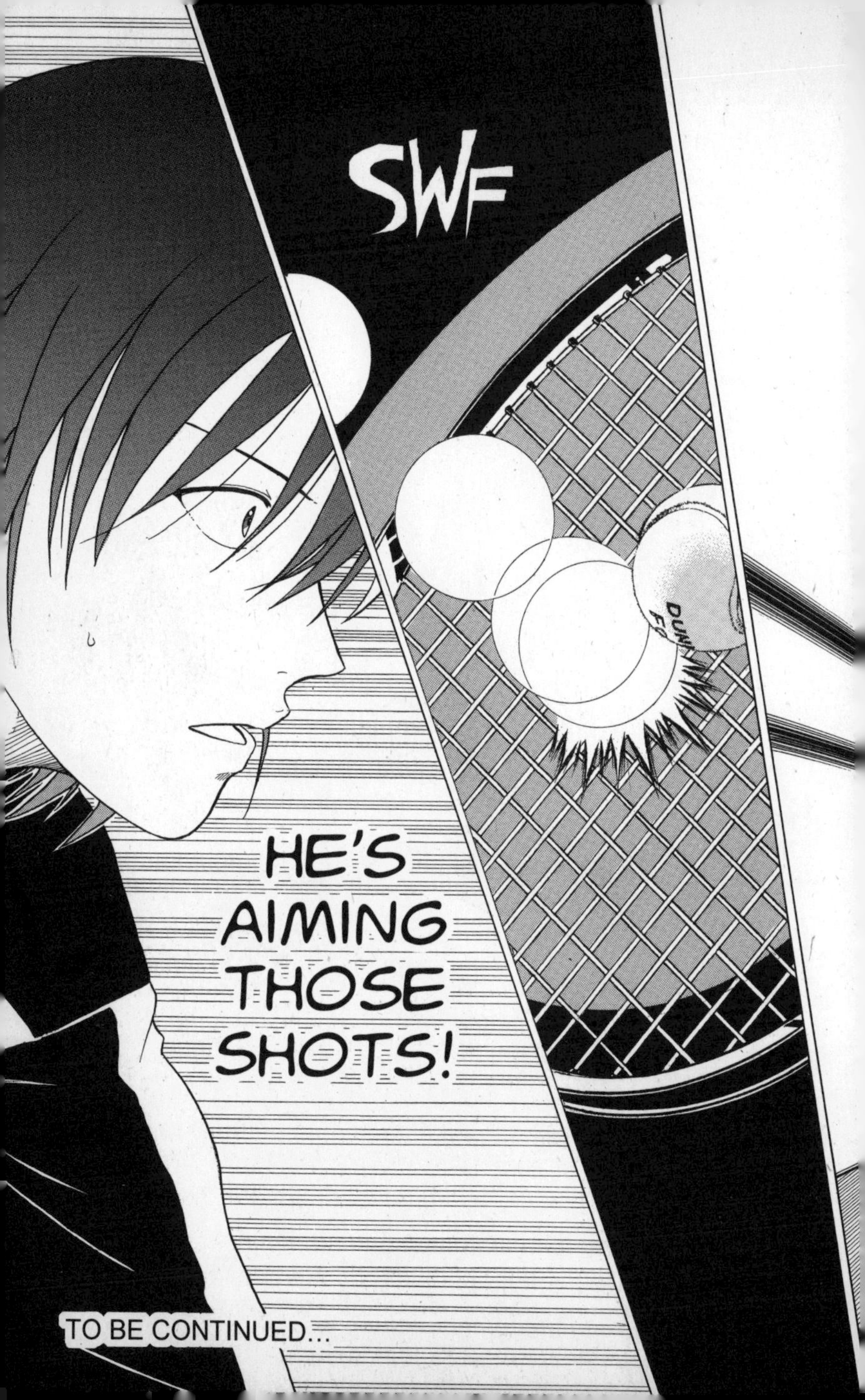
SWF
DUN
HE'S AIMING THOSE SHOTS!
TO BE CONTINUED...

In the Next Volume...

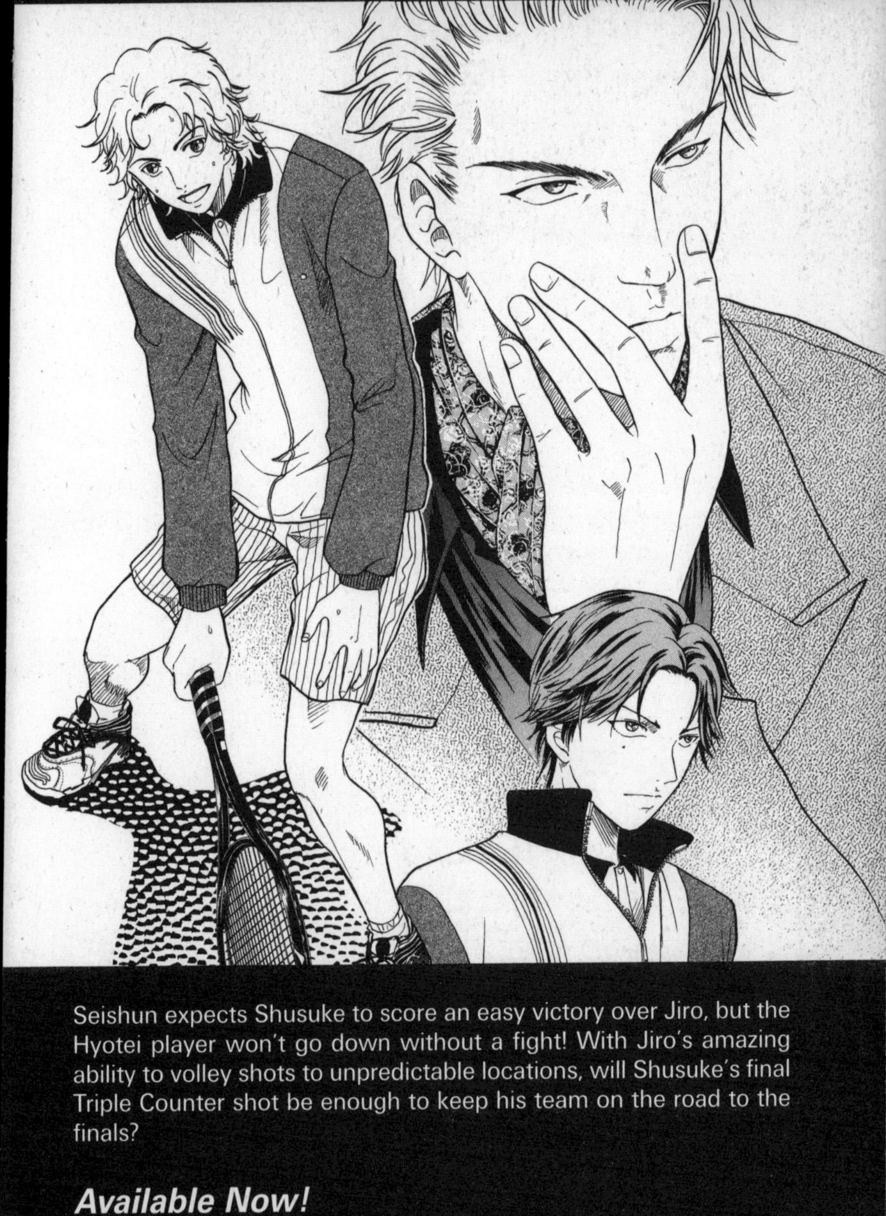

Seishun expects Shusuke to score an easy victory over Jiro, but the Hyotei player won't go down without a fight! With Jiro's amazing ability to volley shots to unpredictable locations, will Shusuke's final Triple Counter shot be enough to keep his team on the road to the finals?

Available Now!

Good things

There are many benefits to writing a tennis manga. These include playing tennis with pro tennis player Fukui, watching the world's top pros at the U.S. Open, and doing talk shows with Shuzo Matsuoka and Naoko Sawamatsu. I am so grateful for their kindness.

- Takeshi Konomi

About Takeshi Konomi

Takeshi Konomi exploded onto the manga scene with the incredible **THE PRINCE OF TENNIS**. His refined art style and sleek character designs proved popular with **Weekly Shonen Jump** readers, and **THE PRINCE OF TENNIS** became the number one sports manga in Japan almost overnight. Its cast of fascinating male tennis players attracted legions of female readers even though it was originally intended to be a boys' comic. The manga continues to be a success in Japan and has inspired a hit anime series, as well as several video games and mountains of merchandise.

THE PRINCE OF TENNIS
VOL. 16
The SHONEN JUMP Manga Edition

STORY AND ART BY
TAKESHI KONOMI

English Adaptation/Michelle Pangilinan
Translation/Joe Yamazaki
Touch-up Art & Lettering/Andy Ristaino
Design/Sam Elzway
Editor/Pancha Diaz

Editor in Chief, Books/Alvin Lu
Editor in Chief, Magazines/Marc Weidenbaum
VP, Publishing Licensing/Rika Inouye
VP, Sales & Product Marketing/Gonzalo Ferreyra
VP, Creative/Linda Espinosa
Publisher/Hyoe Narita

Printed in the U.S.A.

Published by VIZ Media, LLC
P.O. Box 77010
San Francisco, CA 94107

SHONEN JUMP Manga Edition
10 9 8 7 6 5 4 3 2
First printing, November 2006
Second printing, October 2008

THE WORLD'S MOST POPULAR MANGA

www.viz.com

www.shonenjump.com

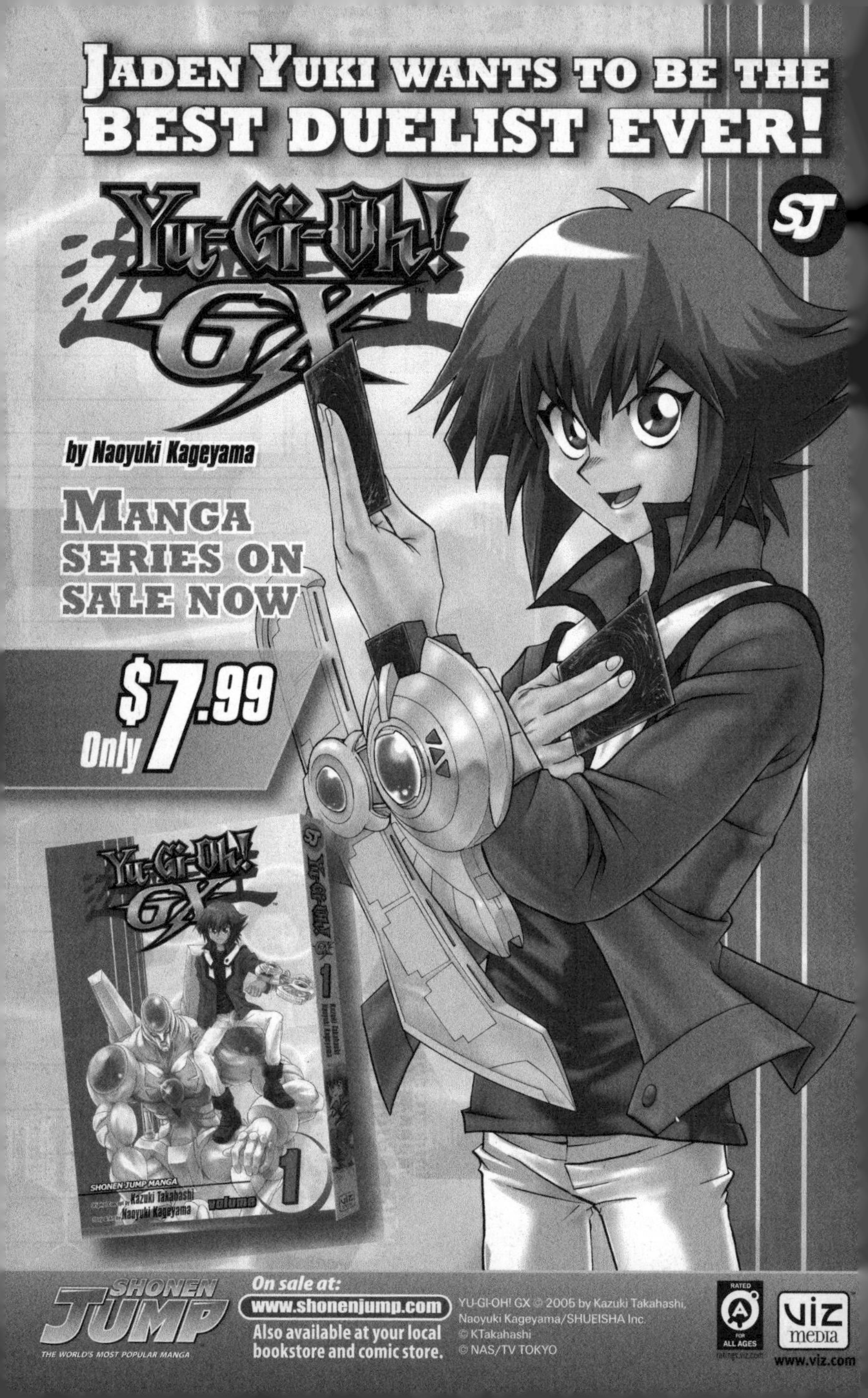
JADEN YUKI WANTS TO BE THE
BEST DUELIST EVER!
SJ
YU-GI-OH! GX
by Naoyuki Kageyama
MANGA
SERIES ON
SALE NOW
Only $7.99
YU-GI-OH! GX
SHONEN JUMP MANGA
Kazuki Takahashi
Naoyuki Kageyama
1
SHONEN JUMP
THE WORLD'S MOST POPULAR MANGA
On sale at:
www.shonenjump.com
Also available at your local bookstore and comic store.
YU-GI-OH! GX © 2005 by Kazuki Takahashi, Naoyuki Kageyama/SHUEISHA Inc.
© KTakahashi
© NAS/TV TOKYO
RATED A FOR ALL AGES
VIZ media
www.viz.com

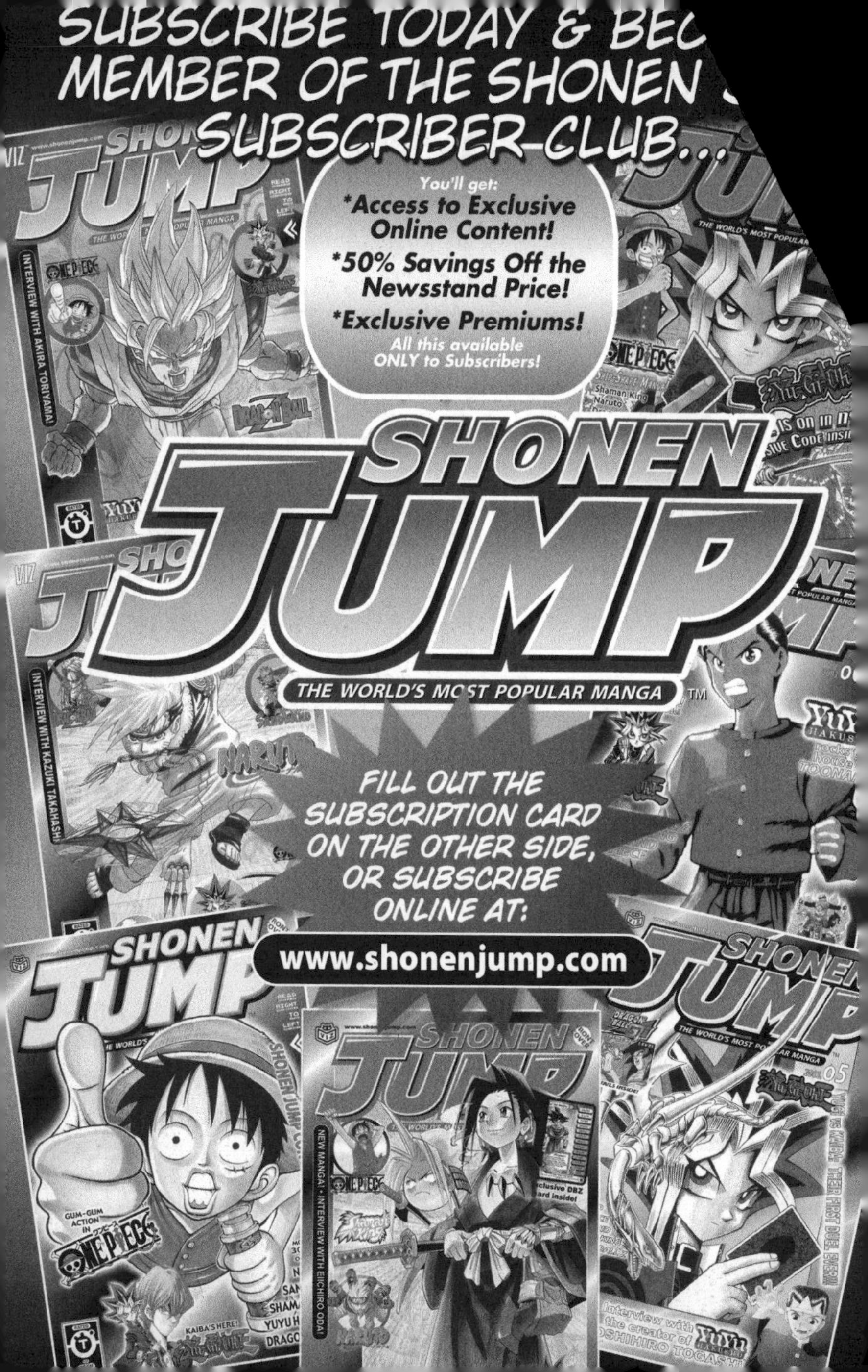
SUBSCRIBE TODAY & BEC
MEMBER OF THE SHONEN
SUBSCRIBER CLUB...
You'll get:
*Access to Exclusive Online Content!
*50% Savings Off the Newsstand Price!
*Exclusive Premiums!
All this available ONLY to Subscribers!
SHONEN JUMP
THE WORLD'S MOST POPULAR MANGA
FILL OUT THE SUBSCRIPTION CARD ON THE OTHER SIDE, OR SUBSCRIBE ONLINE AT:
www.shonenjump.com

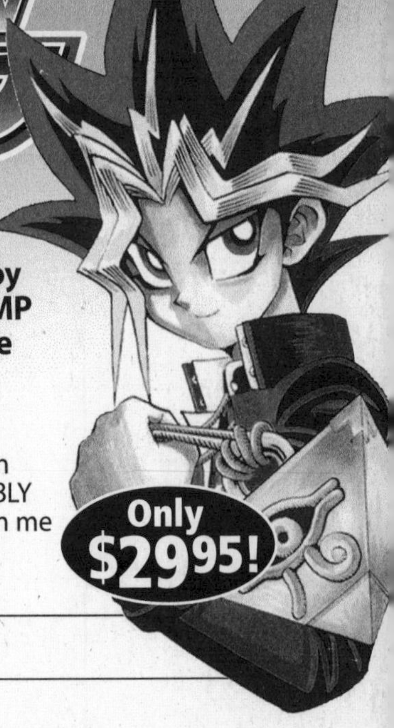